The first edition of Women Working Home was widely acclaimed:

66Women Working Home *helps us make the transition out of the age of the factory and the factory-like office. It is a useful tool for coping with tomorrow.*99
Alvin Toffler
Author of The Third Wave

66*Far and away the best book of its kind . . . a savvy, no-nonsense blueprint for starting and running a home business . . .*99
Family Circle
Gerri Hershey

66*This book is a must for a displaced homemaker who needs to enter the work force and would like to be her own boss.*99
Displaced Homemakers Network, Inc.
Sandra Burton

66*Your information is accurate, well-tailored to your audience and practical. Better yet, the nitty-gritty presentations make it useful. . . . This network of resources is crucial to business success.*99
U.S. Small Business Administration
Michael Moylan

66*The solid business advice given in this book will help women to realize that they really can succeed on their own merits. This volume fulfills a long-standing need.*99
Mary Kay Ash
Founder of Mary Kay Cosmetics, Inc.

66*The 'Bible' of the movement is . . .* Women Working Home.99
Syndicated Column by Phyllis Battelle

66Women Working Home *. . . is a valuable resource for any woman who is in business for herself or who has just given it some thought. The book provides information on getting your own business going—where to get help and what pitfalls to avoid.*99
Handmade

66*The book contains information on setting up and maintaining a business that is widely relevant and supported by a wealth of experience.*99
American Library Association Booklist

66 *. . . contains names, addresses and business experiences of homebased businesswomen, plus tips on getting started.*99
Changing Times

Sandy Aponowich
Word Processor
Credit: Boston Globe Photo

Women Working Home
The Homebased Business Guide and Directory

written and compiled by
Marion Behr and Wendy Lazar

Second Edition

WWH Press
New Jersey
Distributed in the trade by Rodale Press, Inc. Emmaus, PA 18049

Women Working Home, Inc.
24 Fishel Road
Edison, N.J. 08820

Design   Joan Peckolick
Cover Photography   Sally Cooney
Printed in the United States of America

Library of Congress Cataloging in Publication Data

Behr, Marion
  Women working home.

  Bibliography: p.
  Includes index.
   1. Self-employed women—United States.
2. Home-based businesses—United States.   I. Lazar, Wendy
II. Title.
HD6072.6.U5B44   1983   658'.041   83-3487
ISBN 0-939240-01-7

Acknowledgements

This second edition of *Women Working Home* is a tribute to the vast numbers of women and constantly increasing numbers of men throughout the nation who have reached us by phone or through letters to share their desires to work from home, their questions concerning homebased business, and expressions of gratitude and enthusiasm for our first edition. Our second book, from its first page to the last, is a statement of high regard for the professional concerns of those who work, or wish to work, from their homes, as well as a "Thank You" to all those who have shared their triumphs and needs with us.

Success is never achieved by oneself alone. Every successful individual benefits from others who act as support systems, much like an extended family, that can be relied on for professional assistance and emotional support.

We have been very fortunate in the help that has been forthcoming both from individuals and groups. The National Alliance of Homebased Businesswomen has introduced us to an active network of gifted businesspeople in a wide variety of home businesses. The U.S. Small Business Administration provides us with a constant flow of information and a great deal of valuable support.

Specifically, we wish to thank Arleen Priest, Business Manager of WWH Press, for her enthusiasm, assistance, and constant creativity in her approach to business. We are also grateful to Marie MacBride, our copy editor, Nancy Velthaus, our proofreader, and Richard Walsh, for his analysis of our first edition questionnaire. Elizabeth Lyons has given us guidance and counsel with an open mind to new approaches. Anna Manger, P.A., and Albert Barclay, Esq., have answered our endless questions and increased our knowledge of accounting and law. Gerri Hirshey and Vera Stek have followed our progress with continuous confidence in the project. Clare Allen, Adele Kaplan, Lynn Miller, and Al Sinisgalli helped us define so many of our original ideas that, without their confidence at the very beginning, we still wonder if our project would have taken shape. Michael Moylan, Rosemary Mullany, and Juanita Weaver follow our cause from Washington with encouragement and assistance whenever possible. We thank Joan Peckolick for having a strong sense of design and the ability to interpret our ideas; Marlene Pituro and Barbara May for their continuing help with computer and fulfillment services; Ruth Cartlidge for secretarial assistance; and our many supporters in the media who give our work credibility through local and national recognition.

Our families have grown more sensitive and more supportive as we have shared the homebased business concept with those seeking to combine home and business into a pleasing and ever-changing way of life. So, to our husbands, Marc Behr and Martin Lazar, and to our children, Dawn, Darrin, and Dana Behr, and Kim and Jodi Lazar, we give special thanks, for because of them home is a loving setting, and they have made it possible for us to work there.

Marion Behr

Wendy Lazar

Photographer: Lewis Hine
Credit: International Museum of Photography at George Eastman House

WWH

Contributors

Judith S. Abrams
Vice President and head of marketing and business development at The First Women's Bank in New York. Active in developing new business with middle market and professional corporations, Fortune 500 companies, and special interest groups. Analyzes and evaluates loan requests and conducts seminars on personal finances. Formerly, Branch Manager of Chemical Bank and a research analyst with Morgan Stanley & Co. Received her M.B.A. in Finance from the Graduate School of Business at New York University. Lives with her husband and three children on Manhattan's West Side.

Ingrid Fabbe Bauer
Administrator of Futures Network that looks at ways to release human potential at all levels in order to create a better world. Formerly with the Congressional Caucus for Woman's Issues. U.S.-appointed Delegate to the U.N. Mid-Decade Conference on Women, representing rural women and income generation, which developed her keen interest in homebased business.

Dr. Omri M. Behr
Patent attorney—Law office of Behr & Adams—Edison, N.J. Licensed 1967: New Jersey, New York, U.S. Patent Office. Fellow: Royal Society of Chemistry. Member: American Patent Law Association. Practice includes all aspects of intellectual and industrial property law. Specialization: pharmaceutical, biological, and foreign patent law. Author of articles on trademarks, copyrights, and laws concerning patent protection for microbiological inventions of foreign origin.

Roslyn Bernstein
Associate Professor of English, Baruch College, City University of New York. Free-lance writer and editor; poet; lecturer. Editor-in-Chief of *Dollars and $ense,* The Baruch College Business Review. Coauthor of *Ripoff.* Member: New York Financial Writers' Association.

Tina Bobker
Partner in Rainbow Artisans, Inc., a cottage industry manufacturing quality infants' bedding and accessories. B.F.A. degree from Temple University in Graphic Design.

Erma Bombeck
America's bestselling, best-loved humorist. Author of seven books, nationally syndicated columnist, humorist on "Good Morning, America," wife, and mother of three children.

Barbara Brabec
Author of *Creative Cash—How to Sell Your Crafts, Needlework, Designs & Know-How,* and publisher of companion newsletter, *Sharing Barbara's Mail.* Columnist for three craft magazines, contributor to several books, author of *Handcrafts* bulletin issued by U.S. Small Business Administration. Gives craft marketing workshops nationally and serves as private consultant to crafts businesspeople.

Diane E. Burke
Regional Manager of Rutgers Small Business Development Center in Newark, N.J. Provides consulting to small business owners in New Jersey. Also teaches small business courses at Rutgers University, New Brunswick.

Claire Cleaver
Founder and president of Concepts by Claire, Inc., a national creative marketing and communications firm based in Berks County, Pa. and author of *Step into Sales: A Woman's Guide to Personal and Financial Success Through Home Merchandising.* Formerly, VP of Sales Communications & Training for a multi-million dollar direct-selling company. Currently, public speaker, seminar leader, and business consultant. Member: American Management Association, American Association of University Women, National Alliance of Homebased Businesswomen, National Association of Female Executives. Selected for *Who's Who in American Women.*

Carole Dlugasch
Partner in Rainbow Artisans, Inc., manufacturers of quality infants' bedding and accessories since 1976. B.A. degree in Sociology from Rutgers University and M.A. degree in Special Education from Kean College.

Leonard D. Furman
Tax attorney in West Orange and East Brunswick, N.J. Attorney-at-law, New Jersey and New York; licensed to practice before the U.S. Tax Court. Certified Public Accountant in New Jersey and New York. Member: Federal Tax Committee of the New Jersey Society of CPA's. Lecturer on federal tax law, pensions, and estate planning. Previously employed as Internal Revenue Service Field Agent.

Contributors

Mary Jo Gatti
Owner of Dayspring, a mail-order and giftware business established in 1978. Also a professional engraver, using this skill to add the personalized touch to catalog gifts and for business gift and award buyers. Sales generated through local and national direct-mail promotions, display ads, dealers in several states, and sales presentations. Mother of two college boys and wife of a packaging executive.

Gladys Glickman
Attorney admitted to practice in New York and Illinois. Author of *Franchising,* a two-volume work on all legal aspects of franchising for franchisor and franchisee. Full-time position as counsel to a magazine publishing company; part-time home business writing books and articles on business law and representing clients in establishing franchise systems.

Maxine and Kyra Gottesman
Mother and daughter owners of The Shefa Co., Oakland, Calif., a personal services company principally aimed at supporting the use of microcomputers in small businesses. Maxine: former teacher, public planner, and "Jill of all trades." Kyra: presently a senior at Mills College and editor of campus newspaper; also intern at San Francisco bureau of *Newsweek* magazine.

Elizabeth Forsythe Hailey
Author of the best-selling novels *A Women of Independent Means* and *Life Sentences.* Currently at work on a third novel. Lives in Los Angeles with her husband and two daughters.

Sylvia Haydash
Director and Laotian interpreter for CARING Inc., an acculturation project for Indochinese refugees in Prince William County, Va. Graduate of Defense Language Institute, Monterey, Calif. Worked with Indochinese refugees in Bangkok, Thailand, through American Red Cross and American Women's Club.

Steven Kass
Controller of Magla Products, a textile manufacturer in Irvington, N.J. Adjunct professor in accounting and finance at Bloomfield College, N.J. Also, president of CSK Associates, a financial/system/data processing consulting firm.

Marcia Keizs
Assistant Director of External Education Program for the Homebound, Queensborough Community College, New York. Has a special interest in the development of creative employment options for this population. Also a teacher of English: Rhetoric and Literature, a writer of reviews and essays on culture and literature, and editor of *Carib News,* a weekly tabloid.

Marion Landis
President of Ultra-Fine Products, Inc. in Cleveland, Ohio, and developer of Mr. Glass, a heavy-duty, nontoxic glass cleaner for shower doors, windows, and tiles. Product distributed through major national mail-order companies, selected stores, and independent sales agents throughout the country. Has had national TV publicity through *PM Magazine* and *Hour Magazine* and participates in business seminars. Mother of two grown children and wife of a business consultant.

Joan Landsbergis
Owner of The Write Person for Advertising and Public Relations, offering free-lance marketing communications for corporate, trade, industrial, financial, consumer, business, and retail clients. Background includes free-lance journalism; sales and marketing management in textile and translation industries; academic research, writing, editing, and lecturing in philosophy, CUNY; retail fashion advertising; and celebrity public relations. Member: Long Island Advertising Club.

Barbara Lasker
Psychotherapist in private practice in Union, N.J., and on staff of the Institute for Contemporary Psychotherapy in New York City. Earned M.S.W. degree at age forty and Certificate in Psychoanalytic Psychotherapy at age forty-six. Specializes in treatment of individuals, couples, and families. Lectures on midlife transition and stages of family life.

Martin Lazar
Psychotherapist in private practice in Norwood, N.J., and New York City, working with adults, families, children, and groups. Psychiatric Social Work Supervisor, New York Department of Mental Hygiene, doing psychotherapy with children and families. Affiliated with Community Guidance Service, N.Y.C. Developer of programs for the underachieving youngster. Lecturer and consultant in workshops and seminars in interpersonal relations and communications for private foundations, schools, and industry.

Paula Baker Lohrmann
Image and color consultant; professional speaker; owner of specialty store in Charlotte, N.C., providing analysis of total individual: career goals, wardrobe, beauty care, and nutritional counseling.

Dr. René W. Luft
Associate of Simpson Gumpertz & Heger Inc. in Cambridge, Mass. Writes articles, essays, and technical papers. Also writes profit reports for clients and develops price proposals for industry and government. A 1971 Doctor of Science graduate of Massachusetts Institute of Technology. Lives with wife and two children in Bay State.

Elizabeth T. Lyons
Chief of Small Business Assistance Office, N.J. Department of Commerce and Economic Development. Former president of Elizabeth T. Lyons & Associates, a management consulting and training service, and chairperson of N.J. Coalition of Small Business Organizations.

Marie MacBride
Free-lance writer, copy editor, and indexer. Author of *Orange Pages: A Directory of News Media for Bergen County* and *Step by Step: Management of the Volunteer Program in Agencies.* Served as volunteer in many parts of United States and Girl Scout professional worker in program and public relations for ten years.

Lavinia Moore McKee
In insurance business since 1978 as an agent for John Hancock Mutual Life Insurance Company and Sentry Property & Casualty Insurance Company. In July 1981 joined with her father, George Moore, to form the Moore-McKee Insurance Agency in East Brunswick, N.J. Licensed to sell life, health, and all forms of property and casualty insurance.

Lynn Miller
Consultant to women in the arts and media librarian for Rutgers University libraries. Coauthor with Sally S. Swenson of *Lives and Works: Talks with Women Artists,* published by Scarecrow Press, 1981.

George Moore
Coowner of Moore-McKee Insurance Agency. With The John Hancock Mutual Life Insurance Company since 1959. Life member of prestigious Presidents Honor Club and qualified for President's Cabinet; qualifying member of Million Dollar Round Table. Licensed for life and health insurance, variable annuities, variable life insurance, N.A.S.D., mutual funds, auto, homeowners, and commercial insurance. Notary Public. Member: National Association of Life Underwriters, East Brunswick Kiwanis Club, and Agents Advisory Committee of The John Hancock. Married, with two married children.

Alina Novak
Financial analyst with The Equitable Life Assurance Society. Founder of Networks, a self-formed group of Equitable women and men. Pioneered the networking process in speeches and workshops throughout the country. Included in two books, *Networking* and *Networks.* Featured in articles in magazines such as *Ms., Working Woman, Savvy, The Executive Female, Parents,* and *Boardroom Reports.* B.A. in economics from the City College of New York. Listed in current edition of *Who's Who in American Women* and 1980 edition of *Outstanding Young Women in America.*

Frances Gildea O'Neill
President and CEO of Dantec Corporation in Bethel, Conn., an electronic engineering and subcontract assembly firm. Twice elected to Planning and Zoning Commission in Bethel, serving for eight years and twice elected secretary of that group. Member: Bethel Land Trust, French Canadian Heritage Society of Michigan, Greater Danbury Area Women's Network, and Connecticut Chapter of National Alliance of Homebased Businesswomen. In the 1960s, worked in Washington, D.C., for Senator Thomas Dodd and Congressmen James Mackay and Michael A. Feighan, then joined Secretary Weaver's Congressional Liaison staff at the then newly created Department of Housing and Urban Development.

Merrill D. Parra
Director of External Education Program for the Homebound at Queensborough Community College in New York since 1978. Successful in securing state and federal grants to support the operation of the project. Served on the Board of Associates of Teachers College Project for the Handicapped at Columbia University. Member: Commission on Continuing Education of the New York State Association of Two-Year Colleges. Presented workshops at many national association meetings. Coauthor of a number of articles on homebound education and field instructor at Adelphi University School of Social Work.

Lynne H. Pitcher
Coowner, with George Pitcher, of G.R. Pitcher, Inc., in Highland Park, N.J., a firm offering computer consulting and services to small businesses—specializing in custom system design and implementation, including selection of minicomputer hardware, software development, installation, and training. Pioneered in the development of systems using bar code scanners for order processing and inventory control.

Contributors

Judith Pynchon
Former college English teacher turned entrepreneur, creating training programs for business and industry, principally in sales, marketing, and industrial operations. Has developed a unique consultancy specializing in marketing and strategic planning for independent professionals. Her motto: "I can teach anyone to do anything, if someone can explain it to me first." As a single parent, believes firmly in homebased enterprise as the wave of the future and a means to run a successful business while sharing her daughter's growing years.

Beth Ravit
General Merchandise Manager, B.R.I. Corporation, New York.

Marilyn Salmieri
Certified Public Accountant licensed in Connecticut. Maintains a homebased practice in tax planning for the individual and small business. Part-time instructor of accounting at Norwalk Community College, Norwalk, Conn. Member: American Institute of CPA's, Connecticut Society of CPA's.

R. F. Sanford
Member of Western Electric Company's Financial Planning Group in New York. Former evening instructor at Illinois Institute of Technology Graduate School of Industrial and Systems Engineering. Volunteer instructor of accounting and pricing for Workshop in Business Opportunities (WIBO). Bachelor of Science, Mechanical Engineering, University of Illinois, 1963. Master of Business Administration (Accounting), University of Chicago, 1968.

Sunny Schlenger
Director of Schlenger Organizational Systems in Fair Lawn, N.J., a consulting service designed to help busy individuals become better organized. Serves on Board of Directors of Women Entrepreneurs of N.J. and Girl Scout Council of Bergen County. Lectures on subjects of organization and success.

Victoria Sczerzenie
Systems Analyst, Department of Human Services, Trenton, N.J., analyzing data processing system specifications, writing documentary analysis of systems, and developing, maintaining, and troubleshooting systems. Has authored articles on psychology and physiology.

Gonnie McClung Siegel
Author of *Sales: The Fast Track for Women, How to*

Beat the High Cost of Learning, How to Advertise and Promote Small Business, and the *Woman's Work Book.* Combines writing with a communications consulting business, Contemporary Communications, begun in 1967. An early advocate of homebased businesses for women and men because of the tremendous time savings. Sees enormous advantages for women in the future because of the new technology which makes possible more homebased businesses than ever before. A frequent speaker on women and employment. Founder of the Westchester County Women's Council; served as Employment Chair and ERA Chair. Married, with two sons and a daughter-in-law.

Stephanie Solodar-Katz
Owner of SSK Freelance Typing Service in Maplewood, N.J., offering complete and unique secretarial services, including telephone dictation hookups, word processing, printing, original advertising, and stationery setups. Also lecturer, writer, consultant, and certified paralegal in private practice, providing on-call service to clients who do not have need for a full-time paralegal.

Anita Stellenwerf
Certified Public Accountant practicing in Mahwah, N.J. Teaches accounting and taxation at Ramapo College, N.J. M.B.A. from Rutgers Graduate School of Business. Formerly, an auditor with IRS. Member: Beta Gamma Sigma, national business honors society; N.J. Society of CPA's; American Institute of CPA's. Extensive experience with women's personal and business accounting and financial problems. Computerized accounting capabilities available.

Barbara Sunden
National Sales Director for Mary Kay Cosmetics. Received honors in Unit Retail Achievements at $300,000 retail level and $600,000 unit retail level. Twice a member of the Queens Court of Recruiting for Mary Kay. Winner of four pink Cadillacs, diamonds, and a mink coat. Married, with two sons.

Roberta Tasley
Student in The Interactive Telecommunications Graduate Program at New York University, with thesis on New Work Options, particularly addressing the relationship of working at home to the development of community. Administrative assistant and manager of Telecommunications Clinic, a class developed to train advanced graduate students to work as team consultants to not-for-profit community organizations, assessing communications needs and telecommunications systems options.

Thomas Tassini
President and principal consultant of Teleologica, Ltd., a microcomputer supplier to many Fortune 500 companies, as well as smaller organizations. Operates under trade name of Vista Computer, located in Matawan, N.J. Over twenty years in data processing consulting in the United States and abroad.

Christine Van Noy
Owner of The Wordshop, a complete communication service offering typing, word processing, typesetting, and graphic design. President of Van Noy & Associates, a homebased business consulting service, assisting women in the start-up, operation, and redirection of homebased businesses. Founder of San Francisco Eastbay Chapter of the National Alliance of Homebased Businesswomen.

June Walker-Sloat
Budget and tax consultant in Plainfield, N.J. Specialist for people in the arts—writers, musicians, artists—and other self-employed. Financial guidance and planning for women in the process of or newly divorced.

Diane Wenrick
Started her sales career by selling Sarah Coventry jewelry and worked her way up the ladder with a dynamic sales staff of sixty-one people. Traveled extensively throughout the country attending sales seminars. Currently owner of a woman's specialty and bridal shop outside Wilkes-Barre, Pa. Married, with three children.

Sarah Zaleski
In January 1980, founded Everywoman's Bookshelf, a homebased mail-order business to provide women nationwide with books on how to start a new business. Has been written about in local newspapers, national newsletters, and national magazines, such as *Crafts, Working Woman,* and *Woman's Day.* Conducts workshops on starting a small business, consults privately, and speaks to women's business and network groups. Married, with three children.

Donald R. Zoch
Principal of Directions Unlimited Financial Services, Inc., and Zoch & Zoch Associates, Inc., in Fairfield, N.J., providing financial planning consultation to individuals, professionals, and businesses with the aid of an in-house computer system. Certified financial planner and registered investment advisor. Lecturer and adjunct professor at the College for Financial Planning. Member: International Association for Financial Planning and Institute of Certified Financial Planners. Licensed for life, health, real estate, and investment advisory. Selected to Outstanding Young Men of America.

Sharon Zukowski
Senior financial planner of Directions Unlimited Financial Services and head of Directions Unlimited's Women & Money Center, providing women with information, education, and assistance in planning for financial independence. Licensed real estate and life insurance agent. Member: International Association for Financial Planners and Institute of Certified Financial Planners. President of United Charter Chapter of American Businesswoman's Association and acting President of New Jersey Association of Women Business Owners—Northern Region. Also secretary of Board of Trustees of Association for the Advancement for the Mentally Handicapped.

Preface

The second edition of *Women Working Home: The Homebased Business Guide and Directory* is the fulfillment of our promise to expand and update information for women throughout this country who work, or wish to work, from their homes. Our first edition answered questions asked by women who participated in a survey that attempted to define the needs of the "invisible work force" of homebased businesswomen. The book was published in 1981; meanwhile, we have heard from thousands of women nationwide. Our second edition, therefore, addresses the needs of a much broader group—women who are just starting out as well as those who already have successful businesses and want to expand.

This second edition has been updated and augmented. Experts willing to share their knowledge gathered through years of study and practical application have written direct answers to complicated business questions. Since home work is often essential to retired, handicapped, and rural women, articles dealing with specific problems and solutions in these areas are included.

In our first book we were proud (and somewhat surprised) to have discovered over one hundred homebased occupations, but in the past two years that number has more than doubled. We have received letters from and have spoken to women of all ages who earn incomes that vary from modest amounts to six figures, who work from home offices, studios, garages, barns, dens, laundry rooms, basements, attics, and closets; and who are increasing their standards of living and bettering their lives. We pass their stories and statements on to you in profiles and quotes in the hope that their experiences and this book will move you in new directions and enrich the quality of *your* life.

Today homebased businesswomen are earning, in addition to substantial incomes, respect and recognition for their work. We are proud to be part of this movement. In our directory, a diverse group of women are listed alphabetically by state. Occupations and business information are given to encourage readers to purchase products and services from homebased workers. Through the directory we will continue to build a solid, nationwide network.

A report prepared by a task force of independent representatives from eight federal agencies had this to say about women business owners:

> What more vital role can women play in the nation's economy than as entrepreneurs—as owners and managers of their own businesses? In America's free enterprise system, it is the entrepreneur who fuels growth and progress. It is the entrepreneur who innovates, who builds the large industry of the future, who creates jobs and who supplies the goods and services that determine the American standard of living. It is important to a healthy economy that all segments of the population, regardless of gender or race, participate equally in all of these economic endeavors, including entrepreneurship.

Women Working Home is specifically geared to the homebased entrepreneur. In the past few years there have been many positive changes in the development and growth of homebased business. At the back of the book is a questionnaire to be filled in and returned to us, and also reproduced and shared with a friend, so that we may continue to gather and share information on homebased businesswomen and their businesses.

To construct a historical perspective of the development and growth of homebased businesses in America, we would appreciate receiving any information describing your experiences, so that these might be shared with others.

All of us are part of a major trend of tomorrow, and a movement that is benefiting society today.

Contents

Introduction

The Emerging Woman— Integrating Work and Love

Barbara Lasker, Psychotherapist

❝Working from home is the most practical, sensible, and personally rewarding way of life for women today. Those of us who really want to have some sort of career or identity beyond that of housewife/mother and yet do not want to abandon that role and those responsibilities, really have no other good alternative. ❞

Secretary

"The times they are a-changing" are the words of a song popular in the sixties. We are still in the midst of a transition. For women there has been a continuing shift in their assumptions about themselves. Many feel considerable conflict about the new roles in the world of work and in relationships with others.

Some things remain the same. "Anatomy is destiny," Freud said many years ago. For women it remains a central factor of their self-identification. They define themselves in terms of the mothering role: as either without children, or as the mother of a toddler, or the mother of a six-year-old, or the mother of a teenager or even as an "empty-nester." How they deal with this core issue and the way they live their lives has required reassessment in the face of changing social, economic, and personal values.

Let's look at the traditional roles and the expectations of the past. They were clearly defined. Women were raised to be wives and mothers and homemakers. Men were to be the sole providers for the family. Marriages were made to last "until death do us part." The emotional and economic needs of the family were segregated by sex. Mother was the caretaker; she raised the children and provided emotional support for them as well as acting as a helpmate to Father. She depended on her husband completely to take care of both her own and her children's financial needs. Based on this model, boys and girls were raised very differently. Males organized their lives around the work issue. Sentiment, dependency, and feelings were suppressed while aggressive and competitive activities were encouraged. For females, the reverse was true. They were raised more gently, allowed to cry, and discouraged from behaving in ways that were considered dangerous or unladylike. They were protected and sheltered and taught not to take independent risks. Their focus was on activities that fostered the nurturing and emotionally expressive side of their nature. They were taught about looking after children, home, and husband. Competency in other areas was discouraged and so became submerged. This can be seen in a study of academic achievements, made a number of years ago. Girls' level of performance, which had matched or bettered their male counterparts, declined as they became adolescents. They turned from an emphasis on their intellectual capacities to an emphasis on developing relationships with boys, with marriage as the ultimate goal. The dependency on the opposite sex was seen as appropriate. It left little need for the development of other aspects of the self. Passivity, helplessness, and pleasing others were the character traits that were fostered towards that end.

This, then, was the preparation of women for the social and economic arrangements of the past. There have been many changes in recent years. They can be attributed to a variety of sources. Families have decreased in size. The average number of children has been reduced from five at the turn of the century to two in recent times. Women spend fewer years taking care of children. With the dramatic increase in the life span, they have many years to spend without the child-rearing responsibility, perhaps a twenty- or thirty-year postparental period. At one time, a woman needed to spend the entire day in a variety of household chores. With the growth in mechanization of household appliances and technological advances in the preparation of foods, women have been able to cut this down to a few hours. In an era when expectations for a higher standard of living became universal, women have increasingly become involved in working to help meet the family's needs. The statistics tell us that in almost half of the intact families, both parents are working to earn money. The influx of women into the work force is a result of other factors as well. The epidemic of separation and divorce in this country in the last twenty years has left many women as heads of single-parent households, both caretaker and breadwinner. In 1981 there were 3.23 million families headed by single women—divorced, widowed, or unmarried. The various changes in the conditions of family life have led to a dramatic shift in women's roles with regard to paid work. From 1950 to 1980, the number of women working has almost doubled to over 40 million, now comprising 43 percent of the work force.

The occupations that women are currently engaged in have gained in scope and variety. Traditionally, expressing the nurturant side of their natures, women have gone into fields where they serve others or where they meet other's needs. Highly educated women predominated in teaching, nursing, or social work. Women who went into the realm of business could be found in backup positions such as secretary or file clerk. There was little expectation of moving into positions of responsibility or authority. The sweep of change, spurred on by the women's movement, has changed perceptions. It has become more and more evident that women's abilities can be used effectively in areas that were previously seen as suitable only to men. In growing numbers, women are functioning as doctors, judges, and heads of government. They can be seen as taxi drivers, coal miners, and business executives. Few jobs seem out of reach on the basis of sex alone.

With these factors in mind, young women are thoughtfully considering their options in their role as mother and in their role in the work arena. Many young women are seeking an education that will enable them to make vocational choices that are similar to those made by young men. Questions of if, when, and how, are being asked in terms of family life and parenting. The issue for some women is whether to pursue a career and forgo childbearing. Others are trying to balance their career aspirations and their wish to nurture children, by postponement. They are waiting until they are in their thirties and have established their careers before they begin their families. Those women who have careers and who are raising young children are searching for ways to meet their diverse

"Fabric Drawing in Space"
by Dolly Curtis
Photographer: Victor Cromwell

responsibilities. The phenomenon of our time is "Super-Mom"—the woman who struggles to find ways to do it all and to do it all well. For a married woman, the success of the endeavor depends very much on the choice of husband and his capacity to share parental responsibilities and to foster her career. There has been a growing number of men who have shifted their ideas about their roles in life. In search of self-fulfillment, they are seeking far greater expression of their needs in the areas of intimacy through close emotional bonds. Their fathering role with their young children offers them an opportunity to express love and tenderness, a side of their nature that was previously not viewed as important.

For women in the middle years, it is a time of reassessment. As their children grow older and need them less, a restlessness sets in. There is a search for renewal, to make up for the loss of the maternal function. Many who have been primarily homemakers look to the possibility of gainful employment as a new direction. Some find it hard to get started. Several issues arise stemming from women's feelings about their self-identification. Accustomed to meeting the needs of husbands and children before their own, it is difficult to invest in an activity that is for one's self. It stirs up feelings of guilt. They feel that doing something for their own gain violates what is expected of them. Many women are not accustomed to validating their own competency. They have difficulty recognizing the intelligence and capabilities they have displayed in their homemaking tasks and in their community responsibilities. A further restraint for some is the notion developed in childhood that to use oneself in an assertive manner is "unfeminine."

Women who are too fearful to deal with these inner restrictions become stuck, unable to move. They feel their lives take on an empty quality and they begin to stagnate. Often they become angry and then depressed, with no outlet for their feelings.

Those who mobilize themselves to take on the challenges of developing a separate, self-directed work role for themselves face a series of problems; but facing the difficulties and anxieties involved in building a career or business is invigorating. Women who accomplish something on their own, promoting their financial endeavors, relying on their own judgment, gain feelings of independence and self-worth. A gratifying secondary gain is that a woman who feels worthwhile adds richness to her family life. Her model of personal growth and achievement is a healthy one to present to her children.

This is where present-day women find themselves. They are increasingly moving in the direction of financial and emotional independence through the use of previously discredited competencies, talents, and abilities. They are making assertive and self-directed moves towards that end; but always in the foreground are the needs, the gratifications, the rewards, and the demands of motherhood. The complex task remaining is to find a path that allows for an integration of the commitment to work and the commitment to family. For each woman there is the arduous search to find a creative solution.

One way is via the homebased business. Many women have found this ideally suited to their requirements. At home the stress that comes from concerns about the lack of availability to one's dependents is alleviated. There is more ease in the physical proximity to the children. Questions of time and space need to be dealt with so that a structure is established wherein there is a separation of business requirements and the family's needs. With a resolution of this problem, the path towards self-fulfillment seems open. The central issues of work and love can be met in a setting conducive to both.

66 When we first started The Woman's Newspaper of Princeton, our expectations were that the venture would be an adventure and the business a probable failure. Much to our surprise, and partial dismay, the first issue was a hit and cries of 'encore' came in by mail as well as by phone. **99**

Publisher

I Am a Woman Working at Home

Elizabeth Forsythe Hailey, Author

I didn't set out to become a professional. I always enjoyed writing letters to family and friends and when I decided to write the life of my grandmother in letter form, I imagined that my only readers would be my children and perhaps someday my grandchildren. After *A Woman of Independent Means* was published and began to sell, I bought a slim briefcase and turned a linen closet into a filing cabinet. I was now in business.

> **66** My life as a working woman at home is not divided by physical, mental, or emotional 'distance.' Rather, family life and business affairs fuse in a satisfying whole. My husband and I work at it twenty-four hours a day, every day. **99**
>
> Craftsperson

The business grew out of something I was already doing for pleasure—which often seems to be the case with women working at home. To be paid for doing something you enjoy and would probably be doing anyway for free seems to me the ultimate goal for anybody, male or female.

The importance of doing work you love is the special strength that women bring into the marketplace, a strength that should not be forgotten as they struggle to achieve equal pay and equal status. The quality of the work and of the workplace is as important as the size of the paycheck. Women, who for so many centuries have worked without salary or status simply for the happiness and well-being of their family and society at large, are now in a position to bring some of their values with them into the marketplace—and to further humanize the process of working for a living. Working at home, along with shared jobs, flexible hours, maternity and paternity leaves, is one of the many new options available.

How many successful men have suddenly realized at midlife that the children they never had the time to know are grown now? A woman is not likely to experience such a midlife crisis. Even a woman who goes to an office every day does not leave her family behind when she is at work. There is always part of her brain worrying about what to have for dinner, when to schedule a repairman, who will stay home with a sick child. Like the magician's assistant, she often feels sawed in half.

The woman working at home can deal with these problems as they arise and does not have to spend working time worrying about them.

An added bonus: when I was devoting my life to my husband and children and not attempting any work of my own, I sometimes found myself resenting household chores—the endless cooking and cleaning which, no matter how efficiently or expertly you perform it, still has to be done all over again the next day. Once I began using the hours my children were at school to write, I welcomed the change of pace that housekeeping presented. After staring at a blank page and then wondering if there was any merit at all to the words I wrote to fill it, the task of preparing dinner seemed very concrete and satisfying. If I hadn't fixed dinner, people I loved would have gone to bed hungry. If I hadn't written those words—well, there were days when I wasn't convinced that would have made any difference to anyone. The truth was, my work was making an enormous difference to me in the value I placed on my life. Instead of setting up the family versus career conflict that inevitably accompanies a working wife and mother when she begins to seek a paying job outside the home, my writing was giving new satisfaction and meaning to the work of managing a household.

I'm not sure someone who has never worked in an office or for someone else can fully appreciate the luxury of working at home and being your own boss. In the early years of my marriage, before there were children, I worked as a copy editor. I still remember hurrying home on my lunch hour to scrub the bathroom and stopping by the grocery store on my way home from work, cookbook in hand, to pick up the ingredients for whatever new recipe I had decided to try for dinner. This was in the days before slow cookers, so I had to wait for the weekend to try out anything that had to simmer.

Now—though I am generally adamant about saving housework till after writing hours—I enjoy being able to mix bread dough in the morning so it will be ready for kneading and shaping when the children come home from school. I love being there when they arrive, each trying to outtalk the other, showing off test scores and art projects. And yet if I had not been working all day at my own projects, I suspect part of me would resent their glowing sense of accomplishment.

Parents working at home have an unusual opportunity to share with their children, sometimes directly or sometimes just by osmosis, the benefits of their professional experience. My two daughters read my manuscripts in the early stages, make editorial suggestions, proofread galleys, and often accompany me on speaking engagements to lend moral support.

I grew up in a very conventional household. I knew my father was a lawyer, but I had no idea what he did all day at the office. My mother ran the house very capably, but I remember hearing her say that she could not imagine how she would earn a living if anything ever happened to my father. Though she seemed quite content being at home, I sensed in her lack of any professional identity a source of suppressed panic.

My daughters have grown up with the example of two parents who work at home. (My husband is a playwright.) For them there is no mystery or terror connected with the idea of making a living. They have already begun to test their abilities and are secure in the knowledge that they possess skills of value in the marketplace. They have learned that certain aspects of earning a living can be boring and tedious, but the more control one has over the circumstances of work, the more rewarding it will be.

My work and my life are so interrelated it is often hard to tell where one stops and the other begins. Even the things I do for pleasure—reading books, going to plays or movies, traveling—nourish my work. The tragedy of the Industrial Revolution was the artificial boundary it erected between life and work. Work became something you did, often with gritted teeth, for at least a third of each day in order to be able to live the rest of the time. But when work is a necessary and enjoyable part of each day—something which, instead of separating you from your family, can be shared with them, making each member feel important and necessary—it is no longer a dreaded chore but an integral component of human experience. According to Freud, two things are required for a happy life: love and work. Working at home makes it possible to experience both at the same time.

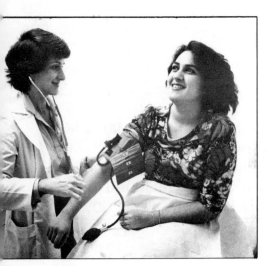

Toni Gloria Novick, M.D.
Photographer: Helaine Messer

Choosing a Home Business

Success means many things to many people—money, fulfillment, self-esteem, but for most, the base line is money and happiness (and not necessarily in that order). The ideal would seem to be feeling happy about what you're doing while the money rolls in! If a person achieves that, then one's occupation is not work but fun. It's a rare combination! How many people do you know who really enjoy their work?

> **"The number of individuals who make all or part of their living by the work of their hands, the ideas in their heads, and the need in their souls is growing more each day. It is often a lonely and discouraging existence and yet the most rewarding way to live a life."**
>
> Craftsperson

Choosing a home business, then, begins with an analysis of your skills and interests. What do you enjoy doing? List all sorts of activities and experiences, work-related or not, from which you can identify skills. Do you enjoy being with children? Playing the stock market? Planting a garden? Shopping? Cooking? Speaking a foreign language? Traveling? Have you a green thumb? A good ear? A discerning eye? Look for skills that overlap in several activities. What appeals to you? Creating? Taking risks? Communicating? Problem solving? Teaching? Persuading? Do you prefer to work alone or with others, under pressure or in a relaxed atmosphere? Analyze values. What's really important to you: making money or making a name for yourself? Filling free time or filling a need? Proving yourself or helping others? Be honest with yourself. When this exercise is completed, you should have a pretty good idea of who you are, which activities and values are most important to you, what skills you have, and the kind of work setting you prefer.

Talk to friends and neighbors. Make a people resource list and use it. Join a network. Check the Yellow Pages. Read trade magazines. Are there already similar established businesses in your area? Does your business fulfill a community need? If there are competitors, what are they doing? How are they failing to serve the public? Where do you fit in? Is extra schooling needed? An apprenticeship?

Cheri Lynn Russell
Furniture Restorer
Photographer: Michael Russell

We already mentioned the importance of enthusiasm. With that goes a sense of purpose and commitment. Are you willing to take risks and make sacrifices? You'll be giving up a certain amount of free time. There will be changing priorities and a changing lifestyle and, because of them, perhaps unexpected conflicts with the family. (On the other hand, family members might surprise you with large amounts of help, patience, and support.) Only you can decide if what you may be losing is worth what you may achieve.

Of course, don't overlook the amount of available capital. This may influence a business decision more than any other factor. Determine how much is needed to pay for stock, equipment, supplies, and advertising. Then figure out how much you can invest and (just in case) how much you can lose.

Anybody can start a business. The trick is to stay in it. Choosing a business—whether at home or an outside location—calls for good judgment, honest advice, and common sense. When the decision is made, jump into the new venture wholeheartedly. Give it everything you can. We all make mistakes, and we learn from every one of them. As the business grows, so you will grow.

Getting Started Right

Elizabeth T. Lyons, Chief of Small Business Assistance Office, N.J. Department of Commerce and Economic Development

66 Getting a new company off the ground isn't easy. We are lucky to have husbands who are generally encouraging and supportive. But, there are so many little obstacles to meet and cover in order to protect and proffer one's talent and to overcome economic roadblocks. 99

Stationery Designer

Getting started right applies to the original start-up of a business and to those times when a change in ownership, expansion, new products or services, financial viability, or other factors provide an opportunity for review and reevaluation of the business plan. A woman whose business grew out of a hobby or personal skill often skips the design of the business plan because it (the business) just grew like Topsy. Without realizing it, an entrepreneur might be ignoring tax or labor laws, licensing regulations, or employer's responsibilities.

If you are thinking of starting a business you will probably find yourself explaining your idea, product, service, goals, objectives, fees, prices, etc., to a great number of people. From some you'll have unenthusiastic or negative feedback or tough questions. A well-thought-out business plan will fortify you for inquiries from potential customers, lenders, and the professionals whose services you'll need. The time you invest in business research and the development of your plan will save you money in professional fees and will improve your ability to sell yourself as a business owner.

A business consultant might be helpful to you in suggesting some of the questions you should ask your accountant, lawyer, insurance consultant, or banker. I suggest you begin your research by writing the answers to the following questions. If you don't have the answers, you'll know where to begin to gather data.

- Why are you starting a business? Is this temporary or long-term?
- What type of business, product, or service do you own or want to own?
- What are the objectives of the business? Your personal objectives?
- What are the financial objectives? Are you profit oriented?
- Do you have the experience or expertise required for this business?
- What disciplines, skills, experience, personality, and other qualifications are required?
- What licensing laws or regulations govern the production and sale of your product or service? Must you be licensed or bonded?
- Is your product or service season- or fad-related (pet rock, hula hoop, etc.)? If so, do you have secondary products or services?
- What is your philosophy regarding customer service, quality, public relations?
- Have you set objectives for the first five years?
- How have others fared in this type of business? Percent of failures and successes?
- How might a recession or poor cash flow affect the firm's viability?
- What are the first year's goals for: sales, gross income, net profit, name recognition, clients, or customers?

- What will your costs be for production and marketing?
- Have you established contacts with potential customers? How?
- Is there a need for patent, copyright, or trademark protection?
- Do you understand enough to keep simple books, collect and pay taxes, take discounts, build and maintain good credit?
- Is a sole proprietorship, partnership, or corporation best for you?
- If you have a partnership, does your contract specify the term of the agreement and how the partnership might be dissolved without endangering the business?
- Which partner holds the greater number of shares? Why? What are the rights and responsibilities of the partners (draw, expenses, etc.)?
- How will budgets be established?
- How will prices and fees be set to insure a reasonable profit?
- How much space will be required for production, inventory, supplies, offices, records maintenance, etc.?
- How will business telephones, mail, checkbooks, and files be isolated from the family activities?
- Have you identified which of your purchases and expenses should be paid from the business checkbook and charged as business expenses, so that you are not spending taxed income from another source on expenditures which should be charged to the business?
- Have you applied for separate credit cards for billings of business-related expenses?
- How much cash will you need to operate your business for the first twelve months?
- What is the span of time from purchase of raw materials through production, distribution, sales, billing, and payment? Can you continue to purchase materials, pay staff, taxes, overhead, during that period?
- Is visibility important in your business? How will you plan to create or enhance a public image?
- Have you budgeted membership dues for business and professional organizations?
- What kind of equipment or vehicle will you require? Have you considered whether it should be purchased, leased, new, secondhand?
- Should you have an answering service or an answering machine?
- Will you require a post office box?
- If operating from home, are you violating any local ordinances?
- What have you done to improve neighborhood relationships?
- Do you have people working for you? How are they paid?
- Are you considered (by them) to be an employer or contractor?
- In either case, do you know how to report earnings or fees paid?
- Have you considered whether you are responsible for payment of employer contributions for social security taxes, unemployment, and disability taxes? Ask your accountant to explain all this in detail.
- Are you aware of the Equal Pay Act, O.S.H.A. (Occupational Safety and Health Act), the minimum wage, age discrimination, and employment of minors laws?
- Have you consulted your insurance agent about liability, key person, and other insurances?
- Have you considered attending selected courses or workshops on business to gain information about entrepreneurship?

Angel Ortloff
Potter
Photographer: Bob Stewart

Please do not become discouraged, just apply the same determination to this project as you've used in getting to where you are now, and you'll begin to ask the right questions of the experts.

Reaching Out

❝I was really at loose ends in the beginning. Fortunately, the Small Business Administration, S.C.O.R.E., and people already established in the business world were more than willing to help. Top resource people provided me with much needed answers and time.❞

Data Processor

Anita Ruslin

*Personalized Stationery
Invitations, Announcements*

15 Warwick Road, Edison, N.J. 08817
By Appointment Only (201)548-5481

A homebased business can be stimulating and rewarding and may help to improve and protect your present or future, both financially and emotionally.

To prepare yourself for new challenges in business, reach out systematically in all directions to acquire as much information as possible about your fields of interest.

Research the library. Contact individuals in your field and listen to their suggestions, experiences, present and future concerns. Listen for ideas on management, advertising, pricing, and marketing. Listen for general statements, as well as small details.

Work for someone active in your chosen field, or a closely related one. Familiarize yourself with price lists, materials, marketing methods, machines available (if any are required), and other pertinent information.

Don't reject outright a field of interest in which you haven't had the necessary education. Consider an apprenticeship or take a course in that subject. Adult education classes can be very useful, as well as special classes for entrepreneurs.

Seek information from available agencies, organizations, and associations, such as the following:

Small Business Administration (SBA)
1441 L Street, NW
Washington, DC 20416
Refer to phone directory for local district office.

The SBA provides free counseling and training to help individuals plan, start, or manage a business. It also helps secure loans through local banks by guaranteeing up to 90 percent of a loan to $500,000. One can apply for a direct loan, providing funds are available. Direct funds are limited to $150,000.

The Women's Business Ownership Office of the Small Business Administration is trying to locate women-owned firms that may be interested in providing a broad range of goods and services directly to the federal government and its prime contractors. If your company has the capability of performing on federal prime contracts and/or subcontracts, you can register on the Procurement Automated Source System (PASS) with over 11,000 other women business owners already profiled in the system. There is a note of caution, however: before considering federal contracting you should have a flourishing business with a guaranteed cash flow that will cover your expenses for six months to a year. For additional PASS information contact Women's Business Ownership Office, SBA.

Service Corps of Retired Executives (SCORE)
1441 L Street, NW—Room 100
Washington, DC 20416
202/653-6279 or refer to your local phone directory

SCORE now has more than 7,800 counselors at work across the nation—volunteers, who are seasoned business executives, providing management assistance to small business owners. (SCORE is a service of the U.S. Small Business Administration.)

Department of Agriculture
Agricultural Co-Op Service
500 12th Street, SW—Room 550 GHI
Washington, DC 20250

This is an excellent place for rural area craftswomen to get information about cooperative craft programs and technical assistance.

U.S. Department of Commerce
Office of Assistant Secretary of Commerce
Washington, DC 20230

This federal office offers business development loans and loan guarantees to individuals, partners, and profit-making organizations.

Farmers Home Administration
U.S. Department of Agriculture
Room 4121S
12th and Independence Avenues, SW
Washington, DC 20250

Lending agency for people who generally cannot get credit elsewhere.

National Economic Development Law Center
2150 Shattuck Avenue
Berkeley, CA 94700
415/548-2600

The Center will answer simple legal questions free of charge and indicate when a lawyer is necessary.

American Woman's Economic Development Corporation
(AWED)
60 East 42nd St.
New York, NY 10165
212/692-9100

Andrea and LaRue RiEcks
Entertainment Specialists
Credit: JED Photo

AWED provides technical training, assistance, and counseling to women business owners and those planning to go into business. (AWED is partially funded by the U.S. Small Business Administration.)

National Alliance of Homebased Businesswomen (NAHB)
P.O. Box 95
Norwood, NJ 07648

NAHB is a network of women who work from home and is dedicated to encouraging, educating, and promoting all women who work, or wish to work, from their homes.

After you decide what to do and how to do it legally, be aware of day-to-day activities that can help your business grow. Word of mouth can bring a substantial number of customers. If you've been active in organizations, let the members know what you're doing. Get a second telephone number with an answering machine or answering service and, as the commercial says, "reach out and touch someone." Newspaper, television, and radio interviews provide marvelous opportunities to reach thousands of people at the same time.

Reach out—so that others might reach you!

Goals: The Ultimate High!

$10,000 net profit the first year!
A college degree!
Six classes, six students per class, within six months!
Five employees in three years!
Nationwide sales representation within four years!
A better mousetrap next year!

And the world *will* beat a path to your door! Goals are important for the growth of a business and for the development of the business owner.

Goals give order and structure to a business plan and define its limits, and they measure progress and give one pride of accomplishment. Since achievement is a motivator, it inspires more work, more goal setting, more success. And, as the old saw goes, "Nothing succeeds like success!"

Think of the mountain climber inching to the top. She throws up her skyhook to a ridge above, then carefully moves upward till she reaches that point of the rock. She reevaluates her position, sets her eyes on the goal, then again throws the skyhook. Inch by inch, step by step, goal by goal—until she conquers the peak and achieves the success so long sought after!

To succeed, goals must be realistic, relevant to the business, and relevant to the individual, as well. One must plan for goals and designate guideposts of achievement, but be able to shift when things are not going as planned. The problem is that goal-setting approaches often fail. Why? There are too many main goals or too many subgoals, resulting in confusion; there are conflicting priorities; there is inadequate built-in accountability—goals must be measurable. When goals are not met, it's easy to say "they probably weren't important anyway." The real problem is that they weren't realistic to begin with, or there was no follow-up. Goals are important, but alone can accomplish nothing. A plan of action to meet the goals, followed meticulously, is required.

Goals are clear statements of direction, targets that have been set for a business in order to fulfill its purposes. They should indicate impacts, outcomes, and effects; they are not strategies, activities, or processes.

If the larger goals seem overwhelming, make your goals more attainable: start small—"I'll sell 2,000 units next year," not 20,000; be specific—"I'll enroll in an advanced horticulture class," not "I'll need more training"; think immediate—next week, not next year; and think positive—"I'll be more confident," not "I'll be less unsure of myself."

Goals are associated with long-range planning; objectives can be here and now. To reach goals, begin with daily objectives: write that long overdue letter; call the supplier you met at the trade show while his memory of you is fresh; pay bills; take action on that pile of papers rather than reshuffling them. Every job is composed of small details, which are manageable if worked at one at a time. With simplification and perserverance a whole task can be completed with definable, successive objectives that lead to the accomplishment of larger goals.

The mountain will be yours, the peak of success attainable—slow but sure, to the very top. Ever upward! Excelsior!

Doranne Jacobson
Anthropologist
Photographer: Pamela W. Sartorelli

The Business Plan

A business plan is written to—

1. establish what your business objectives are and indicate how you will reach them or to describe a company's past and future operations;
2. help you discover, in advance, areas where problems may occur, thereby giving you an opportunity to rectify problems with alternative plans;
3. indicate to your banker or other lender exactly how the monies will be spent and where the profits will be made to further the company's goals and reward the investor.

An initial business plan should help to define all of the following: the exact nature of your business, the product or service being sold, the identity of the competition, why the business is being developed, how much money will be needed for start-up expenses and through the first year, what profit can be made, who your customers are and where they are located, sales strategies, how much time will be devoted to the business, and the various job responsibilities within the business.

In planning, a statement of an anticipated outcome or objective is the first element required. The formal plan itself evolves through writing the strategy needed to reach each goal. Although no two people have exactly the same goals, all workable goals have certain common denominators. All successful plans aim at establishing action steps to achieve desired goals, so that proposed ideas can be analyzed, potential strengths and weaknesses discovered, and pitfalls avoided by providing contingency plans before any actual harm has been encountered.

Clearly, before drawing any map, it is important to know as much as possible about the specific territory in which you are working. Equally important is the evaluation of your business. Write down exactly where you want to go before starting up, taking over someone else's shop, or altering directions in a well-established venture. Setting goals for one, three, and five years down the line will help you choose the wisest steps to move forward systematically.

Planning ahead gives one the opportunity to better understand all aspects of a business. For example, calculating the costs of implementing a new idea while in the thinking stages makes it possible to forecast what funds are required, where they will come from, and how debts will be paid. Careful planning can avoid financial disasters. Lack of direction and structure so often are the reasons given for business failure. Plan to succeed!

Drawing a directional map is conditional upon a logical progression from a starting point to a desired end point. This approach is also true when constructing a plan; therefore, the following questions must be answered, since the resulting information is basic and must be understood before opening any doors to customers.

> 66 There is an unconscious 'businesslikeness' in going to a separate area or room to work in each day. Spouses, children, and friends sense an invisible barrier between your work life and home life, which is conducive to greater discipline and productivity. 99
>
> Craftsperson

29

Planning Your Business

Labarbara Pugh
Linen Manufacturer
Photographer: Fred Nichols

What business am I in?

This definition is essential. Too many entrepreneurs have failed because diversification in their business caused depletion of funds and energy.

Theoretically, a real estate broker could buy lots, renovate older homes, run an agency, and buy furniture at estate sales to resell at auctions; however, an antique business, a real estate agency, or a renovating business each take time, energy, and money to be run properly. Building one business well is financially and psychologically more rewarding than running several businesses poorly.

What product or service am I selling?

Define your service or product in great detail. If you are in a consulting service, describe your area of expertise. This will make you zero in on exactly who you are and what you want to achieve.

A craftsperson may wish to work in diversified areas or select one specialty. In either case, still more definition is necessary. If in one specialty—stained glass, for example—refine your definition still further. Will you create one-of-a-kind, high-priced windows for architects, lamp shades and frames for local stores, or boxes and hand mirrors to be sold in boutiques nationwide?

In planning, as a product or service becomes defined, so does an environment. A homebased glass studio can double as a shop, but perhaps buying or renting a co-op building with a group of artists or craftspersons would prove more beneficial if the others are willing to share financial and sales responsibilities.

Who is my competition?

Imagine planning to start a homebased plant nursery, then discovering five other nurseries in the neighborhood specializing in roses. If selling roses was part of your plan, cross that off your list of potential possibilities and find a replacement. Specialize in mums, daisies, or any other plant that is in demand in your area. Often a great deal of money can be saved on paper by not competing with too many local dealers.

Answer these questions: How large are my competitors? Who are their customers? Do they have employees and how many? What price lines do my competitors carry? Who is prospering or just surviving? How many have recently gone out of business and why? Analyzing why others succeed or fail will help to clarify your own strengths (sometimes referred to as differential advantages), encourage you to capitalize on everything that competitors are doing poorly, and provide an effective means of summarizing selling points to pass on to buyers and prospective customers. The information gathered from observations of competitors helps when making future decisions on what to sell, for how much, and to whom. It can even clarify where to advertise and what hours to be available.

Why am I developing a business?

People build their own businesses for a variety of reasons based on personal needs and business expectations. Under personal needs one might include a desire for independence, a wish to combine family and work into one environment, the necessity for a two-income family, or a single parent's obligation to raise her children and still earn a living. Money, power, fame, or a taste for excitement and adventure—these, too, are personal needs.

When establishing business needs, defining both profit and growth objectives becomes imperative. Realistically, the larger the business becomes, the more work hours will be involved, so carefully balance personal and professional needs. In considering operational and managerial needs, plan who will be the decision makers, advisors, and who can be called upon for help; then indicate who now, and in the near future, will fill every necessary job and how much each will be paid.

How much is needed to operate this business?

When beginning a business, define your start-up costs by listing equipment, equipment installation, starting inventory, home or office remodeling, insurance fees, deposits for utilities, telephone or telegraph, first-time legal and professional fees, membership dues, licenses and permits, start-up advertising, and actual operating cash. Whether start-up money has been saved or borrowed, you and your business will be responsible for paying all these bills and, if monies have been borrowed, for paying back debts!

Next, project business expenses for each month of the first business year and calculate the total of future expenditures. What is your rock-bottom, bare-bones budget?

A budget can help one visualize the dollar amount of anticipated monthly revenues and expenses. Such a cash-flow forecast is a planning tool that can eliminate the anxiety of not knowing where the money is coming from or where it is going. The business owner must be prepared for the financial highs and lows of a business cycle.

Who are my customers and where are they located?

Discovering what customers' desires are, then satisfying their wants and needs with your product or service could bring them to your door provided such potential buyers see or hear about your product.

How can one locate prospective clients? Start by evaluating the source of your competitors' customers and asking friends, colleagues, students, and neighbors to suggest potential customers or give referrals. Identification of your customers, where they live, and what their buying habits are will assist in understanding whether a growth or static market exists and will help in defining your potential market share in your first, second, and subsequent years in business.

In your plan of action, clearly state exactly what methods will be used to reach buyers—how and where and when. Classify customers according to such demographic statistics as age, income, sex, and education. Relating customers' needs to the benefits provided by the product or service increases selling opportunities and business growth, while at the same time allowing you to develop a more personal and effective business strategy.

What kind of sales strategy is needed?

Low prices generally encourage sales but often dictate a need for mass production or low-priced, quantity buying. High prices suggest value but often eliminate prospective customers. Value will always influence pricing, but so does the amount charged by a competitor. Whether your reputation will be built on low-, medium-, or high-priced goods or services, you need a sales strategy. The decision will be reflected in your advertising: "Buy the best product in town!" or "Where else can you find two for the price of one?"

After setting prices, determine methods for payment. Is yours a cash-only business or will a credit card system be used to induce more sales?

66Women owners and managers of construction companies are few and far between. Yet, it is one of the most creative, exciting and satisfying careers a woman could pursue—take it from an old gal who has been there for a mighty long time. The structures I have designed and built stand as monuments for my grandchildren to see. Proof that their grandmother chose a profession with a solid (concrete) foundation.**99**

Builder

Planning Your Business

There are pros and cons to using credit cards, so consider the problems in obtaining and maintaining such a system. You may have to increase prices to absorb the extra costs of providing customers with credit opportunities.

Payment can be cash in advance, cash on delivery, credit card, or payment after delivery—if a service, one-third at onset, one-third when half finished, and the final third upon completion of the work. While cash in advance is, of course, the most desirable method of being paid, you will have to be guided by the customs of your particular business and set up the situation that is best for you and acceptable to your customers.

An important aspect of the overall plan is whether to produce your own goods and services or sell the goods and services provided by someone else. If your intention is just to sell, who will be responsible for production and how will they be paid? Conversely, if you are going to produce, who will sell, at what price, and will a salary or commission be paid? When starting out, many homebased business people are responsible for both production and sales.

How much time am I willing or able to devote to a business?

In developing a home business, it's imperative to schedule working hours into days which often do not have spare minutes. To plan work hours, set daily or weekly objectives. "I'm going to work five hours a day, 9:00 A.M.–12:00 P.M. and 1:00 P.M.–3:00 P.M." Or, "I'm going to work twenty-five hours a week." Now review your present schedule to see how to achieve that objective. By writing down exactly how your hours are spent every day for one week from the hour of waking to the final collapse in bed at night, you will surprise your family and yourself and see opportunities to restructure priorities and to change the schedule to allow time to develop a successful business.

Asking family members to assist your efforts in developing a workable time chart is one way of saying "I need your help to make this work." In many families, becoming involved at the planning stage brings a sympathy and understanding that otherwise might not be established so easily.

Who will do what jobs?

Write a job description for each position within your business. The manager, buyer, star salesperson, accountant, secretary, and manufacturer may all be one and the same person, but it is important to be able to define the specific duties each must accomplish. If, as a business owner, there are one or two jobs you dislike intensely or feel you cannot do, hire someone who has those skills. A business can fail when an important job is simply left undone. Keeping a business functioning depends upon completing all vital jobs.

Along with that goes the responsibility for motivating your workers. We have said that homebased business can be a lot of fun, but no one ever said it would be easy!

When does my plan need to be altered?

A plan must be periodically reviewed and revised. Flexibility is important in an ever-changing marketplace. Tastes and attitudes of customers alter, people move, technologies improve, business conditions vary; a plan of action must be responsive to these changes. A goal or an entire plan may need revision. Meaningful and realistic revisions and adjustments to your plan of action will keep the business alive and lively and help ensure its survival and success.

Ultimately your plan should be like a map drawn to help guide your daily business activities. If you know where you're going and exactly which road to take, it makes the going so much easier.

As your business grows and you want to expand, there is still another type of plan that you, the business owner, will need in your search for equity financing. Such a plan may be the sole basis for approval by private investors, venture capitalists, investment companies, and banks. It describes a company's past and current operations, then shows how the desired investment or loan will enable the company to reach its goals and also, of course, how the investor will be rewarded. The following is a sample business plan outline:

I. Cover Letter

    A Dollar amount requested
    B. Terms and timing
    C. Type and price of securities

II. Summary

    A. Business description
       1.Name
       2.Location and plant description
       3.Product
       4.Market and competition
       5.Management expertise
    B. Business goals
    C. Summary of financial needs and application of funds
    D. Earnings projections and potential return to investors

Ellen and Jo DiMaggio
Photographers
Credit: JED Photo

III. Market Analysis

    A. Description of total market
    B. Industry trends
    C. Target market
    D. Competition

IV. Products or Services

    A. Description of product line
    B. Proprietary position: patents, copyrights, and legal and technical considerations
    C. Comparison to competitors' products

V. Manufacturing Process (if applicable)

    A. Materials
    B. Sources of supply
    C. Production methods

VI. Marketing Strategy

    A. Overall strategy
    B. Pricing policy
    C. Sales terms
    D. Method of selling, distributing, and servicing products

VII. Management Plan

    A. Form of business organization
    B. Board of directors composition
    C. Officers: organization chart and responsibilities
    D. Resumés of key personnel
    E. Staffing plan/number of employees
    F. Facilities plan/planned capital improvements
    G. Operating plan/schedule of upcoming work for next one to two years

VIII. Financial Data

    A. Financial history (five years to present)
    B. Five-year financial projections (first year by quarters; remaining years annually)
      1. Profit and loss statements
      2. Balance sheets
      3. Cash flow chart
      4. Capital expenditure estimates
    C. Explanation of projections
    D. Key business ratios
    E. Explanation of use and effect of new funds
    F. Potential return to investors compared to competitors and the industry in general.

Serious planning is marked by an emphasis on contingency and by a meticulous interest in small details. Through a business plan such as this, investors and bankers will be able to evaluate your business judgment, your fiscal integrity, your management expertise, and your ability to work with others. To be honest, your plan should represent optimism, pessimism, and realism.

Turning Volunteer Skills into Marketable Skills

Marie MacBride, Communications Consultant

The hours you have spent as a volunteer were of great benefit to someone or to some organization. Now is the time to make them count for you.

The traditional twenty-five to fifty-year-old housewife/volunteer more often than not is finding it necessary to seek financial reward for her efforts. She has earned the right to have her volunteer accomplishments recognized by business. One businessman said that any woman who can work successfully with a PTA board has management skills. The trick is to examine the volunteer experience to discover how it can be used to help women who have or are planning to have homebased businesses.

We tend to think in boxes or categories. Perhaps you equate skills with something learned in the classroom or only of real value when it is paid for. The classroom provides theory, but a skill is the proven ability to do something—whether it was learned in the home, in a volunteer position, or in a paying job. The bottom line is the ability you have.

For whatever reason, if you have decided that you need—or just want—to work from your home and you have no special product or service in mind, take heart. Don't ever say, "I can't do anything." You do have a marketable skill. More than one woman, after taking inventory, has identified her own skill and used it as the heart of a thriving business. For example, one woman had a flair for taking bits and pieces of her last year's (and previous years') wardrobe and changing and combining them to express this year's styles. Now she does this for a handsome fee for people lacking the flair or time to do it for themselves. All she knew was how to dress stylishly. Other businesses have been developed from what women learned to do at home: planning/managing weddings, dog sitting or grooming, window trimming, shopping for shut-ins or out-of-towners, sandwich supplier, wake-up service; the list goes on and on. One woman

> 66 ... This volunteer experience, along with my typing and layout experience, enabled me to write the book, do the layout, take it to the printer press-ready, and now I'm marketing it. I'm sure that many businesses have been started because of volunteer involvement. 99
>
> Writer

Betty Marx Dwin
Accessories Manufacturer

who is especially good at organization organizes other people's closets and cupboards, offices, or homes for a fee.

If you already know what business to operate from your home, but are convinced one aspect of that business is impossible for you because "you can't do that," take another look. Bookkeeping, for example, is not a great mystery. Did you ever keep accounts for an event for a volunteer organization or pay the bills for your family? You can do it for your business; at least you can do it until your business grows so that it makes sense to hire someone to keep books for you. But, to start with, you can keep accurate records (bills, receipts, and cancelled checks) of what comes in and what goes out.

Your volunteer habit of giving service is a valuable skill that will show through in your business dealings; service is the heart of good business practices.

If you have successfully managed a large event for a church or a community organization, you have more management skills than you realize. You had to set goals, develop a strategy (or means) for reaching the goals. Then you had to put the strategy into operation and you had measurable results. You probably selected workers, coordinated their activities, controlled the finances, promoted the event, and kept to a production schedule. All of these activities are management skills. You have them.

If you fear you do not have the ability to provide your product or service and then also manage the business end of your endeavor, remember that you have proven you can take care of a number of things at the same time. While you volunteered many hours and days, you continued to keep your home running and your family fed, well, and happy. In order to do that, you had to use your time and resources wisely. Businessmen devote much time and pay large fees for workshops on time management and the husbandry of resources. You have those skills!

Suppose you have taken inventory of your skills and feel you need to add or update communication techniques, or typing on modern machines, or setting up displays with the latest equipment. Take a volunteer job and make it work for you. Seek a well-organized nonprofit or cultural organization that will accommodate your need to learn while you supply volunteer work hours. Increasingly, these organizations are learning that the volunteers have the right to fill their own needs while giving service valuable to the organizations. Shop around until you find a volunteer job that will give you the business experience you need. Start with a Volunteer Bureau or Voluntary Action Center nearest you. They know what community groups will be able to provide the volunteer job to help you sharpen your skills, and they understand that you have the right to learn while volunteering.

There's no need to hesitate using a record of your volunteer work to document your ability in a given area. Such work is accepted as job experience for civil service employment, and business is beginning to look more carefully at the correlation between volunteer work and the same work defined in business terminology.

And finally, use some volunteer help yourself! Members of the National Alliance of Homebased Businesswomen can give you voluntary guidance. SCORE, the Service Corps of Retired Executives, is a volunteer adjunct to the Small Business Administration that gives free advice to people with business problems. The Small Business Administration is listed in the telephone directory under "United States Government."

Volunteering has value for you. Use it!

The Importance of Being Organized

Sunny Schlenger, Management Consultant

The late Bennett Cerf once told his wife, "You could do everything you wanted to in life if you were organized." This is especially true for the woman working at home, who really needs to be an organizational expert at keeping track of all the balls she's juggling; however, there is no value in being organized simply to be organized. You need a framework, an approach that will help you accomplish what you want to do and need to do in the time available to do it. As such, being organized does not mean the same thing as being neat. Neat-looking surroundings can be very nice, but being neat is not the same thing as having a system. Being organized means having a system—one that enables you to find what you want when you need it. For example, an appropriately labeled sloppy-looking file folder is better than a miscellaneous neat pile which has to be gone through to determine if what is wanted is actually in there.

"I manage all of this by making lists. Someone also told me that you shouldn't let a piece of paper cross your desk more than once. When I really get in over my head, I practice this policy and find the work gets done without further delay."

Salesperson

Organization should make life simple. Systems should work for you, helping you to achieve your goals and objectives. A certain amount of self-discipline is called for, but the payoffs are worth it.

So where should you start? Much as you might wish otherwise, you only have twenty-four hours in a day, and the success of your organizational systems will depend, to a large extent, on how well you utilize that time. Effective time management does not come about by accident. It comes about through careful planning, which takes into account your own priorities and the needs of your family. Being aware of your own priorities is important, because as time demands increase, it is usually a woman's own needs that are sacrificed first. It's essential to strike a balance between what activities you consider to be important to your individual growth and development, and those that contribute to the well-being of your family. Careful planning will allow you to devote time to both.

Your Best Foot Forward

Try to schedule your activities to take into account your personal energy level (i.e., how energetic you feel at various times during the day) and external demands on your time. Utilize your changing level to the greatest extent possible, reserving tasks demanding the utmost in concentration for those times when you're willing and able to devote your full attention to them. Likewise, group less-demanding activities for those hours of the day when your energy level is lower, or interruptions tend to be more frequent.

A separate or reserved place to work is also very important. Not only will it enable you to organize your environment more effectively to accomplish the task at hand, but it will also put you in the appropriate frame of mind as a businesswoman. One of the major pitfalls for women working at home is the tendency not to separate business tasks from personal/household tasks. When you enter your office, studio, or even the corner of your dining room, which you've reserved for working, you should be prepared to devote yourself exclusively to your current project without jumping up to dust the shutters or vacuum the rug.

Working at home makes it difficult to ignore the demands of housekeeping, because the results of your inattention will surround you. Unfortunately, housework is a part of our lives with no real beginning and no real ending. It will take up as much of your time as you allow. Housekeeping has to be attended to, by someone, in order that it doesn't interfere with your work. Options include setting aside a limited amount of your time to clean—either in a large chunk or smaller periods, enlisting the aid of your family, or hiring someone to do the cleaning for you. Just remember that if having a perfectly clean and orderly house seven days a week is one of your priorities, then the time or money needed to accomplish that has to come from somewhere. That is, it needs to be planned for in your organizational scheme.

You will find it much easier to get right down to work if everything you own has a place to "live," from your paper clips on up to important documents that will be needed for reference; however, in deciding where something should "live," you want to ask the correct question. You don't want to ask, "Where should I put this?" You do want to ask, "How do I plan to use this?" In answering the question of how you plan to use it, you will very often find out where you should put it. For example: a post card comes in the mail, telling you of an upcoming sale at your favorite clothing store. If you plan to take advantage of the sale, the card should be posted in a place where it will remind you when to go (e.g., in your calendar book, on your bulletin board, on your refrigerator door). Putting it in a pile on your desk will most likely result in your being reminded of the sale after it is over.

It is not easy to change old habits. To be successful, you need to be flexible and maintain your sense of humor, keeping in mind that the appropriateness of solutions will change as your needs change. What is right for you this year may not be right for you next year. What works for your best friend might not work for you. You have to assess your own current situation, determine your objectives, and implement the organizational systems that will get you where you want to go.

Organizing Basics

1. Determine your own priorities and those of your family. Plan carefully to assure proper time allotment to each. Allow enough flexibility to deal with the unexpected.
2. If possible, match your changing energy level to the nature of your tasks. Tackle each task when you're best prepared to get the results you need.
3. Reserve a separate place for your business activities. Minimize distractions in order to concentrate on the job at hand.
4. Schedule a regular housework routine that will not interfere with your office/studio hours.
5. Arrange your work space so that the items you use most frequently are within easy reach. Replace them after use so you won't waste valuable time searching for them.
6. Save only what you plan to use. File or store according to the way you will refer to the item (e.g., by date, name, or subject).
7. Be aware of your own personal style and adapt the available organizational techniques to it. Continually evaluate to make sure that your systems feel right and are helping you to accomplish your objectives.
8. Develop your sense of humor! The more successful you become, the more difficult it may seem to stay organized. It is a challenge, but one that can be enjoyed for its creative possibilities and positive results.

> **66** My biggest problem is procrastination. I tend to put off things until the last minute, then rush breathlessly around trying to get them done and thus feel very pressured. **99**
>
> Newsletter Publisher

Sheila Siderman
Educational Consultant
Credit: JED Photo

Borrowing Time

66 In addition to the business, I was able to take my daughter Kate's chicken pox in stride last winter, train the new puppy, organize and direct a public service project, and produce the usual array of handmade gifts. 99

Tutor

Linda Cox
Sugar Shaper
Photographer: Bob Stewart

One of the greatest advantages that comes from working at home is the ease with which one can sneak into the home office or studio at all hours of the day or night. One of the most difficult tasks faced by any woman with a homebased business is not sneaking into the home office or studio.

In a nationwide study, researchers found that most women in middle-income households who have part-time jobs devote seven hours daily to household duties! These were broadly defined by the women themselves, who listed eighty different activities from child care and car repair to buying clothes and attendance at school meetings. Women with full-time jobs spend five hours daily running their households! These already overburdened women, with ingenuity and determination, can and must plan free time for themselves.

Just as organization and discipline are essential when beginning your at-home business, they become even more important as time goes on. At first you may say: "Don't mop the kitchen floor now, better to spend this time working!" But it is likely that as your business grows and grows, the hours for housework and, more important, time for relaxation will diminish. You will then say: "How can I mop the kitchen floor now—I'm working all the time!" If you don't enjoy housework or can't manage doing everything alone, hire help as soon as you can afford to do so. If you have a young family, write job lists for the children. Stick with these lists. If children help with the chores, it furthers their spirit of cooperation! Don't let chores rule you, either. You're the boss, remember? Skip anything that's not important. Simplify what has to be done—and do it faster!

There comes a point when a business of any nature, if it's going to succeed, takes off! Suddenly you find yourself a workaholic. Your business has grown this far because of your dedication, ambition, enthusiasm, and a lot of hard work. Now you see bigger and better things ahead. As your business grows, invest in adequate household equipment and quality assistance, so you will have more time to do the work that makes your business unique. Twenty-four hours in a day aren't nearly enough for the homemaker/businesswoman. If you can't borrow time, steal it anywhere you can! Wake up half an hour early for your morning exercises. If possible, shop during the dinner hour or at night when stores are empty. Do all your errands at one time. Shop by mail. Learn to say no to nonbusiness demands on your time. Be a two-at-a-timer! While talking on the phone, write your grocery list. Watch TV and catch up on your magazine reading. Set fake deadlines! If you have an appointment at 2:00

P.M., put 1:45 on your calendar and spend those extra minutes reading the newspapers or preparing notes.

If time pressures are overwhelming, you might consider a partnership with someone you trust who has similar interests and varied abilities, so that stresses and strains can be divided. In an expanding business, never forget that its prime purpose is to enable you to enjoy life to its fullest.

Write a list filled with specific objectives for private pleasures.

1. Get six hours sleep tonight!
2. Do exercises!
3. See an exhibition or show!
4. Call a close friend!
5. Read a good book!
6. Lie in the sun!

A museum, a racquetball game, a picnic, a day of pure joy not work related can give you a fresh head to think with, a heart that will endure competition, and the nerves needed to survive in the complicated, hectic, slightly crazy, very exciting time we live in today!

You can borrow time, steal time, and even buy time! Your business is growing. Still you need help. This can come in two forms: people and machines.

Although the capital costs of machines may seem high, they can usually be rented or leased in a very tax-advantageous manner. The rental of a machine is fully deductible as a business expense, but you do not own anything after a long period of rental payments. If, instead, you purchase a machine, you can take deductions for its depreciation plus get an additional first-year investment tax credit. The choice of rental versus ownership depends very much on the expected life of the equipment and the rate at which modernization is expected to occur. A sewing machine could be bought since enormous strides in improvements are not expected. Renting or leasing a computer might be wiser since more efficient models come on the market about twice a year. Clearly, these choices involve quite different cash requirements. This is an area in which it would be wise to receive advice and guidance from other people in your line of work, as well as from your accountant.

The type of people help required will greatly depend on the type of business. A lawyer can increase her output enormously by hiring another secretary or perhaps a paralegal. A weaver might have to bring in another craftsperson of equal ability. A caterer may need an assistant to take over some of the culinary duties while she frees up her time to see customers. The important factors here are compatibility and trust between the newcomer and the original business owner, since dissolving any type of relationship within a small business is a traumatic event, which can be fatal.

As you grow, constantly be aware of how your growth can be supported by personnel and/or machines.

> 66 Being my own boss has been one of the greatest experiences of my life. For others who are under the stress and strain, may I offer a suggestion: take one half hour a day to just write about what is on your mind. I find poetry and prose an excellent release. 99

Courier

> 66 When I have to be out with other clients, printers, etc., I arrange my schedule to do these things during school hours. As a needlecraft designer, much of my work can also be done in the evening while watching television! 99

Designer

Home Is Where the Kids Are

> **"**In my own way, I also hope to illustrate to him by preference and example that not only can Daddies go to work by day or night, Mommies have work beyond just 'house stuff' and that encompasses goals and dreams and successes because Mommies are people, too.**"**

Stationery Designer

It should come as no surprise that a great many of the women listed in this directory began businesses at home specifically because they had children living there. Some could not afford child care; some liked the convenience, comfort, and flexibility of working at home and being with their children; others felt it was important to be around when the youngsters were in their developing years. A theater director and drama coach works at home to be available for her children's needs because she has never met a baby sitter that could match "the mother's touch." A lawyer wrote that being home in case a child needs her gives each one a sense of security and self-esteem.

A divorced jewelry manufacturer now works at home to be with her teenagers. When growing up, she felt that she never saw her mother, who worked away from home, and she doesn't want her own children to have similar feelings.

For the single parent, two reasons for working at home take on special meaning: convenience and security. Home is where a woman can have a maximum amount of time to be both mother and father to her children, yet also be in surroundings that are safe and secure.

These examples suggest why women work at home because the children are there, but they don't explain how to work and mother at the same time. The realities are—you're in the middle of dyeing a fabric when the baby wakes up from her nap crying! You have an important business phone call and your two children enter the room fighting loudly! Just when you have that one brilliant creative idea to tie together a client's advertising campaign, you realize it's time to pick up your son at school and take him to the dentist! Recognize these examples? There are many, many others that are all too familiar. There's no getting away from it! The children are at home at some time during the day. What to do?

If the children are young, have a babysitter come to the house to play with them while you're working. During the summer if possible, hire a mother's helper. From September through June have a teenager come to your home several days a week directly after school to play with your children and free some of your working hours. If and when possible, enlist the help of a child's grandparent or other relative. Try to work out a cooperative arrangement for preschoolers a few half days each week. In many areas there are women who prefer to stay in their own homes to babysit for children. Perhaps you can bring your child to a babysitter's house to give yourself a few hours a day, or a few days a week of absolute concentration!

When children are young, you must be flexible and inventive. At

Twins
Credit: © Helen Keenan Studio, 1983

home encourage quiet games for preschoolers, and quiet hobbies, like drawing and reading, for the school-age set. Enlist the help of your older children! They can stuff envelopes, staple materials, move boxes, and use scissors. A dog breeder with four children, all involved in the family's paying hobby, has the kids do their share of the work after school. Each has his own dog and full responsibility for it.

Request cooperation. "Please give me thirty minutes to finish this painting. I'd really appreciate the extra consideration today." Negotiate, if necessary! "If you give me thirty minutes, I'll take you bowling later!" When the children are older, work during school hours. A great deal can be accomplished between 9:00 A.M. and 3:00 P.M. An editor who needs quiet for concentration puts a red cardboard stop sign on her front door as a signal to neighborhood kids, who like to drop by, so they don't disturb her when the sign is up. Be creative!

Actually, women working at home have a unique situation. Most children never see where their parents work or how they do it; but in the home setting, they can see not only where we work, but how we function within that framework. If the combination of mother and businesswoman succeeds, we may also be passing on a meaningful lesson to future generations. There is often an involvement in the work at home that stays with the child into maturity. We've heard of several successful parent-child teams. For example, a young adult son of a husband-wife photography team is now a partner in the business, so is the daughter of an insurance agent, and so are the two daughters of a woman with her own advertising agency.

Home is a participatory work setting. Just as you must not violate the children's work area, they will learn to leave yours alone. You can draw analogies between homework and home work, explaining why each is important in its own way. Showing respect for their work and their place of business will teach them respect for yours. Having your own room, closet, or basement area for the sole purpose of business helps define your territory for other family members, and you will be able to separate yourself from your work area or from your home environment when necessary. One editor bought a circular expanding wooden gate, set it up in her living room, put her desk and chair in the middle of it, and gave her young son the rest of the house!

There are times when you can play with your children and times when you have to say, "No, this is my time." You have a right to insist that certain hours belong to you alone. It's okay to say that just as you are learning to be independent and creative, the child can also learn to be independent and creative. Obviously, this being on his or her own some of the time must also be balanced with large amounts of love at other times. Children of all ages need time and affection. One writer we know stops whatever she's doing when her girls return from school so they can share the events of their day or discuss any problems. Each also knows that if at any time it's really important that she talk to Mom, she can suggest a hot chocolate break. Her mother will "break" as soon as possible and the two will sit down to discuss whatever is troubling the child.

Successful mothering for the working mother means letting your children know that while you love and enjoy them, there are also things you need as a person that come only through your work. A beauty consultant described it this way: "I believe that operating my business from home, although it may sometimes be inconvenient, has won me admiration from my husband and family because they are directly involved on a day-to-day basis with my successes and frustrations and

> 66 My training has drilled into my head how extremely critical it is for a mother to be with small children while they grow up.... So, I am available to my infant son all of his waking hours and when he sleeps in the evening, I schedule my clients.... I want to be the one to be there when my son has all of his firsts! I'll have plenty of time for a full-size caseload when I have a full-size son. 99

Therapist

seem to be more appreciative of my efforts to contribute to the support of the family and at the same time enrich my own life."

A proofreader expressed it in this manner: "I chose to work at home because of my children. Although they are both in school all day, I still feel it is important to be close by. I tried to work in an office, but sick days, snow days, and early closings complicated things too much. I find working at home simplifies my life quite a bit. A sales promoter wrote, "I wanted to be at home to do all those necessary and vital motherly duties. Working out of the home was the only answer." Commented a typist, "I am thankful for the added time I can spend with my two girls—children need their parents today more than ever." A homebased lab technician with five children had this to say: "I am for equality in women, but I still feel family and all it encompasses is the most important thing in the makeup of a woman, and how the woman handles it is what makes it or breaks it. Certainly [mothering] is the most difficult full-time profession of all—and by far the most satisfying. The dashes in a painting make the highlights brighter—so the problems in a life make the joys more meaningful." A psychologist summed it up when she stated that " . . . having my office at home, sharing my home, my family, and my life with my patients is consistent with the personal style of therapy that I practice. There is integration of my work, my family, and my life. This is my choice and how I want it to be."

Finding creative ways to deal with kids at home while you're working is indeed a problem, but it is also a price of motherhood. Working—anywhere—requires a juggling of schedules. Far better to do the juggling at home. You will benefit from the combination of family, work, and leisure in one setting; your children will know how important home and family are to you.

Women working at home will help daughters feel free to see home as a place where a person can have ambition and a career if she chooses, and it will help her sons see women as people with varied needs and talents. It's okay to want to be a mother and a working woman at the same time. There is time for both, and the woman who achieves that balance is a very lucky, interesting, and fulfilled parent-nurturer and businesswoman who has the best of both worlds.

Marjory Vals Maud
Publisher
Photographer: Kit
McIlroy

> **66 Because I make my sculptures in my kitchen sink . . . the kitchen is my studio/work space as well as the gathering spot for assorted friends and the place where my sons and I sit down to supper and talk a little together about our lives. 99**

Sculptor

Projecting Your Best Image for Ambition, Influence, Impact

Paula Baker Lohrman, Image and Color Consultant

Having a homebased business is a professional, as well as personal, challenge, especially for a woman. Typically, we homebased businesswomen have been stereotyped with an image that says we are not serious or devoted to our careers; however, these presumptions are changing rapidly as more and more of us are reshaping and restructuring the evaluations which society has placed upon women working at or from home. One of the most dynamic areas in which this fact is experiencing positive change is the result of women defining the image they wish to project in their appearance and achieving their own personal style.

> 66 Success to me is the realization of personal dreams. The greatest success one can reach is to find satisfaction in one's work and be fortunate enough to pursue as a viable career what is fun and interesting and keeps life and energy in our dreams. 99
>
> Writer

How we look is the very first thing that another person notices about us. Before we ever have an opportunity to say a word and win someone over with our personalities, we are judged by the appearance or image we present. Stop and think about this fact for a moment. Have you ever asked yourself what another person's reactions might be to the appearance you project at a business meeting and/or social gathering? If you have not, then it is imperative that you begin to really look and to see yourself as others see you.

Step 1: Discipline and Motivation
Pretend that you are a student facing a very important exam. You would

45

probably need to study to make a good grade, otherwise, you might fail the test. Like the student, you must take the initiative to put your best appearance forward. If you need to make some changes, then accept those facts and move on. Change requires risk and action, but imagine the marvelous results you may experience. Being content to follow the same path you always have may be easier, but a too-complacent attitude may also hold back your progress and productivity, both personally and professionally. Yes, practicing discipline and motivation does take work; however, it's really worth the effort when *you* are the recipient—and you feel better, too!

Step 2: Objectivity and Honesty
Once you have decided to take action, the next move calls for you to be honest and objective with yourself. Look in a full-length mirror. How many times has your full-length mirror been your best friend or perhaps your worst enemy? You mean you don't have a full-length mirror?

A full-length mirror is a must for every person to own. If used properly, a mirror tells the truth and nothing but the truth, and you can't find a better friend than that. Many people look in a mirror and see only what they want to see of their appearance. Well, we must look at both our assets and liabilities to see what areas of our image are terrific (and we've all been blessed with many), and which characteristics could be improved upon. Each one of us is a unique and beautiful person physically, mentally, and spiritually. Thus, we should look in a full-length mirror with confidence and know that some things about our being we cannot change, but there are so many things we can.

Stand in front of your mirror and look at every feature you have. Perhaps you have beautiful hair, but you need a more flattering hairstyle. Or your skin is in great shape, but your makeup colors and application could be more effective. Maybe your wardrobe is suited more to your personality than your body type. Whatever areas need improvement, give them the special attention they deserve. You will reap the rewards, and your mirror will definitely be your best friend!

Step 3: Organization and Planning
Have you heard the expression, "If you fail to plan, then you plan to fail?" We homebased businesswomen know that without proper organization and planning in our business activities, we will not achieve or progress in our endeavors; likewise, if we neglect to set aside some time to set goals and develop a plan for our personal style, we may find ourselves projecting an image that's less than our best.

Creating an organizational plan to enhance your appearance is an exciting challenge. The following are simple guidelines you can use to put together an image-improvement program:

1. Take an inventory of your present wardrobe and try everything on in front of the full-length mirror.
2. Decide what items are wardrobe basics, which items need alterations, which items to sell or donate to charity.
3. Make a list of items to add to your wardrobe on a 3x5 card and carry this in your wallet.
4. Purchase items on that list and do not buy impulsively.
5. As a general strategy, remember quality, not quantity. Spend your money on a few well-coordinated outfits, such as two suits and five interchangeable blouses, and don't worry about wearing them repeatedly.

6. If you cannot purchase all the items on your list at one time, then plan to buy one new item monthly.
7. Have your coloring professionally analyzed, so that you will select and wear clothing in your best shades of color.
8. Evaluate the condition of your skin and makeup and the products you have been using. Perhaps the addition or deletion of one product or special color may be all you need.
9. To find a hairstylist you can communicate with, ask a friend or acquaintance whose hairstyle you admire, which hairstylist she uses. Make a consultation appointment with each prospective stylist to discuss your hair needs and questions.
10. Analyze your present food and nutrition program if you are not feeling as energetic or looking as well as you desire.
11. Write down everything you eat for two weeks to see if there are adjustments you must make to lose, gain, or maintain your weight and health.
12. Above all, be thankful for the opportunities we homebased businesswomen have for enhancing our appearance, fulfilling our ambitions, and influencing our world.

In closing, I wish to share with you my personal and professional motto: "What you are is God's gift to you; what you make of yourself is your gift to God." True happiness comes in making your gift the best it can be!

66Smile; maintain your sense of humor; stick to it no matter what; follow up, follow up, follow up; be yourself; don't be afraid of yourself—you're no different or less capable than those who are 'doing it'; start with printing up your business card; buy a large package of manila files, because you must be organized from the very beginning; and stay excited, because that's the best way to turn other people on to your ideas.**99**

Entrepreneur

Client and Donna Prostak (Image Consultant)
Photographer: Robert Jordan

"Here's My Business Card..."

66 My cards say call first or by chance (seven days). We live in a small town...out in the country. Our customers seem to enjoy the change in scenery. We also have customers who ship pieces from all over the U.S. to us. **99**

Wicker Restorer

The first thing that establishes your authenticity and serious intent as a businessperson in the world beyond your home is a business card. This rectangular piece of paper is used for introductions and identification. It is, in many ways, a passport to the business world.

A business card reflects your personality and projects an image of your enterprise. One of quality and good taste suggests distinction and gives the person who sees it a feeling of confidence in your abilities. Cards should be clear and simple, yet professional and eye-catching. Include name, address, or post office box (if relevant), phone number, "by appointment only" (if applicable), and perhaps a logo (symbol) or line of copy to explain what you do. If you operate under a special business name, this should also be included.

Business cards differ. Be creative in your use of materials: a fashion illustrator or textile designer might use a card with cloth veneer; an individual or corporation working with plastics might prefer to have the information printed on a plastic surface; an artist or craftsperson might relate to her medium, as does the woman who etches on slate and whose business card is printed on dark paper with the appearance of slate. Your photograph on your card can emphasize who you are and what you do.

Before deciding on the card that will best represent you, study as many as possible pertaining to your field. Look through a catalog showing varieties in type and style. Go to several printers and look at their samples. Note those that are memorable. Why do they stand out? Placement of words? Type? Catchy copy? Striking logo? Since a business card is a form of advertising, a certain amount of originality can be beneficial. There are choices in the use of color, texture, type styles, unusual paper, logos, photographs, or other special effects. The proper use of special features can make some cards stand out from competing ones, thus creating a lasting impression on a potential client. Draw a small sketch to see what layout seems best. Do a mock-up to help you visualize it. If this is difficult, you might prefer to consult with a graphic designer. When satisfied with the end result, contact the printer of your choice and discuss the final presentation. Remember that the cost difference between good and cheap paper is minimal, but the effect can be considerable. Incidentally, it is a good idea to tie in your business card with your business stationery and advertisements for an overall professional and memorable image.

If you can afford it, engraved cards with raised letters and visible impressions of the lettering on the reverse side are excellent. The clarity of such type is most attractive. If cost is an important factor, there is a cheaper process called thermography, or "imitation engraving," which produces raised letters on the front side but leaves the reverse side flat. Other optional features include: embossed cards, which have lettering or a logo that is raised without being inked; fold-over cards, which open to accommodate extra copy or to allow space for writing a message; hot-foil-stamped cards, which have gold or silver metallic lettering; transparent plastic cards; round-corner cards; textured cards, which simulate linen or other materials; translucent cards, which are made of a durable, high-oil-content stock you can read through; and vertical cards.

While they should never be a substitute for real advertising, business cards are like miniature billboards that can be passed around, tacked on message boards, stuck on refrigerators, or inserted into desk blotters or mirror frames, and are usually small enough to be carried in wallet pockets. Carry them with you at all times. You never know when one might be needed, or when a contact might ask for several to pass around. This is a networking opportunity not to be missed!

Business cards are one of the least expensive, most important items in your budget. They are a simple yet powerful entry into the world of business.

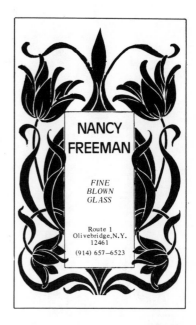

Business Correspondence: A Total Concept

Stephanie Solodar-Katz,
Owner of SSK Freelance Typing Service

> **❝I meet so many potential customers as I move around within organizations that it's essential for me to carry business cards at all times for the important follow-up business. Three trees identify me with what I do—on cards, stationery, and invoices.❞**
>
> **Landscape Architect**

What you say in business correspondence, how you present it in written form, and what the ultimate goals of your written page are, should be given a great deal of thought.

For many, particularly those offering a service, the first contact with a potential customer is through the mail. Your business correspondence can, and should, be turned into a valuable tool for introductions, referrals, and subtle, never-ending advertising.

Everyone in business receives a great deal of mail. One of the first goals for business correspondence, especially when soliciting new business, is to catch the recipient's eye and get an edge on the competition, immediately, before he or she moves on to the next envelope. Try to accomplish this from the onset, by using very carefully designed business stationery to make an indelible impression and tell your story in a split second.

Carry all of the same components (type style, colors, size, logo, page setup, and matching paper) to your invoices, flyers, envelopes, and business cards. The continual and consistent use of printed matter can create the side benefit of instant identification of your company and what you do, and the residual effects of this free advertising.

A word of caution, however. When creating your own unique image through your letterhead, be cognizant of the fine line between professionalism and "way-out." Keep in mind the current postal regulations and try to create the first and best impression.

When you run out of supplies, reprint. With the ever-increasing availability of quick printing, many people are turning to this method to reproduce printed matter to save time and money. This is not necessarily the place to be thrifty. These quick printers make a photographic copy of an original. You have to work with the original each time you print, or your printed matter will eventually appear exactly what it is—a copy of a copy of a copy. . . . The time, effort, and monetary expense to do it right will reap benefits forever.

The same effort that went into the stationery should go into creating the content of your letters. Starting with the most basic items, always make sure the names of the person you are writing to and the company he or she represents are spelled correctly. This sounds so elementary, and yet these items are pointed out time and time again by clients who bring their incorrectly addressed correspondence to me. Do not start your message by offending the recipient. Today, almost anything can be spelled almost any way. Take the time to find out if it is Marlene, Marleen, or Marleene. The same principle holds true for the firm's name. Is it Jane Doe Co. or Jane Doe Company?

Writing a good letter is not easy. Many people become tongue-tied when they try to commit their thoughts to paper. Don't make the task harder than it really is. Decide exactly what message you wish to convey; then place it on the paper in the same straightforward, declarative way. Omit unnecessary words. They distract from the message you wish to communicate. Many people start their letters with a completely wasted line, "I am writing to you because...." The recipient knows you have written; he or she has the letter in hand. Write as you would speak, and stick to the point.

Writing letters is a time-consuming project few enjoy. Good writing requires rewriting. Editing your first, second, or third draft may be necessary if the letter is to accomplish its purpose.

Another important element is to make sure that the statements you make are indeed accurate. Even one inaccurate statement can negate the effect of an otherwise dynamic letter. Also, be sure there are no misspelled words.

Many times homebased businesswomen, as well as those on the "outside," create their businesses on a shoestring. They wear many different hats and try to do it all. Eventually, as their businesses grow, time becomes a problem, and they strive to get ahead by resorting to carbon copies. Think carefully about creating this turnoff. If you don't think the client is worth the time and effort of an original, why should the client think you are worthy of his or her business?

One of the items every entrepreneur wants is instant recall and recognition of his or her business name. It's this instant identification that puts a firm in the desired spot at the top of the list when its product or service is needed. You can aid your quest toward this envious position through the use of subtle advertising in all of your correspondence.

Hiring a professional to type your correspondence is well worth the time, effort, and expense. Do not lose the impact of your thoughtfully designed stationery and carefully thought-out letter by sending correspondence typed by an inexperienced typist who does not know how to set up a proper business letter and types on an out-of-date machine, with a ribbon which should have been changed long ago, on a typewriter whose letters are clogged with ink.

The current availability of various word processing systems has created a new technology in the business world. During its short time in the marketplace, word processing has turned what used to be standard letter-writing practices into no-no's. More and more, it is being used very effectively for "get your foot through the door first" correspondence. There is no longer any reason to send out mass-produced printed letters where the name and address are added later. In these, left-hand margin additions rarely line up and the typewriter ribbon is usually darker or lighter than the printing.

Today, there are a wide variety of processors available. The proper machines used correctly have created a new frontier in business correspondence, and even have the capacity to turn the lowly mass-produced

Secretary and Maria Fiore (Film Producer)
Photographer: © Terri P. Tepper, 1979

form letter into a very potent, personal communiqué each and every time. One cannot compare the effect and response to the perfectly typed and spaced personal letter with its printed counterpart.

There has been a blitz of manufacturers' advertising geared to creating the image that you are somehow not "with it" or are behind the times without one of these expensive machines. Many people do not know the differences and what can be done with electronic typewriters, memory typewriters, word processors, and computers. They were all created from the same technology and have similarities, yet are completely different in the functions they perform.

There are several situations creating additional problems, one of which is the lack of qualified personnel to operate them. Just knowing how to type will not do. This and other deficiencies are in some part being created by the very people selling the products. These items have been sold at a greatly accelerated pace because they bring good commissions. There is no income from service when they break down or from training and retraining when employees change, so these things are neglected.

Explore all areas of these new fields in great detail. Learn what each machine can or cannot do. Then survey your own position very carefully. Many have discovered after purchase that the machine really was not for them. Don't be afraid to be the only kid on the block without the new toy.

Now, spend some time rereading the business correspondence in your files. Try to start without preconceived thoughts. Make notes on the overall appearance and what did or did not attract your attention, and why it was that way.

Next, move to the content of the letter. Again, make notes on the words, phrases, or thoughts that turned you on or off.

Lastly, compare the firms with which you do the most business with notes you made during steps one and two. The end result of a carefully constructed and executed business letter should become apparent. Most of the time you will find that the company whose letters subconsciously attracted you are the firms whose offers you accepted or whom you call upon most frequently.

Now that you know what you like or dislike, it's time to develop your own business correspondence style. In addition to the items pointed out above, keep in mind the uniqueness of your homebased business, the stiff competition, your professional credibility, and the messages you wish to convey as you write.

Don't be afraid to be original, fresh, new. Just because you haven't seen it done doesn't mean it won't work. Conversely, what did not work for someone else may be just perfect for you. Don't be discouraged if the first, second, or third tries are not completely successful. It may take several changes to turn negatives into positives.

One of your greatest assets can, and should, be your correspondence. Make your total communication package work for you in every possible way. You have only *one* chance to make a good first impression!

Pen Notes 134 West Side Avenue / Freeport, NY 11520

Quantity	Catalog No.	Contents
		7901 Italic Calligraphy
		9005 Script Calligraphy
		8003 Learning to Print
		8005 Writing Script
		8006 Telling Time
		7902 Calligraphy Pens

·OF·

Purchase Order No.

Department No.

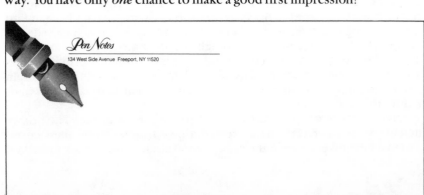

Pen Notes
134 West Side Avenue Freeport, NY 11520

How to Set Fair Prices

Dr. René W. Luft, Consulting Engineer

Congratulations! You've decided to go into business! You know what you're going to do and how you'll go about it. You know whether you'll be selling goods or providing services. Now comes the most difficult part for many businesspeople. What prices? How does one set fair market value?

There certainly is no easy answer. It's a problem all of us have to deal with at some time. Some of us may even have reached the wrong conclusions, then we have had to do some fancy footwork to keep pace with reality.

> **I go through regular periods of battling within myself whether to produce quick-selling items for consumer consumption and thus have a steadier, more secure income or continue to deal with a small clientele that purchases my works as treasures.**
>
> Craftsperson

Consider specific items for sale, products which others may be selling as well, such as clothing, wallpaper, or hosiery. You could set prices comparable to those in area stores, but since you have low overhead and possibly no employees, you can still make a profit by charging less than the store price. A dress that wholesales at $50 is sold in stores at $100. If stores have such a markup, then you can discount. Determine how much profit you want. You can sell a few items and earn a decent amount or sell a great many items with a little profit on each. That same $50 dress can be sold from your home for as little as $60 and up, and you still make a profit! This is true for any product not manufactured by you and purchased from another source. Comparison shop! Know your competition!

If the product is an item you have handcrafted, then the rules are very different—and more complex. The cost of materials and the time required to complete a handcraft must be considered. That time includes not only the actual hours of creativity, but the minutes it takes to drive to the supply house or prepare your working area.

There are three important factors to consider in pricing: labor, materials, and overhead.

Labor includes the salary we pay ourselves and our employees, the salary cost (which includes payroll taxes, insurance, and fringe benefits), and any contract labor for work done outside our home. The salary we pay ourselves must be commensurate with the type of work we do—handcraft, professional service, or other. When starting out, many home-based businesswomen can begin with a salary equal to the minimum wage (in dollars per hour) times the amount of time it takes to complete an item (in hours or minutes per item). By way of example, let's take mythical Annabelle Milligan, designer and creator of wooden ornaments. Each ornament takes about twenty-five minutes to complete, so we took twenty-four minutes as an average time, because it's a nice round 40

53

Managing Your Business

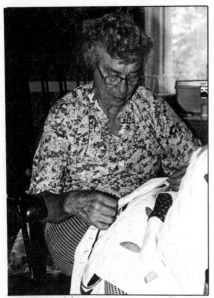

Evadine Garrison
Quilter
Photographer: Bob Stewart

❝It is comparatively easy to set fixed fees for workshops, lectures, and demonstrations, but how does one charge for the hours of creative thought that go into design—not to mention the artwork itself?❞

Designer

percent of an hour. Based on a minimum wage of $3.35 an hour, her salary then equals $3.35 x .40 = $1.34. Annabelle occasionally hires other women to help with the painting and pays them $.60 for each ornament (contract labor). Her labor costs are, therefore, $1.34 + $.60 = $1.94. Annabelle has no employees on her payroll and pays no payroll taxes or workmen's compensation insurance for herself; therefore, she has no salary costs. If she did have employees, Annabelle would find that salary costs are about 30 to 40 percent of the salary she pays her employees, including herself, but excluding the contract labor she pays the painters.

Materials include all items that are used to make a unit for sale. For each ornament, Annabelle estimates that her total price for materials— wood, paint, and trimmings—is $.38. In professional or consulting work, materials include all direct expenses incurred on behalf of a client, such as vellum or Mylar for an architectural or engineering drawing, materials used to build a model, or photographic film and development needed for an advertising design. Consumables used for many clients, such as pencils, erasers, paint, etc., are not included under materials, but they are a part of overhead.

Overhead is the total of all costs excluding labor and materials. That includes tools, office supplies, utilities, telephone, postage, packaging, and sales expenses. If work is done at home and there are no employees on the payroll, the rule of thumb is that overhead is either one-third of labor, excluding contract labor, or one-third of materials, whichever is higher. Since Annabelle has no employees, her overhead cost would equal one-third of salary, that is ⅓ x $1.34 = $.44. If one or more employees are on the payroll, overhead costs run at one-third of labor plus materials for handcrafts and about 40 to 60 percent of labor or 50 percent of labor plus 10 percent of materials for professional services.

Add labor, materials, and overhead for the total cost. Annabelle's total cost for each ornament is $1.94 + .38 + .44 = $2.76.

Now Annabelle must compute a wholesale price and a retail price. If she sells the product wholesale, that is, to a jobber, a distributor, or a retail store, her wholesale price equals the total cost of $2.76. She would add a profit in the range of 10 to 20 percent to her total cost to obtain the wholesale price if she had employees. The same is true for professional services: add a profit to the total cost to obtain the billable fee when you have employees. If Annabelle sells the ornaments directly to the public, whether at a small store, at home, at a fair, or by direct mail, she becomes the retailer herself in addition to being the manufacturer. So, she would do as a retailer does—double the total cost, which for her is $2.76, to get a retail price of $5.52. Then she would look at the market conditions to decide whether to sell for "list price" or "at a discount." Since similar items sell for $5 and $6 in stores, Annabelle decided that a 20 percent discount is reasonable ($5.52 − $1.10 = $4.42), and settled for a retail price of $4.50.

A choice most craftspeople like Annabelle face is whether to sell wholesale or retail. The difference between the retail price of $4.50 and the wholesale price of $2.76 must cover the materials required to sell the ornaments, e.g., gasoline to and from a crafts fair, fees for a booth, price tags, signs, display decorations, and the labor of selling the items. Annabelle estimates the cost of materials to sell an ornament is $.20; this leaves $4.50 − $2.76 − $.20 = $1.54 for labor. Since Annabelle would like to make as much money selling the ornaments as manufacturing them (that is, $3.35/hr), she computes the time allowed for selling an ornament as $1.59 ÷ $3.35 = 0.5 hours or twenty-nine minutes. From past experience Annabelle knows that she sells about twenty-five ornaments a day at a fair, which comes out to about one ornament every twenty minutes. Because she can sell the ornaments faster than one every twenty-nine minutes, Annabelle has made a wise choice in selling retail.

The following chart, *Prices for Handcraft,* summarizes the previous discussion. The first column gives Annabelle's prices consistent with her being a self-employed craftsperson. The second column gives the prices she would have to charge if she had employees who created the handcraft. Each column also shows the prices to the public when she sells wholesale and retail. Comparison of the two columns highlights the dilemma of manufacturing: when self-employed, one can sell for a lower price, but there's a limit to the amount one can sell. What's the solution? Increase the efficiency of labor. If Annabelle's employees could complete an ornament in fifteen minutes instead of twenty-four minutes (perhaps with the help of better tools), the wholesale price would be competitive with that of her working alone. (Can you redo the second column using fifteen minutes per ornament to compute salary?)

Prices for Handcraft

	Annabelle Makes Handcraft	Annabelle's Employees Make Handcraft
Labor		
Salary, 0.4 hrs x $3.35/hr	$1.34	$1.34
Salary Cost, 0.3 x $1.34	-	0.40
	1.34	1.74
Contract Labor	0.60	0.60
Materials	0.38	0.38
Overhead		
0.33 x $1.34	0.44	-
0.40 x $1.74	-	0.70
Total Cost	$2.76	$3.42
Profit, 0.1 x $3.42	-	0.34
Wholesale Price	$2.76	$3.76
Retail Price (list price) 2 x Wholesale Price	$5.52	$7.52
Selling Price (discount price) 10 - 30% Discount	$3.87 to $4.97	$5.27 to $6.77
Annabelle's Price	$4.50	

Remember that any change, no matter how small, in labor, materials, or overhead will also change the wholesale and retail prices; therefore, keep updating your own figures for your specific handcraft. There may be changes from year to year, or even season to season. If your figures seem too high, rethink your process. Perhaps you're traveling too far and too often to pick up supplies that are too expensive. Do you really need to pay someone to do a job you could better afford to do yourself? If prices are too high, you lose buyers. On the other hand, while you may be able to underprice competitors because of a homebased business, if an item is too cheap, it's often looked upon as having little value!

The same is true of services, whether it be design consulting, landscaping, library research, or product testing. Time is money! Know where goodwill ends and good business begins. Don't sell yourself short. You have skills that others may not have, and you deserve to be paid for them. Doctors and lawyers never apologize for their fee scales. Service-oriented businesses must also know what the competition (if there is any) is charging. Hopefully, the service is unique in your area and so fantastic that the phone never stops ringing! Yet, even fees for services must have fair market value or customers will go elsewhere. Labor estimates are still based on a reasonable wage times the amount of time it takes to complete the service plus salary costs. Add to that material costs associated with the service and overhead. Be fair. Don't set a price so high that your service is unaffordable by the people you're trying to reach. On the other hand, business is not charity. You want to show profit or else you probably wouldn't be working. Your personality, competence, responsibility, and judgment combined with the convenience and comfort of your office will make your business successful.

In all cases, whether selling products or providing services, it's important to make your customers feel they are getting some, or all, of the following when dealing with you as an individual in a homebased business: top quality, personalized service, lower prices, and fast service. Word will spread that you're the type of person with whom it's a pleasure to do business. As always, the best advertising is word-of-mouth references from satisfied customers.

Catherine E. Cole
FamilyWorks

Sales: the Bottom Line

Claire Cleaver, Marketing Consultant

We pour our hearts, talent, and money into developing the perfect product or service. Having considered packaging, pricing, order fulfillment, and record keeping, we develop our marketing strategy with the utmost care. Then, hugging our hopes for success close to our hearts, we approach the consumer and deliver our sparkling sales presentation. Just when we are about to clinch the sale, we falter, we hesitate, and sometimes avoid altogether bringing the selling experience to a conclusion. It is at this point that we, as purveyors of products, so often relinquish control to the client and fail to meet our objective—the sale!

> **Knowing I have accomplished many phases of my business which I knew nothing about means success. Creating and doing my best also means success. Self-esteem always building means success. And in our society, making a profit shows others you are a success.**
>
> Fabric Designer

Why? The most likely reason is that asking for the sale poses a threat to our ego. This is the true test of our selling expertise. As we stand face to face with our ability, we recognize our vulnerability. A no from the customer, however pleasantly delivered, strikes a shattering blow to our self-esteem. According to studies, 98 percent of the businesspeople who fail to ask for the order do so out of a fear of rejection.

For women working from home, still struggling to prove equal to the rest of the business world, the fear is sometimes even greater. If you are ever going to neutralize your fears, your first step must be to increase your confidence. Protect your fragile feelings by being professional. Remember that a no is not personal, but merely a decision on the part of the consumer.

Every saleswoman is dealing with the law of averages, and each no brings you one step closer to a yes. Volumes have been written on closing techniques, but you won't overcome your fear of closing simply by reading when and how to close. True success techniques are gleaned from doing. So, read, practice, and do. As your confidence grows, so will your success.

The professional saleswoman thinks of her customer first, last, and always. When you help the customer get what she wants, you'll get what you want. You must be enthusiastic about your product and have confidence in your performance. Where do you get that confidence? First, by knowing what it does, how, and why; secondly, by believing the product will truly benefit the consumer. As a saleswoman you'll take every customer through five steps in your sale: get their attention, maintain their interest, gain their confidence, increase their desire, and close your sale!

To close or not to close is definitely not the question. Your primary concern is when. Unless you've barred the door, your customer is a willing participant in the selling experience and fully expects you to ask for the sale. Knowing when to close most effectively is as critical to your sales

Managing Your Business

Rickey Ezrin
Shoe Store Owner
Photographer: © Terri P. Tepper,
1978

success as knowing how to close. Timing is delicate. Be overly eager and you appear greedy or pushy. Delay too long and you'll talk too much, which may only confuse your customer, make him suspicious, or try his patience.

Closing the sale should not be a traumatic experience for you; that is, not if you have prepared your entire presentation thoroughly. Whether you are selling direct to the consumer or selling wholesale, the same principles apply. Closing the sale really begins with your first approach to the customer. To increase your confidence in closing, strengthen your entire presentation. Let's review your sales call as you are now doing it.

- How well have you targeted your market for maximum effectiveness?
- How strongly have you touched the consumer's psychological need for your product or service?
- How clearly have you stated the logical benefits of your product or service?
- How effectively have you created a comfortable atmosphere by which you show true appreciation for the opportunity to address the client?
- How well have you presented the picture of the knowledgeable, trustworthy businessperson?

If you have given yourself a five-star rating, then the transition to a profitable close should flow swiftly and smoothly.

After a polished and compelling presentation of the benefits and advantages of your product or service, which appeals to your customer's needs, closing the sale will seem very natural. You have created buyer readiness one step at a time. By being a good listener and a keen observer, you can sense the willingness of your customer to close the sale. Your customer's verbal and nonverbal signals are important barometers of your persuasive skill. Be aware of any nuance expressing interest. Has the customer asked specifics about payment terms or delivery time? Has your customer maintained good eye contact with you, smiled, or nodded in agreement? That's the step next to saying yes to the sale. Now that you have the signal, avoid the urge to practice your complete sales pitch. Go for the sale.

If you're not quite sure how convincing you've been, now's the time to test the water. Trial closings help you test the customer's buying readiness. This is accomplished most effectively by asking questions that will almost certainly elicit a positive response. Questions such as the following should seek an opinion, never a commitment.

"Do you like the warm colors in this oil painting, Mrs. Smith?"
"Do you feel this abstract would be appropriate for your room, Mrs. Smith?"
"Do you agree that our frames are a very fine quality?"

Yes! Yes! Yes! Your client has just expressed three positive feelings about the product. You are about to clinch the sale. When people are rolling along in a positive frame of mind, they generally respond favorably to requests. You now have the psychological advantage. Your client is geared to owning that picture. Ask your final question—close the sale.

Be positive. Assume the sale. "I know you'll be delighted with the painting, Mrs. Smith. It would enhance any room. As a matter of fact, you've selected my favorite. Would you like me to wrap it up for you now or would you like to have the painting delivered?" Notice you've not only complimented Mrs. Smith on her good taste, but you've offered her a choice as to how she wants the sale finalized.

Providing the customer with choices is very important. It shows you respect her needs and concerns. Start with minor decisions first. The dialogue between you and your client should be purposefully progressive from beginning to end; the end being an order form in your hand, and your product imminently in the customer's possession. "Would you prefer to pay in cash or with a credit card, Mrs. Jones?" "Would you prefer that we deliver Thursday or Friday?" "Is the morning or afternoon more convenient for you?"

Eliminate customer objections. Planning for objections helps you to close more sales faster and easier. Record those you receive most frequently. Now develop a strategy. Anticipate these objections and counter them in your next presentation.

When you stumble on an objection at any point along the way, pause, listen patiently, and respond positively. "Yes, Mrs. Smith, I understand your concern, but ...." Answer, and then get back on the track. It is important that you maintain control of the conversation. Provide some testimonials of satisfied customers. They're sure to spark some interest. Always reserve a few "goodies" for times like this when the customer is throwing a few obstacles in your path.

If you encounter some firm resistance in your close, identify the objection—the *true* objection. Sometimes a customer tells you what she thinks you're most apt to accept. For example: "The painting is just too expensive." The customer may truly be unable to afford this particular painting. Offer an alternative that is less expensive, but similar in other particulars.

Perhaps the customer is really saying, "I can get it cheaper elsewhere." The small business person often cannot compete with the large business concern, so what you want to do is minimize the price difference by stressing what you are offering at your price—unique, one-of-a-kind service, quality of craftsmanship, guarantees, etc.—that the competitor is not. Make sure also that the consumer is making a valid comparison. You might also consider asking for a deposit to hold the sale rather than requesting the full price that day. Besides, a good salesperson reads an objection to price as a signal that the customer's desire is too low. If she truly wants that painting, the price is of little consequence. You might also try some inducements—a special deal or something extra.

On the other hand, the objection to price may just be to put you off. Perhaps she's looking for something different. Some customers just have difficulty making up their minds and some don't wish to be sold too easily. Remember, not everyone will buy. If you have exhausted all your options and the customer remains resolute, yield gracefully. There will be another opportunity provided you do not alienate the customer now by being pushy. When you fail to close a sale, you will usually know why. If not, ask. "Mrs. Smith, you really seemed to have your heart set on that painting. Is there a reason you decided not to buy it?" When the customer feels the pressure is off because you've obviously completed the dialogue, she is more inclined to open up and provide you with the true objection. It may be one that has a simple solution for you. Don't hesitate. Make the sale! If not, be gracious. Follow through. Set the stage for the next sales contact with this customer. Be sure to thank her for her time.

Remember, a no may be final, but it certainly is not fatal!

Claire M. Cleaver

Step into Sales

A Woman's Guide To Personal and Financial Success Through Home Merchandising

Managing Your Inventory

Steven Kass, Controller, Magla Products

"We sell retail through our studio-shop... wholesale to other shops and galleries nationwide, consignment through the ten League of N. H. Craftsmen retail outlets, and do mail order and craft fairs.... 1983 will be the 13th year we have supported ourselves on craft alone.**"**

Craftsperson

A problem affecting all manufacturing firms, from the largest multinational corporation to the smallest one-person shop, is managing inventory. When you consider that inventory is usually the single largest asset of any manufacturing firm, and that mismanagement of the inventory could lead very quickly to business failure, it is easy to see why maintaining adequate control over inventory is critical to running a successful business.

The goal of any inventory-control system is to ensure that there is adequate inventory to meet current demand and that the inventory is converted back into cash as quickly as possible. This goal is certainly in accordance with the overall objective of any business, which is to maximize return on investment.

To implement the proper inventory-control techniques, it is perhaps best to first define what inventory is. According to the American Institute of Certified Public Accountants, inventory means "the aggregate of those items of tangible personal property which (1) are held for sale in the ordinary course of business, (2) are in process of production for such sale, or (3) are to be currently consumed in the production of goods or services to be available for sale." The distinguishing feature between a manufacturing firm and a merchandising firm is that a manufacturer produces the products while a merchandiser buys its products ready for immediate sale. In manufacturing businesses there are three major types of inventories: raw materials, work in process, and finished goods. Raw materials are those items used directly in the manufacture of a product. Work-in-process inventory represents those products in various stages of production, while finished goods are those products that have been completely manufactured and are ready for immediate sale.

To effectively utilize inventory, analyze the advantages and disadvantages small firms have and their impact upon controlling inventory.

Advantages of Small Business

1. Typically, a small business employs relatively few people. Fewer people usually means less confusion, and less confusion means fewer mistakes, both in the actual manufacture of the product and in the supporting paperwork. Fewer people also means that production can be better controlled.
2. A small company generally produces only a few products, and these products are usually simple in design and easily manufactured. This means that there will be fewer items to keep track of in inventory.
3. Since the typical small business owner is directly involved in the manufacturing, the product will be of superior quality since its production reflects directly on the owner.

4. There is less government and public scrutiny of a small company. This helps facilitate simpler record keeping.

Disadvantages of Small Business

1. Limited manufacturing capacity, in terms of plant and personnel.
2. Limited financial resources, which means that maintaining an adequate stock of inventory will be difficult.
3. In most small businesses, the emphasis is placed on the actual manufacturing of the product. This usually means that the record keeping is relegated to a secondary position, and shoddy record keeping inevitably leads to a poorly controlled inventory.

Maximizing your advantages of being a small business and minimizing the disadvantages will be the key in developing and maintaining adequate controls over your inventory. The controls you establish will vary from business to business, but regardless of the type of product that is made, the methodology used in developing those controls should follow the steps outlined below.

Juanita Bass
Antique Dealer
Photographer: © Terri P. Tepper, 1979

1. Define your product. How is it made? What components does it use? Are there substitute components? Commonly called a bill of material, this is an extremely important step since it will determine how many different components your inventory will consist of.
2. Forecast your sales. If just starting a business, this is usually difficult to do. It may become nothing more than a guessing game; but the results of a poor forecast will be either tying up cash in excess inventory or missing sales by not having enough inventory.
3. Plan the physical layout of your manufacturing area well. If possible, set up the facility in production sequence with the inventory staged at the location where it will be used.
4. Set up a list of suppliers, including alternates. Make sure you always have another vendor to fall back on in case problems develop with your regular supplier.
5. Develop a schedule of lead times for all components that will be used. Lead time is nothing more than the amount of time between the date you place an order and the date you receive the materials. Keeping track of your lead times can mean the difference between shipping an order on time or losing the sale.
6. A simple yet accurate system of record keeping is needed to record all inventory transactions. Get outside help to determine what system will be best. Hundreds are available. Your accountant should be able to set up a system that is more than adequate.
7. Make sure that the person maintaining the inventory records has been thoroughly trained and completely understands what he or she is supposed to. Any system, no matter how sophisticated or computerized, is only as good as the information contained within it. If no one in your organization is qualified to do the job correctly, let your accountant do it.

Whatever system of control you eventually use, try to remember that it is just as easy to do it right the first time as it is to do it wrong; therefore, do not rush headlong into the first inventory-control system that comes along or one that someone else has used and is raving about. What is good for another may not be good for you. Use patience and care in developing your system. A well-thought-out system may require more time and effort initially but will pay off over the long run.

The Bill Collector

"It's difficult sometimes to get clients to pay their bills on schedule. I've tried different ways, from statements on invoices to cajoling and pleading. Times are bad for all of us now; reasonable reminders seem to be the gentlest, most effective way at this time."

Computer Consultant

The bill collector, not a welcome individual, wears many guises. These days, he may be a she, and she may be you, the small business owner. For one's own positive credit profile we know how important it is to pay bills on time. It is equally important for the cash-flow health of your business for you to be paid on time by others. The only money that is usable is money that you have in the accounts payable column of your balance sheet. Money owed (accounts receivable) may look good on paper, but it won't enable you to buy goods or services or pay suppliers.

Often larger customers are paid first, because the small business person does not have the necessary clout. This can mean trouble. Prompt payment of bills can mean the difference between survival and bankruptcy for small firms already caught in a tight credit market.

Two ways of extracting cash are good record-keeping systems that tell who is not paying and polite, personal, and regular phone calls to past-due debtors. To prevent major problems, set a maximum bill that any customer can have and a maximum number of days he or she can be overdue before shipments are stopped. Some general tactics that may be helpful: bill at time of shipment to avoid a lag in paperwork; establish strict credit policies; negotiate in certain cases; consider the size and activity of an account when setting terms, for it may be wise to be more lenient with large customers. Ultimately, you may need the help of a professional collection agent or a lawyer to bring suit, but it is always better if the problems can be resolved before they go that far.

Courts and legislatures have become more sensitive to the rights of consumer-debtors. A creditor may have the right to take reasonable action for payment, but may not use oppressive conduct and unlawful intimidation. To avoid legal pitfalls in collecting bills, learn what practices are not acceptable in your state. Learn, as well, the collection procedures that work for other small business owners to determine what methods will work best for you.

THE
WRITE
PERSON FOR ADVERTISING & PUBLIC RELATIONS

INVOICE

766 S. LONG BEACH AVE., FREEPORT, NEW YORK 11520 **(516) 378-7025**

Marketing Communications

Joan Landsbergis, Advertising and Public Relations Consultant

Without advertising, there is no business, either at home or anywhere else. People can't beat a path to your door for your product or service if they don't know it exists.

The difference between advertising a homebased business or any other is minimal. What's significant is the difference in the way novice entrepreneurs and professionals think about advertising.

> **66** Ad agencies don't seem to want to deal with the really small business owner with the small advertising budget, so I have turned to media publications for help. I've had some winners, some losers; but business is growing and so is my advertising success ratio. **99**
>
> **Restaurant Designer**

Advertising, first of all, is a way of seeing everything you do—from your business card to product packaging, meeting and greeting people, answering the phone, correspondence, product releases, or local write-ups—as advertising in its broadest sense. A better term is marketing communications, because it covers every form of communication between you and your market.

When you buy space in a publication, or time on radio or TV, your marketing communication is called "advertising." When you spend $350 for writing, secretarial services, photography, photo prints, paper, printing, envelopes, postage, and time to prepare and mail fifty copies of a one-page product release with photo to either trade or consumer publications, then it is called "free" publicity.

Secondly, advertising is a language, a psychology, a sociology, an art, and a set of procedures that you'll use at every step of your competitive business life with greater or lesser skill. Learn them well.

Because a marketing communications program takes time and money, it should be figured into operating costs at the start—even if your first ad is months away and free publicity is today's main event. Otherwise you can't truly cost-out your product or service, or know how much to borrow for your first twelve months in business.

Whether you can afford to turn the job over to an advertising agency or you must do much of it yourself, planning an effective marketing communications program starts by establishing the circle of *who* is selling *what* to *whom*.

What Image Do You Project? That's WHO You Are.
Who you are in your public's mind starts with the stationery, signs, ads, commercials, and phone responses you give them. Choose an easy-to-remember business name (after you read about *what* you are selling and to *whom*).

Let a commercial artist create an appropriate logo (a symbol or slogan that represents your business—for example, Elsie the Cow). The artist will also help you select a suitable, easy-to-read typeface, ink color, and high quality paper. The artist will then design a visually matching set of

Advertising, Marketing, and Promotion

business card, letterhead, envelope, and invoice. (Make sure the business name, address, and phone number are clearly shown and correctly spelled on the artist's mechanical before it goes to the printer.)

For reasons of personal security, local zoning regulations, or practical convenience (if a move is anticipated), some women prefer to use a post office box number rather than home address on their business papers. Whichever you choose, use it consistently.

That same visual presentation of name, logo, typeface, and, where applicable, color, should appear on every ad or piece of literature you send out. It takes time and consistent repetition for people to know and remember you.

Visual consistency is only one part of your image. Personal contact is another. Train all assistants to answer phones with your business name and to deal with customers in a courteous, pleasant manner at all times. One rude response can undo a thousand-dollar ad!

A homebased business has some additional image considerations:

1. An adult should answer a business phone during normal business hours. If yours is a busy house full of children, get a second phone and number for exclusive business use. Do not let your children answer it, and close out their background noise. If you or a trained assistant cannot answer, have the business phone connected to an answering machine or answering service.

2. If customers or clients come to your home, the area(s) they enter should be as clean, orderly, and businesslike as any nonhome office or shop. How that area looks, smells, and sounds is also part of your business image.

3. Neighbors in residential areas may complain to the local authorities if your place begins to resemble a warehouse and delivery depot, exudes disturbing smells or sounds, or if the street becomes a parking lot.

   Check local ordinances, use some personal public relations to soothe feelings, and then try to correct any problem. Good community relations is the front line of marketing communications in any area, commercial or residential—especially if the community could put you out of business!

4. A home business can mean working around the clock with unending alternations of job, housework, family, errands, crises, and social life. Sufficient rest, housework, social life, and marital relations—not necessarily in that order—generally suffer first. Single mothers have the added stress of not being able to share chores or decisions with a spouse. Many women must fight family and friends who tell them they are crazy, bad, neurotic, unwomanly, etc., for running a business at all.

How does this affect marketing communications and image? You may choose to create, invent, or manufacture all night long; you may have all sorts of personal stress; but if your business requires customer or client contact, then you must be open for business during normal business hours. Customers who cannot find or reach you between 9:00 A.M. and 5:00 P.M.—or whatever your stated hours—do business elsewhere. So do customers who are lashed by your fatigue, irritability, or frustrations. No matter how good your product or service, its image becomes tainted by your business behavior.

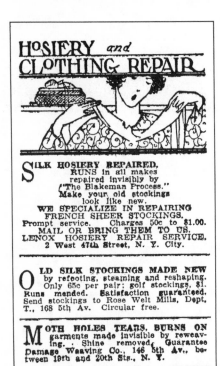

How Do You Position Yourself? That's WHAT You Are Selling.

You are not simply selling a product or service. You are giving your buyers a way to remember your product or service vis-à-vis the overwhelming competition—with an implied or stated benefit to that buyer. Deciding *what* you are selling requires studying the competition and your potential market(s).

You must identify your customers and discover what is important to them in your kind of product or service. Then observe how your competition talks about themselves. There is a hole there somewhere; fill it with what your customer wants.

There are styles in advertising as in anything else. Positioning your product or service vis-à-vis the competition in the buyer's mind is today's dominant style. It is a move away from selling a new or unique feature—as in (ever) *New* Tide; or from creating an image such as the Hathaway Shirt eye-patch man. It is also a move from a language of superlatives to one of comparatives. Some well-known and highly successful examples: (a) Avis. Ranked second in rent-a-cars. "We try harder" (versus Hertz). (b) 7-Up, the uncola (versus Coke and Pepsi). (c) Sanka. "It's real coffee" (versus other decafs). (d) "You've tasted the German beer that's the most popular in America. Now taste the German beer that's the most popular in Germany" (Beck versus Lowenbrau).

The very name of your product or service can begin the positioning process. Choose one that states your product's major benefit—such as Labeleze decal labels, Diehard batteries, Slender diet drink, Spray 'n Wash.

WHO Are Your Buyers?

Corporations? Institutions? Retail stores? Industrial manufacturers? Self-employed professionals? Consumers? *Where* are they—in your town, county, metro area, state, nation, or worldwide?

If corporate, are you selling to the president, marketing/advertising director, v-p of operations?

If retail, are you selling to better department stores or mass merchandisers? Directly or through a professional sales rep? To high-priced specialty shops or better specialty chains? To neighborhood shops, or to distributors to those trades?

If professionals, are you selling to doctors, lawyers, accountants, writers, dentists, or to subspecialties within those groups?

If institutions, are they hospitals, colleges, unions, museums, high schools, banks, libraries, governments? Which departments?

If industrial, what industry? Will you sell to plant engineers, technical communications managers, maintenance managers, sales managers?

If consumer, are you selling to boat owners, artists, teachers, factory workers, housewives, young corporate v-p's? Young marrieds, single parents, or retirees? Male or female? What age range? What income level? Will they pay cash or use credit cards? What price will each income level pay for your kind of product or service?

A market research firm can provide detailed profiles of your market segment including their product or service or price preferences. Many ad agencies also do market research. If you have any friends in marketing and advertising ask for their help and advice; this lets them pay back for the help they received when starting up.

The same product can be sold to several markets, each with a different positioning. For example, a new wipe-clean, learn-to-print workbook is presented to school systems as a way to save money because only five

JANUARY 6, 1917.

Advertising, Marketing, and Promotion

books are needed per class; to young mothers through a mail-order catalog as the way to make learning fun; to a department-store book buyer as a money-maker because it is unique and wanted by parents.

Only when you have pinned down your product or service, its positioning, and your market, will you be ready to develop stationery, signs, packaging, pricing, ad campaigns, promotions, and public relations—all the elements of a marketing communications program.

You will also be ready to appraise advertising media, such as: newspapers, magazines, direct mail, telephone directories, bus, subway, or taxi cards, billboards, theater programs, chamber of commerce publications, radio and TV; also community advertising in church/synagogue journals, school yearbooks, and sports programs—if you can afford them.

The right medium and appropriate direct-mail lists, radio or TV stations, or publications within that medium are determined by your three marketing answers, plus your major advertising goals, your budget limitations, and seasonal timing requirements.

Your goals may be achievable in any of the above listed mediums; however, I'm going to concentrate on an overview of space advertising.

Some major advertising goals, in order of importance, are to—

1. increase sales;
2. build a product image;
3. create market awareness;
4. provide support for sales people or distributors;
5. maintain an awareness level;
6. create new product or brand awareness.

For example, your product is a new kind of workbook teaching children how to print. It is suitable for elementary schools, retail and direct mail-order catalogs, and better book stores. Although advertising to all three markets has the goal of increasing sales, ad campaigns for educators might also reflect goal six, while those to the retail trade will tie in goals two and four.

Your advertising budget restricts you to one market. You choose the educational because research shows products here are bought more heavily during certain seasons—and you are just in time for one of them. Miss the appropriate season and you have missed your major sales for the year.

Whether your market is local, regional, or national, the procedures for locating and choosing the best publications (or radio/TV stations) are very similar. You start with a study of Standard Rate and Data Service catalogs (at library or ad agency), which list every publication, magazine, newspaper, radio and TV station in America, according to classification groupings. Find your classification(s) and read the data. You will soon have a list of appropriate publications to contact for media kits which include more data and current rate cards. Standard Rate and Data Service (SRDS) publishes separate catalogs for business publications, newspapers, consumer and farm magazines, radio and TV stations, and community publications, plus a comprehensive Direct Mail List Rates and Data.

Before you can work up a media plan you must know your advertising budget. You arrive at it by figuring between 7 to 10 percent of your expected gross income. Some small companies average 4 to 6 percent. Your media reps can give you some idea of what your competition is spending. Your accountant will tell you what is actually available.

Your advertising budget covers two kinds of costs: space (publications) or time (radio/TV), and production charges for layout and design,

❝I feel that I have come a long way in six months as I have been accepted by several national magazines and also have done work and have work lined up for a number of yarn companies.❞

Knitter

66

copywriting, typography, photography, talent, sound effects, studio rental, agency mark-up (17.65 percent), etc.

Ideally, an advertising program should be budgeted out monthly for a year, with media space or time bought in thirteen-week runs. Many publications or stations discount for a thirteen-week buy. If you cannot plan for a year, then budget for thirteen weeks, and at the seventh week, start planning the next thirteen. This will give you effective campaigns rather than last-minute impulse buys and helter-skelter messages.

To learn what those media space and time costs are, get the rate card from each publication ("display," not "classified") or station geared to your market. You will be assigned a media rep who can be an invaluable source of information about your market competition.

But buyer beware! Since media reps work on commission, they are inclined to sell their station or publication as the best, if not only, way to reach your market. Do not let yourself be pressured. Ask to see the figures (demos or demographics). All publications and stations have literature detailing how many of *who* are reading, watching, or listening to them. Check to see if those figures are verified by one of the objective, national survey firms, such as—

The Audit Bureau of Circulation (ABC)—general newspapers
123 N. Wacker Dr.
Chicago, IL 60606

Business Publications Audit of Circulation, Inc. (BPA)—business and trade publications
360 Park Ave. S.
New York, NY 10010

A.C. Nielsen Co.—market research
Nielsen Plaza
Northbrook, IL 60062

C.E. Hooper—radio research
566 E. Boston Post Rd.
Mamaroneck, NY 10583

Radio Research
80 Main St.
Warwick, NY 10990

The Arbitron Co.—radio/TV
1350 Avenue of the Americas
New York, NY 10019

Before you make any buys, tell your media rep what you are selling, your budget range, and who your target is, e.g., elementary school educational supplies buyers; executive women, ages twenty-five to fifty-five with incomes over $25,000, etc. Then ask the reps to give you a current rate card; an audience breakdown (professions, ages, incomes, geographical areas, best time to reach each segment); a thirteen-week schedule with recommended placements; costs per month, week, and ad; and a statement justifying their choices.

When you have this information from all your possible media, you will be ready to devise a media plan that fits your advertising budget and a media strategy based on those major advertising goals.

Because of budget limitations, you already limited your reach by concentrating on the educational market; however, you see at least four excellent trade magazines in SRDS for that market. Now what?

Advertising, Marketing, and Promotion

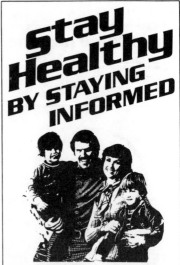
Market studies indicate that (in most cases) frequent advertising in one or two publications will produce better results for the same money than infrequent advertising in more publications to the same market. How do you evaluate the publications? Back to SRDS and/or the even more detailed media kits from your reps.

Check the cost per thousand, or how much it costs to reach 1,000 readers. A $500 ad in a publication with a circulation of 50,000 means it costs $10 per 1,000 readers. This gives a basis for comparison.

If they are all reading! How many of those educational-market readers are the target buyers you are after, or potential users who will recommend it to the buyers—or how many are (irrelevant) high school principals? Look at job function breakdowns.

Is it a controlled-circulation publication (mailed free of charge), or a paid circulation to subscribers only? Paid subscribers imply reader interest and a higher-quality circulation.

In controlled circulation look for the number of personal requests, frequent requalification of mailing lists, and mailings sent to names and titles rather than job functions alone.

Look at geographic distribution. If you want to reach buyers in New England but find most of the readers in the southern tier, save that magazine for a southern campaign later.

When you have narrowed the field, obtain back copies and study appearances and editorial content. You will soon see the difference between quality publications with a content respected and read by your market—versus the junk.

Obtain an editorial schedule for the year so you can run ads to coincide with relevant articles—e.g., anything about children's writing difficulties.

Also check whether your competitors advertise there, and whether advertising is steady over time. Your media reps can tell you how many inquiries competitors' ads generated. (Another way to compare and evaluate publications is cost per inquiry. If a quarter-page ad at $600 pulls sixty inquiries, then cost per inquiry comes to ten dollars.)

While you are researching publications, pay attention to "New Products" sections. Send each one (whether you advertise or not) a professional 8″ X 10″ black-and-white glossy photo with a release describing your product. Include benefits, any technical specifications, price, colors, materials, etc., and where it can be purchased. If the product is new, say so in your headline. Do not forget to add name, address, and phone number.

Consumer and trade publications have different styles of presentation. Copy their style, but always set it up in proper release format, which you can find in how-to books on public relations. An invaluable book to own is *Bacon's Publicity Checker,* which describes the kind of publicity each publication accepts.

Other public relations activities include—

1. sending news releases to your local newspapers (typed, double-spaced, on letterhead) describing your new business or service. Review the various sections of the paper for editorial fit. Send the release to the editor of that section which best suits your product or service, along with a covering letter.

    Also send news releases covering activities such as local speaking engagements, special promotions or sales, classes offered by your business, awards received, donations made, important clients signed on—or anything you do that will put you or your business in your public's eye.

2. becoming active in local community and/or professional groups.
3. offering to speak on your area of expertise to local clubs and schools, or on radio and TV talk shows.
4. holding free how-to classes.
5. setting up contests and awarding prizes.
6. donating your product or services to local charities, affairs, or TV game shows.
7. getting celebrities to use and endorse your product or service. (The mayor of your town is a local celebrity!)

When you have completed media evaluation, set media strategy, and laid out your media plan, you are ready to create (or have created for you) an ad, commercial, sales brochure, direct-mail letter, etc. No matter who writes it, you must first determine the ad's, or ad series', major objective. For example, will it be to—

Bert Garino
Dollmaker

- introduce a new product or service?
- explain how the product works?
- reposition the main competitor?
- stimulate reader requests for more information?
- generate mail orders?
- establish a brand image?
- overcome quality control or delivery problems?
- support dealers', distributors', and reps' sales efforts?

There are more, but the rule of thumb is: one major objective per ad or commercial. All writing and artwork will focus on achieving that objective. (This is one of the first questions an ad agency will ask you. Be ready.)

The Dean and Holtje books in the Bibliography spell out everything you need to know about the creative and production processes involved, including how to hire free-lancers. Study them, as well as other books on the list. Whether you then try it yourself or stay with professionals, you will know the language and procedures and be able to supervise and evaluate outside work profitably. You will have begun to think like a pro!

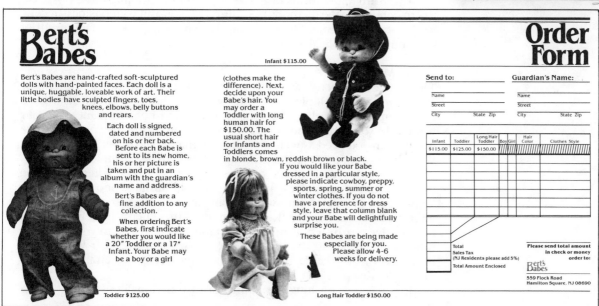

69

Successful Marketing

Christine Van Noy, Business Consultant

> **66** I have my name in the Yellow Pages in small print right now, and it seems to be enough, as word of mouth is my best advertising. I tried a few years of a larger ad in the Yellow Pages, but I found that it only brought more 'price shopping' by phone. **99**
>
> Framer

Successful marketing is a result of one's ability to effectively combine the following skills: (a) to research and properly evaluate the market; (b) to efficiently produce the marketable service or product; (c) to relate and communicate to a specific group of potential clients or customers; and (d) of most importance, to offer a service or product that successfully fulfills the predetermined need of a demanding market.

Each product or service will require a specialized marketing effort, and a demographic survey of potential clients or customers is essential. By determining their demographic makeup, you can successfully gear your marketing campaign toward their needs, continually appeal to their image, and effectively reach them at the most opportune times.

There are firms that offer marketing research, direct marketing, advertising assistance, and market analysis. Some are even homebased themselves! Before you contract professional help, try to project your own marketing plan by surveying all marketing techniques, evaluating your potential clients or customers, and preparing a budget for advertising expenses.

There are many forms of marketing, and researching these possibilities to determine the methods best suited for you and your business will be well worth your time. Listed below are some suggestions. One or all of them might be applicable to your particular needs.

Direct Mail
This can be an effective and relatively inexpensive way to reach clients or customers for developing new business. Purchasing mailing lists from local firms closely related to yours is one way to obtain names for your market. In some cases, however, this method may provide you with more names than you need as well as with some that would never be interested. With the costs of mailing and printing, it is best to be selective.

A free resource available to all is the Yellow Pages. After listing the type of client or customer appropriate for your business, look through the Yellow Pages to determine which companies or organizations might be interested in your service. Keeping in mind that clients usually prefer to find service nearby, concentrate on establishments close to you. Take the time to call and find the name of the department manager who would most likely make the decision to choose your services. Send your mailer directly to that person.

If you're establishing a mailing list of individuals, use some of the following resources for names: city directories (some smaller towns publish their own directories of residents); Chambers of Commerce (write to the organizations they list for membership lists); local school parents' rosters; and merchants' mailing lists.

When using the direct-mail approach, it is important to be consistent. You will be dealing with people who have never heard of you. If your mailings are sent regularly over a period of time, the services provided by your business will probably become familiar to them.

Using a twelve-month calendar to plan your mailing schedule is recommended. It should be structured to comply with seasonal requirements. For instance, if you're marketing gift items, schedule mailings for Easter, Mother's Day, Father's Day, weddings, and Christmas. Educational services should be geared for the public school schedules, and self-improvement products might be effectively marketed around the New Year (for those New Years' resolutions) and for presummer shape-up programs. For services to companies, it might be wise to assist with work overloads during summer vacations. Don't forget the flu season when illness may reduce office attendance.

There are many types of mailers available for this kind of campaign. A well-designed postcard can be quite effective. So can a brochure, flyer, or personalized letter. Whatever type of mailer you choose, be sure it is well-prepared and reflects the image you prefer to project. Sending a flowery piece on pink paper may not be appropriate if you're marketing services to the conservative legal profession; on the other hand, it might be very effective to the beauty-product market.

By being very selective in compiling a mailing list, using well-designed mailers, and keeping your campaign timely and consistent, the direct-mail sales tool should produce successful results in marketing your business.

Yellow Pages

Not only is the Yellow Pages a great resource for researching your potential market, but it is a good place for your firm to be visible—where potential customers will search for help.

Being visible to an awaiting market is your main objective. To accomplish this feat, it is best to be effectively listed in as many places as possible. That's why it is prudent to be listed under every heading that one could reasonably justify. In fact, the more listings you have, the better your chances are at being located by a potential client or customer with a specific need. However, the cost of the listings should be evaluated as to the potential advertising benefit before the selection is made.

With a standard telephone line for your business, you are allowed one listing under a heading of your choice. If you market vitamins, for instance, you may choose the obvious heading, "Vitamins"; however, with the trend toward holistic health, natural living, and the back-to-nature movement, it may be that you will find people searching for your vitamins under the headings, "Health Food," "Beauty Products," and "Health Conditioning."

Evaluate the costs of multiple listings. Weigh this information against using the money for a large display ad within your primary listing. You may wish to display your specialties, hours, payment plans, and any other details that will help promote your product or service.

Take time to read the Yellow Pages. What ads impress you? Why? How many different subject headings are there that relate to your service or product? Use this evaluation when determining what you want to do with your Yellow Pages listing.

> 66 One of the goals I have set for myself is to pick up corporate business... corporate gift programs, for the most part, are not as subject to flux in the economy as are retail stores... their needs are more defined and their input of items wanted is vital to the development of new items for my business. 99

Manufacturer

Advertising, Marketing, and Promotion

Rita Press
LABELeze Labels

Newspapers

Display Ads. Since your best prospects are probably located near you, it may be wise to advertise in the local newspaper.

The Sunday paper is usually a good edition in which to run an ad. Generally, people have more time on Sunday to peruse the paper, and there are more features (such as food, fashion, business, entertainment) to capture the interest of a specific public. Consequently, if you decide to place an ad, be sure to determine the group to which it should appeal and specify the appropriate section in which it should be located.

The frequency of ads will be determined by your budget. Onetime ads are usually ineffective unless they are quite large and/or a once-in-a-lifetime offer. While it is not necessary to advertise weekly, monthly might prove to be an effective way to present your services or products.

One favorable consideration about newspaper advertising is that the cost of the ad usually includes the design, typesetting, and paste-up fees. The newspaper's advertising department is well-equipped and knowledgeable and will usually spend time with you to assist with preparation and copy.

Classified Ads. Check the local paper for headings that relate to your product or service. It may be that "Business Services" or "Employment Wanted" will relate to your service. "Articles for Sale" and "Crafts" are considerations when marketing a product. In the event you are marketing a secretarial service, select the sections that appeal to small businesses or individuals and to large companies requiring assistance.

It may be prudent to begin with a weekly listing, then, if that provides you with a steady flow of telephone calls and work orders, you may decide to increase the frequency of the ad to a daily basis.

News Releases. This is one of the least used but most effective ways to increase your business. News releases are articles written about you and your business at no cost to you.

When setting up your direct-mail calendar, it is a good idea to include some time for sending out timely news releases. When you're offering a particular service or product, perhaps related to a season, write about all the news aspects of your offering. Since these releases are not advertisements or commercials, they must have a *news* appeal. If you are selling your crafts in a boutique, you may wish to write a story on the "Unique Buying Trends of Holiday Shoppers." You might include a brief history of crafts, the practicality of buying one-of-a-kind art objects, the availability of these crafts to the local residents.

Preparing a news release is simple; there are books on the subject at local libraries. If you're in doubt about your newspaper's criteria, do not hesitate to inquire.

Cold Calling

It may be that your particular service or product can only be presented in person and by you. Many people are naturals for convincing prospective clients or customers of the benefits related to their service or product. You are your best asset; only you have the enthusiasm and knowledge to transmit your message.

Always have some well-prepared printed material with you to reinforce what you verbally presented so that when you leave, your prospect will have something to remind him of your product or service.

Some additional marketing techniques that may be appropriate for specific businesses are:

Promotions. A special event can be most beneficial in launching a new business. Plan an open house, a wine and cheese tasting party, or a holiday gathering. This event could include a short presentation of your product or service. Be sure to have each guest sign in so that you will have a way to follow up with potentials. Remember to send in a news release to the local paper notifying them of the event.

Seminars and Workshops. Host a half-day session on a particular subject that promotes your business. If you're an accountant, try "Record Keeping for Small Businesses"; a career consultant may attempt "Effective Resumé Writing". By giving enough information to satisfy the attendees, but not too much information, so that they will still need your services, you have provided a community service as well as marketed yourself.

Television or Radio. Short, well-done commercials can be quite effective. When planning this approach, keep in mind the time of day your potential client or customer will be listening.

Don't forget or discount talk shows. Most locales have radio and television talk shows during the day and evening hours. Write to the producer about the news aspect of your business.

Billboards. Choose an appropriate place. If you're appealing to the business community, find a board that will be seen by commuters. Homemakers may see a sign more often if it is on the way to schools, shopping, grocery stores, etc.

Magazines. Many mail-order businesses find this an effective way to advertise. There are many trade journals and special-interest publications to choose from.

Professional Consultants. Advertising and sales agencies can provide top-notch marketing techniques. If your business reaches the point that it necessitates professional help, shop around for someone who suits you and your business needs.

Inventory your product or services and match them to a market of customers or clients. Present an appropriate and professional image in whatever media you choose. By setting up a basic plan and keeping it within your capabilities and budget, you will see your business grow. It is important to reevaluate your campaign regularly. Your marketing needs will change as you grow.

Corazon S. Watkins
Potter

How Market Research Influences the Marketing Plan

❝I got a restaurant owner to hang some pictures of celebrities in his establishment. He charged no commission, feeling that the pictures decorated his business place and created conversation and comment. At the same time, I was becoming better known and receiving orders for portraits of customers' relatives.**❞**

Artist

Selling is the one element of business that provides an income; therefore—

1. learn everything you can about customers' buying motives: why they buy, what they buy, how they buy, and how much they spend.
2. ask these questions: Who are my customers? Where are they located? What will they buy? Who will not buy? How frequently will my customers buy? What benefits are they looking for? What price will they pay? How can they be reached?
3. get more information such as: How many customers exist to buy my goods or services? How large are their families? How old are these individuals? Where do they live? How much do they earn? What type of education do they have? What do they read? What radio and TV programs do they listen to and watch?

The answers to these questions will provide facts that can be used to determine how a buyer will act under a number of given circumstances. Furthermore, this information will help you advertise in the right places.

Having as much information as possible about your customers is important in any business. In order to keep this information up to date, revise your list of questions every six months or so and update your research.

Answers can be found through both primary and secondary sources.

1. Primary sources:
   A. Talk to people about their likes and dislikes.
   B. Watch what customers buy.
   C. Speak with people in businesses such as yours, located in areas far enough away from you so competition is not a concern.
   D. Learn from what others do well, but also capitalize on competitors' weaknesses.

2. Secondary sources:
   A. Libraries
   B. Reference books
   C. Trade journals
   D. Newspapers and magazines
   E. Credit bureaus
   F. Government agencies
   G. Government publications

As your market research develops, constantly apply the findings to your marketing plan. Determine detailed specifications and, after defining expected results, set goals. Be sure to include the time framework of when and how these goals will be met through the various forms of advertising.

As your promotional campaign progresses, constantly review it to be sure that every action and every dollar spent is moving you closer to the final, stated goal.

Alice Lang
Postmaster
Photographer: Bob Stewart

To Market, To Market

Barbara Brabec, Author, Publisher, Consultant

"Because our items are creative, hand-done, and unique, the bare cost would never allow us to sell in regular stores with the markup they require. So, we explored fairs, advertising, and word-of-mouth discussions and discovered the richness of face-to-face selling."

Photographer

"To market, to market, to sell a fat pig..." Remember that old nursery rhyme? Marketing a product today is no longer as simple as walking to town with one's product in hand, but neither is it the mystery most beginning sellers believe it to be. Now, as in olden days, the key to selling anything lies basically in knowing who needs what you offer and finding a way to communicate with them. Once you've found your market and a way to reach it, you need only offer your product in the right way, at the right price, and at the right time. Learning how to do this is what marketing is all about.

In my twelve years as a crafts marketing writer and publisher, I've received thousands of letters from beginning sellers, and the one that follows is typical of many. Perhaps it describes your current situation:

> At this point, I am ready to either go full force into selling to make MONEY, or I'm going to have to completely back off. Why? Because I cannot locate the right market and I don't know how to go about selling on a bigger scale. How do I go about expanding? How do I find more shows, more shops, more specialized markets for what I make? Also, I live in a small town and suppliers are almost impossible to locate. When I do find them, the prices are terrific, which makes me have to charge more or sell more at a lesser price.

I'm always amazed at how little homework the writers of such letters have done. Whatever happened to the library, for instance? There's a wealth of marketing information in it for any individual who takes the time to look.

If, like the letter writer above, you cannot locate the right market for your product, it may be that you are trying to sell the wrong product. *Know your market!* These words should be forever engraved in your mind, for without a thorough understanding of the people who might buy your product, publication, or service, you will have little success in selling it. Always remember that it is the market itself that determines your product, and nothing will kill the success of a product faster than its being the wrong product for the intended audience. Your success in selling, and thus your profit, will largely depend on how well you have done your market research.

Market research sounds difficult, but it's nothing more than playing detective. You just have to turn up a few clues to solve your marketing mystery. This article contains several of them, and if you'll faithfully follow up on them, then act on the information you discover, I can guarantee that your sales and profits will increase in the future.

Let's assume for the moment that you are selling a service that can best be marketed locally, such as a secretarial, consulting, copywriting, or graphics art service, or perhaps home decorating or child care. How do you find more clients? First and foremost, become more visible in your community. Avidly seek publicity and advertise where your clients are most likely to notice your message. This is not always the newspaper.

Enhance your visibility by giving talks at the library or to organizations and clubs in your area. If you have a Chamber of Commerce, visit it for information and consider joining it if yours is a business service. Make regular calls on local businesses to acquaint them with your service, and follow up periodically with letters and phone calls.

The above tips also apply to you if you sell a product, such as originally designed crafts, toys, or decorative accessories. When selling locally, investigate every retail outlet that sells anything remotely related to what you produce. Visit each shop or store first just to study the merchandise and the price range of items. If your product or line is compatible with other items in the store, make an appointment to show it to the shop owner or buyer. Don't overlook specialized retail outlets such as garden or floral shops, gift shops in hospitals, hardware stores, home furnishing stores, and even restaurants, which might buy certain items to enhance their decor.

Barbara Brabec
Publisher

Again, seek publicity by contacting local media with ideas that are timely and beneficial to the public. Perhaps you can give a demonstration on cable television or do a radio interview that answers call-in questions from listeners. Send an informative article about yourself and your work to your local newspaper, including a photograph of yourself in action.

Here's a tip: in seeking publicity, always remember that editors and producers are not interested in giving you free advertising; they are interested only in giving their readers or listeners information and ideas which will help or entertain them. To learn the tricks of this valuable trade, study a book or two on the subject. (Back to the library!)

In addition to media publicity, take advantage of every bulletin board in your community on which you might post an attractively designed notice. And don't forget beauty shops, laundromats, and church bulletin boards.

Also make connections with every organized group in your area and be sure to tell all friends and acquaintances what you're doing. Good luck just doesn't happen, it is made by expanding your communication channels. The more people you know—and who know about you—the more likely you will be to catch good luck and new clients or customers.

Let's assume now that you are selling, or trying to sell, some kind of product, publication, or service that is related to the broad field of art, crafts, collectibles, gifts, decorative and wearable accessories, needlework, and toys. How do you find more shows, shops, and specialized outlets for your work, both regionally and nationally?

By reading. You are fortunate in that an efficient networking system already exists for these creative industries in the form of periodicals, organizations, shows, and seminars—each of which can lead you to new outlets and marketing possibilities. Your library will guide you to some of these resources.

Although your product may necessarily limit your market to customers and clients in your own immediate area, consider these ways to expand the profits of any small, local business. Your idea may be one that

Advertising, Marketing, and Promotion

could be adapted to the party-plan type of selling, which you could take to nearby communities, or you might help other women set up a business similar to yours, through workshops or lectures. Don't give all your secrets away in a talk; however, consider selling them in the form of a how-to booklet you've written and printed—one that could also be sold nationally through classified ads and publicity.

You might also be able to sell your ideas and know-how in the form of magazine articles, or maybe you've become such an expert in your field that you can sell a regional or national consulting service, or even a newsletter. There is no wall around your town or community, and by looking outside your own area for business opportunities and additional profits, you may well find them.

Branch out to other areas by making an occasional selling trip to a nearby town or city. Enter local and regional craft shows and flea markets that are appropriate for your work. If you do well at them, try a large national show. Show listings can be found in various craft magazines, and there are also specialized publications that publish nothing but this kind of information.

If you sell at wholesale prices, you may wish to hire a sales representative who can get your work into national trade or gift shows or mail-order catalogs. But tread lightly in this area until you know what having a sales rep entails. Mistakes can be costly and extremely frustrating.

You don't need a sales rep to participate in a trade show, of course, but you do need a complete line if you want to make good sales at such a show. Before entering one, talk to someone who has been there before you; it could save a lot of money and heartaches.

If mail order is the way you want to go, be sure to read a book or two on the topic and subscribe to one or two specialized mail-order and direct-marketing periodicals. This will give you the information you're going to need to reach special markets through classified ads, package inserts, direct-response postcard mailings, and cooperative advertising programs, among other things.

To find thousands of other potential outlets for your products, explore the world of library directories. Did you know that you can connect with 14,000 organizations by browsing through the *Encyclopedia of Associations*? Many organizations have periodicals or magazines through which you can reach individual members. Looking for mailing lists of department stores, women's specialty stores, chain stores, craft suppliers, or publishers? Then see *The Directory of Directories,* which will lead you to all these individual directories.

Writers, artists, photographers, and craftspeople will be particularly interested in *Writer's Market, Artist's Market, Photographer's Market,* and the *National Directory of Shops/Galleries/Shows & Fairs,* all published by Writer's Digest.

Before you can effectively expand your business, you must have reliable and affordable sources of supply. Don't overlook *The Thomas Register:* its several volumes include a listing of products in alphabetical order, with the names and addresses of companies that make them. Also investigate *Catalog Sources for Creative People,* which lists more than 2,000 mail-order sellers of art/craft/hobby supplies and materials.

Need a good publicity list? You can compile a great one from library directories, and also find every trade magazine you'll ever need in *Ulrich's International Periodicals Directory.* Newsletters can be an invaluable aid to your business, both as educational and public relations tools, and there are so many these days that they have their own directory, *The Newsletter/Yearbook Directory.*

I'm sure you have the idea by now. The library is a veritable gold mine of information!

I hope you also begin to see that there are many new outlets waiting for your products, publications, and services, but you *do* have to look for them. They will not come to you. Find them by reading everything you can get your hands on and by networking with everyone who knows anything at all about what you're doing. Trade information and ideas willingly, even with competitors, who are often your greatest supporters, particularly if you are helping to expand the market for a specialized product.

Never be afraid to ask what you consider to be dumb questions. Often, that's the only way to learn. (And sometimes you should just play dumb, because you can learn a whole lot more than if you pretend to know it all. Experts just love to help beginners. It makes them feel important.)

In summary, if I had only one word of advice to give to new business owners, budding entrepreneurs, and home-business dreamers, it would be this: *read*. And I'd repeat it like a broken record. There is absolutely nothing you cannot learn from a book, and there are thousands of authorities who have shared their knowledge and ideas in books, which are not only putting money in their pockets, but in book buyers' pockets as well.

I speak from experience, both as the author of a successful how-to book and as the reader of dozens of other how-to guides, which have enabled me to do things I would not have believed possible only a few years ago.

After you've read a few basic business guides and how-to manuals, the next most important investment you can make in your business is a subscription to several periodicals related to your field. Without such publications, you will be unable to learn what your competition is doing, how much they are charging, the problems they are encountering and solving, and which ideas are working for them. More important, periodicals are your barometer to current market conditions. They tell you when consumer interest in something is rising or falling, they alert you to new trends and give you countless ideas on how to develop or expand whatever business you're operating. Periodicals also guide you to additional business resources and marketing outlets.

In short, periodicals enable you to know your market, those three little words which are so important to your success. Without such continuing guidance, your entire marketing effort may be wasted.

66 One of the advantages of living in a small town has been knowing many of the merchants personally and being able to seek their advice on what would sell and how to package. As a wholesaler, I called on merchants in three nearby communities, showing them the products I had developed in the packaging as they would sell them. I also left samples for them to try and a price list. 99

Salesperson

Marketing Your Service

Judith Pynchon, Marketing Consultant

We're independent service professionals: calligraphers, career counselors, wardrobe consultants, caterers, publicists, writers, bookkeepers, artists, typists, photographers, housecleaners; we personally provide services that people need and will pay for. What could we possibly have in common with huge, multinational Fortune 500 corporations? Neither type of business can succeed without *marketing*.

The corporations have an entire department that does nothing but concentrate on marketing the corporations' products and services. Usually, we're one person wearing lots of hats. They have enormous resources for research, a sales organization, an administrative staff, an advertising department, a car pool, a mail room, etc. We do all that ourselves. Still, the basic principles of marketing are simple, and both the independent service professional and the corporation can apply them equally successfully.

The formula is simple: Analyze, Plan, Implement, Control—APIC; make this your alphabet for service business success.

*A is for **analysis**.* Analysis is what you do first, and what you keep on doing. You analyze yourself:

- What knowledge do I have that others need? Where did I learn it? Do I have relevant education? Professional training? A license? Certification?
- What experience do I have to offer others who can benefit from it? Where did I get it? Count experience in years, in hard work, in contact with others in your field, in association with experts, in successes.
- Are my knowledge and experience being used outside of my business? Do I do any volunteer work? Is my service visible to people? How do they know what I can do?

You analyze your service:

- What tangible result does my service produce for my customers? (These are benefits.)
- How is my service different from others similar to it? (These are features.)
- What are the major strengths of my business? What am I best at?
- What are the major weaknesses of my business? What am I not good at?

And, of course, you analyze your market. Your market consists of all the people or organizations who need your services.

- What do my potential customers need? When do they need it? How much do they need? Why do they need it?
- How well are their needs being met by existing services?
- How many different types of potential customers do I have, and how do their specific needs differ?

Analyzing how needs differ from one type of customer to another is called, officially, "segmenting" your market. Theoretically, every single potential customer in your market constitutes a separate segment of that market, with distinct needs you can address. Obviously, it's more efficient for us and the large corporations to group potential customers into segments of reasonable size. Here are some examples.

Your catering business is really suited for weddings because you like the money involved in large parties and because your wedding cakes are creative and popular. So, engaged couples are an important segment of your market, but so are couples who have been married for twenty-five or fifty years, since they too have large parties and special cakes.

Other segments of the catering business include mothers-to-be, retiring employees, public figures, political candidates, and so on. You can segment seasonally, according to the types of parties that occur at certain times of year (holidays, graduations, weddings, etc.). You can segment by geographical area (town versus country, beach versus company town, etc.). You can segment by location; some people traditionally entertain at home, while others rent a public space.

Any market, for any service, can be segmented to infinity, if you so choose.

Spend enough time segmenting your market to come up with two lists: one, a list of opportunities for your service.

For example, you're a photographer, and your analysis reveals that while there are enough competent passport photographers, wedding photographers, and photojournalists in your area to serve the needs of your market, no one specializes in photographs of children and pets. That could be a real opportunity.

One photographer takes pictures of children and their horses exclusively, a decision based on personal interest and good business sense. He is now widely known for this specialty. He located a gap in his market, saw the opportunity, and now practically owns that segment of the photography business.

The second list, while it may depress you, is absolutely necessary; make a list of potential threats to your success in your market.

For example, you've decided that photographing children and pets is a real opportunity, but your research shows that the local department store has most of that business now because their package deal prices are so low. The service the store offers may be a threat to your success.

Follow it through, though; threats can often be turned into opportunities. You may not be able to match department store package prices, but you may be able to shoot at more convenient hours. You may find that customers' objections to the store are the stiff, artificial settings they use, that customers prefer more natural, even familiar surroundings. If you are promoting pictures of children *with* their pets, your offer is a potential threat to the store, because store policy usually doesn't admit pets.

Careful analysis helps you identify the features and benefits of your service; then, it's up to you to make sure your customers understand them.

66We tutor in students' homes—all subjects, elementary through college. I have a staff of 200 teachers working as independent contractors. The agency provides tutors in four countries.**99**

Tutor

81

Advertising, Marketing, and Promotion

Put them in a brochure, demonstrate them in a special event, write an article, get interviewed, make a speech—do whatever you have to to get your message to your customers. I never go anywhere without my business cards; What do you do? is the most-asked question there is.

Analysis also spotlights your strengths and your weaknesses. Play to your strengths (emphasize what you do best), and work on those weaknesses (learn to improve what you're not good at, or stop trying to do it).

P is for *planning.* Every corporation makes plans that are "quantifiable over time." All that means is that you set realistic objectives for yourself and your business, that you write them down, and that you express them in terms of both time and money.

This is how you approach planning. You're a writer offering to write newsletters for small businesses to use as a promotional tool, and your price for this service is based on the number of readers. Your objective for the next quarter may look like this: to secure three clients for the newsletter service, each with a minimum mailing list of 1,000 readers, within ninety days.

That's a real objective, but whether it is realistic and achievable involves more study. How many presentations will you have to make in order to get three definite commitments? How much time will it take to get not only an expression of interest but an appointment with the appropriate decision maker(s)? How can you qualify your prospects (i.e., how can you find out which businesses in your area have at least 1,000 customers, associates, and others who would receive the newsletter)? And so on.

Planning means planning; it doesn't mean predicting or guessing, and it definitely doesn't mean sitting still and hoping. Write your objectives as specifically as you can, devise strategies to achieve them, and create ways to put those strategies into action.

Once you set your objectives, you can go to work on strategies. Strategies answer the question: how can I capitalize on the opportunities I've discovered, and how can I remove or neutralize the threats?

I is for *implementation.* At this point in the marketing process, you put your plans into action. You offer your services to those segments of your market that represent the best opportunities for success.

You're an organizer of spaces and possessions. You've identified these segments of your market as having the most potential:

1. working women homeowners with children;
2. single working people with small houses or apartments with limited storage space;
3. homebased business owners.

All three segments need their living and/or working spaces organized, but your approach to each segment—your marketing strategy—will be slightly different. Segments one and two have a time problem which reorganization could help solve. Segments two and three may also have a space problem. Segment three needs help with both living and working spaces.

Recognizing these differences will help you implement your strategy. You can reach homebased businesspeople through the organizations they belong to and the journals or trade magazines they read, but you would not be likely to reach the others that way. If you decide to pursue the working-mother segment, word of mouth is probably your best strategy, but how

> **66** ...success is working at something I enjoy, utilizing my organizational and creative talents, and knowing I'm doing a good job in providing a necessary and worthwhile service. Making money is the visible sign of success. **99**

Tutor

will you get "the word" into circulation? Going door to door or telephoning at dinnertime is inefficient and would probably get you more enemies than customers. Find a friend or acquaintance whose place needs organizing, do it for her in exchange for her permission to take before and after photographs or for an endorsement you can include in an advertisement, or help her host a party for her work or neighborhood friends to see what you've done for her. Any of these strategies can be the first step in a vigorous and productive word-of-mouth campaign.

The traditional tools for implementing any strategy are direct sales, advertising (for which you pay), and publicity (which is free). Homebased workers and independent service professionals, especially women, are particularly creative in delivering the message, usually because their marketing budgets are so small. So, use your imagination.

Remember that when you're selling a service, you're selling yourself: your brains, knowledge, strength, experience, and all the qualities that make up the unique individual you are. In fact, as far as each of us is unique, independent service professionals have no competition. If you adopt that attitude—within reason, of course—and concentrate on what makes your personal service so special, you'll be well on your way to developing a realistic marketing plan.

C is for *control.* Being creative about promoting your service is fun, but it won't guarantee your success unless you follow up your imaginative ideas with good, solid attention to details. That brings us to the final, but critical, ingredient *control.* To make sure you meet those realistic objectives you set, you must monitor your efforts at regular intervals to see whether you're making progress, spinning your wheels, or falling behind. You can't take action to keep on track if you don't even know your wheels are in the mud. Here are some steps for gaining control.

You're offering office services (typing, filing, bookkeeping) to independent professionals like yourself. You've identified homebased accountants and tax preparers as a likely segment of your market, and set this objective: to secure six clients, each of whom needs at least twelve hours of services each week, within the next three months.

You've decided that your best strategy is to send a brochure describing your services, along with a covering letter, to a target list of 200 accountants and tax preparers in your county and to follow up with a call within a week of their receipt of your material.

In order to control your progress toward that objective, you need to work backwards from the target date: three months from now. In order to get those six commitments by the target date, when will you have to have the first meeting? How long will it take to get an appointment? You may have to stagger your mailings so that you can make all those follow-up calls. When will the brochures have to be ready? When will they have to go out in the mail? When will you have to get copy to the printer? When will you have to have chosen your paper, colors, typefaces, and design elements? All of these events have to be nailed down, on paper, to specific dates. If you don't make those dates, you're off schedule, you're "off plan," and you have to take action to correct your course.

You may spend as much time marketing your professional services as you do performing them, but how else will you be sure that your business is producing what you want it to produce for you? Take a tip from the Fortune 500 and start acting like them.

Pat and Fred Sagarin
Chimney Sweeps
Photographer: © Terri P. Tepper,
1978

Advertising, Marketing, and Promotion

Marketing Your Product

Tina Bobker and Carole Dlugasch, Manufacturers

❝I began doing some local craft shows, taking in customer reactions and comments, and making changes when needed. I also took samples of my creations to local retail shops and started taking orders. Soon I found myself to be a very busy lady!❞

Clothing Designer

You make an item that everyone likes. All your friends buy it, and they tell you that you should sell it to stores. Terrific! But where do you go from here?

A good place to start is with the question: Who will want to buy what I am selling? You must decide who it will appeal to and where these people will go to shop for it. Do you want to sell the product to a gift shop, department store, or craft shop? Perhaps you hope to sell it directly from your home. Also, you must decide if you want to sell it at the wholesale level or the retail level. This will be a factor in determining your price.

Once you have a fairly clear idea of where you would like to sell your product, you must make the initial steps to do so. A very worthwhile place to start is the telephone book if you wish to sell at the wholesale level. You will be able to readily compile a list of local stores in your area that fit your needs. Now you are ready to start some "cold calling." This means simply that you will call a few of these local stores and tell them confidently that you have an item that you are quite sure will sell very well in their store and that you would like to set up an appointment to come in to talk to them further about your product and to show it to them.

Once you have your appointment, make sure that you keep it! Presenting yourself professionally is extremely important. Now that you have the attention of the person who can purchase your product, you must do your best to present it as favorably as possible. Point out all its advantages and uniqueness that make it different from other similar products.

Hopefully you will get an order. When you agree on a completion date (the date on which you promise to deliver the merchandise), make sure it is a realistic one that you will be capable of honoring. You won't get a reorder if you cannot fill the first one promptly and satisfactorily.

You won't *want* a reorder, however, if you do not get paid for the first. That is a good reason to get whatever credit information you can get from the stores you will be doing business with. Find out how long they have been in business, and ask them to give you the name of the bank with which they do business, along with the names of three references that can tell you something about how promptly they pay their bills. Then make sure that you follow up with a letter or phone call to these people. Having this information helps, but it doesn't mean that you will always get paid. If the references do prove to be negative, you may want to discuss prepayment or a COD delivery with the customer. You may even decide not to fill the order at all. It is much better to lose an order than to lose the money from an uncollectable account.

If you can repeat your successful sales performance often enough, you will find that in no time at all you will have saturated the local market with your product. Most likely you will also find that you've exceeded your limit of producing the product yourself. In short, you are ready to *expand*. However, in order to make this transition smoothly and successfully, you must be able to expand in several directions at one time. Needless to say, this is no easy feat.

First of all, you will need to increase your ability to make your product. In other words, it is time to hire some people to help you do some of the work. Decide what aspect of the work you would like to have someone do for you. Write up a description of the job to be done and put an ad in a local paper. Put in as many qualifications as possible so that from the beginning those who respond to the ad will have a fairly good idea of what is required of them. This will help reduce unnecessary responses from unqualified people. Be prepared to interview people and demonstrate to them specifically what you want done. Consider giving them a sample to complete so that you may judge firsthand the quality of their work. You will have to teach them to do it exactly as you want. Expect to find very few people who fill your requirements and don't be surprised if it takes several ads to build up your work force to the point where you feel you are ready to start expanding your market.

You may choose to continue selling your product yourself. Set aside one or two days per week to do your selling. Work within a certain radius and work on each area until you feel that you have pretty much saturated that area. If you are not familiar with the area, perhaps it would be worthwhile to visit the stores first as a customer to see if your product would in fact do well there. Don't become discouraged if you meet with resistance. Sometimes it takes several visits to build a relationship with the person doing the buying before a sale is actually made! Also, take advantage of your telephone to service your existing accounts and get follow-up orders.

It is certainly feasible that you would prefer not to do the actual selling yourself, or that you would like to expand your sales even further into other markets. In that case, it would be to your advantage to hire some sort of sales force. A full-time sales person can be a rather large financial strain on a new business, as he or she will need to be paid a salary. A better arrangement would be to find a sales representative who carries lines related to yours and can sell your products in the same stores. A sales rep generally gets paid on a commission basis, based on a percentage of the total sales of your product.

Sales reps can be found by reading trade magazine advertisements or by going to a trade mart in a nearby large city. You can visit showrooms or you can get a trade-mart directory that lists sales reps in the area. Make appointments to meet them and see how they have set up their organization. Keep in mind that it is extremely important to find a sales rep with whom you are compatible and who has a sales technique that satisfies you as he or she will be representing both you and your product.

Several other methods of selling your product can prove to be worthwhile; however, they can require an initial investment of varying sums of money. Trade shows are an excellent source of exposure to the market you wish to reach; however, booths at these shows are often expensive to rent. Unless you feel confident that you will get many orders there or as a result of the show, consider whether the booth rental fee will severely limit or totally eliminate the profits to be made.

Direct-mail advertising is another way of approaching your market, but the cost of printing and mailing is often too high to make this outlet

66 Have had difficulty with the large corporations, such as General Foods, Pepsico, and IBM. I don't have an agent and must do all the legwork on my own. **99**

Illustrator

worthwhile unless you are able to find an already existing mail-order catalog that will include your product.

Advertising is a useful marketing tool. If you are trying to attract the wholesale market, you may find it valuable to put some ads in trade magazines. If the retail customer is your target, advertisements in local newspapers or magazines are your best bet. It is helpful to have on hand drawings or photographs of your items and a flyer with descriptions and sales information to send to mail-order catalogs, interested stores, or retail customers who express an interest in your line.

There are many avenues for growth; however, a word of caution seems appropriate here. Start slowly. Offer just one or two items at first. This will enable you to benefit from your experience without sacrificing too much time or money. As you become familiar with the market and the various outlets for sales, you can add related products at a pace that is comfortable and one that will not cause so significant a growth in your business that it will overwhelm you and threaten to create a rash of orders that you are unable to fill in the alloted time. Equally unwanted is a sudden growth that will cause a severe cash-flow problem that could drive you out of business altogether.

On the other hand, don't become discouraged if things move along too slowly. As long as you have confidence in your product, you should be persistent. Keep in mind that people have very different tastes. Just because one person does not like the item does not mean that no one will. Don't become discouraged easily and don't give up!

Marketing a Product: View From the Buyer's Office

Beth Ravit, Buyer

Before approaching a buyer, you must decide how your product relates to the existing marketplace. Are you introducing a new product or improving on something that is already available? If your offering is a new item, be prepared to explain why consumers will need or want what you are producing. If improving on an existing product, you must be able to explain why yours is superior—stressing the merits of your item without downgrading the competition! You should also be realistic about any drawbacks to your product. For example, if your cost is higher than existing models, be prepared to explain what causes your product to be more expensive and what the benefits are to the consumer. Don't volunteer the negatives—if the buyer is good, he or she will know them better than you.

> **66 If success is determined by monetary rewards, we certainly are not there yet. However, as a friend of mine, after hearing that Bloomingdale's had placed an order, remarked: 'You've reached the Broadway of marketing.' 99**
>
> **Sales Manager**

Once you understand how your product relates to competitive or similar items, you must decide which retailers to approach. Price point is a major consideration in deciding which stores to sell to. See which stores in your area carry products with the same end use and within a comparable price range. If your item costs a store $10, you will have better luck approaching a store retailing comparable goods between $18–$25 than a store in the $10–$16 price range. A second consideration is the type of customer a store attracts. If your item is young and trendy, you would do better in a boutique store, as opposed to a conservative carriage trade store, though price lines in both may be the same. Decide which stores are competing for your type of consumer and try to sell to them all. A buyer may ask to whom you're selling, and you should mention which other competitive stores are interested in your product. If you are dealing in products at the upper end of the price scale, a buyer may ask for an *exclusive.* This means you agree not to sell to other stores in the same trading area. Before you agree to this type of condition, be certain you will not later regret limiting your distribution.

A strong buyer will ask for as many concessions as the seller will give. These include terms, better prices, return privileges if goods don't sell, markdown money, vendor-paid freight, advertising allowances, anticipation. All of these concessions decrease your profit margins. If possible, speak to someone dealing with your product line and find out what is

Advertising, Marketing, and Promotion

common practice in your industry. Any concessions you decide to give must be built into your price, or you will make less profit than you planned, or in some cases, sustain a loss.

A good buyer is the consumer's representative in the marketplace and is almost in an adversarial position with the seller. Some buyers will appear to be cold, distant, and tough, and some will seem very pleasant. All should be trying to make the best possible deal for their customers; so no matter what your personal reaction to a buyer's method or personality may be, know what you can afford to give up, what is negotiable, and where you cannot move. Once you've mentally answered these questions, you can negotiate without losing money.

Sometimes getting to see the buyer may be your most difficult negotiation. Treat assistant buyers well; they will probably be the first contact you have in the buyer's office and will describe you and possibly your product in a more positive light if you've been professional in dealing with them. Many retail buyers have *seeing days,* which means any manufacturer may wait in line to show merchandise. This is first come, first served; so this can sometimes require a long wait until it's your turn to see the buyer. A telephone call to the buyer's office sometimes can get you an appointment or information regarding seeing days. You can turn this waiting period into an advantage if you find an experienced, friendly seller who will talk to you about your industry in general and this specific buyer in particular. Don't be embarrassed to strike up conversations with your competition. If you're new in the industry, they can teach you a lot.

Take advantage of trade shows or fairs. They can give you a broad audience specifically looking for new product offerings. Use any personal connections you may have to convince the buyer to see you. You should be successful in getting an appointment if you are recommended by someone the buyer respects.

Once you get to work with the buyer, you must sound professional—calm, confident, knowledgeable. Look at the buyer's merchandise in the store before your meeting. This will give you an understanding of where the buyer's emphasis is. Don't discuss specific merchandise (if you praise a potential markdown or knock a best seller, you won't help your cause!), but use the department's current status to strengthen your position. An example: "You have the best assortment in the city in my product line, but I believe mine can outperform the competition," and then explain why. Do not make a comment unless you've done your homework. No one knows better than the buyer the strengths and weaknesses of the current merchandise assortment.

Be aware that a buyer's decision to make a purchase is not based on the salability of the product alone. Timing is an important factor. Sometimes a buyer has no *open to buy* (meaning all the money allocated for a given period has been spent). It's also possible that a buyer feels your product is a duplication of what has already been purchased. The timing of delivery into the store is also important. A great gift item will have a better chance of selling well in December than in July. If you're lucky, you'll find a buyer who will discuss your product, whether or not he or she buys. You can learn as much from a frank discussion with someone who is not ready to buy your merchandise as you can from a merchant who writes an order without making any comments pro or con. Use your contact with buyers as a learning tool. Even if you disagree with their comments, keep an open mind and listen to and evaluate what they say. You may want to start with a store that is not necessarily your first choice as an outlet. This will give you a chance to practice and refine your presentation and learn from the buyer's comments; then approach the store that's your main objective. A buyer may not explain a lack of interest in your merchandise; bear in mind this does not always mean an item is unsalable. Keep trying!

If you are not successful in selling your product yourself, consider the idea of selling through a sales representative. These are individuals who deal with items from several manufacturers which usually are noncompetitive, but have some common denominator. An example would be someone who sells a line of boys' outerwear, a line of boys' slacks, and a line of boys' sweaters. Your boys' shirts would fit right in. The advantage in choosing to deal with a good sales representative is that he or she probably knows the appropriate buyers and has more immediate access than you as a newcomer. You must pay a commission, and your price must be built up to include this percentage. This type of arrangement should not be verbal; there should be a written agreement between you and the salesperson. If you choose to sell through a representative, trade shows can be a good vehicle to find the right representative.

Successfully marketing a new product is dependent on many factors: research, timing, cost, your perserverance, and not to be dismissed lightly, a little bit of luck. Many times being in the right place at the right time will be the break you'll need, so keep trying and good luck!

Glossary

Terms—trade discount to stores who pay for merchandise on time. The percentage is standard for each industry. Example: ladies' sportswear—8 percent; accessories—3 percent.

Anticipation—discount allowed to stores who pay bills before payment is due.

Advertising Allowance—money given to help pay for advertising, usually a percentage of cost value.

Markdown Allowance—Money given to a store to help offset the cost of a markdown if goods don't sell.

Return Privileges—manufacturer takes back goods which have not sold and reimburses store for the cost value of this merchandise.

"Woven Rainbow Environment"
by Dolly Curtis
Photographer: Victor Cromwell

Low Budget Promotions

> **"I'm always certain to donate arrangements to local church and civic groups to keep my name out front. When the N.Y.C. educational TV station has their fund-raising auction, my name is broadcast several times free of charge. I get the credit *and* the business!"**
>
> Floral Designer

Publicity is free. Good publicity can bring you fame and fortune; bad publicity can ruin both your reputation and your business. Advertising is what you pay for—your money, your message. Since homebased businesses are often started on low budgets, obtaining good publicity is essential. Not only that, but working from home can be advantageous for developing an angle for promoting your product or service. A warm and funny story that occurred because your business and home are under the same roof will help local newspapers, statewide magazines, and radio and television programs discover a new human interest story—yours! If at this moment neither print editors nor broadcast producers know you exist, change that immediately!

Begin with a written publicity plan. Magazine stories are finished approximately three months before publication; newspapers, days or weeks ahead; broadcasts, two hours to six months. Analyze customer statistics, then research media audiences. Who is going to buy your product? Where do these individuals live? Is it more productive to publicize your work locally, statewide, or nationally? How much must the customers' income be to afford your goods or services? Is your product or service visual or better described in words? How can you explain the uniqueness of your business in the simplest, most direct manner to get the information across to viewers, listeners, readers?

Once these questions are answered, research in the library for newspapers, magazines, and radio/television programs that reach an audience capable of buying your product or service. Record the name of each publication, address, editor's name, and phone number. It helps to be systematic, for this is a list that will be used many times.

If you're interested in local publicity, check a community newsstand or the Yellow Pages for area newspapers and magazines. Add them to that growing file of contacts. Read the business and women's sections to see how best to slant the press release you're going to write to fit each publication's format. It is important to always send information directly to an editor by name; otherwise, a release sent to an address may wind up in File 13 with the junk mail.

Keep an accurate diary of all correspondence with media people, including contact dates, conversations, and appointments. Confirm appointments in writing on letterhead stationery. In your quest for visual publicity, incidentally, don't overlook local cable TV programs; there's a willing market.

After researching where, to whom, and how you wish to publicize yourself, write the essential—and quintessential!—press release that will introduce you to the media by announcing who you are, what you are doing, how, when, where, and why. It must encourage journalists to want to write about you and your business. You have this one chance to make a favorable impression!

Make the release enticing, interesting, short, and to the point. If it is journalistically well written, it may be placed in a newspaper with no alterations. Stress individual qualities and emphasize the unique characteristics your products or service possess. A little showmanship and imagination can be used to personalize the information.

Type it double-spaced on standard 8¹/₂″ x 11″ bond paper. One page is better than two for an editor's quick read-through, and two pages are the limit. In the upper right-hand corner, type the words *FOR IMMEDIATE RELEASE;* directly underneath, *CONTACT:* followed by your name, address, and phone number. If your release runs more than one page, type *MORE* in the lower right-hand corner. Always simplify the editor's work.

For some businesses, a press kit may be better than a press release. The kit, like the press release, is sent out to interest editors and/or producers in your product or service before you make a phone contact. It should contain a press release with a statement about the uniqueness of your product or service. "Anyone can learn to fly this new ultralite aircraft in a couple of hours. No license is required." Include a letter explaining why your story is of particular interest. You just invented a locust trap. A locust plague is expected in June. Explain why your trap is of value, what it does, and why it's important to all readers in the plague area. A product or service of value, utility, and interest will be newsworthy. Use flair and creativity to demonstrate that. An individual selling health foods might write about the physical and emotional benefits derived from health food packages sent to young adults in college. Or, a clothing designer and manufacturer might describe her clothes for people with special problems.

Include dates you'll be available for interviews. Depending on your product, you might send samples, but don't expect them to be returned. A 5″ x 7″ black-and-white glossy photograph of you at work or of your product can be reproduced for print media and adds visual impact. Some magazines might wish to know if colored photos are available. Your biographical sketch helps personalize the whole thing.

It isn't necessary to send more than a release and letter in a press kit, but if something will help sell a story, add it! Then send the kit by first class mail, which implies urgency and exclusivity.

Don't get discouraged if there is no immediate response. After a week or two, refer back to the publicity list and phone the editors or producers you had previously contacted by mail. Reintroduce yourself. Speak with confidence and authority. Asking each one if your release or press kit was received is a way of starting the conversation. Be prepared to interject additional interesting information. Though you may not succeed every time, follow-up calls can and often do result in an interview. If an editor says, "Sorry, we can't use this story," change the slant of the first release and, six months later, send a second one. Sometimes, after minor changes, a release that isn't appropriate at one time fits the bill perfectly at a later date. Getting publicity means never giving up!

If you're going to be on television, that in itself may be newsworthy. Contact local editors, as well as editors of the papers where the interview takes place. Tell each why you're appearing on TV and try to have articles appear close to interview dates. It's often difficult to have contact addresses announced on the air; newspapers are more willing to provide

Advertising, Marketing, and Promotion

this information. When people see, then read, about what you are doing, they tend to remember the details better. What is written can be clipped and filed.

Word of mouth is one of the most effective ways of promoting and selling your product or service. A catchy name, one people like to use, can perpetuate business. Be your own publicity: talk when it counts and let people know what you're selling and why it's terrific. Whenever possible, state how and where your goods can be purchased. Give lectures. Teach courses connected with your business. Build a reputation that proclaims your honesty, reliability, conscientiousness, and skills, and people will purchase whatever you sell!

Anything favorable said about your product can help promote it. When someone who is known or respected endorses your product or service, that statement can be translated into publicity. Endorsements of our work appear on the back cover of *Women Working Home.* We are proud of the positive responses given by people whose opinions are valued. These endorsements sell the book to individuals and to the media and can be printed on flyers, quoted in letters, and blown up on display posters. When your work is favorably presented by the media, that, too, is an endorsement. Any recommendations from respected sources, whether printed or spoken, sell!

Flyers and brochures are another method of reaching customers. They can be tacked on bulletin boards, distributed at meetings, and mailed to potential customers. A brochure, like a letter of solicitation, should contain a description of the product, price (but not always), and purchasing details. Since the customer is being talked to through this brochure or flyer, it must sell the product or service and motivate the reader to buy! Use a slogan and/or visual to encourage opening and reading. Use a headline that announces something, describes a unique quality, or promises something. A brochure lets you quote endorsements, relate special product or service features, and define special qualities. Design it carefully. Include essential information, but keep it clear and concise—it is one more opportunity to project a professional business approach. (If you lack skills in graphic design, you can hire a professional, but this will definitely add dollars to your low budget campaign.)

If you will be sending a great deal of mail, consider obtaining a bulk mail permit. The bulk mailing privilege can cut down your mailing costs considerably, although there is extra work involved in the required sorting of mail by zip code.

For pennies apiece, brochures can be included with merchandise that someone else is mailing out; flyers, with an organization's newsletters.

Setting up your own displays is another way of drumming up business. Every Christmas a designer friend arranges her beautiful hand-made dolls in a boutique set up in her home. Just in time for the holidays, friends and neighbors come to shop! If your product is wearable, wear it! If you have a service rather than a product, arrange letters of praise in a portfolio. Exhibit it with photographs, artifacts, or other visuals at places such as business expositions, trade shows, civic functions—anywhere customers might gather.

In summary, promoting a business attracts new customers and reinforces your good image with present customers. There are so many good, inexpensive ways to promote a homebased business:

Word of mouth. Nothing sells an item better than having a trusted friend say how good it is! Encourage satisfied customers to pass on all positive feelings and to share the names of their friends and neighbors (potential buyers) with you.

If my work displeases you, tell me.
If my work pleases you, tell a friend.

Display. Let people see how good your products or services are and what benefits they can provide. Products should be clearly priced and within reach (fragile and valuable items, such as blown glass and gold jewelry, exempted). Services can be promoted by showing results through a portfolio of letters and/or photographs. You want to show your customers what they can get for their money.

Signs. Whenever the opportunity arises—at meetings, fairs, or business gatherings—display signs to remind people what you do and where you are located. A listing in the Yellow Pages or in the *Women Working Home* directory is like a sign. Calendars, T-shirts, and pencils with your name, address or phone, and a slogan effectively encourage customers to buy. "Have a Coke!"

Samples. Give customers a taste of what you're selling so that they desire more. Samples only count when they are likely to lead to sales. Giving one free flower-arranging lesson is likely to bring in students; handing out sample brownies in a location too distant from your home bakery will not bring buyers. Qualify your prospects!

Sales. Always try to increase your total profits. (That's why you're in business, after all!) If discounting a product or an aspect of a service will bring in more customers, try that approach. Send postcards (rather than letters in envelopes, with their increased postage) or pass out handbills to keep costs down.

Publicity. Get your product or service promoted in any media that will reach potential customers.

The last word: test. Always test each promotional approach carefully. Try each method on a small scale first to see which low budget promotional approach works most effectively for you and for your business.

Lois Winston
Graphic Design and Illustration
One Asbury Avenue
Melrose Park, PA 19126
(215) 635-3471

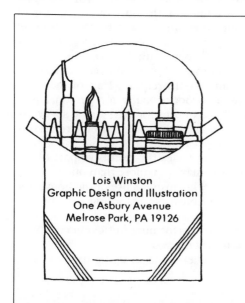

Lois Winston
Graphic Design and Illustration
One Asbury Avenue
Melrose Park, PA 19126

1982·USA·THE NETHERLANDS

Lois Winston
One Asbury Ave.
Melrose Park, PA 19126

The IRS and Home Business

66We found a fairly large, old Victorian house with two living rooms, which made an ideal set-up for me. I have a separate entrance into the studio from the front of the house. This works well to meet the IRS requirements as a separate space used totally as a work area.**99**

Fabric Artist

A taxpayer may be able to take sizable business deductions if she uses part of her home exclusively and regularly either—
1. as her place of business, or
2. as a place of business that is used by patients, clients, or customers in meeting and dealing with the taxpayer in the normal course of her trade or business.

An employee may claim a deduction for business use of the home only if all exclusive and regular use requirements are met and if such use is for an employer's convenience. If the business use of the home is only appropriate and helpful in the employee's work, the deduction cannot be taken.

Exclusive use of a part of the home means that one must use a specific part of the home only to carry on a trade or business. If a writer's bedroom has a corner set apart for work with a desk, typewriter, and phone, she cannot claim a deduction under present law because the room is also used for personal purposes—in this case, sleeping. A seamstress who does alterations on the sewing machine in her den cannot take the deduction. An artist who paints in her sunny kitchen cannot take the deduction. An exercise teacher who conducts classes in her family room cannot take a deduction.

The one exception to this exclusive use rule that applies to persons working at home is that of storage of inventory. The inventory must be held for use in the business; the home must be the only fixed location of the trade or business; and the trade or business must be the selling of products at wholesale or retail. The storage space must be used regularly and must be a separately identifiable space suitable for storage. An example of this is the storage of clothing in boxes and on racks that a woman who sells clothing from home would require. Half of the basement is used for inventory storage and occasionally for personal purposes when she does the laundry. The expenses for the storage space are deductible even though this part of the basement is not used exclusively for business.

Regular use means that the taxpayer uses the exclusive part of her home on a continuing basis, though she may have more than one business location. For her to deduct expenses for the business use of the home, she must determine whether it is a place of business according to—

1. the total time ordinarily spent in performing duties there:
2. the degree of business activity there; and
3. the relative amount of income received from doing business at home.

An example of this is a woman who works in a corporate office as a secretary, and evenings and weekends in her home office as an artist. Her home office qualifies for deductions because it is the place for conducting a particular business (assuming it meets the other requirements). It no longer matters whether the home business is the principal or secondary trade or business—a 1981 change that is retroactive to 1976. (Check with your accountant to see if amended returns should be filed.)

If, in the normal course of business, you meet or deal with patients, clients, or customers in your home, your expenses for that part of your home used exclusively for business are deductible. Individuals with occupations that generally meet this requirement are doctors, attorneys, therapists, and other professionals who maintain offices in their homes, as well as those who operate businesses such as beauty shops or clothing outlets.

The expenses for a separate, freestanding building next to one's home, such as a studio, garage, or barn, are deductible if the building is used exclusively and regularly for business. It does not have to be the principal place of business or the place where one meets patients, clients, or customers. Examples of this would be an artist's studio, a florist's greenhouse, or a riding instructor's stable.

UPDATE: In August 1983 the IRS issued a revised set of proposed regulations favorable to homebased business that reflect several changes in the law, as well as current IRS interpretation of older regulations. The first is that it is not necessary for a room to have a permanent partition for that part of the room used for business purposes, but must be a separately identifiable space. Second, the exclusive use test will be satisfied even though the room is used for a nonqualifying business that does not fit into any of the excepted categories, such as the principal place of business or place to meet clients. If a school teacher, for instance, corrects papers in a room used part time as an artist's studio, a portion of that room, limited to the amount of income from the artist's business, may be taken as a deduction. Check these proposed regulations with your accountant before filing.

What's deductible?

The part of your home that is used for your business is treated, for tax purposes, as property separate from the personal part of your home. You must divide the expenses of operating your entire home between the personal and business uses of your home. Some expenses are divided on an area basis, others on a usage basis. Certain items are totally deductible; others, totally nondeductible. You must have proof to show—

1. that part of your home is used exclusively and regularly for business;
2. that the part of your home used exclusively and regularly for business is either your place of business or the place where you meet with patients, clients, or customers in the normal course of business.
3. the amount of depreciation and expenses for keeping up that part of your home which is used for business.
   To substantiate deductions claimed, keep canceled checks, receipts, and other evidences of paid expenses for at least six years.

To figure the percentage of your home that is used for business, divide the square footage utilized for business by the total square foot area of your

> **"It's a challenge to juggle work while caring for the children. I believe in paying a student to clean my home twice a month. This keeps me feeling good about my place and is a tax deduction. In fact, my in-home business provides incredible tax deductions!"**
>
> Nutrition Consultant

home. Or, if the rooms in your home are all about the same size, simply divide the number of rooms used for business by the number of rooms in the house. Translated into actual figures, that means that if you use one room in your home that is 10' x 12', or 120 square feet, for business, and your home has 1200 square feet, you are using 10 percent of the total area for business. If the rooms are about the same size and you use one room in a five-room house, you are using one-fifth, or 20 percent, for business.

There are always certain expenses required to maintain and operate a home. Some of these expenses are directly related to the business use of your home—painting or repairs to the specific area or room used for business, for instance. Others are indirectly related—painting the outside of the house, repairing the roof, lighting, and air conditioning, for example. These must be allocated to the part of the home used for business. Others are not related at all—a swimming pool is an example.

A capital expenditure is an investment of money either to get property that will be useful for more than one year or to improve property already owned. Examples of capital improvements are replacement of electric wiring or plumbing, a new roof, a new addition to your home, or remodeling existing space. The cost of such property may not be deducted entirely in one year, but must be depreciated and allocated to the part of the home used for business. Homeowners must distinguish between repairs and improvements and keep accurate records of all expenditures.

If it sounds confusing, that it is! And that is why a homebased businesswoman would be wise to seek professional advice. We are dealing with strict rules and regulations set up by the Internal Revenue Service. Tax laws and tax return forms can be a maze of confusion to the uninitiated. Besides, tax laws are constantly changing and unless you intend to keep fully informed on all these matters, you had best get the help of a competent tax adviser. That individual can often save you far more in taxes than the amount charged for services, and the fee itself is tax-deductible. The adviser will help you prepare returns, tell you whether you must file quarterly tax returns, and calculate the amount of money due each quarter—payable January 15, April 15, June 15, and September 15. Use his or her services fully—but wisely. To save time and money, be well prepared with facts, figures, and orderly files pertaining to your home business. Have a receipt for everything, even if it's only 30¢ for an eraser. Save bills and canceled checks. Maintain simplified, accurate records that balance costs against sales, money out and money in. Standard account books for small business can be purchased at any business stationery store. You may even be able to find one especially designed for your particular business. The IRS is not specific in the type of records it requires. That is up to you! But you must include whatever is needed to determine tax liability and to support statements made in tax returns. You don't want to lose valid tax deductions and credits, or pay taxes if they could be deferred to another year.

Still Life
Photographer: Helaine Messer

Tax Information for the Homebased Businesswoman

June Walker-Sloat, Budget and Tax Consultant

Whatever the reasons—inflation, unemployment, grown children, or a desire to return to the work force—self-employment among women has been on the rise in the last few years. Many women opt to supplement their own or their husband's full-time income with part-time, nonsalaried work. For others, self-employed income is the only family income.

For tax purposes you are self-employed if the company or people for whom you work deduct no taxes from your pay. At the end of the year you will not receive a form W-2 from your place of work but, in most cases, a form 1099. Sales commissions, consultant fees, and craft sale income are examples of self-employed earned income.

Some regard the money they earn in this way as a matter of no importance. "Why do I need to report it, since it doesn't amount to much?" goes the refrain.

The first point in rebuttal is that it is illegal not to report earned income; it must be reported to the Internal Revenue Service.

Second, it may be to your advantage to report it, because once you are forced to look at your self-employment as a business, you will grasp the amount of expenses you incur related to that business.

The salaried mathematics teacher, who does craft work on weekends and during the summer, might, for example, earn $3,000 over the course of a year. When she begins to tally the cost of her supplies, use of her car, her home telephone, and electricity to run her equipment at home, she may find that her expenses exceed the $3,000 she earned. That excess in expenses can be deducted from her salaried income, for example—

Salary from York School District	$20,000
Craft expenses	3,500
Craft income	3,000
Loss on craft work	500
Net income	19,500

The same accounting is not used for hobby income.

Whether you deal in a product or a service, whether your self-employed income is supplemental or principal, it is to your advantage to

> **❝I use the one-write system for my expenses and checks. It's so simple; there's absolutely no hassle with it. I send the information to my accountant twice a year, though he has told me that four times a year would be better.❞**
>
> Fulfillment Service Director

Financial Advisory

look upon what you do as a business and upon yourself as a businessperson. To develop this outlook so that it becomes habitual will take some self-training. You will realize its value, however, as your serious attitude is reflected in your work. If your long-term plans are for growth and expansion, such an attitude can aid in the realization of those plans. An immediate result will be seen at tax time when less money ends up in Uncle Sam's treasury and more in your own.

Deductions/Legitimate Business Costs

Research Events. Any event related to your business which provides material or background intended for use in current or future work that you expect will produce income is a research event: as a craftsperson, attendance at a craft show; an animal breeder, a trip to the zoo. These expenses are legitimate business costs. If you're an advertising consultant, astrologer, investment counselor, or any of a number of professionals who use the services of the library, town clerk, or the like, such trips are deductible. If it is necessary for your work that you keep abreast of local affairs, subscribing to local cable television is also a legitimate business expense.

As a dance instructor, music teacher or performer, photographer, or artist, your sources of inspiration and your business contacts are blended into your total life. Concerts and dance performances, while entertainment for most, are business experiences for you and are in most cases deductible.

As a real estate broker, horticulturalist, or gardener, your ride through the country on a spring day may be business oriented. If the ideas and information you acquire are necessary in your business, that would make the trip deductible.

Donated Work. If you donate your work, either a book you've written or patchwork pillows you've made, for sale by a civic organization, you can deduct only the basis of that work and not its fair market value. By basis is meant the actual cost of producing that work—paper, fabric, travel costs—not what your hourly rate would be were you to charge for your work, nor what your work would sell for in the marketplace.

Office in the Home. Recent changes in the federal tax code have established new and stringent rules for deducting the costs of maintaining an office in the home. As a self-employed individual working out of your home, your work area, if used *exclusively* for your work, is deductible. It must be your principal place of business or where you meet your clients or customers. If it is a complete room, a percentage of your living expenses can be deducted. For example, if one of your four rooms is used exclusively for your work, then one-quarter of your rent, insurance, and heating bills are business costs. The IRS sets income limitations on this deduction. Special rules apply if your home is used as a day-care center.

Regular Expenses. Could you carry on your business without your telephone or your answering machine? How many of the calls you make are to fellow professionals to discuss business? Those, all your business calls, and a percentage of your monthly service charge are deductible.

The cost of all the equipment necessary for pursuing and practicing your business are deductible—typewriter, tools, sewing machine, tape recorder, paper clips. If you get more than one year's use out of an item, you should not deduct the entire cost of the item in the year it was purchased. Rather, you depreciate the cost over several years. In that way you spread the deduction over the *useful life* of the item. For an item with a useful life of three years or more, you can take an investment credit. The credit, equal to six or ten percent of the item's cost depending on its useful life, is a direct offset against tax liability in the year the item was first put to use.

Any books, magazines, or publications useful to your work are deductible. Also deductible: advertising or promotional expenses, business cards, newspaper ads, flyers, postage, photocopies, agent fees, employment agency commissions, dues to professional organizations, legal and accounting fees, copyright fees, and interest on business loans.

Local Transportation. When you meet with a client or a potential client to pick up or deliver work or confer about work, travel to speak at or attend a conference, or run any business errands, your transportation expenses are deductible. If you used public transportation, you may use actual costs; if you use your own car or truck, you may calculate the cost in number of miles, plus parking fees and tolls. (The 1982 rate was 20 cents or 11 cents per mile, depending on the age of the vehicle. Check for current rates.) If you do a lot of business traveling with your own car, you should keep all of your car expenses—gasoline, oil, tires, repairs, insurance, even the cost of a new car—and take the expense as a portion of the business mileage against total mileage. If your total mileage for the year is 15,000 and 5,000 was for business, then one-third of all car expenses are deductible, including one-third of the yearly depreciation of the new car and the proportionate investment credit.

Travel. When you travel away from home overnight for business reasons, you may deduct the ordinary and necessary travel costs, as well as lodging, meals, laundry and cleaning, tips, baggage, and telephone. Good records are required.

Business Gifts and Entertainment. Business gifts are deductible up to $25 per year for each business associate to whom a gift or gifts are given. If you incur expenses to entertain someone for reasons directly related to the active conduct of your business, they are deductible. They might include meals, tickets, drinks, or business-related entertainment at home. You must be able to show an expectation of income or other business benefit as a result of the occasion, and accurate records must be kept.

Education and Training. If you attend seminars, conventions, or school for the purpose of learning more about your profession (not, however, to learn a *new* profession), your expenses—admission fees, tuition, books, and transportation—are deductible.

Record Keeping

Good records can be simple and still satisfy all the legal and practical requirements. Some self-employed fret that record keeping is time-consuming, but a simple and efficient method can take only a few minutes per week, can save you or your tax preparer hours at tax time, and will also ensure that you take full advantage of all deductions due you.

The following is the simplest acceptable method for the beginning self-employed. The most important mental note you must make is to pay by check and to save receipts. At the end of every day put all your receipts in one box. Label a number of envelopes—"Postage," "Research Events," "Supplies," etc. Once a week sort your receipts from the general box into the appropriate envelopes. Then at tax time, all you have to do is add up the receipts and canceled checks. Be sure to mark the receipts "lunch with Jane Smith re dress designs" and the like, to satisfy IRS requirements. If a receipt is not available or convenient, you are still entitled to a deduction, but you must keep the expense logged in a notebook, which

66 I have cleared out the lower level (family room) for my studio. The bar is now the area I mix my dyes in, bricks and boards fill the space to the ceiling for storage, and my husband has helped build waist-high frames to stretch my silk. **99**

Fabric Designer

can be kept in your glove compartment, purse, or pocket (e.g., 7/14/83—used books on home catering, $14.50).

Your journal is also a good and convenient place to list your income as it is received. Taxable income is money paid you for a service you perform or a product you sell.

Once you've mastered this system, or if your business grows enough to warrant it, you may switch to a more formal system.

Why Record Keeping
The chief reason for keeping records is to enable you to complete your tax return. Records are required by the IRS in an audit. Tax laws do not specify what forms records must be in, as long as they are permanent, accurate, and complete, and they clearly establish income, deductions, credits, etc. It is remarkably easy to overlook deductible expenses unless you record them at the time they are paid and keep receipts for them. Good record keeping has other advantages:

1. It helps you monitor how well your business is doing and thereby helps you keep out of financial hot water.
2. Records help you to borrow. In the estimation of banks and other lending institutions the self-employed are at a disadvantage. They are often considered unemployed for lending purposes. Even if a salaried steady job produces less income, it is considered preferable for lending. With accurate records you will be better able to present your income statements in proof of your solvency when seeking a loan.
3. Accurate records are needed for legal action, whether you initiate it or respond to someone's suit in which you are involved, including divorce and child-support cases or monies owed you by a client.

How to File Your Tax Return
As a self-employed individual, you will fill out your Form 1040 tax return as usual. You will also need a Schedule C (Profit or Loss from Business or Profession) on which you will subtract business expenses from your gross business income to determine your net income or loss. You will also need to complete a Schedule SE (Social Security Self-Employment Tax) which calculates the amount of Social Security tax you must pay on your self-employment income. No Social Security tax is due if your income is less than $400, but the Schedule SE must be completed anyway.

Under IRS rules your business should make a profit in two out of five years. There are exceptions, however, so contact your accountant or financial advisor.

How to Pay Taxes During the Year
If you earned wages or a salary, your employer would withhold taxes from your pay and send them to the government. As a self-employed person, you are your own employer and must remit your own taxes to the government. By the time you file your tax return you should have paid at least 80 percent of your total income tax and Social Security tax due for that year. You do this in quarterly installments. Payments are due on April 15, June 15, September 15, and January 15. Obtain Form 1040-S (Declaration of Estimated Tax) and pay your taxes to the IRS based on your income for that three-month period.

Final Note
There are many specific limitations and requirements regarding income and expenses, and tax laws change from year to year. If you have questions, consult an experienced tax preparer.

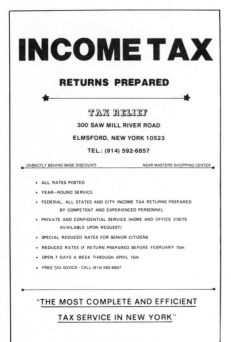

Simplified Record Keeping

Marilyn Salmieri, Certified Public Accountant

Why Keep Records?
- To insure that you will pay only the tax that you owe and no more.
- To accurately assess cash position.
- To allow for projections into the future based on past history.
- To insure no errors in the payment of invoices from suppliers or the request for payment from customers.

What Type of Records Are Necessary?
First consideration must be given to what is required by the Internal Revenue Service. Although the IRS specifies no particular format, the following must be considered:

1. Source of receipt. Keep records that indicate the source of cash. Some may not contribute to taxable income, such as capital investment in the business or loans from outside the business. Others may indicate taxable income, such as sales, refunds, or interest income.

2. Source of disbursement. Record all disbursements of cash, whether through the checkbook, petty cash, or any other miscellaneous expenditure. Each disbursement may or may not be related to taxable income. Some that are not are repayments of loans to owners or outsiders. Some which reduce income are payments for office supplies, travel, entertainment, postage, etc. Be sure to retain documentation or receipts. If there are no receipts, the item may be lost forever either in the initial preparation of a tax return or in the subsequent audit of a tax return. A major mistake of a small business is to lose track of fully deductible expenses.

Single Entry Versus Double Entry System of Record Keeping
For the small business, the simplest method is single entry, i.e., using the checkbook to determine which receipts and disbursements contribute to taxable income. Obviously all receipts and disbursements contribute to cash flow. This method is simple but may not fully reflect business activity and return on investment. The single entry system can readily be converted to the more refined double entry system by someone knowledgeable in accounting. The single entry system relies on the checkbook and a summary of cash receipts and disbursements done on a continuing basis.

The double entry system provides a method of checks and balances to insure accuracy. Since business transactions are an exchange of one thing for another, double entry bookkeeping shows this effect by recording each transaction as a debit entry in one account and a credit entry in another. The total of the amounts entered as debits must equal the total of the

Financial Advisory

amounts entered as credits. If not, an error has been made and steps can be taken to correct the error even in the simplest system.

At the end of the accounting period, the income statement and balance sheet may be prepared. The income statement reflects operations for the current year. The balance sheet shows the financial position of the business at an exact point in time.

An outside accountant can provide instruction and a simple worksheet approach for the continuous record keeping of a business with only minimal supervision required.

Cash Versus Accrual Accounting

There are two basic accounting methods that may be used to record your business transactions: cash or accrual.

Using the cash method, you report income when the money is actually received and report expenses when the bills are actually paid. Using the accrual method, you report income when it is earned (whether you've received payment or not) and report expenses when they are incurred (whether you've paid for them or not).

You may use either the cash or accrual method or a combination of the two as long as you apply your accounting method consistently and your records clearly show your income; however, if the production, purchase, or sale of merchandise is an income-producing factor, you must keep inventory records to clearly show income, and you must use the accrual method to record your purchases and sales. Many personal-service businesses use the cash method because it is relatively simple since there is little or no inventory involved.

Setting Up the Books

Before buying elaborate ledgers and journals, which are quite costly, it would be wise to consider the following:

1. What level of activity is the business likely to attain during the first year or years? What type of business? If the business is part-time, service-oriented, has one or a few large customers, the bookkeeping system would tend to be more simplified than a full-time, manufacturing or retail business dealing in an inventory of many small items manufactured or sold.

2. What level of expertise is possessed by owner or staff members related to accounting? Often an outside accountant is consulted initially who sets up the books but does not continue on a regular basis due to cost considerations. If the owner does not understand the system, many time-consuming and costly mistakes may result by the use of an overly elaborate system, even if such is needed in response to considerations in item one above.

3. Also consider whether the business will utilize a computer in the future. If so, it might be wise for the first records of the business, i.e., cash receipts and disbursements, to be maintained by an outside computer service bureau. This will relieve the owner of needless drudgery and will quickly provide the owner with financial reports long before he or she would have the time to do them manually, particularly in the start-up phases of the business.

Business Bank Accounts

Even when first thinking about a business, it is wise to establish a separate checking account for that purpose. While it may seem unnecessary at the

66 When I get too far behind on filing and recording, my husband bails me out. 99

Camp Consultant

102

time, expenses related to the business idea rapidly occur and are most evident when separated from a personal checking account.

As the idea develops and income is produced, all receipts should be deposited only in the business account. All expenditures should be paid by check if at all possible. This does not mean that you need retain only canceled checks as evidence of business expenditure. Also retain backup information to support the canceled checks. Avoid making checks payable to cash. Make checks payable to yourself only if they are income withdrawals or repayment of loans; indicate such on the check stubs. Also fill in all check stubs with a description and purpose of the disbursement and enter dates on the stubs. Payments made to replenish a petty cash fund should be documented by petty cash slips and receipts. Supplying the appropriate information when the transaction occurs is time-consuming, but less so than trying to reconstruct missing information later when needed, most often at tax-preparation time.

In addition, do not overlook the importance of keeping bank reconciliations current. A much better check is kept on cash flow and possible bank or recording errors if done properly and promptly.

Petty Cash

A petty cash fund is important to cover those situations where writing a check is unjustified, i.e., usually an amount too small to record in the checkbook; however, even though the expenditure is made in cash, proper documentation is necessary to make even small items deductible for tax purposes. Always try to obtain receipts. If no receipt is available, use a petty cash slip which, if properly filled out and retained, can substitute for receipts for small items.

It is best to maintain an imprest petty cash fund, i.e., a fixed amount is maintained in a separate container to cover small expenditures. As expenditures are made, the cash taken out is replaced by either a receipt or a petty cash slip for the same amount. The result is that the fund always has the same amount in it, usually composed of some cash and some receipts. As cash becomes low, the receipts and slips are tallied and a check is drawn for that amount to petty cash to refurbish the account. Those receipts and slips are then removed from the container and retained in the permanent files of the business to serve as necessary documentation for tax purposes.

Jane Poston
House Sitter
Photographer: Hazel Froud

Worksheets

The following are some guidelines to worksheets that might be prepared on a continuing basis. How often and to what complexity they are prepared depends on the volume and type of business. The list is not all-inclusive.

Daily Summary of Cash Receipts. Cash sales for the day are summarized either from cash register tapes or cash sales slips received for the day. Cash receipts should be deposited in the business checking account as quickly as possible, even on a daily basis if necessary.

Monthly Summary of Cash Receipts. This summarizes the month's activity of cash received from such items as net sales, sales tax, refunds, other receipts and deposits, all in separate columns with monthly totals at the bottom.

For tax purposes, the most important total derived from the monthly summary of cash receipts is the amount of monthly taxable transactions shown as net sales. If applicable, figure total monthly net sales by reducing the total monthly receipts by the actual amount of sales tax to be turned over to state or local taxing authorities. Sales tax payable would then appear in a separate column not to be included in gross income. Another way to handle sales tax is to include the total sales tax collected in your gross receipts and to take a deduction for sales tax when it is paid to the state.

Cash Disbursements Journal. All expenditures that are paid by check should be recorded in a cash disbursements journal. This may be done on a daily basis in this journal for each check written. Each entry should show date, check number, payee, and amount of the disbursement and should be spread to various expense and other classifications by extending each entry into the appropriate column on a monthly basis. This type of journal may be created by either posting each check stub consecutively and regularly to a line in the journal or by using one of the one-write systems which are readily available from business forms suppliers.

Fixed Assets and Depreciation Schedule. As capital assets of the business are purchased, a permanent record should be established on a schedule maintained for a particular type of asset, i.e., furniture and fixtures, equipment, or transportation equipment. The information on these schedules is of importance when preparing tax returns to determine the appropriate depreciation expense and any related investment tax credits that might be available.

Employee Compensation Records. A record is kept for every employee showing number of hours worked in a given pay period and total pay for the period. Also record federal and state taxes withheld from pay to arrive at net pay for the period. All these calculations are needed in the preparation of quarterly and annual payroll tax returns and monthly or quarterly tax deposits.

Record Retention

It may seem premature to worry about record retention during the start-up phases of a business, but remember that once records are discarded, it is unlikely they can ever be replaced when they are needed again. Following are some simple guidelines:

1. Records directly related to the preparation of tax returns should be kept a *minimum* of three years after the due date of the return; better yet, they should be kept six years to substantiate gross income if a false or fraudulent return is suspected. Better still, retain records for eleven years, when all statutes of limitation expire.
2. Keep all tax returns as filed and amended indefinitely because these are also difficult to replace even through the Internal Revenue Service. Such returns are often important for carry-overs of tax credits and operating losses.
3. Records that are permanent should be kept in a fireproof file or room. Examples are cash books, fixed asset and depreciation schedules, general ledgers, journals, and financial statements.
4. Canceled checks, bank statements, accounts payable and receivable records, inventory schedules, payroll records, sales, and invoicing details should be kept six to seven years.

All of these suggested procedures can quickly become quite standard, with some outside guidance and training from an accountant. Do not become overwhelmed by the record keeping, but be aware that it is very important to the ultimate function of a business—to generate sales and produce a profit and return on the investment.

Managing Your Cash Flow

R. F. Sanford, Member, Financial Planning Group,
Western Electric Co.

Sooner or later every businessperson comes to learn that there can be a big difference between earning income and making money. We have all heard stories of people whose business is prospering (income) yet they can't buy a pair of shoes. Conversely, businesses can be showing losses on the income statement, yet the bankbook balance may be booming.

Ultimately all income becomes money; and, in the long run, all expenses use up money, but it is the interim period in which we usually operate. This article will focus on the relationship between income and cash flow (money) and discuss ways to manage money. Prudent money management can make your business life much easier and more pleasant.

The first place to start is where you are going to keep your money. The place you choose will depend on the specific terms and conditions offered by various banking institutions. Some banks offer free checking with a minimum balance (which earns no interest). Others charge for each check, but require no minimum balance. You can keep your surplus in an interest-bearing account elsewhere. Although there is no one answer for all businesses, one thing is clear—the place to keep your money, after providing a method for paying your bills, is where you can earn the most money (interest). In order to make this choice, you will have to consider at least two factors: the average amount of cash you expect to have on hand (average cash balance), and the frequency of your payments.

Big business will actually transfer funds *daily* in and out of money markets to maximize their interest incomes. Smaller businesses won't normally have this option, but the principle is still clear. Keep your money earning money!

One other point. Life will be a lot easier and cash-flow management less difficult if you can start with an adequate cash balance. Starting a business on a shoestring is rough. Therefore, you should plan to have cash available to pay all bills until your sales become self-sustaining. Of course you also need to pay all start-up costs (acquisition of equipment, facilities, and inventories, for example).

Having obtained an adequate financial base and having set up the most efficient and profitable way to handle the cash transactions, it's time to talk about getting that money. Whatever business you're in, you aim to sell your own goods or your own personal services to obtain money (cash). If your sales are already on a cash basis only, then sales equal cash flow; however, most businesses offer at least some portion of their sales on

> **❝I never publish strictly for money—though the temptation, when the checkbook is at zero, is there.... I do not accept any book I don't personally feel strong affection for, and that's meant turning down some friends, some well-known writers, and some books that might well have become commercial successes.❞**
>
> Publisher

credit. It may be credit-card sales or longer-term accounts receivables (whereby you bill your customer and wait for his payment by return mail). Although credit sales promote business, there is also a cost associated with extending credit. It may result in lost sales (default by customers) and will certainly cost money, because some credit card companies charge for their services and/or because you will have lost the use of your money (to earn interest) during the period while you're waiting for the cash. Regardless of the cost, credit sales take time to flow through an interim balance sheet account before becoming cash.

There's an opposite side to this coin. Just as you may have to make credit available to your customers (and wait for your money), you can probably get similar credit from the people from whom you buy goods or services. Let there be no mistake about what you are about to read—*you must always pay your bills.* You may, however, be able to take advantage of the short-run credit terms offered by your suppliers (as opposed to long-run time payments plus interest). You should never pay your bills until they are due. If the terms are "net 30" (payment in full is due 30 days from date of the invoice), do not pay that bill until that time. Keep track of your bills in an accounts payable system. You can be sure that your customers will do likewise. This will help maintain a cash-flow balance between customers paying you and you paying suppliers.

There are exceptions to this rule. If your supplier offers discounts for early payment, like "2% 10 net 30," this means that you can pay 2 percent less than the bill if you pay within ten days from the date of the invoice. Otherwise, you must pay the full amount of the invoice. You should generally take advantage of these savings. In fact, you may want to consider providing similar incentives to your customers to improve your cash flow. Another way to encourage your customers to pay their bills is to charge interest on overdue accounts. Obviously, you should avoid incurring late payment charges for your purchases. Finally, remember that many suppliers offer trade discounts or volume discounts. Always ask for, and take advantage of, these provisions.

Not only do you want to look at the *terms* of your purchases in order to maximize discounts and extend the interest-free use of their money, but you must look at the dollar level of your purchases. Inventory control is a crucial element of cash-flow management. If you buy too much inventory, you are draining your cash-flow position because paid-for inventories don't make money until they are sold. If you buy too little inventory, you may be limiting your ability to make sales and thereby hurting both your profit and your cash-flow positions. Because inventory control has a significant impact on the success of your business and because there are no fixed rules for controlling inventory, it merits your ongoing attention. If your inventory can be obtained quickly, you can probably maintain minimum quantities on hand. Buy as you go. If your inventory requires long intervals to obtain or if you need larger volumes on hand, try to arrange consignment deals where the material is delivered and stored by you, but where you don't pay for the material until it's actually used or sold.

There is not much that can be said about labor expense. People need to be paid regularly whether or not you have received cash income. Obviously, you shouldn't hire until you need help and don't pay in advance of pay date. Use the payroll account to hold these monies until payday. You may wish to consider paying your salesmen on a commission basis in order to more closely correlate sales and cash flow.

One last cost element that has a major impact on cash flow is depreciation. When you make a capital plant investment (one that will have an average useful life that is greater than one year), you can write off, or depreciate, that investment. Depreciation is a noncash expense which is deducted from your taxable income on your income statement; therefore, since you do not have to pay tax on that amount of income, you will save cash in the form of paying less tax. The cash drain has already occurred upon purchase of the equipment, but your business does get an ongoing cash-flow benefit each year via the depreciation.

Of course, you need not always buy your equipment outright. You can buy it on time, paying interest but reducing the cash-flow impact, or you can lease it. This author does not generally favor leasing, primarily because lease payments will always include a factor of profit to the owner (for the use of money). You should seek to keep this profit in *your* business. If the machine or equipment is truly a good investment, it is worth your investment; however, if your company is really financially strapped, or if there is a question of the long-run viability of your business, you may be forced to consider leasing.

This article addresses the more perplexing aspects of how income and expenses flow through the various balance sheet accounts on the way to your cashbook. A funds statement will also show that. It is essentially a restatement of your cash balance (bank account), except that it uses a different format (see Figure 1). The funds statement is one of the three basic statements that your accountant should prepare for you (the income statement and balance sheet are the other two). You, as a businessperson, should understand each of these three statements and how they are related.

Remember income and expenses do not, and need not, translate into cash immediately; therefore, you should seek to get the most money you can, as fast as you can and pay the least money you can, as slowly as you can while earning interest on the difference in the meantime.

Figure 1
SAMPLE FUNDS STATEMENT

Sources of Funds

Net Income	xxx
Depreciation	xxx
Decrease in Inventory	xxx
Decrease in Accounts Receivable	xxx
Increase in Accounts Payable	xxx
Other Borrowings	xxx
Capital Stock	xxx

Total   xxxx

Uses of Funds

Capital Plant	xxx
Increase in Inventory	xxx
Increase in Accounts Receivable	xxx
Decrease in Accounts Payable	xxx
Dividends Paid	xxx
Repayment of Borrowings	xxx

Total   xxxx

Increase (Decrease) in Cash Balance   xxxx

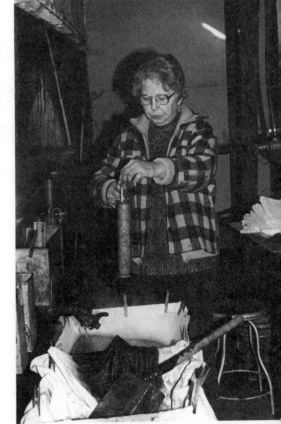

Maud Finch
Syrup Maker
Photographer: Bob Stewart

Credit: How to Get It and How to Keep It

66 I got my Visa/MasterCard credit through my bank. I deposit the charges to my account, and the companies take out a small percentage for their payment. It's a convenience for my patients, and I'm assured of getting my money. **99**

Optometrist

Credit is permission to pay in the future for money, goods, or services received now. It is used by businesses to facilitate trade, solve temporary cash-flow problems, and increase sales. It allows an individual of limited means to engage in a business of her own, and it encourages the growth and development of all business.

The ability to secure credit affects your life more than you realize. Credit is a convenience, a budget stretcher, and sometimes a necessity. Establishing a good credit record is an important step to creating an independent financial identity.

While women constitute almost half of our nation's work force, comparatively few have established credit histories. Although in some cases women have no financial identity simply because they have not needed credit, in many other cases it is because until recently they have been refused credit.

In October 1975, Congress passed the Equal Credit Opportunity Act to put an end to unfair discriminatory credit practices. Specifically, a creditor may not deny credit on the basis of sex or marital status nor disallow income received regularly from alimony, separate maintenance, or child support, or because the woman is of child-bearing age. Under this same law a woman may have credit in her own name, based on her own income, if she is creditworthy; keep her own accounts and credit history if her marital status changes; build up her own credit record while married, because new accounts must be carried in the names of both husband and wife if both use the accounts or are liable for them; apply for her own credit without providing information about her spouse or having him cosign (unless property rights are involved); get a copy of her credit record.

The lender is not required to disclose certain information on a credit report, so don't be upset when you are referred to a credit reporting agency. There will be no charge if you tell the agency you've been turned down on a credit application within the past thirty days; a slight fee if you are merely checking your report. TRW is one of the five major credit reporting agencies, with eighty-six million names on file. Each credit profile lists only accounts receivable (how you pay your bills); it does not have checking accounts, savings, or a person's sex or race. Negative information is legally removed after seven years; bankruptcies, after ten. If you have a dispute about your report, the agency will go back to its subscriber (banks, stores, etc.) for verification. If the customer still feels information is incorrect, she can include her own 100-word statement on the report. These reports, or profiles, are not rated or evaluated.

When building your credit history, be consistent in using your own name—that is, your first and middle names and either your maiden or married last name. The use of "Mrs." before your husband's first name, while legal, is only a social title and should not be used for building a separate credit history.

There are five transactions that will help you build a credit history.

Open a checking and savings account. Your local bank can play an important role in your credit future. Although opening a checking or savings account does not give you a credit background, it does help you establish an independent identity at a bank and demonstrate your ability to manage your own finances. Opening an account will also give you an opportunity to get acquainted with bank personnel who may be able to help you with future transactions.

Apply for a department store charge account. When using your checking account at a local department store, ask for a charge account application. You will probably be approved if you have your own verifiable income and if your application meets the store's other credit requirements. If you have previously had a joint account, point that out, stating that you now want to establish your own separate credit account. It is a good idea to apply for charge cards first at larger department stores. Such stores are likely to subscribe to a credit reporting agency which will record your transactions for future credit reference. Once you receive your charge cards, use them to build your credit rating and repay each obligation promptly. (Usually, if your bill is paid by a certain date, you pay no interest.)

Apply for a bank charge card. Since the credit standards of a bank are more stringent than those of a retail store, and since bank credit transactions are always listed with a credit reporting agency, the value of a bank charge card such as MasterCard or VISA in building a credit identity is greater. In order to secure a bank charge card, you may be required to have held your current job for twelve months or more, but applying at the bank where you have your checking and savings accounts increases your chances of obtaining the card. Again, once you are approved, build your credit history by using your card and paying your bills promptly.

Secure an installment loan. A successful record of installment (monthly payment) borrowing can be an impressive part of your credit history. Just as with a bank charge card, your chances of obtaining this type of loan are greatest at the bank where you have your checking and savings accounts. You probably wouldn't consider applying for a loan if you didn't need the money. Yet it is often easier to secure a loan when you don't need the money than when you do, and it's a good way to improve your chances of gaining future credit. You will lose money in interest charges, but by placing the loan in your interest-bearing savings account, making prompt payments for about twelve months, then paying off the obligation early, you will have earned a good payment record at the credit reporting agency and at the bank. While this may not be a wise method for everyone, it is another way to approach credit.

Apply for an overdraft checking account. Overdraft checking accounts provide a relatively new form of credit for banks' more established customers. Such an account protects you when you overdraw your checking account by advancing you money from your approved "line of credit." This type of loan requires fixed monthly reductions from your checking account unless you pay it back in one lump sum. Overdraft

66At this time, my partner started stealing money from the business. Meeting the bills was difficult so I kept my other job. Through divorce, I finally was able to balance both my personal and business debts. My clientele grew.**99**

Courier

109

checking accounts have many advantages—your good name is protected from returned checks, you have the convenience of merely writing a check when you want to borrow funds, and you can repay the money you borrowed in a day or two if you like, therefore eliminating extensive interest charges.

The way a bank loan officer reviews credit applications serves as a good example of the evaluation procedures used by most lenders. You should approach the lender with two predetermined facts—the amount of money you wish to borrow and the purpose for which you want to borrow it. You will also be asked for other pertinent information, such as your date of birth, social security number, credit references, bills outstanding, number of dependents, telephone number, employment history, salary, and prior residences. When you have provided the basic information, don't underestimate the importance of the personal interview. Lenders are looking closely for extras. Their impression of your character and honesty makes a difference in the lending decision. Be sure to disclose all borrowings. Lenders receive a credit agency report of your credit history, and an undisclosed loan can weigh heavily against you.

Banks are not the only source for loans. There are other types of lending institutions: finance companies that make high risk loans at higher rates of interest; credit unions for smaller amounts; and government agencies.

Among the ways to build a financial identity, there is one common denominator—installment or monthly payment obligations. Most lenders consider the regular repayment of installment debt as one of the more important factors in establishing a credit rating. Regular monthly reductions in accordance with a preestablished agreement are a good indicator of your financial stability. Most people run into occasional financial difficulties and your response to these ups and downs becomes a vital part of your relationship with a prospective or current lender. This doesn't mean that you will always be able to meet your monthly payment obligations, but merely that you react in a responsible manner.

It is not our intent to be the bearers of bad tidings, but it is unfortunately true that in many areas credit is exceedingly difficult to get these days. Because of the double whammy of a usury ceiling (the maximum interest rate a bank can charge) combined with present economic conditions, banks are not as willing to loan money out for high risk situations or to those who are first-time borrowers. It is wise to shop around, be cautious, and know your lender. An imaginative individual should be able to suggest various kinds of loans appropriate to your needs, as well as various kinds of repayment plans. It is your business, however. You alone will know if what you are planning is workable.

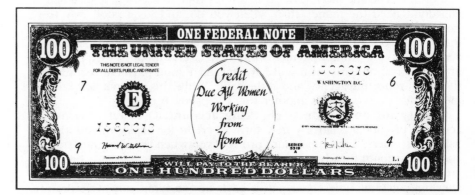

The Relationship Between Banker and Businesswoman

Judith S. Abrams, Vice President, The First Women's Bank

The First Women's Bank was established in October 1975 to provide equal access to credit and full commercial banking services to women as well as men, to companies and corporations, in a personal, efficient, and nondiscriminatory manner. It was before the passage of the Equal Credit Opportunity Act and at a time when it was difficult for women to obtain credit or financing in their own names, regardless of income or position.

> **"I've been very fortunate in that the financial rewards of my business have greatly exceeded my initial expectations, and I foresee a potential of $25,000 per year in the near future—or much more, should I decide to get into word processing, an area I'm considering."**
>
> Typist

Soon after the opening of The First Women's Bank and, we feel, partly as a result, the Equal Credit Opportunity Act was passed, which made it illegal to discriminate on the basis of sex or marital status against women who applied for credit. In time, race and national origin were added to the law.

How does a bank today view a woman's homebased business applying for credit? It views a woman's homebased business the same way as any business and needs proof of a track record in order to consider a loan request.

If you are an established business and are ready to apply for a loan, whether you are a homebased business, professional corporation, or an officer or president of a company, the initial requirements are the same. You will need to provide your bank with the following:

1. Two to three years' financial statements on the company;
2. Two to three years' tax returns;
3. Projected cash-flow statements going forward for the term of the loan requested;
4. Completed business loan application;
5. Personal financial statements and tax returns of the principals;
6. Other pertinent data, depending on the nature and business of your firm, such as an aging of receivables (showing how long your receivables have been outstanding), copies of invoices on equipment purchases, or a copy of state certification if applicable.

Additionally, there are three basic questions all lenders will ask when you come to borrow.

1. The amount of your loan—how much are you asking to borrow?
2. The purpose of the loan—why do you need the money? Is it for short-term working capital, for periods of tight cash flow? Is it for paying accounts payable before your receivables come in? This would require a line of credit, due and payable normally within a year. Or, is it for renovation of your office, or a long-term need, which would require a loan of two to three years or longer with monthly payments of principal and interest?
3. The source of repayment—how do you plan to repay the loan? The bank will look at your projected cash-flow statement and your historical financials to show the ability to service debt payments. For the short-term loan, if your business is seasonal or if you're waiting for accounts receivable to come in, an aging of your accounts receivable will help to show the flow. For a long-term loan, the projections and an extension of your historical performance will help show your ability to repay the loan.

Be professional in your presentation. It represents you.

Before you can apply for credit, you need to produce financial statements which demonstrate that you have been in business two to three years. If you're not yet at that stage, you should:

1. Establish a banking relationship, so that your bank is familiar with your business in advance of your application and understands your banking needs. Your banker should be knowledgeable about your company, your industry, and your market, and understand your product. You should meet regularly to discuss your business and to review the services the bank is providing for you.
2. Have a clearly defined business plan and review it regularly.
3. Keep your records in good order.

If you follow the above steps, when you are ready to apply for financing, your records will be in order, your banker will know you and your needs, and you will be able to get a quick response from your bank.

Can you obtain a loan if you need it now and can't wait to establish a track record? Yes.

1. You can go to your family. That is usually the best place to get a loan if you do not have enough capital of your own. If your family does lend you money, it is essential that you structure the loan in a professional manner, with a formal payback period and interest schedule.
2. You can go to friends, as long as you structure your loan as above.
3. You can obtain a bank loan if you provide your bank with acceptable collateral, which includes marketable securities (stocks, bonds) a certificate of deposit, passbook or statement savings account. Financing your business in this way will start your company's credit history at an earlier stage.

I'd like to emphasize again that no matter what stage you have reached, a good banking relationship is an absolute necessity. The importance of this cannot be overstated. This relationship is built on trust, confidence, and open communication. It's one where you can speak to your banker as things occur, not after the fact. Regardless of what business you are in, it is essential that you get good professional advice—a qualified attorney, accountant, and banker—so that you can devote your time to running your business.

66Being an artist, preferring to place my emphasis on creative time, I've found it crucial for me to employ the help of trusted accountants, bankers, and reps—freeing me to relax and work (to me, not a contradiction of terms).99

Artist

Financing Sources

Diane E. Burke, Small Business Consultant

Every small business needs money to survive and grow, and homebased businesses are no exception.

Planning for the financial management of a business should be an ongoing process. Requests for loans are often denied because of inexperience in financial planning and control. The first step in financial planning and control is to separate personal and business funds for record-keeping and spending purposes. At the very least, you should have separate business and personal checking accounts to make this process easier. The second step is to determine what your money needs are and whether they can be met by your personal funds and income from the business, or whether you need outside funds (loans).

If you are going to need a loan, there are several basic questions you must answer to determine how much money is needed and when it can be repaid.

- How will the money be used?
- How much is needed and when?
- What are the financing costs (interest rates)?
- How will the money be repaid?

Answers to these questions will help you plan for what you want to do with the loan and your capability for handling the costs. Think in terms of renting the money.

Before seeking outside capital, you should develop a financial plan and then determine the best methods and sources of financing. A complete business plan is best. Preparing a business plan will force you to look at all aspects of your business rather than just the financial aspect. If you take the time to do a business plan—in the long run it is well worth the effort—you should do it yourself or with the assistance of your accountant, rather than hire someone to do it for you. The preparation itself is an educational process that will help you better understand the strength, weaknesses, and needs of your business.

Most financial lending institutions, whether private or government, are reluctant to lend to small and homebased businesses for these reasons:

- There is usually little, if any, collateral to secure the loan.
- Most small businesses are undercapitalized and there is little equity in the business.

> **“Working with my accountant, I developed a business plan for getting additional finances for my growing business. . . . The whole idea of the new product was a gamble, but it's been successful, and I'm well on the way to paying off the substantial loan.”**
>
> Manufacturer

Financial Advisory

JACKPOTUNITIES

Vol. 4 No. 4   *Oct-Nov 1982*

Sweepstakes

Contests

Freebies: Etc.

You too can be one of thousands who will learn how to increase your odds for winning sweepstakes and contests. We put it all together for you in an easy to follow guide.

Published by Shirley Liss

66 I guess I had beginner's luck, because I won $25,000 cash from Johnson & Johnson Baby Powder after only four months of contesting (and that was after I sent in only three entries). Needless to say, I have been hooked ever since. **99**

Publisher

114

- The small loan amounts requested are costly for lenders to process and service; larger loans are more profitable for lenders.
- Many small business owners do not practice financial planning and control and come to the lender as unprepared applicants. This increases the chances that they will be perceived by the lender as too much of a risk for a loan.
- There is a greater risk of default on the loan. This is especially true since new bankruptcy laws have made it easier for people to declare personal and business bankruptcy. Lenders are assessing loan requests more carefully in light of the growing use of bankruptcy. Banks are even requiring that personal loans, which are generally easier to get than business loans and for smaller amounts—$1,000 to $10,000—be secured by second mortgages and other guarantees.

In general, lenders are interested in:

- character of the loan applicant;
- personal and business credit history;
- historical earnings to the business;
- ability to repay the loan;
- sufficient equity in the business to sustain some setbacks or losses;
- ability to operate the business successfully.

At a minimum, before requesting a loan you will need:

- amount and use of loan funds;
- list of collateral to secure the loan (house, life insurance, stocks, and other holdings);
- brief description of your business;
- income tax statements for previous three years;
- financial projections for next three years to show planned sources (income) and uses (expenses) of the business. Projections should include an estimate of loan payment schedule because this will be an expense of the business, and you must indicate your ability to repay.

Banks provide more loans to small businesses than to any other source; so it is important to cultivate a relationship with your banker. Most people wait until they need money before they meet their banker. You should establish a rapport before you need money, so that your banker is familiar with you and your business.

Government loan sources are shrinking due to government economic policy and recent budget cuts. Most of the agencies that have loan programs now offer only guaranteed loans rather than direct loans. With guaranteed loans, the participating bank provides the loan, and the agency guarantees up to 90 percent of the loan; in effect it acts as your cosigner in the event that you default on the loan. You must, however, meet the criteria of the agency's loan program.

You can improve your chances of obtaining loans under government programs by following a few general guidelines:

- Know the agency's goals and limitations before going through the application process.
- Have on hand the details about your business and personal finances described above.
- Apply for financing before you have a critical need for it; processing times can be lengthy. Note that processing of your loan application does not begin until the agency has received *all* correctly completed

application forms and all the relevant information about your business. Being prepared will save you the time and trouble of having your application returned to you for additional information.

The U.S. Small Business Administration is the most active government source of loans to small businesses. The SBA is a "lender of last resort," which means that you must first be turned down from a bank for a regular loan; then ask the banker whether the bank will participate in an SBA Guaranteed Loan. The average SBA loan is $100,000 with the majority of the loans granted under $50,000.

The SBA has a time-saving program in most states called the SBA Lender Certification Program. In an effort to reduce paperwork and expedite the guaranteed loan program, SBA initiated a Certified Lenders Program. Under this program, the SBA essentially relies on banks to investigate credit and determine whether the loan should be granted and the amount of the loan. If an SBA Certified Lender participates in the loan, the procedure takes only three days. In addition, in most states, there are designated participating banks where the procedure takes about thirty days. This is after receipt of the correctly completed application forms.

Other government agencies provide loans to small business, but these will most likely not meet the needs of homebased businesses. Generally, for these agencies, the amount of the loans provided are larger; processing time can be lengthy and expensive; and they are often targeted to business types (retail, manufacturing), designated areas (urban areas, areas of high unemployment), or for targeted uses (land, building, construction, fixed assets).

The Farmers Home Administration guarantees loans up to 90 percent for businesses located in communities of less than 25,000 to a maximum of 50,000 population. Unlike SBA, you do not have to demonstrate that other financing is not available. The purpose is to create or preserve rural employment; so you must show how many jobs will be created or how it will benefit the community. The average loan is usually greater than $500,000, and there is a one-time charge of 1 percent of the guaranteed portion of the loan.

The Economic Development Administration of the U.S. Department of Commerce guarantees loans up to 90 percent to expand or locate businesses in economically lagging areas of the nation. Loans are generally above $500,000 and available only in areas deemed to be in need of economic development. The important criterion for approval is providing new jobs.

If you are not able to secure a loan from a bank or government agency, other avenues you may want to investigate are:

- **Credit cards.** You can use your business or personal credit cards to pay business expenses or to obtain cash for working capital. You should work to build your credit ratings and increase your credit limits.
- **Leasing.** Leasing of equipment (typewriters, copiers, etc.) may be a source of financing where the leasing company retains ownership and title to the assets as collateral. In the long run, the lease payments may total more than the purchase price of the equipment, but leasing rather than purchasing frees cash for other requirements of the business. It also provides fully deductible tax benefits as payments for leased equipment.
- **Life insurance.** These policies have cash value and can be borrowed against for business purposes. The borrower should realize that the loan drains the dollar worth of the policy and that should the

Nancy Finch
Finch Grocery Store
Photographer: Bob Stewart

115

life insurance be needed, the policy will cover only the amount not loaned.

- **Supplier credit.** Manufacturers and wholesalers permit small businesses to buy inventory or equipment on an open account for thirty to ninety days. Inventory is usually financed for thirty, sixty, or ninety days with discounts for prompt payment. Equipment is usually financed for up to five years with a 20 percent to 30 percent down payment. Trade credit is usually available to established businesses with good credit ratings.
- **Overdraft checking.** This is a type of checking account which, in addition to regular services, can provide you with financing by advancing you money from an approved line of credit. Overdraft checking not only protects you from having your checks bounce if you overdraw your account, but you can also write a check when you want to borrow funds from your credit limit. Repayment can be by monthly deductions from your checking account, or you may pay it back in larger installments.
- **Personal loans.** For small amounts of cash, you may be able to get a personal loan more easily than a business loan. As mentioned earlier, however, many banks are now requiring that personal loans be secured by collateral also.
- **Internal financing.** This should not be overlooked as a source of financing. Retained earnings and profit from past operations are the most attractive source of funds. These funds should be reinvested in the business to provide adequate cash flow for operations and to provide for growth.
- **Stringent management.** Another source of internal funds can be from stringent management of business operations. This includes: control of salaries and money taken out of the business; control of purchases and business expenses; collection of past due accounts; leasing of equipment; and sharing services and equipment with other businesses.

FARM AND FIRESIDE, FEBRUARY 1918

"FROM the beginning I found that our trade name, 'The Home of the White Hen,' attracted inquiries, and once you receive inquiries it isn't difficult to make sales. So I began to figure how we could further arouse curiosity and make our advertising different from the rest. Ever hear of an '& Daughter' partnership? I never had, but I couldn't understand why mother and daughter couldn't constitute a firm as well as father and son. Mildred had become a real partner. She was keeping the books, helping with the incubators, and selecting breeding stock for shipment like a veteran poultry woman every week. So the firm became Mason & Daughter that fifth year. I played up the name, and inquiries poured into our mail box every day.

"Step into this laying house and take a look at our method of trap-nest record-keeping," was the next request. On the white-washed wall I saw a neatly kept record giving band numbers of the penned hens and the number of eggs produced by every fowl. But what interested me most was the printing on that card. Attractively displayed, here is what it said: "Jennie Mason, Mildred Mason. Mason & Daughter. Single-Comb White Leghorns and White Wyandottes. At the Home of the White Hen."

"One of these days it's going to be Mason & Company, for Ted is eager to join the firm," and Mrs. Mason smiled down at her dark-eyed son.

Saving for Retirement

June Walker-Sloat, Budget and Tax Consultant

As of January 1, 1982, saving for retirement became more financially attractive for almost everybody. Tax experts suggest that under the new rules anyone who earns an income ought to establish a retirement account. The benefits from such an account are immediate. If you can spare any money that you do not need for living expenses and will not need until you are 59½ years old, you should seriously consider a retirement account.

> **66** My husband died three years ago. Thank God I am independent and can keep my home. I have a studio large enough to do my work and a finished basement for larger groups. I work along with frequent helpers who apprentice for small wages. **99**
>
> Antique Restorer

Retirement accounts are tax-deferred. When saving—call it investing —your money in a designated retirement account, you may deduct that money from your total income and pay no income tax on it. The money, however, must be earned income—that is, money you have worked for— not lottery winnings or stock dividends.

You do not pay taxes on your investment or its earnings until they are withdrawn at retirement age. At that time your income may be considerably lower than during your working period, putting you in a lower tax bracket. At that time, less tax will be paid on your investment than had you kept your money in a taxable, nondeferred account during your lifetime.

There are two types of retirement accounts, one for the wage earner or salaried person and the other for the self-employed.

Individual Retirement Account. An IRA fits the needs of the wage earner or salaried person. You may invest as much as 100 percent of your income up to $2,000 per year in an IRA. If you are married and your spouse has no earned income, you may invest an additional $250. You would then have two IRAs—a standard and a spousal IRA. The $2,250 investment may be divided between the two however you choose as long as neither account receives more than $2,000 annually. If both you and your spouse have earned income, you may each set up an IRA with a $2,000 maximum on each.

You may establish an IRA even if you belong to a profit-sharing plan or a pension plan where you work. Upon retirement you would then have three sources of income: Social Security (we hope!), a pension from your employer's plan, and your IRA.

Some employers' pension plans allow employees to make additional voluntary contributions instead of establishing an independent IRA. The same $2,000 limitation applies, and the contributions have the same tax-deferred status; however, there is no tax deduction for contributions you are required to make to a company pension plan.

If you are divorced and were the non-wage-earning spouse (say it, the wife), you can contribute as much as 100 percent of your alimony (but not child support) up to $1,125 into your already existing spousal IRA, provided the account was set up at least five years before the divorce and contributed to in at least three of those five years.

Unless you become permanently disabled, you cannot make a withdrawal on any IRA until you are 59$^{1}/_{2}$ years old. At that age, you may withdraw all of your investment or portions over a period of time. The withdrawn amount is taxed at your then current tax rate. If you must withdraw from your IRA before that age, you will pay a 10 percent penalty on the withdrawn amount, as well as the income tax on it.

You must begin withdrawing from the account by the end of the year in which you reach the age of 70$^{1}/_{2}$. At that time you must withdraw at such a rate that all will be withdrawn by the time you reach the end of your life expectancy, as established by actuarial charts. The manager of your account will advise you of that rate. If you continue to work after 70$^{1}/_{2}$, you may continue to contribute to the plan while withdrawing from it. The funds remaining in your IRA are payable at your death to your designated beneficiary.

If you wish to switch your investments from one IRA to another, perhaps from an insurance company plan to a bank, you may do so once a year, but no more than sixty days may elapse between closing one and opening another. Such a transaction is called a rollover. If you leave a company and receive your pension funds in one lump sum you may roll over that sum to your own IRA. A rollover is not considered part of your contributions for that year.

Keogh Plan. A Keogh plan is a tax-deferred retirement plan for the self-employed. It allows you to contribute 15 percent of your self-employed income up to $15,000. In order to contribute the $15,000 maximum you must earn $100,000 per year. The withdrawal regulations for a Keogh are the same as for an IRA.

Even if you have a company pension plan and an IRA, you may also establish a Keogh if you have self-employed income as well. If you are qualified and able, therefore, you may contribute up to $2,000 to your IRA and $15,000 to your Keogh, for a total income deduction of $17,000. Your spouse has the same possibilities.

Retirement accounts for both husband and wife are especially advantageous when one spouse is the high earner and the other the low earner. Let's say the low earner makes $2,000 annually as a free-lance writer. Added to the joint return with a high earner, much of that money may go to the government. If your joint tax bracket is 50 percent, half of the $2,000 earned would go to Uncle Sam. If, however, the $2,000 is put into a retirement account, none of it will go to the government until it is withdrawn. Since $1,000 of it would have been paid in taxes anyway, the loss in money available for living expenses for the year is only $1,000.

Opening the Accounts. You can open an IRA or Keogh account just as you would open any other account. They are offered by insurance companies, banks, savings and loan institutions, mutual fund companies, and brokerages. The manager of the account will provide you with the forms you need. Fees, if any, vary with the type of investment and institution.

A Keogh plan must be established by the end of the tax year. You may make contributions, however, up to the time for filing your federal income tax return for that year. For 1983, your account must be set up by December 31, 1983, but contributions for 1983 may be made up to April 15, 1984.

An IRA may be established for a given year any time up to the due date of the tax return for that year. For example, an IRA based on 1983 income

CAROL SCHWARTZOTT

623 BUFFALO AVE., NIAGARA FALLS, N. Y. 14303 / 716—285-8392

may be set up and contributed to any time from January 1, 1983, until April 15, 1984.

If by mistake you contribute to your retirement account in excess of the allowable amount for a given year, you may withdraw the excess on or before the due date of your tax return for that year and pay no penalty. If you do not withdraw the excess, a 6 percent penalty is charged against it until it is withdrawn.

In deciding whether a retirement account is for you, consider the financial implications and your own lifestyle; then consult a professional. Ask about defined-benefit Keoghs, self-directed retirement plans, and, if you are an employer, your responsibilities to your employees.

To determine your tax bracket, which varies based on your income and your marital status, call any accountant. Have your most recent tax return handy so that you can supply any needed information. If you are in the 40 percent tax bracket, forty cents of every dollar you earn goes to Uncle Sam. You would pay $800 income tax on $2,000 income. If you start a retirement account at thirty years of age and contribute $2,000 per year until you are sixty-five and that investment earns 12 percent interest, at sixty-five you will have $966,926 for retirement—as well as having saved $800 a year for thirty-five years in income-tax payments, assuming that you were in the 40 percent bracket for all those years.

Even if you contribute only small amounts to your retirement account, if the contribution earns 12 percent interest, it will double itself every six years—tax-deferred.

As attractive as a retirement account looks, remember first that you must be able to get by without the money that you've laid aside. Think hard about whether you are prepared to lock the money away until you are 59½ years old.

> **"Like so many women of my age, I often feel frantic about the lack of time left in my life to accomplish the things I want to accomplish and never even considered attempting until this year."**
>
> Knitter

May and Ken Glover
Caners
Credit: JED Photo

Computerizing Your Finances

Sharon Zukowski and Donald Zoch, Financial Planners

> **66**In our society, power is measured by the dollar; without an income of my own I fell into the trap of thinking less of my capabilities. . . . The money in my bank account is tangible proof that I am a vital, accomplishing individual.**99**
>
> **Caterer**

Ms. Doris M, a successful homebased business owner, steps into our office at 10:30 A.M. sharp for her scheduled appointment. Allowing a few moments for the appropriate introductory protocol, Ms. M starkly breaks into the reason for her visit: "I'm making more money today than ever before, but I don't seem to be getting anywhere financially. . . ."

The ensuing discussion unveils a number of personal- and business-related obstacles that she is having problems overcoming: high taxes, inflation, poor cash flow, no liquidity, poor investment results, ill-defined goals, poor budgeting and money management. The inability to adequately cope with these problems has bred a sense of financial insecurity and stress for this otherwise confident businesswoman. Seeking solutions has been costly in terms of dollars spent and time lost. "I am not unsophisticated when it comes to finances," Ms. M offers, "but I am having trouble analyzing all the different advice I receive from various sources."

Indeed, the usual fragmented approach to planning business and personal finances has left her in a state of financial confusion. She receives proposals from various insurance agents attempting to solicit her business, recommendations on stock purchases from her broker, and inducements into savings instruments from her banker. She has not seen her attorney since he drew her will three years ago. Her accountant stops by twice a year. She has been receiving sales literature on an assortment of investment opportunities but cannot reasonably weigh the pros and cons. Her accountant is not trained in this field, and she is leery of the motivations of company representatives.

Ms. M realizes that a firm foundation for the future is laid only by proper planning in the present. Yet her path to financial peace of mind has been clouded by confusing choices:

1. What will I have left after taxes to plan with?
2. How do I plan for retirement costs and education for my children?
3. What's the best way to manage my cash flow and income?
4. What is the most appropriate tax strategy for me?
5. Should I incorporate and start a benefit program?
6. What's the most appropriate investment for my Keogh plan?
7. Should I refinance my home?

"Nothing is coordinated; I keep receiving different advice from different people. I need to know where I stand and where I'm headed. I have to develop an overall program. But I'm afraid that I can't afford the cost of a complete analysis."

Computers to the Rescue

Ms. M is not atypical of many small business owners. She has developed the expertise to handle the day-to-day problems of her business and the ability to successfully market her service; however, when it comes to strategic financial planning she is understandably a neophyte. Today's rapidly changing, complex economy coupled with continuing inflation and rising taxes have created a financial wilderness. Ms. M, desperately mired in this seemingly endless maze of confusion, has attacked her finances in a piecemeal fashion, relying on the input of a series of "advisors," many of whom, in her own words, "had an ax to grind."

Ms. M is astute enough to realize that no area of finance operates in a vacuum. There are legal, tax, cash-flow, risk, and comfort ramifications to each and every financial decision that is made. Fragmented planning or poor advice in one particular area can produce severe repercussions in another. A comprehensive, coordinated financial program entails a thorough analysis of six specific areas:

1. Personal and business financial affairs
2. Risk management
3. Tax planning and management
4. Investment planning and management
5. Retirement planning
6. Estate planning and conservation

Reesa Abrams
Software Quality Consultant
Photographer: Don Hinckley

Unfortunately, neither her attorney nor her accountant have the capabilities to coordinate an entire package. Ms. M has a feel for the amount of time that would be involved in such an analysis and is rightfully intimidated by what she thinks might be the cost. She, too, works on an hourly fee basis.

Fortunately for Ms. M, and thousands like her, computer technology has made comprehensive financial planning affordable to most. Today many financial planning firms are equipped with the computer software that enables them to thoroughly analyze, project, recommend, modify, and alter financial plans in one-twentieth of the time it had taken their predecessors. A computerized financial plan will be more thorough and precise than one in which computers were not utilized. In order to clearly illustrate the impact of computers on your business and/or personal finances, we will examine the elements of sound financial planning in more detail. In most instances, these concepts can be applied to both personal and business planning.

Personal and Business Financial Affairs

Setting goals. The first area of concern for the homebased business owner is the establishment of financial goals and priorities. Goals should be developed for both the business and personal life. After goals are established and ranked by priority, a realistic time frame for meeting them is developed. While setting goals, it is important that a realistic idea of the amount of money needed to accomplish these goals be decided upon. In other words, you need to find out how much money it will cost to reach those goals.

In planning for future goals, such as buying a house, retirement, or providing an education for your children, the effects of inflation must be considered. If it would cost you $30,000 a year to live comfortably if you retired today, how much will it cost you when you retire in twenty years? A computerized planning system will be able to project future costs. If there is an average inflation rate of 6 percent over the next twenty years, it will cost you over $90,000 a year to have the same comfortable retirement that $30,000 a year would provide today.

Budgeting and cash management. After goals are set, the financial planner will work with the client to identify all sources of income and all areas in which the money has been spent. Through the use of the computer system, the planner will be able to track out an entire year's spending and present a month-by-month analysis of expenditures. An annual summary is also provided.

An analysis of personal and business spending is vitally important to the homebased business owner. Used efficiently, it can help alleviate the problems caused by poor cash flow and no liquidity. It will also point out areas of spending that must be changed in order to achieve stated objectives. Once the analysis is completed, it is used as a basis for a budget and cash-management system for business and personal finances.

Risk Management

What types of insurance does the homebased business owner need? Is there need for a properly constructed buy–sell agreement? If the business is incorporated are tax-advantaged insurance products being utilized? Is the business underinsured? Overburdened with premiums? Has a coordination of business and personal protection been developed? What companies offer the most attractive packages for the various lines?

These are only some of the questions that the experienced financial planner can answer. A hard-copy integrated computer printout will identify all areas of potential risk, analyze current protection, recommend alternative solutions, and drastically cut costs.

Tax Planning and Management

Indeed, one of the most important areas of finance for both personal and business finances is tax planning. Business taxation has a direct effect on personal returns. Current tax situations must be analyzed. It is then necessary to project tax burdens for the next five years utilizing certain income and deduction assumptions within the framework of the present business structure. It is only after such a projection that alternatives to reduce tax burdens can be investigated. Business and personal tax planning is an extremely comprehensive and complex procedure. Tax planning is in a continuous state of flux due to ever-changing tax legislation.

Different forms of business ownership must be investigated along with the viability of qualified retirement plans, tax-sheltered vehicles, shifting of incomes, stock option and deferred compensation programs, leasing arrangements, and a wide spectrum of other considerations. Necessarily, all tax planning takes into account the current risk management program, the retirement plans, estate plans, investment strategies, and management.

Investment Planning and Management

Within the realm of investment planning, it is of utmost importance that funds be allocated to the goals and needs established. Again, an analysis and projection is in order. Projections must be made using reasonable yield expectations and time frames as well as realistic tax and inflation discounts.

It has been our experience that most business owners do not take into account the tax and inflation ramifications of their various holdings. Certainly, most were "sold" various investments on a projected return basis. Yet a fully taxable 12 percent return in 1980 for a business owner in the 50 percent tax bracket produced a negative 2.5 percent return after taxes and inflation. Marching backwards is no way to achieve financial goals.

Generally, the asset mix must be altered or redistributed based on stipulated objectives, time frames, yield expectations, and emotional suitability. The newly established program must be reviewed and modified periodically to reflect changed circumstances, e.g., economic conditions, life cycle changes, health, lifestyle, and income.

Retirement Planning

It is a truism that only 5 percent of the American population reaches the age of retirement with any degree of financial independence. No doubt a lack of planning in this area is the main cause. Proper retirement planning calls for a projection of the amount of income one will need at retirement based upon the lifestyle desired and the anticipated inflation rate. Once this figure is determined, an analysis of the present retirement program is in order. The amount of income that one can expect at retirement from various sources is then projected using reasonable yield estimations. Included in this projection would be future estate values, anticipated social security payments, and income from all other sources: qualified plans, annuity, profit sharing, business value, etc. This analysis will graphically display anticipated shortages. If a shortage does exist under the current plan, then a modification is in order. A specific course of action can then be planned and implemented, allowing for appropriate degrees of flexibility.

Estate Planning and Conservation

The homebased business owner must realize that working hard and accumulating assets during a lifetime is not enough. Improper estate planning can result in assets being frozen, double taxation of the estate, or a young, inexperienced heir who will squander it all. Careful planning can help avoid these problems and save you and your heirs from taxes.

Marlene Pituro
Data Processor

Estate planning begins with a determination of your estate value and a projection of its future value. Assets are classified as those that are a taxable part of your estate and those that would be available to your heirs for settlement of debts and income production. Liabilities are subtracted from the total amount available, leaving the gross adjusted estate. Projections must also be made of current and future estate-tax liability. Once the tax liability is determined, a plan can be developed for the transfer of the estate utilizing an appropriate mix of trusts, gifting, and testamentary transfers. The estate plan must be reviewed and modified on a periodic basis to reflect changes in tax regulation and personal circumstances.

Putting It All Together

Ms. M has found a solution to her problem of haphazard planning of business and personal finances. With the aid of a computer system, her financial planner can link together budget, insurance and investment data, tax information, and financial goals and desires. After calculating her retirement needs, social security benefits, estate taxes, insurance needs, and children's education cost, the financial planner will work to develop a program to help Ms. M achieve her financial objectives.

Once the program has been developed, the financial planner will continue to work with her to review and change as necessary. Changes in Ms. M's objectives, income, and legislative updates will all be evaluated for their effect on her program. Happily for Ms. M, and many others, computer technology has made this type of planning possible and affordable. A comprehensive business and personal financial plan, developed through the aid of specialized computer programs, will help Ms. M achieve her financial objectives.

The Business of Business

66 The most frustrating problem I have encountered is the discrimination from wholesale supply houses. Although I have a retail tax number, most wholesalers refuse to sell to me because my business is in my home.... If I am willing to pay their minimum order and pay my taxes to the state, I should be able to buy wholesale. 99

Art Teacher

Sales Tax

Most states require a sales tax, and in some places, there are city and county taxes, as well. If you make anything for sale or buy goods for resale, you must apply for a sales authorization certificate. This document has a resale tax number that will enable you to buy, without paying sales tax, any materials at wholesale prices for resale.

Once you have that important sales tax number, you will be responsible for collecting sales tax on everything you sell directly to consumers and then remitting these monies to the appropriate state, county, or city offices.

Sales tax information and forms to apply for the tax number and for making returns may be obtained from your State Department of Taxation and Finance, Sales Tax Bureau.

Licenses and Permits

Many different types of businesses—whether small or large, at home or away from home—are subject to government regulation by licensing.

A license is formal permission granted by state governmental authority to a person, firm, or corporation to carry on some business, occupation, or activity that would otherwise be unlawful. A license usually requires a fee and may also involve some form of examination to see if the recipient can qualify under certain standards (usually based on education and/or experience). The license is a tool of regulation to control a course of conduct relating to public health or safety—for example, plumbers, physicians, hairdressers, marriage counselors.

A permit is similar to a license but is granted by local authorities. It is often required for businesses involving food, door-to-door selling, and home shops.

Prospective businesspeople should be sure to consult local, county, and state ordinances to see if their particular business is included, so that they are in full compliance with the laws. Check with your town administrator or at city hall.

Choosing a Name

The name you choose should be unique. To be assured of that, if your business is local, do a name search in the office of the county clerk to see if the identical name is already being used; if statewide, check with the secretary of state. If yours is an interstate business such as mail order, the name would have to be checked in each of the fifty states. This can be done by a trademark attorney.

Choose a name that is both pleasant and easy to pronounce. If the name needs an explanation every time it is mentioned, people might remember it, but negatively, if at all.

When choosing a name, it is best to be farsighted. The Silversmith is a good name until a jeweler wants to work with gold or beads. The Fruit Bin is limiting if vegetables are sold, too. Baby Gear only applies to small sizes. What if the business expands to include larger children's sizes? Select a name that will work now and in the future. It is easier and cheaper to plan ahead rather than correct mistakes down the road.

Business Name Certificate
If a business is conducted under any name other than the owner's real name, a business name certificate must be filed with the clerk in the county in which the business is transacted to enable creditors and others to determine actual ownership of the business. This certificate, available at most business stationers, must be filled out in triplicate. The county clerk will file the original and certify the other two copies, if requested. Keep one copy in your files; or, depending on the type of business, you may prefer to frame and display it. Take the other copy to a bank and open a commercial checking account in your business name; the bank requires this copy by law.

Corporations do not need to file a business name certificate unless operating under a name other than the official name of the corporation.

Federal Trade Commission Regulations
Truth in advertising is serious business with the Federal Trade Commission in its attempt to stop practices which are unfair or deceptive. One cannot in any way misrepresent a product, service, or business; use deceptive prices or bait-and-switch techniques; or imitate the trademarks or trade names of others. All packages and labels on goods must conform to the federal Fair Packaging and Labeling Act and must identify the product; name the manufacturer, packer, or distributor; and show the net quantity of its contents.

FTC laws also pertain to consumer safety and the labeling of textiles, fabric, clothing, and items with concealed fillings.

Mail-order businesses are also covered. All orders must be shipped within their stated time or, if no time is stated, within thirty days of receipt, or the customer is entitled to a refund. If an order cannot be shipped within that period, for whatever reason, the seller must advise the customer and provide an opportunity for the order to be canceled or indicate a date beyond which shipment will not be accepted.

For more complete information, write to the Federal Trade Commission, Washington, DC 20580.

Exporting and Importing
New market and profit opportunities in international trade are open to American producers and marketers as never before. The U.S. Department of Commerce provides information, marketing assistance, and counseling to businesspeople. There are forty-seven district offices in industrial and commercial centers throughout the country that can tell you about trade and investment opportunities abroad, foreign markets for U.S. products and services, financing aid to exporters, tax advantages of exporting, international trade exhibitions, foreign exchange regulations, economic facts on foreign countries, and export licensing and import requirements. You can also write to the International Trade Administration, U.S. Department of Commerce, Washington, DC 20230 for information.

Your state Department of Labor and Industry may have an Office of International Trade that informs businesspeople of opportunities in the international field and offers free assistance to companies interested in developing an export business.

You, the Employer

Social Security

The Federal Social Security Act is designed to provide for a worker's old age and to assure some income to her dependents after her death. This is the old age and survivors insurance system, the cost of which is borne by both employers and employees.

Every individual who employs one or more persons is liable for this old age tax and must apply for an employer's identification number on Form SS-4, available at the nearest office of the Internal Revenue Service. An employer currently pays a 6.7 percent tax on wages up to $32,400 a year for each employee, and the employee pays a like tax on all wages up to the same amount. The employee's share is deducted by the employer at the close of each pay period.

Social Security taxes enter into the obligations of a smaller business, as well. After the end of any year in which there are net earnings of $400 or more from a home business, an individual must file a self-employment form along with the regular income tax form and pay into her Social Security account.

If you do not already have a Social Security number, you must apply for one at a Social Security Administration office.

Federal Identification Number

A business must identify itself on tax forms and licenses by either a Social Security number or a federal identification number. The latter is mandatory if there are employees and is available free of charge from the IRS. After receiving a Federal Employer Identification Number, the IRS will automatically send quarterly and year-end payroll tax returns which must be filled out and returned even if there are no employees.

Employee's Withholding Allowance

That's IRS Form W-4. Each new employee must fill out a W-4 indicating marital status and number of exemptions claimed. The W-4 is kept in the employer's files and taxes are withheld from wage payments at prescribed rates.

Occupational Safety and Health Act (O.S.H.A.)

It's the obligation of employers to give their employees a safe place to work, free from recognized hazards that could cause death or serious physical harm, and to follow specific health and safety standards adapted by the U.S. Department of Labor. To find out your responsibilities under O.S.H.A. contact a regional office of the Federal Occupational Safety and Health Administration, U.S. Department of Labor.

Wages and Hours

Details concerning wages and hours are available from the regional office of the Division of Labor Standards, U.S. Department of Labor. They will provide information on minimum wage rates, wage payments, overtime pay rules, laws governing discrimination and minors, and record-keeping requirements.

Workmen's Compensation

Most states require that every employer must carry workmen's compensation insurance to provide wage, disability, and death benefits for employees injured or killed on the job. The employer must have it before an employee works for the first time.

Owners of sole proprietorships are usually not covered under the Workmen's Compensation Law. As a partner in a partnership or an officer in a privately owned corporation, an individual may elect to be included in most states. If you are not covered, you should carry your own accident and health insurance.

Unemployment Insurance

This, too, is required. You'll have to submit an application, a Report to Determine Liability, and receive an insurance rating. Rates vary from state to state and from occupation to occupation. Check with your State Department of Labor.

A Word to the Wise

Surely at this point you must realize how much more difficult it is to have even one employee. It is said that hiring employees just about doubles one's paperwork and that means more time spent working through the papers. Also, businesses with employees are more closely controlled and regulated than those without. Government laws are strict, and the IRS is inflexible when it comes to payment of payroll taxes. This is not to say that you shouldn't hire employees. They can be essential to the growth of one's business. Just be very aware of your responsibilities as an employer before you hire your first employee.

The Alternative: Hiring an Independent Contractor

Many homebased businesswomen could use additional help—clerical, secretarial, fulfillment, etc.—yet not have the need for a full- or even part-time employee. The simpler solution is to hire an independent contractor. There is a big difference between the two classifications. An employee is one over whom you have some control in terms of her working at your convenience, with your tools, and at your location. You are responsible for Social Security taxes, unemployment taxes, worker's compensation insurance, and year-end earnings statements for each employee. An independent contractor is in business for herself. She sells her services to the public and chooses her own hours as well as location (her home *or* your home). You pay the contractor her fee in full and do not withhold taxes (your state may not even have an income tax on wages), pay employment taxes, or file payroll tax returns. You must, however, file a Form 1099 with the federal government to report payments totaling $600 or more within a calendar year to any nonemployee.

Maria Fiore
Film Producer
Photographer: © Terri P. Tepper,
1979

Idea Insurance: Patents, Copyrights, and Trademarks

Dr. Omri M. Behr, Patent Attorney

"The drawings were printed as postcards; the cards were the basis for tile designs; the tiles were made into grandfather clocks. Because my copyright was on the drawing, I collected a percentage on everything sold."

Artist

You protect your business, your life, and your health with insurance policies, but do you know that the United States government will help you insure the most valuable property of all—the products of your mind? Depending on the type of idea, these insurance policies are called patents, trademarks, or copyrights.

One of the first needs of a business, after working capital, is the need to make a lasting and recallable impression upon customers and clients. Even the smallest business should have a word, phrase, or picture to remind people of that one business and no other. It should be unique and should suggest the business activity but not describe it. For example, Women's Insurance is unregistrable for insurance for women, but WomanSurance is a mark which suggests insurance and women. As a fanciful phrase, it would be considered registrable by the Patent and Trademark Office.

Registrable—what's that? Most states and the federal government have laws that define registrability, or the conditions under which it will protect a trademark and prevent others from using it. The widest protection is granted by the Federal Lanham Act, which will protect a mark used for goods or services passing across state lines. If your business, services, or products remain solely within one state, then you need only apply for state protection.

Choose your mark carefully. Have an attorney search it for you and then use it as widely and prominently as you can. Always emphasize the mark in print. Most marks should be capitalized (either totally or just initial letters). If your mark has been chosen deliberately in lower case, then it is preferable to print it in a bolder face type than the rest of the text or advertising material. Use the mark as an adjective but *never* as a verb. The people in Rochester will never ask you to xerox a letter but suggest you make a Xerox® copy. The ® tells everyone that the United States insurance policy—the Federal Registration—has been granted. If interstate use of your mark is required, an attorney will prepare the papers for you. The grant takes about two years (most of it just waiting), but you can and should use the mark in the meantime. The ® cannot be used until registration has been granted, but you may use the letters TM next to the mark to emphasize trademark use—though these letters have no legal effect.

Between the fifth and sixth year after registration you can confirm continued use of the mark. That is done by filing a declaration in the United States Patent and Trademark Office under Sections 8 and 15 of the Lanham Act. The mark is then clear for a total of twenty years from registration, at which time it must be renewed.

No matter how small your business, choose a good mark for it, and as the business expands, use that mark alone or in conjunction with new marks for each new, important line of goods. Over eighty years ago, Coca-Cola was a small Georgia brand. The product is still going strong and so is the mark.

Your trademark identifies the quality and origin of goods and services to your business. But what if the products are unique? If the uniqueness is artistic, then copyright may be appropriate; if it is technical, then perhaps a patent.

A copyright will protect any artistic or literary work from the moment it is "fixed." Fixing supposes a form in which the work can be detected by others such as writing, printing, painting, a sculpture, phonograph records, electronic tapes, and the like. The time of protection is long—expiration is generally fifty years after date of author's death. To be able to enforce this right, the copyright must be registered with the Copyright Office of the Library of Congress as soon as possible. Copyrights are not examined for novelty or originality—only a court can determine that. Registration identifies the work and its date of fixing by you. Where artistic or literary works are published or offered for sale, national and international protection is available by additionally affixing the copyright notice, usually ©, your name, and the date of first publication. The exact requirements vary with the type of work.

This type of protection covers the right of reproduction. It does not protect the thoughts, ideas, or intellectual approaches contained in the work. It is, however, very inexpensive. For certain works, compliance with the notice provision is enough, and registration is not actually required unless litigation is to begin. Copyright advantages should be considered by those whose business is in the literary or artistic world.

If you have developed a product or a process (but not a method of doing business) whose nature cannot be kept as a trade secret, a patent may provide appropriate protection.

For copyright registration, the services of an attorney, while helpful, are not really necessary; for trademark protection they are advisable. For patents, a registered patent attorney must be consulted as patent rights are very strictly defined by the law and can be easily lost.

A patent can be granted for an invention which is "new, useful, and unobvious" and which has neither been sold in the United States nor described in a printed publication anywhere in the world more than twelve months prior to the time an application for patent is filed. The invention must have been made by the person or persons who apply—joint inventorship is quite proper. While in the United States a twelve-month grace period for application is available, it is better to proceed as if this grace period did not exist. Merely use it as a fall-back safety measure if needed, since it does not exist in most other countries, and sometimes you may wish to obtain foreign patent rights, as well.

A patent can be granted for a thing (product) or a way of doing something (process) provided this involves a physical activity. A method of heating ceramics in a kiln to achieve a particular glaze effect is

The Ritz™

Lovely ladies and gentlemen adorn the Ritz line from Hello Studio. Their look is reminiscent of an earlier elegance now being re-introduced into American life. The new opulence of the eighties is captured here. Arrayed in bold, contemporary colors, they are striking. The Ritz is designed to appeal to sophisticated consumers at all price points. The Ritz adds that touch of class with its own special △™ symbol appearing on all designs. A truly elegant and distinctive touch, the very essence of the Ritz.

Hello Studio, inc. Fleischmanns, N.Y. 12430 phone 914-254-4666

Shelli Lipton
Designer

PATENT PENDING

"**Anything GRoes** will have a greater effect in making more people successful in the growing of plants than the total of all other available products in horticulture."

ANYTHING GROES
RR #3
Columbia City, IN 46725
(219) 244-3247

Sherrill Boggs
Plant Counselor

How to Run a Housesitting Business

jane poston

Jane Poston
Personal Services Specialist

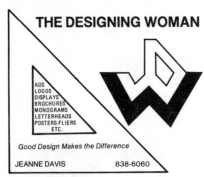

THE DESIGNING WOMAN

ADS
LOGOS
DISPLAYS
BROCHURES
MONOGRAMS
LETTERHEADS
POSTERS-FLIERS
ETC.

Good Design Makes the Difference

JEANNE DAVIS   838-6060

Jeanne Davis
Graphic Designer

patentable, but a system of sales promotion is not. Computer programs are in a never-never land right now, but generally are not considered patentable. Asexually produced plants, i.e. roses, apple trees, tulips, etc., may be the subject of plant patents. Design patents are granted for the appearance of a useful object. The line between copyright and design patent is often very close—it required a decision of the United States Supreme Court to define it. A sculpture by itself may be copyrighted, but where the sculpture is incorporated with a lamp fixture, the entire lamp may be the subject of a design patent. On the other hand, if you have created a new type of switch for the lamp, then a regular patent would be appropriate.

When you have an idea that you think may develop into an invention write it down, preferably in a bound notebook with numbered pages. Avoid scraps of paper. Sign and date the idea and have it witnessed by a friend you trust who can countersign and date with the words "read and understood by. . . ." Write down everything in the same way—ideas, experiments, results, both positive and negative, until you have something you think will work. It is not actually necessary to have built the device or practiced the process to get a valid patent.

At this stage, consult a patent attorney. He will advise you if you have enough information for him to conduct a search. A search is an unavoidable expense and will vary with the complexity of the invention; $300 to $600 should be considered proper for most ordinary inventions.

If the invention is deemed patentable by your attorney, he will prepare the application papers and negotiate with the United States Patent and Trademark Office. Costs over the two or three years of the process will run about $2,000 to $3,000, of which at least $1,000 to $1,500 will be for the initial application.

Properly handled, a patent is a valuable means of enabling creative individuals to protect a special share of a market for themselves. It has formed the bedrock of successful enterprises, but it must be handled strictly according to the rules, so let the professionals advise you.

When you have made an intellectual creation, please remember some of the **Do's** and **Don'ts.**

Trademarks
Do pick a mark that you think is unique.
Don't use a mark that is descriptive.
Do emphasize your mark in print.
Don't use the mark widely, i.e., in a large advertising campaign, before having a search done.
Do use the mark as an adjective; **don't** use it as a verb.
Copyrights
Don't publish without the copyright notice.
Patents
Do write down your ideas in a notebook.
Do keep good records.
Do be fairly certain the idea will work.

Before you see an attorney—
Don't disclose your invention, orally or in writing, to anyone (except in your notebook as mentioned above and to a trusted friend who witnesses it, and, of course, eventually to your attorney).
Don't give newspaper interviews about the invention.
Don't sell the invention.
Don't offer the invention to any company or sales organization.
Don't think you can protect yourself with a description mailed to yourself in a registered envelope.

Zoning

Frances Gildea O'Neill, President and CEO of Dantec Corp.

Zoning regulations have the same endearing qualities as tax regulations—what you don't know can put you out of business! Therefore, stop ignoring them and learn what you need to know. Zoning is a local process, so you must learn what applies in your town.

Step 1: Find out if your town has zoning. Most urban and suburban areas do; many rural areas don't. Call your city or town hall and ask. If your area doesn't, relax, but keep your ears open for any proposal to introduce zoning. If such a proposal is made, a legal notice will appear in your local, general-circulation newspaper (daily rather than weekly) stating that a public hearing will be held. Attend all hearings and make yourself heard so that you can influence the regulations dealing with home businesses. The public hearing is your chance to speak. By the time a meeting is held to vote, it is too late—in fact, usually at the voting meeting, the public is not allowed to speak.

Step 2: If you are in an area with zoning, find out your local structure. Most areas will have an equivalent of Connecticut's three basic functions: planning, zoning, and appeals.

The planning board (may be combined with the zoning board) sets the goals, develops a long-range plan for growth, and reviews land divisions and large-scale plans (industrial and commercial) to assure that they are in conformance with the overall long-range plan of development.

The zoning board develops and enforces a set of zoning regulations that have been written with the intent of achieving the goals of the long-range plan of development. In theory, this board has no discretionary powers. Once they have created a set of regulations, they are met or not. In practice, this description of the zoning board may not be accurate.

The appeals board exists to: (1) waive zoning regulations if they have created a hardship on an individual piece of property and (2) review a decision of the zoning enforcement officer. Some towns also cover review of the decisions of the building inspector.

Example 1. Zoning regulations require one acre of land to build a house in your zone. You have nine-tenths of an acre. Each of the adjacent parcels of land has exactly one acre with a house on it. The zoning office will not give you a permit to build since you cannot meet the one-acre regulation.

The appeals board may look at the fact that you did not create the problem; that you cannot correct it by purchasing adjacent land; that you can meet all other requirements; that the parcel can support a well and septic system (or has water and sewer); and that no damage will be done to the town or other property owners by allowing you to build. They can then grant you a variance of the one-acre requirement and the zoning office will give you a permit to build.

> **❝I have gotten my share of grief from our township, and I try to ignore it because I feel that as long as I comply with regulations such as 'no signs,' no off-street parking, no trucks making deliveries, etc., there should be no reason I can't do this.❞**
>
> Framer

The Law

Example 2. The regulations allow "the office of an . . . artist. . . ." You are a woodcarver whose primary work is large items such as altars, church doors, etc. You are issued a "cease and desist" order by the zoning enforcement officer, who says what you're doing is not allowed.

You appeal the decision of the zoning officer to the board of appeals based on the fact that you are an artist, which is allowed by the regulations. You also present them with a list of references to your work in publications dealing with art and a list of places where you have exhibited your work. The dictionary defines an artist as "a person who is skilled in any of the fine arts, such as sculpture" and a sculptor as "a person who carves or models figures"; therefore, you fit the definition of an artist as allowed by the regulations. This logic should have them overturn the decision of the enforcement officer and lift the "cease and desist" order.

Step 3. Read a copy of the zoning regulations. (All of it! Odd requirements seem to be sprinkled through them in an apparently random fashion.) One should be available at your library or zoning office, probably at little cost. Find out what zone you are in from the zoning map or inquiry. You don't have to tell anyone why you are asking; it is public information. Most towns are divided into residential, commercial, and industrial zones. The zones may be broken further into subcategories (light versus heavy industrial, single family versus multi-family homes). Read the section that deals with the zone you are in. Check the permitted uses in that zone. (See Appendix A for typical regulation.)

If exactly what you're doing is listed as a permitted use, relax. If you're not sure that what you're doing is covered by the list of permitted uses, reread Step 2, Example 2 and interpret what you're doing in a similar manner. Save what you've written in case you ever have to defend your interpretation.

If what you're doing is not listed as a permitted use and is not similar to a permitted use, look for something similar to "all uses presently existing in the zone," a so-called grandfather clause. If your business or a business similar to it existed at the time of adoption of the regulation, this clause makes it legal. If the date of the regulation indicates it is a revision of an earlier regulation, go back through the revisions until you find the first one that said, in effect, "you can't do that here" (may even be the first regulations that introduced zoning in your town). If your business existed prior to the date of adoption of the first regulation that said "you can't do that here," you are "preexisting, nonconforming"—legal even though you don't meet the current regulations; however, this status can affect you if you wish to expand your business. Don't stop reading until you've made sure there is no time limit on "preexisting, nonconforming" situations.

If you are illegal, you'd better consider the possibilities. You can be issued a "cease and desist" order at any time by the zoning enforcement officer. This means you must stop what you are doing immediately or face the possibility of a per-day fine. If this should happen, either: (1) file an appeal immediately with the appeals board (if you interpret the regulations differently than the zoning enforcement officer); or (2) submit a change in the zoning regulations to the zoning board to allow your type of business. Either will allow you to continue without fines until the board or boards reach a decision. If you are thoroughly familiar with the regulations and working of the boards, you probably won't need a lawyer. If you aren't, you will.

In reality, you'll probably never face this unless someone complains. Most zoning officers don't have time to chase people who aren't bothering anybody.

However, to defend yourself against this possibility and/or prevent it from happening:

1. Don't annoy your neighbors.
2. Start keeping a list of every business you know that is violating the zoning regulations (look for small signs in front of houses, ads in the Yellow Pages, etc.). The size of the list will tell you how many allies you might have.
3. Read the regulations dealing with business adjacent to a residential zone (these really don't apply to you but deal with places where the business and residential zone lines meet). These will tell you what the board considers reasonable when home and businesses are next to each other. Be sure you can meet their intent, since logically the situation is the same.
4. Read the regulations concerning businesses that *are* allowed in a residential zone and compare your business to them.
   Example 3. If a doctor is allowed—Do you generate more or less traffic, noise, etc.? Do you have adequate off-street parking for cars and trucks? Does your business alter the appearance of your house?
5. Attend a meeting of each of the boards and identify the person who appears most active and logical and might be sympathetic to your position.
6. If you're an activist at heart: *(a)* volunteer for the next open position on one of the boards. Traditionally women have not been interested in these positions. (It is presumed that you are a registered voter.) Contact the town committee of your party or your mayor's office to find out how to volunteer. In a large city this may be difficult; in smaller municipalities where these jobs take long volunteer hours, it is frequently easier; *(b)* write a regulation allowing home-based businesses and submit it to your zoning board, or planning board, for consideration. (In Connecticut, if it is submitted officially, a public hearing must be held and the change considered; however, you pay an application fee and a legal notice fee.) If it is submitted as a suggestion and the board likes your proposal, they may look it over and bring it to a hearing as their proposal (no fees). Since these boards are usually up to their ears in work, changes that have been fully researched and written for them may be welcome if the board is inclined to your viewpoint. I have included an outline for a model regulation (Appendix B); however, you will have to read all of your local regulations so that you may add and delete the necessary sections and number them properly for submission.

Remember, the zoning board is not the enemy. Most often, they are a group of volunteers, putting in long hours for no pay, trying to the best of their ability to keep your town a nice place to live and work.

APPENDIX A

Typical Regulations for Homebased Business

Zoning Regulations—Danbury, Conn. "The office of an accountant, architect, artist, dentist, designer, engineer, lawyer, musician, physician, surgeon, teacher, real estate and insurance agent or other person qualified through professional training to perform services of a professional nature, located in the same dwelling occupied by such person as his residence, and employing not more than two (2) persons not resident on the premises."

Trusting in a woman's intuition

By M. CEU CIRNE
Staff Writer

SHAVERTOWN — Diana Wenrick of 82 Perrin Ave. says she learned a valuable lesson while fighting to open a fashion shop in her home.

"When you have a project, never let others discourage you," she said. The 36-year-old mother of three trusted her instincts.

Now, two and a half months after opening, her shop is on its way to success and her neighbors' complaints have stopped.

Mrs. Wenrick obtained a temporary zoning exception in February to open a dress shop in her family room, despite opposition from six Perrin Avenue families who claimed the shop would increase traffic in the neighborhood.

The special variance was issued by the Kingston Twp. Zoning Hearing Board on the condition the permit be reviewed after six months, when it will either be renewed or cancelled.

Mrs. Wenrick, a former jewelry retail saleswoman for a Newark, N.Y. firm, said she is expecting the permit will be renewed because her neighbors seem to have accepted the shop.

"I feel confident," she said. "We've remodeled this entire home. We wouldn't do anything that would not blend in with the neighborhood."

Her neighbor Dorothy Lawson of 86 Perrin Ave. said traffic has not increased.

The shop "really hasn't made one bit of a difference," she said.

Mrs. Wenrick says she's spent "thousands of dollars" setting up Diana Designs. She said she invented that much money because she never doubted she would succeed. She said she planned the project well and with determination.

"I've always wanted to own my own business," she confessed. "I am much happier now than I have ever been in my life."

Part of her satisfaction, she says, comes from knowing she can be a full-time businesswoman without shortchanging her family.

She said her husband, Thomas, and children, Rachael, 8; Brian, 14; and Joey, 16, appreciate that.

It is not unusual for her to keep the door from the shop to her private living room ajar. If one of her children needs her, she said she excuses

herself from the shop.

Diana Designs offers sportswear, lingerie, blouses and dresses "moderately priced to better." Mrs. Wenrick says.

Alterations are free and she said she offers appointments for customers who would like to shop privately.

It's "a new shopping experience," Mrs. Wenrick writes in her business cards.

The shop is open from 10 a.m. to 5 p.m. and until 9 p.m. Mondays and Thursdays.

Diana Wenrick outside of her Shavertown home-turned-dress-shop.

TIMES LEADER-RICHARD SABATURA

Diane G. Wenrick
Sales Manager

❝I work out of my home, designed by me and completed in 1980. It is energy efficient—with solar heat for the house and water.... I am concerned about quality of life—working at home saves gasoline and its air-polluting problems. It saves time going to and from a workplace. And the design gives me a businesslike showplace for my work.❞

Solar Consultant

"A customary incidental home occupation such as dressmaking, millinery, preparation of food products, watch repairing, television and radio repair, beauty parlor, barber shop or similar service occupation carried on within a dwelling and exclusively by a resident of the premises in accord with Section 1.H 'Home Occupations in Residence Zones.'"

Zoning Regulations—Brookfield, Conn. "Customary Home Occupation: The offices of a physician, surgeon, or dentist provided no patient is hospitalized or housed overnight; the office of an architect, lawyer, registered surveyor or engineer, accountant, realtor, artist, musician or teacher located in the same dwelling occupied by such person as his residence and any home occupation which is customarily or may be properly carried on for compensation entirely within a dwelling by the occupant thereof which (a) is clearly secondary to the use of the dwelling for dwelling purposes, (b) does not change the residential character of the dwelling in any visible manner, (c) does not create objectionable noise, odor, vibrations, or unsightly conditions visible off the premises, (d) does not create interference with radio and television reception in the vicinity, and (e) does not create a health or safety hazard. The conducting of a clinic, tea room, antique shop, or similar use shall not be deemed to be a customary home occupation."

APPENDIX B

Outline for Zoning Regulation for Homebased Businesses

Permitted use in residential zone:
A home business or home office operated by the resident of a dwelling as an accessory use which meets the following requirements:

A. Is clearly secondary to the use of the dwelling for dwelling purposes and does not change the residential character of the dwelling in any visible manner;
B. Does not create any objectionable noise (0 dB above ambient—that is, average or normal—at the property line), noticeable vibration, or objectionable odor at the property lines;
C. Does not create waste or unsightly conditions visible off the property;
D. Does not create interference with radio or TV reception in the vicinity;
E. Does not employ more than two persons who are not residents of the premises;
F. Has no display visible from the street, except signs allowed in this regulation;
G. Sells no articles, not made, raised or grown on the premises;
H. Does not occupy a total floor area exceeding 25 percent of the dwelling floor area (excluding the basement from all calculations);
I. Has sufficient off-street parking for both the residential and specific business use as defined by this regulation;
J. Does not create a volume of traffic inconsistent with the level of traffic on the street on which it is located.

> 66 Success is to enjoy my work, put out good quality items, and see others receive pleasure from my work. . . . success is whatever a person makes of herself—and I intend to make something of myself. 99
>
> Quilter

A Modern Approach to Old Laws

It began simply enough.

Audrey Pudvah, mother of two young children, knits, teaches swimming during the summer months and, because she herself has a black belt in karate, occasionally teaches the sport to children. Her husband is supportive of her working but does prefer Audrey to work at home. For that matter, so does she. In the cold Vermont winters, their primary source of heat is a wood stove, so being at home also enables her to literally keep the home fires burning. Two large gardens occupy her spare summer hours. She cans and freezes vegetables and, from home-grown berries, makes jams and jellies.

Audrey found a ready market for her knitted products even before she bought her knitting machine in 1979. She knits primarily for one company that provides her with yarn and pays her to make hats or sweaters. As an independent contractor she sets her own prices, and if the company won't pay them, she won't knit for them! When not knitting, she fills personal orders, working from her own patterns or her customers' designs. She earns $6–$8 an hour for her knitting.

Vermont is not exactly "the land of opportunity for working women," as Audrey puts it. "If a job can be found, the pay is generally not too great!"

There are many women like Audrey in that state who have purchased knitting machines and have chosen to work at home while earning supplemental incomes. The women, who are aged, infirm, or mothers of young children, are happy for the opportunity to earn money without leaving home in a state where transportation is difficult and jobs scarce, even for the able-bodied and carefree. Companies using the women's skills are pleased with their products, and taxpayers are relieved of the possible burden of welfare support for the women and their families. Seems like an ideal situation, doesn't it? It was—until 1980.

It was then that the United States Department of Labor brought suit against one of the companies, citing violations of the minimum wage law and of a department regulation restricting employment of homeworkers. The law was not recent but dated from the early 1940s when it was revealed that employers in seven women's apparel and related industries (embroidery, buttons and buckles, jewelry, knitted outerwear, gloves and mittens, and handkerchiefs) were avoiding the then relatively new

> **❝**I love working at home. I can be with my kids more and work when I feel like it, which is most of the time, between the housework and cooking. I have to reveal one secret—I could not do half of what I accomplish without my dear, supportive husband. I consider this to be extremely important.**❞**
>
> Needleworker

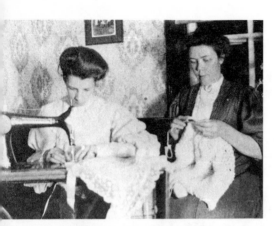

Women Sewing in Townsend House
Collection of Mary Searle
Fleishmanns, N.Y.

Jo Ann Miller
Designer/Manufacturer
Credit: Schiavone Studio

minimum-wage requirements by farming out factory work to unsupervised homeworkers. Rather than attempt to police the industries on a case-by-case basis, the government simply banned the use of homeworkers except in certain disability cases. The regulations were originally implemented largely for the purpose of protecting workers from minimum-wage violations, child labor abuses, and sweatshop working conditions in many segments of the largely urban garment industry.

Forty years later the law again made headlines and attracted the attention of big business, small business, big government, labor and consumer groups, public interest law firms, and officials in almost a dozen states. There were hearings in Burlington, Vermont, and Washington, DC, and national media coverage over many months.

For major apparel companies, their trade associations, and the unions representing their workers, the issue was much broader than a few hundred rural knitters. If the restriction against industrial homework was lifted, they contended, it could open the door to the urban sweatshops of the past, exploitation of the poor, and unfair competition for the firms that use in-house labor and comply with minimum wage, overtime, and workers' compensation requirements. For the Vermont employers, the major concern was the "unholy coalition" of big business and big unions, backed by an "unreasonably oppressive government wrecking the chances for small business and individuals." For the Vermont knitters, it was seen as excessive intrusion of federal laws and regulations into the lives of individual Americans.

The trouble comes in the failure to adapt regulations to a changing marketplace when industrial homework is spreading to more industries in this age of increasing technological change. "Failure to recognize that pursuit of a person's chosen occupation as a vital component of this nation's inherent strength and vitality would be to foreclose economic opportunity and the future," according to the Center on National Labor Policy, a national, nonprofit, nonpartisan organization chartered as a public interest, legal foundation to engage in national litigation in matters affecting the public interest.

The end result of this complex affair came in a decision by Secretary of Labor Raymond J. Donovan in 1981 after no documented evidence was offered to establish any violations of the minimum wage in the knitted outerwear industry in Vermont. He lifted the ban on industrial homework for knitted outerwear only. There was not enough support to remove restrictions in the other six industries. Secretary Donovan said, "It is not the department's intention to deprive Americans of job opportunities at a time when unemployment is already too high." He added that he did not believe that "working at home should be an underground or illegal activity."

"Amen to that," we say. And to Audrey Pudvah and other Vermont knitters and to all those who worked to gain this victory, homebased businesswomen in all fifty states add an enthusiastic and sincere "Thank you!" and "Keep up the good work!"

Direct Sales

Barbara Sunden, National Sales Director,
Mary Kay Cosmetics

Direct sales is truly the ideal career for women today, whether they have children and stay home to care for them or they have a career already. In today's society, women need more challenges and are looking for opportunities to use their talents, and more and more women will join the job market as our economic situation demands more dollars for the average cost of living.

❝I already earn enough to support our family, plus a company car and several expense-paid trips to San Francisco, Pennsylvania, and next June—to the Bahamas! It's a fantastic business, especially the benefits. I am my own boss and can work my own hours.❞

Direct Salesperson

Even though all this points to direct sales, most women look past this field or wind up in direct sales accidentally, planning to stay with it only for a short time.

In the ten years that I have been in direct sales, I've noticed that people don't regard direct sales as a serious business because it is a nonstructured business. But that, in fact, is the beauty of it. You are your own boss; you can make your own hours allowing your family to come first; you can be there for the children when they need you; and yet you can have that necessary time for you to be recognized and rewarded for your creativity and talent. To be able to remain feminine yet have the income commensurate to a man on the corporate level is certainly an ideal situation.

Today women are crying out for more independence, a more flexible schedule, no ceiling on their income, a career, and a family—and the only way to reach all these demands is to be in charge of your own business.

I love the dual role I can play as a wife and mother and also a successful career woman. I set the pace of my career and no one suffers.

You don't necessarily have to have had any previous training in business or sales, because in direct sales the first part of your activities is out in the field selling the products. The training is on the job and always under the guidance of a seasoned associate. Yes, we are independent sales contractors, but in direct sales you are on your own but not alone.

If you are looking for a direct sales career, analyze alternatives. The product is the first consideration. What product do you like? What product do you truly feel good about endorsing? What product do you get so excited about that you want to tell everyone about it? What product do you like so much that you want everyone to have it and you'd like to explain the use of it step by step?

The second consideration certainly is the type of service that company's product offers and the type of benefits the salesperson with that company gains. How far can you go? How much must you do on a daily basis? Are there quotas? What advancements are there? How many people can you work with? What are the investments? Are there any territories? What is the training program? Where are the products delivered? Where are they manufactured? What are the product guarantees?

Whatever the product—vinyls, plastics, copper, bowls, brushes, pots, clothing, stitchery, wicker, or cosmetics—remember that when you join the direct selling industry, you represent that product 100 percent. You are the name to everyone you meet. If the product is good and the enthusiasm is high, success is the next step.

Join the millions of women that are already in direct sales for the time of your life!

Planning for Expansion

Direct Sales

Diane Wenrick, Owner of a women's
specialty and bridal shop

❝I show these high-quality educational toys to parent groups, teachers, hospitals, libraries, and any other groups of people interested in education. I also teach these people how to use the toys and help them understand some very basic child development.❞

Direct Salesperson

Educational Toys, Books and Games

JUDY ANDERSON DAHLKE
Educational Consultant

9606 Yorkshire Lane
Eden Prairie, MN 55344
(612) 941-0549

From plastics to lingerie, cleaning products to jewelry—the merchandise varies, but more than four million people in America today (80 percent of them women) are racking up sales volume for a 7.5-billion-dollar-a-year industry. Incomes derived from the party plan concept or person-to-person method of sales run the gamut from part-time people, earning a few extra dollars, to full-timers fortunate enough to earn six figures—and there are many such successful people. In the party plan, a hostess invites ten or more friends into her home, serves dessert and coffee, and receives free merchandise in exchange for the sales. Of the people who are recruited or hired in direct sales, 90 percent come through the home party. The person-to-person method uses individual contacts, as in private makeup sessions or door-to-door sales.

In direct sales, problems are minimal; rewards are great; and one can expect to meet people from all walks of life. The best advantage is being one's own boss. Hours are flexible and compatible with other full-time or part-time employment or family responsibilities. A homemaker can earn a few hundred extra dollars each week.

Direct salespeople need little experience or capital to enter the field and are able to tailor their efforts to other commitments, whether personal or professional. For those who enjoy being with people and enjoy the "selling game," the financial rewards are excellent, and, in some companies, one can drive away with a new car every year or write one's own paycheck, depending upon one's desires and individual performance. Enthusiasm is the greatest factor in success. For the woman with few hours, part-time weekly earnings can vary from $75 to $300. For the career-minded person who loves a challenge and has an eye on moving up, one can work a forty-hour week in managerial positions.

According to the Direct Selling Association, 90 percent work part-time; over 80 percent work less than half-time; and over 60 percent work less than ten hours a week. There are presently 3,200,000 women in the sales force, 600,000 minorities, 200,000 over sixty-five years of age, and 400,000 disabled.

When you zero in on one company whose product and marketing plan appeal to you, talk to more than one recruiter from that company, for the one you choose will be your supporter, teacher, and contact. She can influence your earnings considerably.

Some companies require a small investment for a starter kit. Once a kit is purchased, a limited training period is required to acquaint the new salesperson with the marketing concept and method; this is usually done by a field salesperson or manager.

There are three- to four-hundred direct sales firms in the United States; 120 of them are members of the Direct Selling Association adhering to a strict code of ethics. If you are researching the field, you can write to the DSA (1730 M Street, NW —Suite 610, Washington, DC 20036) for their membership listing that includes name, address, phone, contact individual, and product lines.

Mail Order as a Homebased Business

Sarah J. Zaleski, Owner of Everywoman's Bookshelf

When you mention that you sell by mail order, a lot of people visualize you sitting in your basement opening letters and then laughing all the way to the bank. These people also think of mail order as an easy way to get rich quick, but in fact, it's also a very quick way to go broke.

What do you need to know to maximize your chances of succeeding and to minimize your financial risk? You *can* start and operate a mail-order business from your home. You can start small, experiment as you go along, control the growth of your business during the start-up period, keep flexible hours, raise a family, and manage a household while you are developing your mail-order business.

How do you lay the foundation for a successful mail-order business? *Study* mail order as an industry and study individual companies that sell products similar to yours. Learn the laws and regulations that will govern your mail-order company. *Specialize* and try to capture only a very tiny corner of the market that you have identified. *Test* the market by advertising very cautiously and risking the least amount of money possible. *Plan* your business, calculating the numbers towards profitability and developing a one-year advertising campaign and a second-year publicity campaign.

What is success in mail order? It's generating volume sales, building repeat business, and making a profit.

What is failure in mail order? It's running ads that generate sales but do not result in a profit (also known as owner's salary). Running an ad and receiving no orders is considered experimenting and is chalked up to experience; it is not failure.

To succeed in mail order, all you have to do is to advertise the right product at the right price in the right place to reach the right customer at the right time!

The Right Product
The right product is something not readily available elsewhere; is easily described and illustrated in an ad; is priced to give the impression of good value for the money; is easy to produce in quantity; is nonfragile, and easy and inexpensive to mail. As a general rule, it is easier to sell a kit, a pattern, or a design than a finished creative product. It is easier to sell a recipe than to sell a packaged food item.

> 66(My business) was started as a feasibility report for my business writing class in school. ... After three months of doing a research paper on starting a mail-order fabric business, I decided to give it a try, with a loan from my parents. Since all the legwork was done doing the paper, I simply put the wheels in motion.99
>
> Salesperson

Planning for Expansion

Terri Lipman
Folk Artist

The best product for you to sell would be something that is your creation: a product that you designed, can manufacture, and can control the source. It is extremely difficult to be a middleman in mail order.

Preferably, you have some experience selling this product before attempting to sell it by mail. You will have an edge if you have sold it to stores or at shows and fairs. Then you will know how much it costs to produce and will have solved any manufacturing difficulties. You also will have had some sales success and customer feedback.

Most important, the right product is one around which you can develop a line of related products, which means you can build your business on repeat sales.

The Right Price

The right price will give the impression of good value for the money and will generate enough cash flow to cover your operating costs and pay you a salary for your efforts. Before you run your first ad, you should do some calculations and give the numbers careful thought.

The markup for your mail-order product needs to be five times your cost. Assume that you have a product that costs $2 to manufacture. You mark it up times five and price it at $10. Then you have $8 for overhead and profit. This sounds terrific, but stop a minute and think.

How much is it going to cost you to operate?

The number-one myth in mail order is that you can operate a mail-order business from home with virtually no overhead expenses and no staff. First of all, advertising can consume fifty cents of every sales dollar. That immediately reduces your margin to $3 on each item sold. You will need to hire additional people during the peak periods. You will need to cover the cost of the space you use in your house. This last cost won't actually be paid out of pocket when you are starting up, but before you can make a profit, the money has to be generated to repay your household account for rent and utilities.

Serious questions to answer include how many items will you have to sell to cover an overhead of $100, $300, $500, or $1,000 per month? How many will you have to sell to meet your monthly salary goal of $100, $300, $500, or $1,000 per month? Add both these answers together and multiply by twelve. This is your sales goal for the year.

One factor that will affect your ability to reach your sales goal is that mail order is definitely a peak-and-valley business. There will be months, such as during the summer, when you may have no sales, but you will still have overhead expenses. When business is booming, you will have to hire people to help you with sorting mail, keeping records, typing, and packing orders. Even if you recruit family members, they won't work for long without pay.

The Right Place

The right place to reach your mail-order customer is through specialized magazines. To find these magazines, go to your local library, browse through *Writer's Market,* look through the magazines you read now, ask your friends and neighbors if they buy anything by mail. If so, what magazines do they read and from which one did they order?

Use classified ads for experimenting. Display ads will not generate enough sales to cover their cost.

The Right Customer

The right customer is a mail-order buyer.

The Right Time

The right time to advertise is during the prime mail-order months of September and October for holiday gifts; February and March for self-improvement items.

After you have some success with advertising and have worked the "bugs" out of your fulfillment operation, it's time to implement a major publicity campaign. Write a press release announcing your product or your catalog of related products. Send it, along with a cover letter and a sample of your product or the catalog, to an editor at the specialized magazines you have identified. You will have no control over when they might mention your product, but any mention will build your business.

Managing your mail-order business requires a thousand little decisions. Following are some helpful hints:

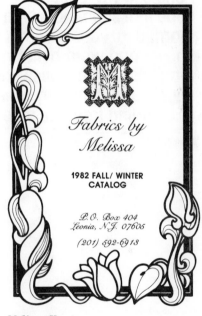

Melissa Kuntz
Salesperson

1. Use a two-step method of selling, which is to advertise a catalog or have the customer write for more information; then you do your selling through sales literature on your reply to their request.
2. Begin your business with one product, but develop a line of related products that you can sell in a catalog. At first, half a dozen is easy to handle. Increase from half a dozen to a dozen. Do not make a drastic jump in the number of items or your headaches will increase ten-fold as you try to manage the inventory.
3. Be careful about giving away your catalog. Production, printing, and postage are very expensive. It doesn't seem like much when you are mailing to hundreds, but when you are mailing to thousands, the cost becomes prohibitive. Besides, a prospective customer who sends you one dollar or so for your catalog is much more likely to buy than the person who writes for a free catalog.
4. Be aware that there is a bell curve to sales. Sales start slow, increase significantly, and then drop back down to a trickle. It's very easy to get caught up in the enthusiasm of the peak sales period and to re-order or to produce too many of the product. Reorder very cautiously during this sales surge after a new ad is run or a catalog is mailed. Otherwise, you will be stuck with extra quantity when the sales drop off at the end of the cycle.
5. Keep track of your results: how many requests for your catalog or flyer did you receive? How many of those who requested, ordered? What was the dollar value of their orders? What was the cost effectiveness of the ad or mailing? Key everything. Repeat your successes and learn from your mistakes.

Mail order is a business that requires that you live and think and plan six months to a year in advance of today—all the time. You can't just say, "Well, today I think I'll open a mail-order business." You have to plan when you will run your ads, create them, submit them four to six months before the magazine will hit the stands, then wait until you do, or don't, get some results four to six months later. Patience and unending optimism are definitely necessary.

It's difficult to get a mail-order business started, but it's harder to kill one. You will still be getting orders or requests for your catalog long after you no longer have it available. Years later, someone will run across an old ad she has saved and write to you. We hope the letter will find you laughing as you stroll into the bank!

Case History of MR. GLASS

Marion Landis, Manufacturer

> **66** ...this is a long preamble to my confirmation of today's order for a case of MR. GLASS. I enclose my check as per your instructions. I hope that soon more women in America will get married a second time without polygamy as I have; and what better name for an additional man about the house than MR. GLASS, and I might add with my one and only husband applauding from the sidelines. **99**

Customer

Marketing strategies have a way of coming full circle sometimes. That is exactly what has happened with my product, MR. GLASS.

The oxide film from screens on my house windows was the catalyst that led me into business. Unable to find anything on the market that would remove it, including the use of professional window cleaners, I decided to give it a try. (Please don't be misled, I really hate to clean.)

After experimenting in my kitchen with the aid of a twenty-six-year-old electric mixer (I'm not too fond of baking either), I came up with a formula that was most effective and nontoxic. The fact that I didn't have a chemical background did not deter me. There is a wealth of information available from research departments of chemical companies and trade publications—it just takes time to glean what you need.

Next came a period of testing the cleaner on every difficult-to-clean glass surface, such as shower doors, auto glass, and tile, in order to expand the market. I spent hours at a local wrecking company looking for badly stained window glass.

My formula was ready, now what? I knew I couldn't make it in my bathtub, so with the aid of the Yellow Pages I set out to find a specialty contract packager who would do the mixing and filling. The company I chose has been extremely supportive, and I was fortunate that its owner saw some merit in the product. There was much to be learned, and his willingness to share his expertise has been invaluable. This underlies the fact that, contrary to popular belief, most businesses are receptive and helpful—provided your approach is appropriate. Doing your homework beforehand pays off.

How would I market it? What would be the best medium for getting it into the hands of the consumer without the cost of advertising or expensive mailings? I decided a mail-order company would be my first contact. A national firm that does its buying in New York was the target for two reasons: they carried many household items, and if I bombed, no one in Cleveland would know about it!

The appointment was set up by phone; I made a mock-up of a label; and got down to the serious part of it all—what would be a realistic retail price that would allow for the markup needed by the mail-order firm, plus a reasonable profit for me.

This required getting bottle, filling, packaging, and shipping costs. There was very little investment of money—just lots of time. Again, all the businesses contacted were helpful. After all, they too are looking for potential new customers. Quotes were given over the telephone, by mail, and some came to the house personally to show me samples.

At my meeting with the mail-order buyer, I demonstrated the product; he was sufficiently impressed; said it would be reviewed; told me an order would probably be in the mail in approximately thirty days; and sent me on my way with several forms to fill out. Total shock set in. That was the longest thirty days!

Incidentally, it isn't necessary to call on mail-order firms in person. My largest mail-order customer contacted me after reading about the product in the new-products section of a trade magazine. I sent them a sample of the product plus a small piece of dirty glass to test it on. Transactions were all done by mail and phone. If your product is attractively packaged and/or unique, business can be conducted in this manner. An introductory call to the buyer enables you to obtain pertinent information to help you quote a price. As I have subsequently learned, buying practices vary among firms—i.e., who pays shipping charges, markup percentages, terms of payment, advertising charges, if any, etc.

Next, the decision was made to explore the retail scene to gain more credibility. I was fortunate that Marshall Field's, a major department store in Chicago, liked the product, and plans were made for a late spring promotion. This gave me the impetus to approach a major home-center chain, Forest City, based in my home city. Retail establishments for the most part must be able to see the possibility of quick product turnover in order to justify buying an unknown item. Therefore, some publicity or advertising is a must.

I have been pleased with the activity at the retail level till now. It is very difficult to rely on distributors if you have one product with limited advertising monies. You must have people checking the stores every so often, and must maintain contact with the buyers. This can be time consuming, frustrating, and costly if it involves several cities.

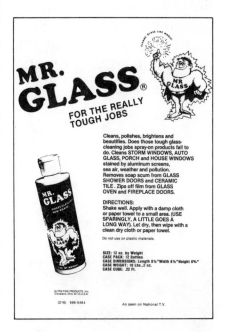

In comparison, my experience selling mail order has also been productive, but much less time-consuming. This has led me to the decision to pursue starting my own mail-order program. Knowing that the product has already proven itself in this medium makes me more comfortable about investing in a mail-order advertising campaign.

Here again, the telephone played a vital part. I contacted the publisher of a large advertising company that puts together inserts for Sunday newspapers. They in turn put me in touch with an advertising firm that specializes in mail order. This became a crash course in the ABC's of a mail-order business. I learned one has to figure the cost of order forms, mailers, the cheapest postage, the best wrap to protect the product, and even the fee charged by the bank for making numerous check deposits at one time!

Another avenue of distribution that is closely related to mail order is selling to sales agents, who in turn sell directly to the end user. These sales agents can be found by an advertising campaign in specific magazines, such as *Spare Time* and *Money Making Opportunities*. This requires finding ways to maintain contact with the agents to keep them enthusiastic with new ideas and incentives to market the product. Once a network of sales agents is established, it becomes a viable channel for adding new products. They buy the product outright, whereas manufacturers' representatives work on a commission basis, and you don't receive your money until the rep sells it to a retail outlet.

Little did I dream when I started mixing chemicals in my kitchen four years ago that I would now be head of a company and that my product would go as far as it has. MR. GLASS is sold nationally both in mail order and through retail stores. I plan to vigorously pursue these marketing channels next year to broaden our distribution and to make the product more readily available. As a result of mail order, I have received letters from all over the U.S.A. telling me how much they like the product and asking me to please try to have it available in their local stores. Mail order has definitely enhanced the marketing possibilities for MR. GLASS.

Planning for Expansion

Case History of Dayspring

Mary Jo Gatti, Owner

66There are limitless ways to be a mail-order entrepreneur. Fundamental good business practices, common sense, a willingness to learn and work, family support, and money are needed, in varying amounts.**99**

Giftware Consultant

Mary Jo Gatti
Giftware Consultant

144

"I did it my way," Frank Sinatra sings, and I'm still doing it my way. I truly believe that the only essential ingredient to build a successful mail-order business is desire.

There are limitless ways to be a mail-order entrepreneur. Fundamental good business practices, common sense, a willingness to learn and work, family support, and money are needed, in varying amounts.

I've often thought: "If I knew then what I know now, I'd have done it differently." Despite my mistakes and setbacks, such as wrong timing for a display ad or choosing a gift item that was too unusual, my choice of business career has been extremely rewarding. Flexibility of hours and work schedule, the challenge of structuring the business to fit my style, and the opportunity for unlimited moneymaking appealed to my spirit of adventure. Each risk I carefully took inched me forward in know-how, confidence, or both.

I was fortunate to have good friends willing to help a serious novice. Their support was invaluable; yet I learned early that the financial risk belonged to me alone, and I really liked being the decision-maker.

I believed in my first mail-order item—back in 1979 no one had heard of a digital pen watch. With assistance from advertising-agency professionals and the advice of my mail-order-pro friend, I prepared and mailed almost a half million flyers and was off to a flying start. Other items have not yet matched my first success, but I have continued to learn through my own experiences. I have also enrolled continually in courses and seminars on starting, maintaining, and expanding one's business, and on selling techniques, marketing, and financial management. My next course is titled, "Time and Territory Management for Salespeople." Joining trade associations, attending trade shows, and reading extensively have been invaluable in leading me to sources of supply and to new marketing ideas. Quite a turnaround from my college training as a speech therapist!

I began working from home when my sons were in high school, since I wanted to develop and expand gradually. I find the challenges fascinating. I enjoy being my own boss, setting my own hours (from 11 P.M. to 4 A.M., if necessary), and working with so many people of my own choice in related fields, such as advertising, mailing houses and list managers, manufacturers, and printers.

To add personalization to the gift items I offer I learned the art of jeweler's engraving and have incorporated this option into my gift catalog. Dayspring now specializes in creative personalized giftware, enhanced with brass plates with custom-engraved personal initials, titles, and/or messages.

My greatest reward has been the growth and success I've had the good fortune to achieve. In addition, I've been delighted to have the opportunity to network, whenever I can. And best of all—it's fun!

Franchising

Gladys Glickman, Attorney

Franchising is primarily a method of financing the expansion of an existing business. Despite its recent popularity, franchising is not a new concept. It has for centuries played an important role in the distribution of goods and services.

Basically, it works like this: a person develops a product or service and protects his or her rights in it by registering a trademark or trade name for it, as well as by patenting or copyrighting any designs or other elements that can be patented or copyrighted. The developer (franchisor or licensor) can then license to another independent business person (franchisee) the right to market the product or service under the developer's trademarks, trade names, and business style.

A franchise agreement can be a simple agreement authorizing another person to use the product owner's trademarks and trade name in marketing a product that is purchased from the franchisor. Or it can be an elaborate agreement in which, for a franchise fee and continuing royalties, the franchisor offers training, a marketing plan, and promotional assistance to the franchisee, and requires that the franchisee conduct his business in accordance with the franchisor's standards.

The usual, more elaborate form of franchise agreement contains provisions *(a)* granting the franchisee the license to use the franchisor's trade names, logos, and other rights in conducting the licensed business; *(b)* restricting the location from which the business may be conducted or the territory it may serve; *(c)* setting forth the obligations of the franchisee to the franchisor and the public; *(d)* enumerating the training, if any, the opening assistance, and the continuing promotional assistance the franchisor will provide to the franchisee; *(e)* permitting the termination of the agreement, either at the end of a specified term or under specified circumstances, and providing for the settling of accounts and the disposition of the assets of the business upon termination; and *(f)* requiring the payment to the franchisor of an initial fee (frequently referred to as a franchise fee) and a continuing royalty based usually on gross sales or revenues.

The franchise agreement may contain, or be accompanied by, additional agreements regarding the purchase of product or equipment either from the franchisor or from others or the leasing of premises.

A lot of law goes into the development of a franchise. Trademark, contract, and antitrust laws must be consulted in drafting these agreements. Additionally, there are federal and state laws directly applicable to franchise offerings and to the provisions of franchise agreements. An attorney knowledgeable in these areas of law must be consulted.

A Federal Trade Commission trade regulation rule requires that, if a franchisee is required to make payments of $500 or more within the first six months after entering a franchise, the franchisee must be given a disclosure statement at the first personal meeting between the franchisee

> **"All in all, I am doing what I love most! I was truly motivated into trying by the negative outlooks of those with whom I discussed the idea and set out to prove them wrong and happily ended with a whole new life!!"**
>
> Knitter

Planning for Expansion

and the franchisor or ten business days before any payment is made or binding agreement signed. Ten states require the registration of franchise offering statements with a designated state agency before a franchise can be sold in the state.

Thus, to expand your business by franchising, you must—

1. protect your rights in your product, service, or business concept by developing and registering trademarks, logos, service marks, and trade names giving your product or service a unique identification and by patenting or copyrighting any original designs involved;
2. market or test market your product or service yourself for a period sufficiently long to determine public acceptance;
3. develop a franchise agreement along the lines suggested above;
4. develop a plan for advertising and selling franchises.

Sara Addis
Home Sitter

Several companies recruit franchisees. Although franchise opportunities are offered in virtually every field, including child day care, residential real estate brokerage, and local magazine publishing, there are few franchised businesses that can be operated from home. Moreover, unfortunately, certain types of fly-by-night operators use the word *franchise* in offering home work opportunities which merely invite the *franchisee* to purchase merchandise or equipment that may not be resalable.

The purchase of a franchised business is an investment which may require a large initial outlay, continuing capital investment, hard work, and risk of loss. It is important to investigate any offering carefully and to consider carefully whether you are personally and financially ready for the responsibility involved.

As noted above, the Federal Trade Commission requires every franchisor of a franchise requiring an initial outlay of $500 or more to give a prospective franchisee a disclosure statement (sometimes referred to as an offering circular or prospectus). Be wary of any franchise offeror that does not have one. The offering circular tells you the actual name and business experience of the franchisor, the names under which it does business, and the business backgrounds of its officers or principals. It also gives the litigation and bankruptcy history of the franchisor. It then outlines *(a)* all of the opening costs the franchisee incurs, e.g., the franchise or initial fee, the cost of any necessary equipment or furnishings and supplies, and the cost of initial inventory, if any; *(b)* the franchisee's obligations to purchase inventory or other materials from the franchisor or a franchisor-designated source; *(c)* the opening and continuing assistance the franchisor provides in marketing, management, record keeping, etc.; *(d)* the details of the franchisor's training program; and *(e)* the conditions under which the franchise can be terminated and the franchisee's rights and duties after termination.

The disclosure statement must also include sample copies of all contracts the franchisee will have to sign and the franchisor's audited balance sheets and profit and loss statements for its latest three years. A list of franchisees in your state or local area must be included. If the franchisor makes any projections as to future earnings, the data on which those projections are based must be provided. The data must show whether the projections would apply to your local area.

It is important to read these documents analytically—if possible, with the aid of an accountant or attorney. It might be wise to visit or at least talk to one of the listed franchisees in your area.

A franchisee is the owner of a business and thus, he can sell his interest in that business, albeit with the franchisor's consent. A franchisee selling his own franchise is not required by the FTC rule to furnish a disclosure statement. If you are buying an existing franchise, however, you should insist on obtaining the franchisor's disclosure statement as part of your investigation of the franchisee's business.

There are two advantages of buying a franchise opportunity: you are selling a product or service that has a recognized trade name or trademark, and the franchisor usually offers training and opening assistance as well as marketing, advertising, and record-keeping assistance during the entire franchise term.

The disadvantages? Most franchise offerings require substantial up-front outlays. Virtually all require payment of a continuing royalty during the entire term. This is usually based on *gross* revenues or sales, thus cutting into net profits. Some franchises are so structured that inventory or equipment has to be purchased from the franchisor or a designated source, even though the contract does not require this. This can increase costs. You may be restricted to selling the franchisor's products exclusively, thus limiting your flexibility.

In going into a franchise relationship, remember that contracts are negotiable. Don't hesitate to question any provision you deem disadvantageous. Before signing, consider not only the public acceptance of the franchisor's product or service and the franchisor's economic viability, but also whether you have the financial capital, the time, and the energy necessary to start up and maintain a business and are prepared to face the risks involved.

> **❝I think as we begin to realize and achieve in areas unique to us, up to our full potential, we achieve personal success and satisfaction. I'm getting closer all the time.❞**
>
> Sales Manager

Sara Addis
Home Sitter

Understanding a Microcomputer System

Victoria Sczerzenie, Systems Analyst

66 My new computer is terrific! It took a while for me to catch on to all that it can do for me, but at this point it has simplified my life and freed me from time-consuming, boring, and expensive tasks! **99**

Advertising Consultant

For someone whose home business has grown large and complex enough to require computerized record keeping, saving the extra money to buy a home computer system may appear to be the major obstacle to solving paperwork and organizational problems. One may imagine that, with cash in hand, purchasing a computer would simply mean locating the nearest computer store and describing one's business to a salesperson. That accomplished, he or she would wait for large boxes of components to arrive, plug everything together, push some buttons, and watch enthusiastically as the cost-benefit ratio associated with this major purchase improves. Troublesome, time-consuming paperwork would disappear. The number of customer accounts that could be handled would skyrocket while bills would be promptly issued and paid. If you are in a similar situation with similar expectations, forget the money obstacle and examine some facts about how microcomputer systems work and can work for you. You may find some strange concepts to deal with once you have financed yourself into the world of the home computer.

First of all, it may surprise you to encounter the need to know something about data processing in order to choose a microcomputer system that will be an asset to your business. Computer store salespeople seldom communicate clearly and effectively to the customer what he or she should know about computers in general or about a specific system. They also may not be able to fully appreciate facts about your business, which should influence you in selecting a system. More likely, you will have to learn the general structure and functions of microcomputers to understand the sales talk and make your own choices of both hardware and software. This means becoming familiar with some major principles and terminology, but unless you enjoy thick technical exposition and endless jargon, learning even the basic principles of computer use won't be simple or natural.

While overconfidence about the ease of buying a microcomputer system may quickly disappear, don't replace it with a belief that only a math or electronics wizard can understand computer functions. That computers are approachable by only a select group of egghead programmers is simply not true. Thinking they are can lead you to demand that any system you buy be completely prepackaged and as easy to control as a can opener. Such a system, even if it exists tailor-made to your business needs, will be costly. It would be better to start out believing that you can, by mastering a set of basic concepts, handle the computer sales talk, the software system commands, and even a simple computer language.

We'll begin here with general ideas which should give you a helpful orientation into the details of owning and using a microcomputer system.

A computer solves problems by means of symbols: letters or numbers, which exist temporarily inside it in the form of groups of electrical charges. Each group of charges is held by substances which take up some very tiny amount of space. For this reason, each letter of a word or digit in a number that the computer uses requires space to be worked on, space to be stored, and a means of moving back and forth between these two spaces. Human information processing is analogous. When you read a book or solve a math problem, the printed page is the storage area, the brain is where the symbols are used, and the connection between the letters on the page and your brain is the light bouncing off the page into your eye. So, too, with a computer. There are storage areas (magnetic disks or tapes), central processing areas, and connections by means of tape- or disk-reading devices. Also, for humans and computers alike, this system for information processing (storage, work area, connection) must be capable of holding at once all the information necessary to solve problems or answer questions asked of it. For a human, this capacity is generally limited by experience, motivation, and access to information. For a computer, the limitations are space and the type of software it is given. The computer's space limit is not measured in feet and inches, but in the number of groups of electrical charges, i.e., characters the computer can work on and store. You will encounter this concept under the term "K" words of memory or storage. The software, the second limit on the processing capacity of a computer, are sets of instructions, written by humans, by which the computer does things. The complexity of these instructions can vary greatly and is limited by the amount of space the computer has in which to execute those instructions. Therefore, in considering what computer system to buy, it will be important to think out thoroughly what tasks you expect the computer to perform and the form of the data which you expect the computer to work on. These two factors will determine the complexity of the task the computer will perform. For example, if you want the computer to give gross sales for the year, the task could be adding twelve numbers or 365 numbers. Or, if the question is your net income for the year, the task might be the sum of the differences between twelve or 365 pairs of numbers. Because computer systems differ by space and software, a system may be large enough to handle the first task with no problem, but have trouble with the second.

Another important basic is the concept that a task which seems unitary to a person, such as computing sales for the year, seems so only because the human is already familiar with all the separate steps required to prepare for and carry out the task. To illustrate this to yourself, try to make a detailed list of all the equipment necessary for brushing your teeth and of all the actions that are involved. Then imagine that a computer begins similarly mundane, routine tasks without any "experience" or "equipment." The operating software adds the ability to receive, store, and act on information; the language software gives the ability to understand a small set of commands; and the applications software uses those commands to detail what actions to take. Thus each task the computer completes is broken down into many elementary steps which

❝It is not necessary to go out and buy a computer to handle inventory. ... until your business reaches a certain size, such systems generally go underutilized. Also, your time and money will be needed elsewhere initially.❞

Computer Consultant

Planning for Expansion

are carried out by the different instruction sets known as software. Considering this mode of functioning for a moment will make it apparent that the most basic requirement for completing a task by computer is that the steps taken include all that is necessary. This requirement is remarkably difficult to fulfill. Often while working with a computer you won't even recognize that you've left something out. Even using prepackaged applications software (the most likely case for the microcomputer user) a great many troubles will stem from not knowing some essential step in procedure or from reversing the sequence of some steps. To avoid this, keep a log book of the steps you follow to accomplish each task regularly done at the computer. Enter in this log book each action you take and record the result the computer gives you. This may sound tedious, but there is nothing more hapless than to have a computer spew out gibberish while you sit unable to recall what you did to produce the uproar. After a time you can simplify things by working up a checklist of steps followed for each task. This list should include the parts of the job done by hand, such as where to get the data to enter and where the results are to be recorded. Make enough copies to have a fresh sheet each time you do the work. Keeping the used sheets will create a record of what you have done, with what data. The use of such a log will prevent your computer area from becoming a morass of disks, tapes, printer output, and scratch paper and leave you with a firm idea of what you and the computer did.

After spending this time analyzing the tasks the computer performs so that everything is done correctly, you should spend as much time preparing for when things go wrong. This may sound strange, but the third principle of computers is that something will go wrong, and probably frequently. Your task will be to recognize what is wrong and what to do about it. This principle is an offshoot of the stepwise nature of computer problem solving described above in connection with how to avoid mistakes. Just remember that all mistakes cannot be avoided. First you must realize that the computer, in and of itself, can't say when data or an instruction is incorrect. To solve this communication problem, software systems have ways of checking input data before further action on that data is allowed ("edits") and responses to improper commands ("error messages"). These parts of the software screen two types of mistakes: entering incorrect data (sales of $.43 instead of $43.) and asking the computer to do the impossible (dividing by zero or reading data that doesn't exist). Without edits and error messages, the computer, given the first type of mistake, will continue its task and just report a disappointing sales balance for the month. Given the second type of mistake, the computer may stop functioning entirely. These outcomes should be prevented by the screening of input by the software. To use the system effectively, you must learn what mistakes will be recognized and what result or message will happen in response to them. An even more important puzzle will be what happens when a mistake of either sort is not screened by edits or error messages in the software.

After you have selected and studied your microcomputer comes the time to apply the knowledge acquired, as well as yourself, to the job. At this point you may face the fourth major principle of computer systems: computers thrive on organization. The computer takeover of the job you want done may be impossible without a major reorganization of your papers, files, and books. The machine's mere presence in your office won't produce an organized and efficient billing or inventory system. The machine can't sort stacks of bills or refile misfiled orders. Depending upon how much complexity your system can handle, it will be more or less able to impose an organization on information put into it in a disorganized sequence. For instance, for a monthly inventory report, you may need to transform by hand your alphabetical vendor/customer file into a monthly vendor/customer file before entering any data from it into the computer. In general, be prepared to spend some time organizing the manual system of your office to join smoothly with the data-entry requirements of the computer system and with its output format. The time required to enter data and the speed with which you can use what comes out depends on whether your office papers exist in an organized state and whether that organization coincides with the software's data entry and output sequences. Simply put, the magnificent inside organization of the computer won't help much and will probably just add more paper to the fire, if there is not a good outside organization. The computer is just an element in a stream that begins and ends with humanly executed procedures.

This objective look at your office procedures can also provide a background for informing the computer salesperson about your needs and for evaluating the systems you consider purchasing. At the store, find out what the system will give you, exactly what percentage of the tasks you now perform will be replaced, how many questions can be asked about the data you have to enter; then, after a thorough demonstration, return home to examine your office procedures again. Ask yourself how the software system will be of use to you, what you would do to enter data right then, whether you have the right data to enter, and how you would use the computer answers.

The problems mentioned are minor compared to the ones you've tackled in building your business, but they may prove more annoying and frustrating because the talents you have used—a sense of business and your product's marketplace—don't mean much when dealing with a computer system which isn't functioning acccurately and smoothly. For example, you can't ask it out to lunch or compliment its choice of office furnishings. It doesn't care that you look your best and sound positive about your abilities. That your product or service for which it is printing bills is the top of the line doesn't matter. The result is that if you are the one who will have to solve the computer disaster when it occurs, then some new skills must be acquired; and in acquiring and working with these new skills you must use again the qualities that you used in building your business to the point of needing a computer—a willingness to work steadily and patiently without giving up and with a sense of adventure.

Tina Yagjian
Data Processor
Photographer: Helaine Messer

At Home with Microcomputers

Maxine and Kyra Gottesman, Computer Consultants

66 To me I will be successful in the word processing service if I develop a large enough clientele to allow me to hire an operator during the day, so that I could do some of the work in the evenings but not have to stay up until midnight doing it. 99

Word Processor

There is no doubt that day by day microcomputers are becoming more and more integrated into our society. They are obviously versatile since they are used for both entertainment ("Have you played Atari today?") and for business ("An Apple a day. . ."). Soon they will be as commonplace as a telephone or typewriter and as inconspicuous—noticed principally when they are absent from an office. Right now you may be wondering— just as your mothers and grandmothers did years ago about telephones— do I need this? Perhaps you feel that you've managed without them so far, so why get one.

If you presently earn your living from a business at home, or your business contributes substantially to your family's (or your own) well-being, or you are building the "business of your dreams," then there is no doubt that you should purchase and use a microcomputer for yourself, your family, and your business—and don't wait.

The average cost of a microcomputer system will vary from as low as $1,800 to $20,000, depending upon such variables as type of software purchased, amount of memory available, or whether the screen is in color. An expensive system is not necessarily the best. Your research, inquiries and *intuiting* will support your correct choice. Incidentally, a perusal of the classified ads will show that resale prices remain strong and are, for an informed buyer, a source for a good buy.

A question that often arises concerns obsolescence—won't a purchase now be out of date soon? No. Look at the car market. Does each of us drive a state-of-the-art auto? No. Does our ability to select the appropriate auto increase with each purchase? Yes. Do you begin to see what we're driving at? Consider the farmer who continued to plow his fields by hand after the first combines, reapers, and other machines became available, because he was waiting for the most advanced machines before he would buy. What likely happened is that he was bought out or forced out of farming by other farmers or agri-businesses before he knew what hit him.

So, given that you are committed to the success of your business, how do you go about making a selection? Some guidelines are suggested below; first, however, realize that any choice you finally make will not be all you will need for all time. It will be your best choice at that point in time. Begin at a general computer store; both games and business software are available, and the personnel are usually well informed. Acknowledge that you are seeking information or exposure. Pick up a copy of such publications as *Infoworld* or *Computer Age* and spend some time developing a glossary of your own (maybe jot down words in a tiny pocket notebook—byte, bit, RAM, ROM, disk, binary, analog . . .). Find a class in your community, through a store or community college, which gives hands-on experience on any microcomputer. Read books on the subject.

In your inquiries, also ask about service. With the purchase of a new system you will find that there will be a warranty, that whatever repairs are needed will be done at the dealer's site (like a typewriter), and that most often there is an 800 toll-free service number. If you are at a standstill, you call that number, describe the apparent problem, and the technician at the other end will tell you how to fix the problem yourself. It's not easy to break a computer, but a beginner can find some peculiar things on the screen.

Finally, why is a microcomputer (or micro) important? What can it do for you? It has programs which, when assumptions are put in, will reflect the impact of those assumptions on a wide range of data in the system and does this quickly and accurately; it can play a game or run a budget with the change of a disk; it is marvelous entertainment for friends; and you will have to beat the kids away once they catch on. You will also produce more work more quickly. But these are not the reasons you should have a microcomputer for your business.

There are two better reasons. First, as a user you will have a vote in the types of software being demanded and, thus, the way in which computers will be used in the world. You will be a part of demystifying this wonder-filled world, thus controlling it, utilizing it, shaping it. Second, the world of possibilities open to you through electronic networking is, quite simply, thrilling. Let us amplify that: if the membership of the National Alliance of Homebased Businesswomen were users of micros and we all bought the same electronic mail service, we could be in daily communication cheaply, marketing our products and services to one another and to each other's client base, and we would not be restricted by time of day. We could read our electronic mail at the time of our choosing, answer it, and *mail* it unhampered by time zones, weather, or mailboxes.

Finally, you might be concerned that micros further isolate us from one another or are new tools to keep women at home; yet those of us in homebased business have chosen to make the home a powerful place from which to produce first-class products and services. We will use the micro to benefit our lives and businesses and our relationships with other people. It will free up our time so that we can be with people, communicate more efficiently as needed, have more time to market our services and products and, in general, perform at a higher level because we have opted to be businesswomen at home with our microcomputers.

Joan Lechner
Computer Consultant
Credit: JED Photo

Microcomputers: Their Value for Small Business

Thomas Tassini, Microcomputer Supplier

66 Since there is a sweeping trend toward homebased work, particularly in computer-assisted production, maybe I will see the day when I don't have to cringe when someone asks 'where are your offices?' **99**

PR Consultant

Increasingly, people running small businesses are attempting to utilize small computers—microcomputers—to help them use their time more efficiently, make their business grow more rapidly, or gain control over some aspect of it. This has, in some cases, been less than successful. Sometimes due to overestimating what can realistically be expected of a small box full of electronic circuits, more often due to a lack of familiarity with the entire field of computers, the potential user is forced to rely on computer salespeople or neighbors to make what is a decision of real significance to the business. How to start? Please do not learn to program unless you are the kind of person who would like to learn how to install spark plugs in a car prior to buying one. It is something to do, but probably not the right thing for you.

First, let's look at some missions of the small computers.

Word Processing. This is a familiar use—as in producing many letters where the body of the letter remains largely unchanged but where variations occur in the name and address or a paragraph. Text processing is similar—it is the writing of articles, books, and contracts with common clauses.

Information Management. This requires the computer to store information in electronic form which can be retrieved very rapidly from a number of points of view. A personnel file is an example. If you wanted to review a person's qualifications, you would look up the name alphabetically. But what of the search that would be made for someone who has a degree in social psychology? The electronic card file can be accessed and looked at from any number of directions. Preplanning is a necessity.

Financial Management. A computer can be used to do the typical accounting functions of general ledger (income statement and balance sheet), accounts payable (invoices received from suppliers), accounts receivable (invoices sent to customers and the monitoring of their payment or nonpayment), and payroll.

Decision Support. By using the computer to provide information, refined by mathematical formulas in some cases, one can manage more effectively, consistently, and objectively. A simple case is inventory management. By applying well-known formulas, you might be able to have the computer tell when stock of a given item is low and should be reordered and how much to reorder (EOQ—Economic Order Quantity).

Another example would be the budgeting process where various assumptions are made about sales, expenses, inflation, etc., prior to setting up a final budget.

Telecommunications. Here the computer is used to talk to another computer for the purposes of exchanging information. This could be accessing Dow Jones stock information, receiving a letter left in an electronic mailbox, or getting orders from salespersons in the field. This is probably the area of usage that has the most potential for innovation and future development.

Education. There is no question that the microcomputer has application to the field of education. It is still hampered by the fact that some of the best programmers are not good teachers, and the best teachers may not know how to program; nevertheless, for drill and practice in subjects such as arithmetic or typing, it is a superb instrument.

Most of us have something in the above *menu* that we would like to have our own computer do. This wish list is a potential problem since many people have lists that are far too long ever to be accomplished. If you find yourself in that position, the next step is to prioritize. What are the two or three real payoff areas? Concentrate on them.

After selecting what you want to accomplish, the work begins in analyzing it from a systems perspective. Let's define a system, any system. It is formed of parts, placed together, connected into a whole. The parts become a unit. This is exactly how to analyze the work the computer will do. Its parts are input, processing, output, and files. As an example, look at the four parts of a simple name and address file looked at from a systems perspective. See Figure A. It lists within each part the detailed breakdown of its contents. You will need to do this for each area the computer must operate in; it is really dissecting the work to be done.

There are several hints to help you analyze the intended uses of the computer within this framework. First, list all the information elements that are flowing out of the system *output*. (Flowing is the way of thinking about how this system functions, very much as plumbing works in your home!) Then determine where that information comes from and list it in the appropriate box. You may have several sets of these flow diagrams, and they may get a little messy—that's okay. You are determining what you really want to do. Once the flows are completed, you will determine what the expected volumes will be with some kind of an expansion factor (10 percent or 20 percent is not unusual) to allow for the growth in your business. Using the example in Figure A, we would determine how many names and addresses there will be in the file.

Don't worry too much about obsolescence. Your computer will be obsolete in some sense the day you buy it! There will always be a newer one on the horizon. Knowing what you want it to do and correctly estimating the volumes of work that it will do is most important. The next step is looking over available software in the light of your flow diagrams so you can select suitable software. This is where you will need some assistance. Current business-oriented or trade magazines, a good full-service computer store, or a consultant—all can be of assistance. Before you finally settle on your software, see it run and have the person who will use it try it. The very last step in the process is selecting and buying the computer itself. Be sure the place you buy it from will set it up for you and give you after-sale support. No matter how careful you are, you probably will need it. Lastly, apply a good dose of skepticism and common sense.

NAME AND ADDRESS EXAMPLE
Figure A:

System Input:
New Names
Street
City State Zip
Telephone
Deletions
Changes

System Processing:
Sorting
Selecting
Deleting

Files:
Names (3,000 total)
Street
City State Zip
Telephone

System Output:

TV:
Name
Telephone

Printed Reports:
Mailing Labels (500/week)
Alphabetical List
List by Zip Code
Etc.

Planning for Expansion

Telecommunications

Roberta Tasley, Manager of NYU Telecommunications Clinic

❝ Computer homework nowadays doesn't necessarily refer to what computer science students do after class. For more and more people, computer homework is a lucrative way of escaping commuting, 40-hour work weeks, and day-care costs. **❞**

J. D. Solomon, *The Daily News*

What sort of productive, profitable activity is environmentally healthy, energy-conservative, community-oriented, interpersonal as well as individual, central to the new information economy, and highly productive?

What new work option is open to scientists, computer programmers, data base researchers, accountants, insurance reps, word processors, research assistants, and securities analysts? The answer is *telecommuting,* a term coined by University of Southern California Professor Jack Nilles to describe the use of telecommunication and computer systems as a substitution for commuting to work. Those who telecommute work at a remote site (at home or in a satellite work center) and communicate to one or many centralized work centers by computer and telephone networks. Though currently relatively few people choose to be in the forefront of this shift in work patterns, it is conservatively estimated that as many as 7.5 million workers (that is 15 percent of the information industry) can telecommute. What phenomena have contributed to the emergence of new work patterns? And what is a new work option related to these changes?

An Information Economy

Call it an emergence of an Information Society, a Technological Revolution, the Electronic Revolution, a Service Society, the New Information Order, or the Third Wave Info-sphere. Label it as you will, we have moved from an industrial to an information economy.

Statistics tell us that information occupations engage over 50 percent of workers in the labor force. Professor Nilles describes these workers as "those persons whose primary job is to move, manipulate, and/or transform information in some way or other." Central to the maintenance of an information economy is high-speed, complex communication equipment and those persons who wield the specialized skills to operate it.

The overnight development of highly sophisticated communication technologies including microcomputers, their peripherals and specialized software and the growth of telephonic networks and satellite systems are technological determinants of the information economy. Concurrent to technological change, we have entered a period of environmental alarm—fuel costs are escalating and we know our energy resources are finite. Additionally, there seems to be a trend, some say a remnant of the "me generation," that more and more people who are able are considering the issue of quality of life in their career decisions.

It appears that there is necessity—and opportunity—for a telecommunications-transportation trade-off, and the trade-off can have positive socioeconomic implications. The possibility of new work options is the result of the storage capacity of computers.

The Development of the "Electronic Cottage"

By simple electronic means computer information can be manipulated from decentralized sites twenty-four hours daily. There are no longer geographic nor time constraints on where or when work must be done, which has led Alvin Toffler to lay great emphasis on the "electronic cottage" as the "center of society." There may not be social recognition of the shift from centralized to decentralized economy, nor even agreement that the shift will be as important as Toffler predicts, but there is certainly recognition that the home can be the locus for bona fide, paid work. This emphasis may be a result of a need for qualified telecommunications workers: professional computer programmers, experienced systems analysts, precise word processors.

As the heart of the information economy, computer work is conducted around the clock, and the result is a serious scarcity of skilled, experienced computer specialists. It is estimated that in the 1980s there will be a shortage of 10,000 programmers and data analysts. The computer industry is short staffed at present, and a good number of the jobs can be manned by *women*.

There is no longer need for many women to make a choice between raising a family and remaining on the career ladder. The information industry is a perfect place for women to exercise control over their time and space while having the freedom to pursue a very profitable and fulfilling career path.

Indeed, across the country there is a growing tendency for enlightened (and needy) service-oriented corporations to experiment with homeworkers. Often the experiment was initiated when a valued, long-term data processor became pregnant or wished to stay home during child-rearing years but did not want to cut all professional ties. Corporations such as Continental Illinois Bank and Trust, Control Data Corp., Digital Equipment Corp., Blue Cross and Blue Shield of South Carolina, Mountain Bell, Apple Computer, and Aetna Life and Casualty all have homeworkers in different capacities. In some cases, the corporation supplies communication equipment and pays for a dedicated phone line; in some cases, workers lease the equipment from the company; and in some cases, workers own their equipment. Most information about these experiments is proprietary and fraught with speculation.

One of the most interesting companies in this field is not conducting an experiment at all. It is Heights Information Technology Service Inc., a firm that acts as broker between homebased free-lance computer experts and businesses in need of computer expertise for ad hoc projects. It is a prototype for homebased business in the information industry.

Out of two small offices in Tarrytown, N.Y., and Oakland, Calif., Heights maintains a pool of about 200 panel members and managers who work at home and are assigned to work on projects ranging from writing computer programs to designing complete data processing systems. Not by chance, Heights employees are 70 percent female. It is their basic philosophy that there are many persons, especially women, who need a flexible work schedule; and intrinsic to the computer industry is flexibility in employment patterns.

To maintain quality control Heights requires three years experience from prospective programmers and five years from its systems analysts. The task of the Heights project manager is to analyze client needs and panel member capability, to project the extent of the job and time frame. Additionally, the project manager must maintain an esprit de corps among remote workers. This is accomplished by constant telephone contact and through training seminars and social gatherings. Though the evidence so far is merely anecdotal, personal interviews indicate that worker productivity is improved by 100–300 percent!

Not So Much Blue Sky, Please

Despite blue-sky predictions, telecommuting is not for everyone. Toffler neglects to recognize that there are other people in the electronic cottage—other people with different schedules, physical and ego needs, and often with conflicting expectations on what should be done in the home. He also ignores the fact that more than 15.5 million people live alone and the figure increases yearly. Personal isolation is an important research issue that must be addressed and dealt with.

Another kind of isolation—professional isolation—exists when workers are excluded from the work center. Traditionally, one must be seen to remain on the corporate promotional ladder, one must meet with professional peers to learn what's new, and a lot of innovative thinking takes place in impromptu moments during the day. Though the computer has a special capability to stage synchronous meetings between numerous participants, it doesn't pat you on the back and offer a convivial drink at day's end. Special attention must be made to keep in touch with professional peers.

Certain practical issues such as workers organizing, benefits, and tax deductions have not been consistently resolved.

The Individual and Sense of Community

One issue which has not been dealt with in any of the literature is the development of an enhanced sense of community. It is my particular premise that people who work at home will save certain resources— especially time and money—which were previously spent on job-related activity (commuting, clothing, entertainment) and that these resources will be spent by homeworkers with flexible hours in their local community. Parents can contribute to school and church activities; political activists can join organizations; environmentalists can work to reorganize use of resources. In a society that has become increasingly nomadic and idiosyncratic, this work option can be a positive social contribution as well as personally and financially satisfying.

> "THE OUTPUT DEPENDS ON ME;
> THE INPUT STILL DEPENDS ON YOU."
>
> SIGNED,
>
> COMPUTER

Chart of Advisors

Advisor	What They Can Do	How to Locate One
Lawyer	Can help select the form of business, draw up contracts and agreements, guide you in legalities of operating a business, arbitrate disputes within the business and for the business against others, advise you of your rights and obligations under the law.	Lawyer can be referred by friends, other businesspeople, suppliers, consultants, trade associations, local bar associations, or through Yellow Pages listings. Fees are based on hourly rates, depending on complexity and extent of services.
Accountant	Can set up a bookkeeping system that is simple for a business owner to follow and that an accountant can work with at audit and tax time.	Accountants are listed in the Yellow Pages, but it's better to get a reliable recommendation from your banker, attorney, or friends. The accountant is like a doctor in that he or she knows your business from the inside out. Speak with several; check their experience and references before selecting one. Fees are based on hourly rates, depending on complexity and extent of services. Many Certified Public Accountants will give you an initial consultation free.
Banker	Has financial knowledge of loans, business accounts, bank services, and credit systems; is familiar with the community and may be able to suggest individuals and institutions that might be helpful to you and your business.	Confer with bankers. Some are more conservative than others; some specialize in certain types of loans and industries; some have different concepts of loyalty to customers. Find a bank large enough to satisfy your needs but small enough to value your business.
Insurance Agent or Broker	Will evaluate insurance needs and set up packages to cover specific types of business. May be an independent (dealing with several insurance companies) or a direct writer (employed by one company and writing policies only for that company).	Talk with several to compare coverage, costs, and convenience to select a plan that suits your needs comprehensively and economically. An agent requires complete information on business operations as they relate to insurance coverage and must be kept up to date on changes that may affect insurance needs. Agents and brokers are listed in the Yellow Pages.
Management and Marketing Consultant	Can help the new businessperson deal with the many facets of starting a business: products, inventory, pricing, advertising, filing, hiring. Has access to other resources and contacts that could be beneficial.	Consultants are listed in the Yellow Pages or can be referred by other business owners and colleagues. Consultants may charge on hourly, daily, or weekly basis, or on a monthly retainer fee.
Computer Consultant	Can determine if your business would benefit from computerizing part or all of its operations and identify the choices of computer hardware and software.	Get referrals from business associations and businesspeople who have used computer consultants, or follow up advertising in computer publications and the Yellow Pages. Establish what consultant will do and what will be required of you. Get estimates of time and charges.

Selecting a Business Entity

Leonard Furman, Tax Attorney

Whether you are starting a new business or are already in a business, one of the most crucial decisions to be faced is determining the best structure for your enterprise.

There are four basic forms of doing business:

1. Sole Proprietorship
2. Partnership
3. Corporation
4. Sub S Corporation

Sole Proprietorship

The easiest form to use to operate a business is a sole proprietorship, a one-person operation. It will often be appropriate for persons setting up a part-time business or a personal service business.

Many people have not made a strong commitment to a new business activity and yet must choose a form for operating. A sole proprietorship saves both legal fees and accounting fees for organizational documents and tax return preparation. No legal forms or agreements need to be drawn up, and the business can be closed down at the owner's discretion.

The most significant tax considerations are the following:

1. Any operating losses or investment tax credits from the business can be directly passed through to the owner, thus reducing the amount of individual income that is subject to tax.
2. Certain fringe benefits available to corporate shareholder-employees are not available to sole proprietorships. These include tax deductible payments for up to $50,000 of group term life insurance coverage without any income to the insured, tax deductible payments for medical insurance premium and medical expense reimbursement plans.
3. Qualified retirement (Keogh) plan contributions can be made by sole proprietors up to $15,000. In addition, self-employed individuals will be able to place up to $2,000 into an Individual Retirement Account using the same self-employed income.
4. Transfer of partial ownership would ordinarily require a change in business form, to either a partnership or a corporation.
5. A sole proprietor who hires his or her spouse or their own children under age 21 need not pay social security tax or federal unemployment tax on them. (Family corporations do not get this break). The spouse and/or the children can then open up an Individual Retirement Account on the wages received.

In summary, a sole proprietorship seems most appropriate for small individual undertakings with no significant capital requirements.

Partnership

If there is more than one person involved in a business, the choice is between a partnership and/or corporate structure. The various individuals involved share the income or losses from their common business. The partnership acts as a conduit and does not itself pay any federal tax; instead the partners pick up their share of the income or losses on their individual tax returns. A partnership has most of the tax characteristics of a sole proprietorship.

Partnerships can also be rather simple from a tax viewpoint. Transferring assets and liabilities between a partnership and its partners can be accomplished with relative ease and generally with no tax consequences.

In the past, the IRS generally required partnerships to conform to the tax year of the principal partners or to use a calendar year. The IRS has adopted a policy, however, whereby it will normally allow a partnership to adopt a year (ending September 30, October 31, or November 30) differing from that of its principal partners.

A partnership can be used by the partners to give income to each partner who will be subject to the self-employment tax.

While you can have an oral partnership agreement, it is recommended that you have a written partnership agreement that covers such things as the percentage allocation of the profits and losses, amount of salary to each partner, amount of money (capital) to be invested in the business, provisions regarding death, disability, retirement or termination from the business,etc.

Corporation

An individual who owns a business can form a corporation. He or she transforms the individual proprietorship by transferring the assets of the business to the corporation—personal property, real property, and/or goodwill—in exchange for shares. The stockholder is an owner who has invested in the business but does not necessarily have the responsibility of management, while the managers are employees on salary who do not necessarily own controlling financial interest. Though they are classified differently by law, there is no reason why manager, stockholder, and a member of the board of directors cannot be one and the same.

A corporate entity has numerous nontax advantages, such as limited liability, ownership interests which are easily transferred, and conventional hierarchy. There are also numerous tax advantages available for regular corporations.

1. Income tax savings at corporate rates are generally lower than individual rates. Also taxes can be saved by an allocation of the taxable income between salaries that are taxed to the individual and income that is taxable to the corporation. The income that is retained by the corporation can then be loaned interest free to the shareholder.
2. The regular corporation (other than a Sub S) has the most attractive qualified pension and profit-sharing plans available. Loans can be made by the qualified plan to the participant. Loans from Keogh plans to self-employed individuals are not permitted without tax penalties.
3. The corporation can provide group life insurance to its employees. The premiums paid are fully deductible to the corporation and, up to the first $50,000 of coverage, the premiums are not income to the employees.

66My husband became a partner. My hobby had become our livelihood. We are doing what we love and making a living home. It's a dream come true.... If it hadn't been for my husband and his support and confidence and love, I'd never have been able to come this far.**99**

Wicker Restorer

161

Business Advisors: Your Team of Experts

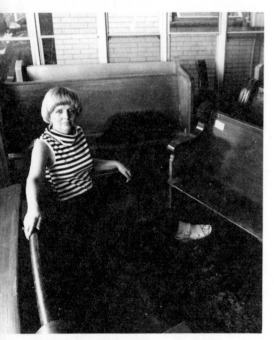

Lorie Warner
Saleswoman
Photographer: © Terri P. Tepper,
1977

4. The corporation can provide a medical reimbursement plan under which it could reimburse the employee for any medical expense which he or she or anyone in the family might incur. This sum would be fully deductible by the corporation and would not be taxed to the employee. The self-employed individual, however, is left to the regular income tax deduction for medical expenses. Thus, self-employed individuals may deduct only those medical expenses exceeding 3 percent of their adjusted gross income, plus 50 percent of the cost of any medical insurance up to a total of $150.

5. Disability insurance can also be paid by the corporation for the employee, without the employee being taxed on the premiums paid. This insurance is known as "income insurance." It is not a deduction which is allowable to the unincorporated business, but to the person who has incorporated his practice, it may be purchased with pretax dollars.

6. The corporation is entitled to exclude from its income 85 percent of the dividends received from investments in other domestic corporations, whereas an individual would be taxed in full after an initial minimal exclusion.

7. It is easier to obtain capital-gain treatment on the sale of corporate stock than on the sale of a partnership interest.

8. The need to make estimated tax payments on Form 1040-ES may be eliminated since withholding can be set up to cover the individual's taxes. Possible underestimation penalties can be avoided by additional withholding at year end.

9. A corporation can select a year-end of any month.

If a corporation form is chosen for a new business venture, the owner/employee should strongly consider not drawing a salary until the business becomes profitable. If the business operates at a loss, a salary to the owner simply increases the loss; in essence, money is borrowed to pay a salary which is subject to income tax. It is much better for the owner to simply borrow the money required for living expenses and to save the income tax expense. Even with a Sub S corporation where the losses are passed through and deducted on the owner's return, the payroll tax cost, which can be substantial, must be considered.

Sub S Corporation

Sub S corporations can provide attractive tax benefits and opportunities for planning, but you should use an accountant who is familiar with all of the rules governing election, operation, and termination.

An election can be made to be a Sub S corporation within the first seventy-five days of the taxable year. Therefore, you can see how your business is performing before you determine whether to make the Sub S election.

A Sub S corporation should usually be used if losses are incurred, and if the shareholders have sufficient investment cost (basis) to permit deduction of the losses and the shareholders have sufficient taxable income to effectively benefit from the losses.

Unlike a partnership, a Sub S corporation can select any month for the end of its fiscal year. A Sub S corporation with a January 31 year end defers tax on eleven months of its income each year.

Sub S corporations are inflexible when it comes to allocating income or loss among the shareholders. Since one class of stock is outstanding, all shareholders are treated equally. Losses must be allocated to all shareholders based solely on the number of days they owned stock. This is a strict arithmetic calculation, made without regard for the economic realities of the business. Income and investment credit are allocated to shareholders based solely on their stock ownership on the last day of the corporation's fiscal year. This could provide interest opportunities for shifting income to lower-bracket family members after the income has been earned.

The following chart will briefly outline the basic factors in selecting a business entity:

Basic Factors in Selecting a Business Entity

	Sole Proprietor	Partnership	Sub S	Corporation
Which tax rates apply	Individual	Individual	Individual	Corporate
Paperwork required	No organizational documents; no separate tax return	Partnership agreement desirable; separate tax return required	Incorporation papers; separate tax return	Incorporation papers; separate tax return
Timing recognition of owner's income	No flexibility	Some income deferral possible	Some income deferral possible	Some income deferral possible
Allocation of income among owners		Possible	Must be in proportion to ownership share	Must be in proportion to ownership share
Character of losses in disposition of business	Ordinary or capital	Ordinary or capital	Usually capital	Usually capital
Who may claim losses	Owner	Owners	Owners	Corporation
Character of gain at sale	Depends on assets sold	Depends on assets sold	Usually capital	Usually capital
Consequences of passive investment income	None	None	Endangers election	None

Great care should be taken in the selection of the type of entity to use for your business. You should be aware of the advantages and disadvantages of the entities and should participate in the decision.

A final update: the Tax Equity and Fiscal Responsibility Act of 1982 (TEFRA) is intended to raise revenues and make sure every taxpayer bears a fair share of the tax burden. The following provisions summarize some of the important features that affect all corporate plans:

1. The maximum annual contribution to a profit-sharing plan has been lowered from $45,475 to $30,000. The maximum annual pension that can be received from a pension plan has been reduced to $90,000. It is effective for years beginning after December 31, 1982, if a plan was in existence prior to July 1, 1982; otherwise, plan years ending after July 1, 1982.

2. Previously loans to members of a corporate profit-sharing or pension plan were made on a tax-free basis, regardless of the amount. Effective 1984, loans made after August 13, 1982, cannot exceed $50,000 and must be repaid within five years.
3. Also effective in 1984, there will be special limitations to plans known as "Top Heavy Plans" that provide more than 60 percent of their benefits to key employees. This will affect almost all small employers as to minimum contributions and the amount that an employee will be entitled to receive from the plan every year that he or she works.

Changes with respect to self-employed individuals, partnerships, and Subchapter S corporation pension and profit-sharing plans effective in 1984 are:

1. The basic contributions, benefits, and loan amounts allowable will be increased to match those under corporate plans.
2. An individual will be able to be the trustee of the plan, whereas previously one had to use a bank or similar institution.

Your accountant and/or attorney should be consulted in order to determine the effect of this law on your business. In fact, the advice and guidance of an attorney and tax accountant are always important when establishing a business.

Several factors determine the choice of a business: your personal financial situation, your marital status (and, if married, your husband's tax bracket), the type of business and its possibilities for growth. While the tax laws and other aspects of regulation are not designed to influence your choice of the form in which you do business, the fact remains that the structure of such laws does influence choice.

The business and everything that relates to it is your business. Only you can decide what is best for you and what form will best protect both you and your business. Legal guidance in these matters will insure that you understand the various aspects of tax obligations involved, that you will be in compliance with local, state, and federal laws, and that the articles of incorporation and the bylaws (if you choose to go that route) will be tailored to the needs of your particular enterprise.

Francine Fierstein and Sylvia Wolff
Artists
Photographer: Marilynne Herbert

An Accountant— Why Do You Need One?

Anita L. Stellenwerf, Certified Public Accountant

Everyone in business wants to know how he or she is doing. Am I making money? Am I making as much as I can for the effort I am investing in my business? In order to answer these questions you need two things—a good set of books and a good accountant. Needless to say, often the two go hand in hand. Both are important for the operation of a successful business.

When a business is started, there are usually several objectives one hopes to achieve, not the least of which is making a profit. In order to get an accurate picture of how you are doing you must have a well thought out and organized way of measuring business transactions. This means you must have a good set of *books.*

Books are records which enable you to track the transactions of business from day to day. These will eventually enable you to prepare financial statements over specified periods of time, telling you how the business is doing.

There are many different types of records one may keep. Each business must maintain those records which will be most meaningful to it and which will give the owners the necessary information to make good decisions and to run the business well. The record-keeping system should be easy to operate, easy to understand, and flexible enough to change should the need arise. The cost of keeping a particular set of records should not exceed the benefit received from those records.

A bookkeeping system should, in addition to providing you with useful information about your business, be adequate enough to provide the various taxing authorities with the information required to determine proper tax assessments on the business. This includes income taxes, payroll taxes, and others.

If you are unfamiliar with setting up books, this would be a good point at which to hire an accountant. An accountant can and should be an important asset to you in the operation of your business. An accountant is trained to help you in many facets of your business operations. Certified public accountants can provide you with services in the following areas:

1. Auditing financial statements. This means providing an independent opinion as to the fairness of the presentation of your financial statements in accordance with generally accepted accounting principles. For large publicly held corporations, an independent audit is required. A

> 66 My accountant has patiently sat with me explaining the basics of record keeping, cash flow, and balance sheets. Understanding it all hasn't been easy, but I'm grateful for her help and feel that without her guidance my business would be nowhere at all! 99
>
> Salesperson

small business may never need a certified audit or may need one only for a specific purpose, such as obtaining a loan.

2. Providing accounting and review services. These are less thorough than an audit, more than adequate for most small businesses.

3. Tax return preparation and tax planning. Your accountant can prepare all necessary tax returns, both business and personal, and, in addition, help with tax planning to minimize your tax bill. Tax planning should start at the beginning of the year, where possible, to obtain the maximum benefit.

4. Advice on management and accounting aspects of your business. Management advisory services are a fast-growing area of services provided by certified public accountants. This may include areas such as developing information systems, improving profitability, and forecasting. As a business grows, so does the need for these services. Often it is these services which help it grow.

5. Preparing financial reports. This includes preparing statements such as an income statement, balance sheet, statement of changes in financial position, and specialized statements for special needs.

6. Assistance in securing loans. In addition to providing the financial reports lenders may require, many accountants have good relationships with lending institutions. This may help ease the way to borrowing needed funds to keep your business operating and growing.

7. Designing accounting systems. This may be as basic as setting up a simple set of books or as complex as setting up a system to run a large company.

8. Advice on personal affairs. This includes personal finances, budgeting, and estate planning.

Seeing the wide range of services a certified public accountant can provide may bring other questions to mind:

1. How do I select an accountant? Locate one through the Yellow Pages, the recommendation of a friend, banker, or lawyer, the state CPA society directory, and the American Institute of Certified Public Accountants' (AICPA) Directory. Select one with the qualifications to fit your needs. Interview those on your list, asking questions about their education and areas of experience.

Not all CPA's acquire expertise in the same areas, and therefore not all accountants supply the same services. You must determine which of the previous services you require.

2. Should I use a certified public accountant (CPA) or a public accountant (PA)? All CPA's must pass the Uniform CPA Examination and meet the educational and experience requirements of their state. This is not true of a PA. A PA does not have to meet the same requirements and is therefore limited in the services he or she can perform. If, for example, you needed a certified audit, you would have to go to a CPA to obtain one. Only a CPA can perform that service.

3. What can I expect to pay? Each firm sets its own fee schedule based on time spent, experience of the CPA, complexity of the work performed, and prevailing cost of conducting a practice in the community.

4. How do I get the most value for my money? The AICPA suggests:

- Be prepared to discuss your plans and objectives.
- Explain clearly what you are hoping to get from the accountant's services.
- Keep good records.
- Keep your accountant informed of changes and new directions.

Dorothy Squires
Antiques Saleswoman
Photographer: Bob Stewart

The Basics of Insurance

George Moore & Lavinia Moore McKee, Insurance Agents

Homebased businesses are fast becoming important and big business. With the proper planning and advice, you can have a sound and profitable future. Insurance can help you safeguard your business against crippling financial losses and promote its continuation, growth, and profitability.

> **❝I love my work; and I've always had a homestead, usually thinking of it as living where I work. Actually, for two years I lived in the back of a former church, using the sanctuary as workshop. The baptismal was converted to a shower, since none of the four bathrooms had one.❞**
>
> — Artist

When starting up a business, you and your accountant should discuss the division of personal property versus business property. Much the same kind of division occurs with your insurance needs. The area in which you run your business in your home has separate needs for special insurance.

The basic homeowner's insurance required by mortgagees on homes includes several restrictions regarding businesses that are located on premises. You may, in fact, be voiding the coverage under the homeowner's policy by running a business in your home. This can be corrected by replacing the coverage on the dwelling.

If your business is strictly an office, a school, or a studio, you may be able to have this type of "Pursuit" or "Occupancy" endorsed onto your current homeowner's policy. If the primary use of your home is for business and you still maintain your residence there, you may need a renter's policy to cover your personal belongings.

Be sure you obtain "Nonowned Auto Liability" to cover your business if your employees ever use their own cars for business use. Your family auto policy would not even cover defense costs in case of an accident.

Liability insurance protects you if you are sued. Your homeowner's policy covers you for personal liability, but it will not cover you and your business pursuits. You should check the limits of your homeowner's policy and increase it to its maximum limit. If you want to go beyond the homeowner's limit you can purchase an umbrella policy, which takes over when your regular liability policy stops. This policy usually costs about $100 for an additional $1 million of coverage. This will give you a large base of personal liability.

You will still need a commercial liability policy to cover your business for claims arising out of your responsibility for injuries or damage caused by ownership of property, manufacturing operations, and sale or distribution of products. This liability coverage can usually be put in a "package policy" along with the coverage on your business property. You may in addition have a need for errors and omissions, products liability, host liquor liability, and malpractice insurance.

Workmen's compensation coverage is required by all fifty states and applies to all part-time, temporary, and seasonal help. The coverage provides benefits to employees for injuries sustained as a result of their employment regardless of blame. It pays the cost of medical care and weekly payments to the worker, or if he dies, to his dependents. The policy is issued for an estimated premium based on salary estimates, and the total premium is compiled at the end of the policy period after a payroll audit.

Business interruption insurance protects you if your business breaks down due to physical damage. This coverage will take effect when a fire or other specific peril forces you to totally or partially suspend operations. It will give you the money needed for operating costs, mortgage payments, taxes, payroll, payments on equipment, and other expenses. If money is needed to move your business operations to another place, you would also need extra expense insurance, which would cover the extra expenses incurred to maintain uninterrupted service.

Just as your business interruption insurance would protect you if your business breaks down for physical damage, "disability income protection" would protect your income if you became disabled. If your business is a corporation, you would be covered by workmen's compensation; however, under a sole proprietorship or partnership, only employees are covered by workmen's compensation. The self-employed individual needs to obtain a disability income policy. This valuable protection is not easy to obtain, especially if your income is irregular, below certain minimums, your health is impaired, or you are in certain job categories.

Group hospitalization, major medical, and group term life insurance are now available with some companies for as few as one person. Of course, the more employees the more favorable the company will consider the application. Hospital insurance covers medical expenses in the hospital and some doctor's office expenses; major medical will pick up where hospitalization leaves off after a deductible. The higher the deductible the lower the cost, but with today's high medical cost the coverage is essential. Dental coverage, eyeglasses, and prescription drug cards are all available, but each benefit has an added cost.

A life insurance policy to provide the dollars that you meant to provide in event of an unlikely death could be used to guarantee a loan at the bank (mortgage insurance); to hire and train a replacement in event of a key employee's death (key man insurance); to purchase your partner's share of the business in event of death (buy and sell insurance); to purchase a deceased stockholder's stock to retain control of your corporation (stock redemption); to provide additional income at retirement (deferred compensation).

In the early stages of your business, the type of life insurance is not nearly as important as the amount you can afford and the job you want it to do. You may start with a term policy, which is the least expensive in the beginning but may become very costly in the later years; therefore, look for a policy that may be converted to another policy without evidence of your medical history in the future—always leaving you in the position to make the necessary changes as your needs change and the business grows.

*George Moore and
Lavinia Moore McKee
Insurance Agents*

Computer Consultants

Lynne H. Pitcher, Computer Consultant

You may wish to acquire computer capabilities for your business, but be uncertain as to how to proceed. Using the services of a professional computer consultant will ease your introduction into the world of computerized systems.

We are all aware that using a computer can offer great time, energy, and money savings to our businesses. We know too that we can buy, for very affordable sums, amounts of computing power that could not be had, even for considerable sums, just a couple of decades ago. Advertising tells us that we have a wide range of computer makes, sizes, and capabilities to choose from. This world of computers can be a very complex and difficult world to step into the first time. A professional computer consultant can help you define your needs, establish priorities, and select the right combination of equipment, software, and/or services to accomplish your goals within your budget.

Computer consulting is a fairly new, dynamic profession developing in response to business and personal needs for assistance with the choice and usage of computer systems and services. You will find both generalists and specialists in this field. To find your consultant, tap these sources for recommendations:

1. Acquaintances who have successfully used a consultant's services;
2. Businesses and business associations;
3. Advertisements in computer publications and the Yellow Pages;
4. Your local library's business directory;
5. Retail computer stores, being aware that a bias will exist here.

Be willing to spend some time and care to choose the person or firm that's right for you, one with whom you feel comfortable. Your initial meeting should define the consultant's role from beginning to end. You should obtain a clear understanding of what will be required of you during the process. Also determine how the consultant will charge and get an estimate for the entire job. Finally, get an estimate of the time required.

As a first step, you and your consultant will determine if your business would benefit from computerizing part or all of your operations. Are you currently devoting too much time to repetitive administrative chores which could be handled more efficiently with a computer—chores such as bookkeeping, maintaining client lists, maintaining an inventory? Are there integral areas of the business where a computer would be helpful? For example, a writer will want a system with word processing capabili-

> **❝**I think I'm at the point of getting a computer; it would certainly help me to keep track of my customers and their inventory. There are so many to choose from, though, I have no idea what would be best for me and my business in terms of capabilities and dollars.**❞**
>
> Distributor

ties; a designer, interior decorator, or architect can use graphic techniques. Are recreational and educational capabilities of a computer important to you and your family? Will your needs be served equally well by using computer services or buying time on a computer, rather than by owning a computer? Answers to these questions, and many others not posed here, will be important in deciding whether you should acquire a computer system.

Assuming you decide to computerize, you and your consultant will then consider factors that will determine your possible choices of computer hardware and software. Today hardware is more standardized than software; therefore, since a particular type of software can dictate your choice of hardware, it may be desirable to choose the software first. Your software choices will be determined by the processes you decide to computerize. You should plan to proceed in easy steps, doing the most important function first and proceeding downward. For example, if you are maintaining a large inventory and few employees, you will want to computerize your inventory before your payroll. Your consultant will identify those areas, if any, which are unique for your business and thus require customized programming and will estimate the cost for you. You may wish to explore the possibility of writing your own programs; your consultant can recommend suitable training for you.

Three broad categories of computer hardware are (1) the mainframes used by large corporations; (2) mini-computers, which have many features of the mainframe and are priced in the range of $20,000 to $500,000; and (3) microcomputers, or personal computers, which generally can be used by only one person at a time and are priced in the range of $1,500 to $30,000. Knowing your budget, the amount and types of use the computer will be subject to, the volume and complexity of operator input, and your printing requirements will, among other things, enable the consultant to select possible hardware choices for you.

A further consideration should be the estimation of your future needs. Your system should fit your current needs within your current budget and be capable of being upgraded for increasing needs. If there is the possibility that your growth will obsolete your computer too quickly, your consultant may recommend leasing equipment.

Before you make your final selections you will want to know that satisfactory repair arrangements are available. Most hardware manufacturers and some software distributors will offer maintenance contracts. Your consultant will review these with you to ensure that you are satisfied with the price, the repair site and arrangements for getting the equipment there and back, the availability of substitute equipment, and the estimated repair time.

Finally, you should see and operate your semifinal selections in a situation relevant to your proposed use. This can be arranged by your consultant.

The consultant's job may end with your acquisition of a system. Certainly, large firms who require consulting services to choose a computer plus custom software services should consider separating these two functions. For a smaller business, however, this separation is often not necessary nor even feasible; to hire a new firm and retread much of the same ground can be counterproductive. As a small firm you may wish to retain your consultant to ensure proper implementation of your system. In any case, you have reached the point where you are now ready to enjoy the excitement of the computer age at first hand.

The Three-Hour Class

Gonnie McClung Siegel, Communications Consultant

"I'm on 52nd and Mad," said the man in a pin-striped suit sitting opposite me on a train bound for the New York City suburbs. He used the well-known, and some feel accurate, abbreviation for busy Madison Avenue. "Where are you located?"

"My office is at home," I replied, carefully measuring his reaction.

"Oh," he replied, thrusting his *Wall Street Journal* between us.

> **"**Why do I live at work/work at home? I find it very sane—emotionally, economically, and ecologically—to commute to work by walking down the hall, fueled by caffeine, not petrol! ... You work your own hours, call your own shots, and have no one breathing down your neck.**"**
>
> Artist

This small encounter occurred twenty years ago, when it was hard to impress a stranger by talking about your homebased office. At that time only historians and very old people remembered the days of the cottage industry, when just about everybody worked at home.

By the 1950s the cottage industry had vanished, replaced by city offices and suburban malls. Women who worked at home were housewives. Men who worked at home were failures. Neither could cover the rent—the only reason anybody settled for a home office. Even writers rented expensive city offices. "Peer feedback," they claimed. Peer feeding (lunch), I suspected.

The suburbs, from the 1940s to the 1970s, mushroomed into a lifestyle filled with dogs, cats, parakeets, silver candlesticks, lawnmowers, children, station wagons, credit cards, and cramped sportscars. Each gingerbread house came equipped with its very own chauffeur and caretaker—Mom. The suburbs had become a place for women and children to live and fathers to sleep over.

Today, a conversation about a home office on any commuter line produces a reaction akin to announcing you've just won the Irish Sweepstakes. Terminally tired travelers become energized with hope. Home offices are in and wheels are out as thumbnail-sized silicon chips turn science fiction into reality. Former housewives have become the fastest-growing entrepreneurs in the country, half of them operating new and exciting businesses from their homes. Cottage industry has been revived and trotted out as The Electronic Cottage. Think tanks bubble with ideas from important thinkers and office-of-the-future conferences fill up with paying participants.

Other success signs of the home office boom are unmistakable, as a new jargon proliferates into another language of acronyms. IRS agents, who once red flagged home offices for a house call, have thrown in the towel. They seldom inspect except for a claim of a Rolls-Royce and 2,000 feet of office space in a cottage by the sea.

Futurists' projections for the home-office boom boggle the mind as technology makes distance irrelevant, and the second cottage industry emerges from the ruins of the iron horse. Within a short time, it may not matter whether your office is at home, in the middle of Bombay, or on a

Kăthe Ăna
Storyteller
Credit: Fhawano Evening Leader
Carol Ryczek

ship at sea. As distance becomes irrelevant, however, time becomes much more critical.

Pondering the lonely suburbs and crowded rail stations that technology will soon reverse, I recently computed my projected time savings while bouncing along on a dreary commuter train. Each time I go to the city, the trip takes me three hours, office to office. Daily commuters, however, claim the trip takes them an hour less. Until I fully understood them, I thought I had hit upon another brilliant idea for a homebased business: producing rose-colored glasses for commuters.

I discovered, however, that what a commuter means by a one-hour commute is the time somebody once made it during optimum "if" conditions. For example, from where I live in Westchester County, it is possible to get to New York City in one hour *if* nobody else uses the highways that morning; *if* each traffic light turns green upon the approach of a silent object traveling faster than the speed of sound; *if* the ice and snow stay in Buffalo; *if* your Aston Martin parks itself after catapulting you over two sets of stairs into a waiting train; *if* the express shows up on the dot and resumes full speed thirty seconds later; *if* those who disembark at 125th Street are thrown from the train; and *if* your office is located in the men's room at the underground level of Grand Central.

Since in twenty years I've never been able to get all these if's together, I figured my savings at three hours a day times five days a week times twelve months a year times a career that begins at age twenty-five and ends at age sixty-five. This adds up to a whopping ninety days a year, which adds up to almost ten years. An incredible lost decade! It's depressing to think of spending a seventh of a lifetime in a dingy boxcar, memorizing graffiti on passing trains. Imagine what you might do with the extra time? Think of the permanent tan you could get from a ten-year cruise. You couldn't afford it? The savings, at current commutation rates, add up to more than $40,000. A beginning commuter could retire a millionaire by putting the money into an IRA instead of commutation tickets.

Compare this with the tiny cost in time and money of my home office. The total? Only two months in over forty years of traveling from my bedroom to my office. The savings? Not enough to buy a new pair of running shoes.

Did I gild the lily by underestimating my home commuting time? No way. I overestimated by 50 percent. I figured twenty seconds a day starting from the head of my bed, traveling down the hall and into my office. I can actually make it in less than half that time at a fast trot.

If I marathoned it the way commuters race up and down the staircases, huffing and puffing, hurling themselves into the crowds, collapsing in the aisles, gasping for oxygen, pleading for somebody to put them out of their misery, I could get to work in five seconds a day; that adds up to a mere two weeks over forty years.

What's more, if I left my office door open, bought Adidas and trimmed down a bit with little Richard Simmons, who knows how much additional fat could be cut.

Go for it? No way. Because, when you have an extra ten years, a home office, a brand new computer, and nary a share of Conrail, it's un-American not to flaunt it.

Whenever you step back in time by riding any kind of commuter wheels, make sure you take along your copy of *Women Working Home*—just for the status symbol.

And get the driver's autograph. At the rate the working world is coming home, it'll be hotter than an old Wonder Woman comic book by the year 1984.

The Female Entrepreneur: Is She Different?

You bet she's different!

Women are more independent, capable of making decisions without committee support. Many have a greater degree of perspicacity—that necessary ability to see the overall business picture rather than just its parts. They are better able to integrate and synthesize information, and that's important in this world of constant change. Undercapitalization would seem not to be an advantage, but for the homebased entrepreneur starting out, it might be. If a woman is married and supported by a husband, she has an opportunity to operate a business during the shaky start-up phase without draining money from it. A business often begins with *sweat capital,* and women are better able to improvise and keep things going while it builds. Aren't they the ones who accomplish miracles at home with food and decorating budgets? Watch them go in business!

According to one writer who, for reasons of personal safety, has chosen to remain anonymous, there are a few ways to tell the difference between a businessman and a businesswoman:

> A businessman is aggressive;
>   a businesswoman is pushy.
> He is careful about details;
>   she is picky.
> He loses his temper because he's so involved in his job;
>   she's bitchy.
> He's depressed (or hung over), so everyone tiptoes
>   past his office;
>   she's moody, so it must be her time of the month.
> He follows through;
>   she doesn't know when to quit.
> He's firm;
>   she's stubborn.
> He makes wise judgements;
>   she reveals her prejudices.
> He isn't afraid to say what he thinks;
>   she's opinionated.
> He exercises authority;
>   she's tyrannical.
> He's discreet;
>   she's secretive.
> He's a stern taskmaster;
>   she's difficult to work for.

> **"**Our goals are, of course, to be able to support ourselves from our business. The outlook is good although it won't happen overnight. The secrets? None, except hard work, self-discipline, sensitivity, and luck.**"**
>
> Newspaper Publisher

173

That may be the way some people see it, but there are reasons to believe that women, though different, may have the edge. When a woman does a job well, she's noticed, and that visibility is one of her best assets. There is plenty of research to show that in competition with men, women have equal or superior reserves of strength and stamina. Think about this. A full-time wife and homemaker becomes a full-time mother (still maintaining that role of full-time wife and homemaker) and then decides to start a business which will also demand full-time effort. (She will work harder for herself than she has ever worked for anyone else!) She needs all the energy she can muster and the willingness to work hard at difficult, as well as menial, tasks.

Owning and operating a successful business requires some of the following:

An irrepressible streak of independence.

An imaginative and open mind that can create a good idea, see it at different angles, then develop it into a workable concept.

The energy to maintain both physical and emotional health.

An adventurous and courageous spirit.

Patience to lay a sturdy foundation.

The wisdom to plan carefully.

Self-confidence to believe in your plan and know it will work.

Determination and discipline to pursue your plan.

Time to get it all together, to deal with last-minute deadlines, to handle unexpected problems.

Resilience, or bounce-back.

An ability to cope with financial insecurity.

Poise to keep your cool under pressure.

A sense of humor that can help you through the rough times and lift the low points.

Good judgement to evaluate facts and make decisions quickly and effectively.

Individuality, flair, and creativity to set you apart from the competition.

The experience necessary to succeed.

A responsiveness to people's needs.

Understanding for and from your family. (Women with family support are more successful in business; women without it, may be forced to choose between family and business.)

Very few women are lucky enough to have all these qualities. That is not to say that failure is inevitable. Not at all! There are successful women who have a great rapport with people and good judgement but do not have tremendous reserves of energy, and there are those who have difficulty making decisions but are able to stick with a plan of action once it's been determined. (When evaluating your strengths and weaknesses, maybe this is a good time to consider working with a partner who has what you lack!)

Above all, what a woman needs is the desire to succeed—it's not the earning power but the yearning power—thorough knowledge of her business, and a love for what she is doing. Important, too, is that differential advantage you have over your competitors because you're more innovative, charge less, work faster, whatever. Today there are more female entrepreneurs than ever before in history. Women who build their own businesses have a great deal to gain in life—and a great deal to give.

Vive la difference!

A Changing Lifestyle

Martin Lazar, Psychotherapist

Women are at the forefront of many revolutions in this twentieth century. With the changes taking place in the woman's family role, one of the more subtle types of change is the development of new areas for work which some women have quietly and creatively found. For centuries women have been the chief executives in their homes with slight acknowledgement. Some women these days are obviously capitalizing on that experience and becoming chief executives in the home in more ways than one.

> 66 As my work progresses and my outlook on designing and life broadens, I am experiencing a sense of well-being as never before. I find that all of life, including spiritual life, takes on new meaning and purpose. I am growing as an individual! 99
>
> Knitter

The woman working at home has had the rare opportunity in our sophisticated times of carrying on the traditions of the individual entrepreneur. With this role has gone the ego benefits of individuality, autonomy, decision making, creativity, and self-worth. It is interesting that these are the very factors so often cited by experts as necessary for ego development. The ego is that part of the psyche which helps us strike a balance between ourselves and our environment. When the balance is comfortable, we are considered well-adjusted. For the balance to take place, there must be ongoing stimulation of a positive nature from ourselves and from those we value around us. We feel important when our ego synthesizes this input, and we conclude that we are on par with our goals, expectations, and background pressures.

The woman working at home must realize her special opportunities and nourish her ego with the knowledge that she carries on a real American tradition—that of the individual entrepreneur. To do this she must develop a cadre of peers, with whom she can easily communicate, who are equally individualistic, independent, and resourceful. The ultimate goal of a consciousness-raising group—that technique so germane to the women's movement—is to achieve those very freedoms that the woman working at home already has. While resisting the seductive corporate advertising, which suggests glamour for women in the corporate cubbyhole, she must continue to explore her own individuality with more self-confidence and security than she has shown in the past. Beginning, more often than not, as a problem-solving device because of family responsibilities or limited capital and hours, she has built a career, but not a mental attitude of the rugged individualist. She has been given this opportunity, however, and must begin to realize how ego-appropriate her functions are.

Women are stereotypically not used to this responsibility and technique. Professional women often refer to the "women's syndrome" while chatting with their colleagues over coffee. By this term they refer to the

Special Reports

66 As the wife of a naval aviator, I find myself moving from town to town every two or three years. Consequently, I also must change places of employment with that move. ... I believe I've found the solution to my employment dilemma as I move around the country—working from my home! A very simple answer to an often very frustrating situation. **99**

Craftsperson

Joan Peckolick and Thea
Graphic Designer
Photographer: Sally Cooney

way little girls are not trained to make decisions or develop their own sense of identity. They are trained instead to cater to the dictates of others, to be someone else's commodity. The woman working home has independence as part of her job and needs—to make a bad pun—to capitalize on it in building identity, to seek out others in similar careers, and to feel good about herself.

Not only does the woman working at home stay at home with all of the usual problems; she plays the role of her own supervisor as well. While we have been a nation truly strengthened by our individual entrepreneurs, most of us have been raised to work in groups—especially women, trained to handle large families. With modern changes in family roles, some women have now looked elsewhere for their life tasks, supervision, and groups. One of the subtle and somewhat seductive expectations of the past has been the suggested sense of freedom that has always been associated with the marketplace. In mythology, men were leaving home to partake of this marketing delight while the women drudged at home. Reality, however, has now placed the greater number of women, often leaving spacious and comfortable daily home surroundings with relative freedom of choice in their time schedules, into cramped, often uncomfortable spaces; with continual psychic stresses; with increasingly rigid time capsules; and at the beck and call of bosses they don't like and who have made all kinds of servitudinal demands upon them. They have, therefore, traded a role in life, perhaps imperfect but of obvious worth and importance, for one most often lacking in individuality, coglike, and of passing value at best. Health problems have increased; happiness has not. Working away from home has been a mixed blessing at best, and there has been no indication that "getting away" has produced mental health. Often it has been just the opposite. Margaret Mead talked about the schizophrenic nature of modern man, commuting from nowhere to nowhere and spending the day performing meaningless tasks in between. Women do that now, too.

Women have been using their experiences of working at home to solve their problems since long before the fictional Penelope wove her famous rug, waiting for her husband to return from his travels and keeping other suitors away. But the phenomenon sweeping the country today is significant in providing for many an attractive choice in the general movement of modern woman into the labor force. In these changing times with changing lifestyles, an option is presented to women, who would otherwise feel quite shy, or unaggressive, or fearful, or uncompetitive. It has, for example, been the experience of workshop leaders that women, more so than men, have begun the process of entering the world of work with a demonstrated lack of self-confidence, and a general feeling of reticence. The feeling of success that has gone along with the establishment of homebased businesses has, however, brought concurrent feelings of growth in other areas, so that self-confidence and necessary competitiveness or assertiveness have grown apace.

Not long ago a woman came into my office burdened with problems and, in the midst of telling her woes, happened to mention that she had established a homebased business—a typing company in which she employed five women. It was soon apparent that the homebased business was the one bright spot in her life in the past few years. That she felt that way was no surprise; nor that she attributed to it a sense of well-being and purpose, without which she felt that she would have been in much more serious trouble. She was, in fact, quite right. Her experience in establishing her service, dealing with clients as well as staff, solving problems, making decisions about business matters, and, of course, making money, had brought her satisfaction, and helped her to the point where she could face the fact that she had, indeed, other serious problems. It was interesting to note that when she talked about her business, her voice got louder, her tone firmer, and she clearly felt in control.

In psychotherapy our job is often to help troubled clients learn how to sustain a fragile ego balance with some continuity. For the woman working at home, the job becomes one of isolating those factors that can lead to ongoing ego satisfaction. It is ironic that women working at home do not generally feel the kind of importance and excitement that their chosen careers offer them. One of the principal reasons for this problem may be the isolated position that the woman working at home has had vis-à-vis her peer group (other women working in their homes). Isolation is an immediate red flag for the therapist. One must presume that the current efforts for setting up a network providing for information, communication, recognition, and possible social opportunity—as represented by this book and the growing National Alliance of Homebased Businesswomen—will go a long way toward helping to solve this problem across the nation.

Women at home should use this tool extensively. They should plan to make contacts with other women listed in the book and build them into their business schedules. They should develop business referrals through it to other women listed here, expecting the same in return. Women in local areas should visit each other and meet with each other regularly. They should spend much time sharing their feelings—their joys in business, their successes, their fears, and frustrations. The ephemeral social contact that corporate women have can be developed by women at home. Together with the independence and achievement of their own business, this activity should provide women working at home with opportunities for mental health and ego balance second to none.

Rosemary Summers
Beauty Resource Developer

177

Homebased Work and the Homebound Disabled: Creating Your Own Opportunity

Merrill D. Parra, Director, and Marcia Keizs, Assistant Director, External Education Program for the Homebound

❝I think people should know how hard it is for a legally blind person to make a place for himself or herself in the world. You see too much for the non-seeing people, and not enough for the seeing world!❞

Typist

The American Coalition of Citizens with Disabilities estimates that there are more than three million homebound disabled people in the United States. The figures are never conclusive, but the message is clear: for the most part, the homebound disabled remain a forgotten group closeted away in home or hospital, underserved by voluntary organizations or by government agencies.

In the area of education, the homebound disabled person is usually excluded from higher education, because most college administrators still think that in order to earn a college degree, you must physically attend classes on campus. In spite of this prevailing opinion, the External Education Program for the Homebound at Queensborough Community College in New York has, since 1973, provided students with an opportunity to pursue postsecondary education. A combination of telephone instruction, supportive services, and special equipment have made it possible for more than 250 homebound individuals to participate in the program since its inception.

Individuals who are confined to their homes seek education for the same reasons as others: personal enrichment, employability, and professional advancement. Yet, over the years, many have raised serious doubt about whether we can expect this population to become employed.

Recent data indicates that 50 to 60 percent of qualified Americans with disabilities are unemployed. This figure includes many who, discouraged by repeated rejections, devastating economic and pyschological disincentives, and offers of obviously unsuitable employment have retired to situations of relative dependency. Even when they are employed, as Bernard Posner, Executive Director of the President's Committee on Employment of the Handicapped reported in 1978, their incomes are meager. Approximately 85 percent of people with disabilities earn less than $7,000, and 52 percent of these make less than $2,000 per year. Current studies confirm that two-thirds of working age disabled adults exist near or below the poverty level. This presents a great challenge to the providers of social, educational, and vocational services.

These facts and others confirm that homebound persons' employability has been severely limited in the past, but the stories of our students begin to provide us with a new emerging picture of what the employment future can be for the disabled. There are a number of indicators that encourage fresh hope.

The recent enactment of federal legislation requiring the establishment of affirmative action programs and the resulting incorporation of some disabled individuals into the work force has helped to reduce many of the fears that business had with regard to this population. In fact, many firms, when surveyed, found that initial concerns about increased insurance rates, worker safety, or the need for expensive accommodations were unfounded. As a result, we are now seeing disabled individuals employed in capacities that five or ten years ago were unthinkable. Furthermore, recent changes in social security laws now allow disabled persons to experiment with work while at the same time continuing to receive a monthly Supplemental Security Income check. The Small Business Administration is also guaranteeing loans to disabled individuals who are interested in starting their own businesses.

On another front, the handicapped, especially the homebound handicapped, are being affected by expansion in the electronic medium. The age of computer technology is changing the work patterns of many people. More and more the computer and its technology have enabled us to change the traditional work site. In 1975, nearly 2.6 million Americans worked at home according to the U.S. Census Bureau. The rising trend in telecommuting is made possible by the growing sophistication of the computer industry. Though telecommuting has not caught on everywhere, several corporations have started to offer this prospect to a variety of people who, for one reason or another, prefer to work at home. This possibility provides homebound persons with a real alternative to high-cost transportation.

Another factor encouraging homebased work is the acute shortage of workers in certain skilled areas and the burgeoning cost of space. Consequently, personnel managers are turning to previously untapped sources to meet the growing demand for people with office skills.

These changes are already altering the employment opportunities for qualified homebound disabled persons in such industries as publishing, communications, and data processing. Neither the disability nor the inability to travel will prevent the qualified homebound disabled person from working. What is needed now is training that will ultimately allow the disabled person to improve his economic circumstances, making him or her independent of governmental ties.

The women whose profiles constitute the remainder of this essay are typical of the kind of women who have passed through the Queensborough's Homebound Program and of many women—able-bodied or

66My decision to work at home started when my first child was born and after I was diagnosed as having Systemic Lupus Erythematosus.... Having two small children and a disability, I find it difficult to have a regular work schedule. My special interest in art, however, keeps me working from three to five hours of studio work every day.99

Craftsperson

disabled—throughout America. Like their able-bodied counterparts, work for them is not merely an option; it is an economic necessity. Being at home for them also is a necessity, not a social choice, since the nature of their disabilities prevents them from moving freely in the marketplace. The women presented here are not, however, homogeneous. They are quite individualistic and are at varying points of acceptance of their disabilities as well as at varying levels of career pursuit. Because of the complexities involved, some are ready to go public, while others feel that some caution must still be exercised.

Eileen Anglia (a pseudonym) spent the first thirty years of her life as an active, engaged person. Nine years ago she was raising two children and running her own interior design company, but life collapsed for her in 1973, when polymiositis struck; thereafter, she became bed-ridden and isolated. Her active life was considerably reduced. In time Eileen realized that her illness would not go away. Since it would persist, how could she adjust to it?

Eileen decided that she had to modify her expectations and her life. At first she tried to improve her mind by reading on her own. Then she tried New York State-sponsored independent study. After a year, her frustration grew; she really wanted a more structured academic setting in which to grow.

She enrolled in the Homebound Program and found her years at Queensborough rewarding and enriching. An excellent student, she will graduate in 1983 from Barnard with a B.A. degree and is already making plans to explore a homebased career, for though she can function well in the limited environs of her home, she cannot travel unassisted. She may continue to work in the area of editing and proofreading which she now does on a part-time basis for a large publishing house.

Mary Otruba's home business bears her name. It is an office management business which offers a broad range of office services to a select group of clients in the Great Neck, N.Y., area. Starting her business through advertising in local papers, she first attracted a number of small business persons who were starting their own businesses while working at a job. With growth and expansion, she finds that her business is attracting larger and larger organizations with a wider variety of work.

Today, Mary singlehandedly runs an office that offers services to her clients, who represent groups of homeowners and property owners of varying types. The services include mail and correspondence, legal-secretarial work, payroll, taxes, bookkeeping, and accounting. Mary puts in some thirty to forty hours of work per week and from time to time hires her children on a part-time basis. As her children grow up and move away from home, she is considering the necessity of hiring outside help.

Mary sees the growth of her business as a real challenge. Although she is often tempted with seductive offers to come back to an office away from home, she knows that that is not a workable option, since her disability, a collagen disorder, is characterized by easy exhaustion and short endurance. Working at home and being her own boss allows for flexible scheduling of work shifts as well as the hassle-free opportunity to take a rest whenever she needs one.

Again, her experience with the Homebound Program has opened up new areas of competency for her. She has recently obtained a new piece of office equipment, a computer, which she will be applying especially to the accounting segment of her business.

Though Mary sometimes laments the lonesomeness of the homebased work (she misses the social atmosphere of a bustling office), she nevertheless is exuberant about being her own boss and working at her own pace.

"I find prayer and maintaining a positive attitude make all the difference. Rather than seeing a situation as a terrible problem, I choose to see it as a challenging opportunity."

Nutrition Consultant

To cut down on alienation, Mary has obtained a real estate license and is affiliated with a group of local realtors. This takes her out of her home office for a few hours a week; and thus she fulfills a need to share ideas and socialize with colleagues and clients.

Laura Donato (a pseudonym) is a new student of the Homebound Program. She brings to it a lifetime of experiences, abilities, and skills.

Six years ago, as the result of a divorce, she became responsible for supporting herself. She suffers from a neuromuscular dysfunction, a highly unpredictable condition which leaves her fatigued and weak.

Laura is currently engaged in two homebased ventures. Starting where she was and with what she had, she accepted the job of housing and supervising two mentally disabled female adults. When she entered into this arrangement her own disability was less severe, and she spent many hours providing care, supervision, and companionship for these two persons. In the beginning it was quite difficult. Today, with her diminishing strength, she wonders whether she would assume such a task again. Laura's second venture is that of proofreader for a local commercial printer. She started this about a year and a half ago in response to a local ad. She picks up the work at 5:00 P.M. each evening and starts to work immediately, working straight through until it is finished. At 8:30 A.M. the next morning the work is returned and reviewed by a supervisor.

Laura is paid an hourly wage, with semiannual reviews, vacation and sick days, and an opportunity to join a major medical plan if she works thirty or more hours for three months consecutively. She sometimes works as much as forty to fifty hours per week. Most of 1982, however, was lean. She took that in stride since her health took a turn for the worse. Now she hires a local person to pick up and deliver her work. For a while she also hired a local teenager to help with certain clerical functions so she could save her meager strength to do the actual proofreading. Work is picking up again and thankfully, Laura is able to do it, but there is terrific pressure to finish the work each night. She compares herself to a fighter in training: each day she must conserve her strength and nap in the afternoon so she can work that night.

Laura makes as much money as many more physically able persons, but it's still not good enough. With rapidly increasing expenses her income must increase also and in such a way that she can earn more money and expend less effort doing it.

These women are like other women, both able-bodied and disabled, working from home by building on the abilities they have. We hope their profiles will encourage and inspire others.

For information about a homebound college program in your state, please write to the authors at:

Queensborough Community College
Homebound Program
56th Ave. & Springfield Blvd.
Bayside, N.Y. 11364

> 66 The flexibility of working at home is wonderful—and due to a partial disability (hip injury) is just perfect for me. 99
>
> Poet

The Woman Artist and the Home Studio: Pros and Cons

Lynn Miller, Author of *Lives and Works: Talks with Women Artists*

> **❝I like working for myself, especially at home. I am not bored and find my social contacts with other artists and art-related people at the ever-present art openings and panel discussions and art happenings. ❞**
>
> **Weaver**

For some women artists, the medium they choose reflects the need or wish to work at home. When space limits are imposed, fabric arts, such as quilting and other traditional or portable media, provide flexibility and compatibility with working at home. The recent return by many women artists to traditional arts, in both form and medium, illustrates how far we have come toward accepting women's traditional arts (weaving, basket-making, quilting, and others) as fine arts and as valuable and valid contributions and how women artists, after sojourning in the world outside, can learn to become comfortable with traditional forms and have the security to do so if they choose. Work patterns vary from individual to individual and also in a given woman's life over the course of time. As Faith Ringgold has said:

> I was always painting. When the kids were very little, I did water-colors, because I could carry my watercolors around in a little package. I could go out in the country, use paper and put it away easily. . . . [By the time] I had graduated, had my master's degree, the kids were getting older; they were eight or nine. If I was to be an artist, I was going to have to make a studio in my house. I knew I had to take my art out of the closet. I was separated from my first husband, so I was living only with the kids. . . . I came back and I opened up a studio. I really loved it. . . . [After remarrying] and we moved, . . . I set up my studio in the back. Actually there's no back here but just a corner of the apartment.

For many women in circumstances similar to Faith Ringgold's, the home studio is ideal. For others it is a necessity. For still others, at a certain point in life, working in the home setting becomes frankly impossible for a variety of reasons. Combining home and studio for an artist with small children and not much money is a necessity fraught with the perils of the demands those children make. As photographer Amy Stromsten poignantly points out in *Lives and Works*:

> Since I've been in New Jersey I've met so many women who apologize for not working and not being feminists, and it's so silly, because

someone has to raise children. That's also a great joy. I have gotten more pleasure out of my daughter than out of my work. I love her; she's delightful; and I have a great time with her. I take her with me on trips all the time. She doesn't like photography very much. I'm glad I have her. It's very hard, though. For instance, I have to spend half of what I make on child care; I always have that expense. . . .

You must have good child care. I did have her in day-care centers when she was little, and it was very bad. Disastrous. So I finally settled on what's comforting to me, to have someone live here and take care of her. After she's ten maybe I won't need that help any more. In her early years I felt that having live-in help was one way I could feel I wasn't making her life worse. With children you go through all kinds of problems, and you can never be free. You have to worry about them all the time. When I go into the darkroom, she can't open the door because it will ruin the prints. . . . So it's very isolating for her. But it's worked out. I feel that it's OK.

Judith Wadia
Artist
Photographer: Daniel Habib

Work underway cannot always be interrupted. On the other hand, the parent is there, available to the child, for better or for worse. Working at home often means fitting one's art into a corner where it won't get in the way.

A home studio is convenient and reduces the time and effort invested in going to work, which can then be directed into making art. Living and painting in the same space allows great independence and an integration of life and work.

An important issue, that of the worker at home taking herself seriously and being taken seriously by others, is compounded in a particular way for women artists who have home studios, since art making is not viewed as work by the society at large. Many women I've spoken to feel that both in order to take their own work seriously and to have their work life as artists respected by their families it may become necessary to separate home and studio, to compartmentalize the private, family aspects of their lives away from the creative, art-making aspects.

One reason is simply practical: for some painters the size of the work may become a problem in home studios, which sometimes cannot accommodate very large canvases. For others, care may be necessary in separating family from art materials, for health and safety reasons as well as aesthetic ones.

There are no ideal solutions to the woman artist's need for a good work place, no easy choices. The Soho loft, where many New York City artists live and work, is often glamorized by contemporary legend, but it is after all just a home studio. The good thing is that it is in New York, a major, if not *the* major, center for the arts. The suburban woman artist working at home may feel isolated from other artists, but this is more a function of cultural geography than of whether she is at home or not. In both instances, networking informally with other women artists or through an organization like a Women's Caucus for Art chapter reduces the isolation.

Ultimately, of course, each woman artist makes her choice of work place based on economic and family reality—what she wants and needs as an artist, as a family member, and as an individual with a certain work style, balanced against what she can and can't afford. For many women, the home studio is the ideal combination at those various points in their lives when they want or need to be at home and still continue to work as active artists.

❝Success = strokes. I find it very satisfying that people will part with their hard-earned dollars, in these inflated times, to own items produced by my humble hands.❞

Artist

Rural Homebased Industry

Ingrid Fabbe Bauer, Administrator, Futures Network

❝We have a family business—my sister does the bookkeeping, my brother does the training. A business from the farm is like any other until a foal is born. That is a very special time when we can fully appreciate the rewards and challenges.❞

Horse Breeder

I've been studying the needs of rural women for four years. My interest stemmed from my personal experience as a single parent living on an island in Puget Sound, WA, two hours by ferry from the mainland. It was difficult for me to support my family. Not only were the available jobs low paying and often seasonal, they were also boring, dead-end jobs that provided no room for personal growth and creativity.

I wanted to improve my life situation, but I also wanted to stay on the island with my twin girls. Evergreen State College awarded bachelor degrees for certain off-campus experiential learning situations and approved of my work-study plan with the State Department of Social and Health Services (Public Assistance Office). I started to earn credit for my work with low-income rural women in my job as a clerk typist.

These women were just like me! They lacked access to good-paying jobs but did not lack incentive. We formed a small group and worked together on self-esteem building, career counseling, and job-search skills. We started to feel good about our futures. One of the major breakthroughs was the recognition that skills learned in the home were transferable into the work place (budgeting, time management, planning, etc.). When the class ended, the participants went looking for work.

What a disappointment! There were no jobs. Employers refused to recognize the transferability of homemaking skills into the marketplace. There was sex discrimination in the nontraditional, good-paying trades. The available jobs were the typical *women's* jobs—secretary, hairdresser, clerk, and salesperson. None of them paid enough for the single parent welfare recipients to get off welfare even if they worked full time.

It was then I realized that if women in rural areas wanted to make enough money to be financially independent, they would need to create work for themselves and work out of their homes or through cooperatives. This way they could manage their families and make a living as well. Thus began my study of the feasibility of homebased industry for rural women.

It seemed important to find out what rural women thought about homebased industry, so I sent letters to the editors of many rural magazines and newsletters asking women to write me. I asked for information on existing homebased industries as well as the need for training to start such a business. I was flooded with mail!

"I design and sell patterns," a woman from Montana wrote. "My husband and I build made-to-order greenhouses," wrote a couple from Oregon. The variety of homebased businesses was amazing: free-lance writing, folk-art painting, stained glass and pottery, teaching, a mail-order women's self-help program, houseplant doctor, services to the home-bound, drying and selling herbs, weaving, spinning and wool dying, making instructional yoga tapes, basket weaving, writing books on oral histories, making bridles and saddles, and making dulcimers.

Four basic patterns of business development emerged. Women taught what they knew, learned a craft and sold the product, performed a service, or developed a hobby into a vocation. Marketing seemed to be the major difficulty in the rural area. The most successful marketing techniques were getting mail orders through advertising, use of major craft catalogs such as the *Goodfellow Catalog of Wonderful Things,* consignment sales at stores in nearby towns, and the development of cooperatives with their own storefront.

Cooperatives often serve as an intermediary step between women forming their own businesses and the larger, more hierarchical work place. They can provide a supportive atmosphere, access to bulk-order prices, shared profits, and flexibility. Since time contribution in a cooperative is shared, members have the time to develop their own businesses while earning some money through the cooperative. Cooperatives such as HOME (Homeworkers Organized for More Employment—in Hancock County, ME) can even give women a means of earning money by teaching them a craft and selling their products. They provide a safe environment in which one can learn business skills while offering such support services as an answering service, advertising flyers, business cards, and a display area. Most important for women living in isolated areas, cooperatives provide communal warmth and caring.

I received many letters from women who wanted to work independently in their homes but did not know where to begin. "I feel strongly that there is a great need for exactly the type of cottage industry you described in your letter," said a woman from Farmington, ME. Another woman from Troy, KY responded, "If I could make a little money from a home business or projects, maybe I could stay home with my newborn child."

It occurred to me that rural women wanted more training than was presently available to them. Why not get cooperative extension and other rural service providers to develop workshops on career counseling, skills development, small business management, marketing, and cooperative development? I contacted the Department of Agriculture, 4-H, church groups, and the Rural Electrification Committee to determine the amount of emphasis being given to rural women's business needs in their research and development programs. These organizations are just beginning to realize that women are interested in more than homemaking skills. The economy is forcing many women, single and married, farm women and small town women, into the labor force. These women have to carry the double burden of maintaining the home and working outside of it at low-paying jobs. Rural women are further burdened by isolation and transportation problems. Rural service organizations want to be more responsive to the changing roles of women and are thankful to receive recommendations and input. I suggest that rural women write and telephone their cooperative extension agent, 4-H leaders, home economists, community colleges, rural electrification cooperatives, and church groups, requesting workshops on subjects that will help them meet their economic needs.

Homebased industry is a natural solution for rural women. It overcomes the isolation and transportation problems and maintains the balance of the family. Rural women share a desire to earn an income, remain in their rural areas, and be independent. Homebased industries provide women with that opportunity.

❝Our business is located in a rural area in a country setting, not a commercial area. We owe our retail success to unusual, high-quality craft which people are willing to go out of their way to find. Visiting our shop is a pleasant occasion.❞

Craftsperson

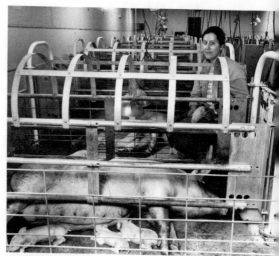

Kathleen Barbier
Pork Producer
Photographer: © Terri P. Tepper,
1979

Refugee Women: The Laotians

Sylvia Haydash, Director, CARING, Inc.

> **66** I feel that success is mainly measured in excellent service and pride in how you do what you do. I do not turn work over to a client unless I am satisfied that it is my best. If *you* know you're good, then you can tell potential clients that in all honesty. **99**

Bookkeeper

They escaped from poverty, war, hunger—from large cities and small villages—bringing with them the clothes on their backs, children of all ages and sizes, and little marketable skills for an English-speaking society.

They came with their dreams of a new future for their families—the proverbial thought of streets paved with gold and plenty of everything for everyone. They were not quite prepared to enter our new world after months or even years of waiting and soon found that if they don't work, their poverty in America will be more severe than what they faced in Indochina.

They escaped from firing guns, only to be frightened by cars that backfire and rambunctious Fourth of July celebrations. They can relate in detail the times they had nothing to eat or drink and survived with a strong determination, only to find the cost of survival in America is dear. They can't fish without a license; they can't garden without permission; and the fascination with electricity ends with the reality of the first bill. They are dead-ended in a country that can't understand them because of their strange language and different culture. The large number of children in their families, a sign of prosperity in Laos, is where they place their hopes, for somehow the children can make sense out of English, understand the monetary system, decipher labels in the market, and acculturate with American life very quickly. The women will take any job so that these children will have a better life.

The first English phrase they master for survival is, "I need a job." They are willing to do anything, but their marketable skills are minimal. They need day care, orientation to so many American products, and much more English tutoring. Job placement for many is difficult at best.

Most of the Laotian women were taught how to weave and embroider at a very early age. Their colorful dress and traditional needlework have always caught the eye of travelers to their country, and it is quite common to see women selling embroideries along with fruits and vegetables in Indochina. We had been so busy trying to westernize these women that they tried to efface their culture in the process. It was up to us to determine if any of the Laotians in our community had this talent.

At a Laotian wedding ceremony the culture emerged. The women came dressed in intricately embroidered silk and cotton skirts—the stitches more even than machine work and every repeat of the intricate pattern a mirror of the previous one, without a missing stitch. They proudly displayed their handiwork, and it was obvious that there was great value in their culture. In their minds, stored along with the jumbled ABC's, how to clean house, and how to use a washing machine, were the patterns and the knowledge of weaving silk. Where did one begin?

We started with a donation from CARING Inc., our organization to acculturate the refugees. (CARING is an acronym for Community Action toward Refugees for Introduction to New Growth and is located at 880 Sudley Road, Manassos, VA 22110.) A local department store was closing out a line of embroidery thread and gave us a good price on an estimated 800 skeins, which by actual count became over 1,700. An initial purchase of ten yards of count cloth completed the business, and we were ready to start making samples. Once orders started coming in, it was hoped the women would start their own businesses. How naive is the entrepreneur with a good idea but no sense of corporation!

Every woman wanted to get in on the act. They chose their own colors, design, and product. It was to be their business, using their ideas. There were times that it seemed as if this might have been a mistake, because, in the initial stages of embroidery, the colors seemed to clash and were so much brighter than most Americans prefer; but the finished products were truly works of art. The designs were unlike any known in America, and the beauty of the designs spoke of the beauty of these women. The colors that clashed initially were now blended artfully in the finished product.

Laotian Women
Photographer: Marilyn Muse

Marie Farmer, an English as a second language teacher, volunteered to teach the women how to finish edges and to make the product more marketable. We envisioned pillows and table runners for the home, along with bell pulls and place mats. The positive aspect of this tutoring was that the women who took advantage of the sewing class were able to find work in a sewing factory in the area. They are cooperating with child care and transportation, and many positive results can be seen. That still didn't solve the embroidery problem, however. An appeal was put out to a voluntary agency to find someone with marketing know-how and free time. No one volunteered, but through word of mouth and displays of embroidery in churches and at women's meetings, something is starting to happen.

Colage is a group of businesswomen who would like to market the Laotian women's embroidery. It has designed several western suits and dresses with the extraordinary and graceful counted cross-stitch and hopes to successfully market a line of women's apparel. If a market is not found for this work, it is felt that the art form will be lost, for Colage has noticed that many Laotian women are beginning to embroider prestamped American designs in the hope of selling these craft pieces. It is difficult for them to understand that the intrinsic value of their art lies in its freedom of line and color rather than their skill in embroidering.

Quite apart from the immediate concerns of placing the clothing is the need to recognize the depressed state of the garment market. Colage hopes that one or two outlets will be found for these clothes and that design adjustments can be made to satisfy both the artisans and the buyers. We are not giving up our visions of the women's ability to do it on their own. Now, as this is written in fall 1982, there is a lack of sufficient knowledge of how to start their own corporation, although we are learning ways to help them. We are trying to preserve their culture, so much of which is evident in their needlework. Given time, money, and knowledge, these women will also be a part of America and the melting pot of talent. They have forgotten the past, struggle with today, and have set their sights on the future.

At Wit's End

Erma Bombeck, Syndicated Columnist
Reprinted by permission of Erma Bombeck
Field Syndicate

❝Sometimes, I torture myself by wondering what it must be like to fill a wastebasket you don't have to empty, and the peace of not having to let a dog in and out 175 times a day.❞

Erma Bombeck

The President and I are the only two people in this country I know who work from our homes.

He's got the best of it. Surrounded by all that security, having a desk that locks, and no one ringing his chimes in the middle of the day to sell him pastry brushes and lip gloss.

Oh sure, he has his share of interruptions, but does he ever lift his phone and discover someone has entwined a Popsicle stick in the cord? Does he ever get involved in a high-level phone conversation and have to excuse himself to turn the timer off on the ham? Is he ever in the midst of drafting a piece of legislation that will change the history of the world and hear a yell from the other end of the house, "We're out of toilet paper!"

The big problem with working from your home is no one treats you like a professional. Pest control men shuffle in and out spraying insecticide on my feet, children draw faces on my calendar and color my roll of stamps yellow, and at least once a day, my husband calls with instructions to "Go to the garage. Turn the power mower over on its back. On the bottom, just under the right rotary blades, is a serial number. Copy it down and call it in to the repair shop so they'll know what they're dealing with. When you're out picking up my cleaning, you can pick up the part."

As a humor writer I can only reflect on the flashes of wit that might have been had I only had a typewriter with set margins, paper clips that weren't strung into a necklace, a dictionary with all the vowels, and a pen and pencil by the phone for messages.

Sometimes, I torture myself by wondering what it must be like to fill a wastebasket you don't have to empty, and the peace of not having to let a dog in and out 175 times a day.

But the real kicker is convincing your friends and family you are really working. The telephone calls that begin, "You busy? So, what's happening? Still working for that crazy lady who won't let you go to lunch or play tennis? So, let her fire you. Ha. Ha."

Like the President, I too have my Camp David. It's calm, serene, and private. I tell no one I'm going there. I just slip off with my work and sometimes just a few hours makes all the difference in the world. When I return, things are in perspective, and I am once again ready to do battle with the steady stream of interruptions.

The IRS is questioning my expenditure of a new shower curtain for my office, but what do they know?

Erma Bombeck
Syndicated Columnist
Photographer: Rod Moyer

The Writer

Roslyn Bernstein, Free-lance Writer

Several years ago I attended a round table discussion given by five well-known free-lance writers, all women. They faced an audience of perhaps 200 aspiring writers and their alleged mission was to tell all—to reveal the deep, dark secrets involved in becoming a successful writer.

66 There are so many things I want to say about life and love, history, and relationships. I'm able to transfer experiences and memories to paper so that others can share them. Before my first novel was completed, I had begun random jottings on two more. **99**

Writer

The first four speakers did what one might expect them to do. They gave lively, anecdotal accounts of the ups and downs of their careers: their triumphs, punctuated by lots of applause; their catastrophes, followed by tears and handkerchiefs; the story that almost was; the stolen idea; the article that was bought, but which never appeared.

The fifth speaker, however, took another tack. She began with words that I will never forget. "Every time that I sit down at my typewriter," she said, "no matter how many stories I have sold or how many checks I have received for my by-line, I always face a *blank page.*"

Blank page. Philosopher John Locke's *tabula rasa,* empty space that is both inviting and intimidating. The place where every writer begins— the place where every homebased writer begins too. Long before the official query letter and the phone calls to the editor, long before the marketing process, comes the idea, the thinking, and the creating.

For both the beginning free-lancer and the established one, the initial burden is always the same: generating an exciting idea, researching what has been done within the last two years, shaping the idea to suit the readership of a given magazine, and allowing for a three-to-six-month lead time before publication.

Of course, ideas have many potential sources. A two-inch news brief in a local newsletter on federal aid for artists yielded a story I wrote for *New York* magazine on CETA (Comprehensive Employment and Training Act) Funding for the Arts. An animated conversation at a cocktail party regarding changes in college students' career patterns resulted in "The Class of '82" for *The Village Voice.* A casual remark overhead on an uptown bus produced a little feature on a previously unheard-of Soho arts event. There is no one source for ideas, and the free-lancer must read widely and listen carefully. The two go hand in hand.

Many years ago when I worked on staff for a national magazine, the editor-in-chief required all editors to submit a list of ten to fifteen original ideas every Friday afternoon—or else. It was serious business. Editors sat behind closed doors, rummaging through newspapers and magazines, reading books, racking their brains in the competitive scramble to come up with something terrific, something unique. In the end, the best ideas were assigned to the brightest free-lance writers, all very established.

Times have changed since the sixties. Magazine staffs have shrunk, and many publications are now largely staff-written. The tables have turned, and most ideas flow from writer to editor and not from editor to writer.

Dawn Sangrey
Writer
Photographer: © Terri P. Tepper, 1978

Special Reports

❝I feel that one of the main difficulties encountered is that the profession is not taken seriously enough. If I am only able to devote part time to writing, it is no less a profession. It is not expendable time that can be used for other, household purposes when they arise. ... This is not to say that I can abandon the household; after all, I am the primary 'housekeeper.' But I must take the time, every day, to write: when the time is best (for me, first thing in the morning), daily, trying to avoid interruptions that can wait.**❞**

Writer

The burden now falls upon the free-lancer to make up her own list of ideas and to update it constantly. My own manila folder has a simple title, "Ideas in Progress," and it includes lists, clippings, quotations, etc. Hopefully, it contains the germ of my next story in case the one that I am presently writing falls through. Once a week, or at the very least every two weeks, it needs weeding, like my summer vegetable garden. Although you run the risk of being stereotyped, the beginning free-lancer is wise to develop a specialization, some area in which you are an expert.

Once you have your idea, where do you go from there? To an editor? Not necessarily. For the novice, the better route is to do research, to build up a small clipping file on your subject, and to do perhaps one or two interviews in search of quotes. A lot of work, you might say, especially since you have not yet contacted an editor and determined whether there is serious interest in your proposal. Not really. In my experience as a free-lancer the legwork pays off. It alters the nature of your query letter because the more you know about your subject, the more you are able to sell it to someone else.

If you are thinking of pitching a story to a national woman's magazine on the obsolescence of the secretary, for example, it really helps to have handy statistics from the Labor Department and a quote from the president of a national secretarial association. It can make all the difference between a vague, say-nothing query letter and one that works. For the novice writer who often has few or no clippings to enclose, it can perform miracles.

A basic rule is to send your query to the managing editor or to the articles editor and to keep it succinct, one or two typed pages. Your focus is on your idea, with a couple sentences of biography thrown in as a coda. If the story has visual appeal, accompanying photos can help sell it, too. The worst query letter that you can possibly write is one that merely offers a title without background documentation or some indication of the story's drawing power for the publication's readers. Spend a great deal of time on your letters. They should be intelligent, well-written, and compact. And, lest you forget, always keep a copy!

What happens next? Sometimes, alas, nothing. You wait and wait. You wonder whether your letter has been filed in a wastebasket or ever received. You wonder whether you should write again or call.

My own advice is to call after waiting at least two or three weeks. A friendly follow-up call asking whether there is any word on your proposal is entirely in order. If you are lucky, you may be told that your idea is interesting and that it has been passed on to Associate or Assistant Editor Y, whom you should now contact. If you are not, you may be told that they are not interested this time around but that you should keep trying them. The hardest message of all is a bare "No thanks!"

Let's suppose that you have captured their attention and are now working with Editor Y. If you are a complete beginner, you may be asked to write the piece on speculation with no promise of payment if things don't work out. Payments are exceedingly variable. A friend of mine who does interviews and feature articles for a local newspaper on the North Fork of Long Island receives $25 to $50 for her pieces, which often run over 1,000 words. Most magazines pay a flat rate, not by the word, and the fledgling free-lancer can expect anywhere from $200–$500 for a story of about 1,500-2,500 words. With a few clippings and a string of writing credits, you can probably command at least double this rate ($400–$800) and you will most probably be offered a "kill fee" of about 25 percent of the full payment if they don't accept your manuscript. Not much, but at least enough to cover basic expenses. Experienced writers can receive as much as $1,000–$2,000 for a 3,000–3,500-word article.

You should receive a letter of assignment from your editor even if you are only writing on speculation. Such a letter can be a helpful entree when arranging difficult interviews. Executives and public relations people understand the power of publicity and it helps to say, "I'm writing an article for *New York* magazine or *Family Circle*."

You are now "on assignment." Some basic rules: do more interviews than you think you will need. Learn as much about your subject as you possibly can. Look beyond the obvious for the earthworms hiding under the rock. Try to set a reasonable timetable for yourself and, above all, follow it.

The pulls of family are always there. As a widow and single parent, I wear my writer's hat for short, intense periods of time. I am forever juggling full-time mothering, full-time college teaching, and my home-based free-lance writing.

I have trained myself to endure noise although I much prefer quiet. I have a big desk, which an artist friend helped me build, lots of book shelves, two white file cabinets, and a well-used electric typewriter. My only other investment over the years has been $20 for an invaluable business card which I designed myself.

It is never easy to write and it is certainly harder when there are numerous distractions, but my children have learned to accept the sound of my typewriter as the normal background music in our home. As often as I can, I try to involve them in my work by letting them listen to my first drafts and by asking for their opinions.

You have to be determined and, I might add, tough, to write. Rejections are hard to take; they feel like personal criticism, especially in the beginning. After a while you develop calluses and understand that it is not always your fault when things don't work out. Another magazine scoops your story. An expected interview just doesn't pan out. Your original idea proves a bit faulty. New regulations make your article dated. The magazine has a backlog of materials, making the space for your Christmas feature never available. Rejection slips, like pink notices on the job, tend to be short, cold, and ever so incomplete.

My advice is to toss them into another folder, far from Ideas in Progress, and keep writing. Most of all, try to build a working relationship with a number of editors so that you can continue to test new ideas.

I confess that when a poem of mine appears in a small poetry journal I expect no pay and am happy. The satisfaction lies in being in print, in being read. But in the business of writing, I agree with the great Dr. Samuel Johnson, who once wrote: "No man, but a blockhead, ever wrote, except for money."

With one correction, however. I amend Dr. Johnson to read: no *woman* either.

66 To work and create by communicating visions to others through words and to pass on new concepts and ideas are rewards in themselves. **99**

Writer

66 I've lost the buzz and the relationships of the 9 to 5'er. When I pick up the phone in the quiet house to do an interview, my voice sounds so loud to me, like I'm waking up the world. **99**

Writer

The Networking Process

Alina Novak, Founder of Networks

> 66 I am part of a five-women group called Third Generation. We all do different types of artwork or sewing, so there is not inner competition, but we are a support group; we share booth fees at shows, and yet are independent of each other. ... I like the collective; it stops a lot of whistling in the dark. 99

Craftsperson

Networks are a new kind of group, structured in a formal or informal way, whose main goal is to facilitate the networking process. This process can be defined as the planned acquisition of contacts for mutual support, the exchange of information, and the transaction of business.

Over the past five years, the concept of networking has been popularized by women who have emulated the good-ole-boys' networks. The good-ole-boys have met, played, and studied in the right Ivy League schools, on team sports, and in exclusive, all-male clubs from childhood to adulthood. In contrast, women have only recently begun to use the process. Whether they have joined existing networks or set up their own, women are meeting each other as adults and trying to experience the team and club atmosphere. Although the experience of connecting is predominantly restricted to other women, men are part of the networking process.

This process is a crucial part of business success. Knowing the right people at the right time is a skill that can be developed and maintained. Successful men in business have always known how to use each other to get ahead. As women move up in business, they are expected to develop connections. In fact, the process is often so informal that men are unaware of women's historical isolation and assume that women are connecting when, in fact, they aren't.

It has been said that girls play with other girls because they like them, while boys play with other boys because they bring skill to the game. The good-ole-boys' networks that endure are based on need and skill rather than on popularity. The skills that are prized in boys' sports are part of the goal of winning. Through these games, boys absorb the art of goal setting. In the past, girls usually lacked this experience while growing up. As women, they often have had a hard time setting goals other than personal ones. The business environment demands clear goal setting, as does the process of networking.

As women have made decided strides in their progress over the last decade, they have become aware of the powerful results men achieve through networking. In addition, the enriching experience of women supporting women through consciousness-raising groups and in assertiveness training has been a precedent to women's networking. In business, women are using the networking process in two ways. The formal route involves joining a network as a member who attends meetings, pays dues, and links up with other network members. The informal way is to individually set up one's own system of networking. Most men have done both; women are learning to do the same.

One of the primary ways that the process of informal networking can be activated is by exchanging business cards when meeting people on a one-to-one basis. For many women, getting business cards is an exercise in assertiveness because it means self-promotion. For others, it signifies creativity by designing one's own card and having it reflect one's profession or avocation.

Contacts made by trading business cards can be classified according to the nature of the contact, date, and place met, and anything else that might help identify the person. Often this is a game of odds; in the insurance business, the chances are that out of 100 cold calls, sixteen will visit with the insurance agent and one will buy an insurance product. These numbers are similar for the person who exchanges 100 cards at a convention or seminar. Perhaps a dozen of these new contacts will produce a lunch or dinner appointment. Depending on the exchange, one or two will become part of one's network.

The scheduling of lunch or breakfast has always been a favorite with businesspeople. Women are now regularly connecting and sometimes inviting a few people on a regular basis. These kinds of informal luncheon or breakfast groups are a way to network without setting up a formal organizational structure. Top-level women will often reserve a private dining room for a select group of women with whom they can meet to exchange ideas and lend support. By invitation only, these get-togethers provide a mentoring experience for the group. Also, the top-level woman acts as a role model.

Networking between men and women is often a function of the industry they are in. More and more men have supported women's networking as they have realized that it's an important ingredient to all business success.

So far, for the most part, the networking process has been developed and implemented by women seeking to better their chances in the business area where who you know is as important as what you know.

During the initial encounter, a number of questions are asked between the lines. What information might be exchanged? Can mutual support be developed? Is a business connection possible? How can we support each other? These and other questions are explored further in subsequent meetings. Further analysis will usually focus on where the contact fits in with respect to one's relative position. In other words, are you networking horizontally with a peer, vertically upward to a mentor/expert, or vertically downward to someone junior or less experienced than you?

Networking goals clarify the outcome. People network for a variety of reasons. One reason is to practice making contacts with people at all levels, somewhat in a random fashion. Others have a specific need to make connections around a particular project. This could be part of the exploration of a career change, running a political campaign, getting increased visibility to demonstrate executive skills, or just keeping up with office politics.

Somehow, setting a goal for one's networking is not enough. One must also estimate the correct mix of needed contacts. Most women want to network upward and find someone who will mentor and support their careers. Almost everyone finds the exchange with one's colleagues to be a crucial part of getting ahead. Oftentimes, peer support can make a difference in moving up. Leaders usually cultivate a following of supporters in addition to their relationships with peers and mentors.

The number of people one cultivates depends on many factors. Some situations foster networking for quantity. Sales and public relations are

> 66 I subscribe to the national trade journal *Sew Business,* and from that magazine, I obtain leads and information on trade markets and trade shows. I then joined the National Needlework Association, based in New York, and attend the markets they sponsor.... Attendance at the markets brings orders for my needlepoint designs and quilt patterns plus leads for features in national magazines, etc. 99

Needlepoint Designer

Special Reports

examples where knowing many people is paramount; however, it is in the quality of contacts that corporate payoffs begin to reach women. Finding a mentor or having the support of the right select few is a special kind of focus that women in particular need.

At this point, the person interested in networking on the individual level should set up a special file of index cards for the 100 most important contacts in her career and personal life. If there are not 100, start cultivating them. These 100 contacts should be broken down, using a management system of prioritizing, which simply means to establish groups by priority.

The first group should contain all the contacts that you consider vital over the next twelve months. Examples would include people with whom you work closely, your mentor, key contacts, personal friends, and family. The second group is made up of those people who are part of your two-to-five-year career plan or long-term networking strategy. This category would include past supervisors, members of your social club and professional organizations, and acquaintances. The third includes a miscellaneous classification for anyone who doesn't fit either of the first two groups. Your lawyer, neighbors, or country club friends might fit this category. Finally, the last group is made up of enemies and people who are not to be trusted. These contacts are often dangerous but necessary and need to be handled carefully. Sometimes, an alliance is possible.

Once you have defined who you know in addition to what you know, you'll be ready to consider who's who and which way is up. The next step is to develop a networking plan of action that takes into account your time commitments, budget, and lifestyle. An exercise listing the ten people with whom you spend most of your time, either face-to-face or on the phone, can be revealing. Good networkers are disciplined and organized; they add contacts as well as discard them.

Women often are concerned about using people. Confusion exists with respect to the difference in using versus abusing someone. Often, the mutual support of other women can make it easier to clarify the situation. Networking is not "making nice." It's not necessarily being friends. Sometimes friendships develop, but not as a rule. It's not even necessary that you like the person; respecting someone is the key. Using each other is a win/win situation for both.

Part of the networking process is to identify one's financial emergency network. Here, a list is made of the people you could call out of the blue for financial assistance or, better yet, a list of the people who would be willing to extend credit in a crisis.

Another important network to consider is that of people who can help you make your next career move. In this case, developing a strategic plan is a must. Office politics, timing, and support from the right people can pay off. In fact, the hidden job market has been estimated at 70 to 90 percent of the jobs above entry level. The good-ole-boys' network usually manages to corner the market on filling these jobs. Women are trying to be part of this inner circle to whatever degree possible and are setting up parallel good-ole-girls' networks.

Most men respond to money, power, or fame in their quest for success; until the last few years, women did not react well to these goals. In seminars, women pick money and power, 50 and 40 percent respectively, with fame trailing at 10 percent.

The identification of people in our networks who are driven by money is valuable, especially if one then presents ideas to them with a bottom-line orientation. Power-hungry people should be approached with a different agenda; those seeking fame hear another drummer.

Success in making contacts can depend on your networking style. Here you should analyze the way you sell yourself. If you wanted to meet a few new people in the next month, would you call, write, use a referral, or approach them face to face? Some people always call; others write. Those who use others to introduce them are different from those who would walk right up and introduce themselves.

Since networking is a two-way street, researching someone's networking style is invaluable. There are phone people, and there are those who you'll never see unless the right person introduces you. Others respond best to something in writing. Finally, there are those who prefer a face-to-face approach.

Relative strength plays an important part in deciding one's strategy. It also helps to know how that profession or industry operates. Proper networking necessitates a firm grip on the goal of the encounter.

Since goals are essential to the success of any endeavor, you must ask yourself these questions: Is your goal reasonable? What about the timing? Has the preparation been adequate? What are the risks?

The networking process assumes an agenda. People who practice networking soon refine the topics they want to discuss. Gossip, trade secrets, and anything politically suicidal is usually avoided. Personal confidences are also a no-no.

One way that you can prepare is by making a list of ten subjects to discuss and then pair up with a buddy to role play. Advancing the role play to bragging, each person talks for five minutes nonstop about herself and why she is successful. The experience of bragging is foreign to many women who have a restricted task orientation and prohibitions against bragging about themselves. Men often socialize where bragging is part of the process. Too often, however, the listeners are women. Some executive search people feel that anyone unable to brag about their accomplishments for fifteen minutes will not get the job.

Studies show that women have not been socialized to brag or promote themselves. Their self-confidence often is unrealistically low. A support network usually helps in raising a woman's self-esteem.

Knowing and using basic self-help survival skills are what networking is all about. Knowing someone from whom one can get support is vital. Exchanging information hones one's communication skills, and transacting business creates a successful climate for winning.

Finally, setting up one's own informal, individual network involves setting goals, assessing one's contacts, and developing a networking plan of action.

THE WOMAN'S NEWSPAPER OF PRINCETON

A Woman's Place Is Where She Wants To Be

VOLUME 1, NUMBER 1   © 1982 The Woman's Newspaper of Princeton   MARCH 1, 1982

Arri Parker
Publisher

The National Alliance of Homebased Businesswomen

66My membership in the New York Chapter of NAHB has been very valuable—I've met interesting and vital women who share some of the same problems and successes that I have, and I find that our meetings are lively, interesting, and fun.**99**

Manufacturer

The National Alliance of Homebased Businesswomen is growing at a remarkable rate. Why? Because this nonprofit, professional organization is dedicated to the needs of homebased businesspeople who have long been in search of a support group of their own. In addition to a very active network among its members, the Alliance encourages economic, professional, and personal growth for those who work from home.

Members now exist in forty-eight states of our country, and chapters are constantly developing. If its present growth is any indication of its future potential, the Alliance will be one of the most influential organizations in this country in the years ahead.

Peter Rodino, chairman of the Judiciary Committee of the House of Representatives, recently wrote to us saying that the formation of the National Alliance

> ...was an admirable endeavor and an important step in encouraging women to work for more rights in business and in public life. Its expansion [at the time this letter was written] into forty-five states seems to indicate a rising awareness of the needs and requirements of homebased businesswomen.
>
> You can count on my support to expand and improve your program.

In the past year the Alliance has also received recognition from the Senate and the White House. Bill Bradley, United States Senator, wrote:

> For too long Federal government has not been sensitive to the needs of those who chose to work at home. As indicated in your memorandum, other government policies including tax and labor laws, also fail to recognize the legitimate and productive work that is based in homes.

President Reagan recently invited a representative from the Alliance to a White House Conference on the creation of Rural and Inner City Enterprise Zones. This gave us the opportunity to introduce the concept of homebased businesses in this new area.

Considering all the recent attention we have generated for home-workers, it is difficult to believe that in 1978 this work force was still unrecognized. At that time a survey was designed to uncover the "invisible work force" and identify: Who works from home? What are home-workers occupations, their greatest joys, and most severe frustrations? What type of earning power is available to most homebased businesspeople? The initial survey responses came from New Jersey, New York, and Pennsylvania. Finally, in reaction to an article which appeared in the preview issue of *Enterprising Women,* responses came from all parts of America.

What was discovered? More than two hundred homebased business occupations exist. Ambitious, inventive entrepreneurs in a wide range of ages from diversified geographical locations are creating homebased businesses by selling products or services which give them extra spending money or incomes up to hundreds of thousands of dollars each year. Many respondents wrote that their homebased businesses offered the best of both worlds. Low overheads, less commuting, and flexible working hours provide women with an opportunity to be homemakers as well as income earners; however, definite problems also became increasingly evident. One was that more business advice was needed; to fill this demand we wrote the first edition of *Women Working Home.*

At the same time, many women expressed a desperate need to meet with others on a personal level to exchange business information and ideas. The survey results pointed out that running a homebased business often brings with it a tremendous sense of isolation. Homeworkers need an opportunity to gather together to exchange information on pricing, marketing, advertising, employment, and zoning problems. This need to overcome the isolation factor resulted in the formation of the first national organization to bring together homebased businesspeople.

On June 16, 1980, in Edison, N.J., a town where many years earlier Thomas Edison had invented the light bulb, nine women first met to form the National Alliance of Homebased Businesswomen.

In July 1981, NAHB was incorporated as a not-for-profit organization with tax-exempt status. By our first general members' meeting in November of that year, we had members in all but twelve states and chapters developing in more than two dozen cities.

Membership in the Alliance is $30 a year, for both established and new business owners. As a member of NAHB, one is entitled to a quarterly newsletter containing excellent articles pertaining to home-based business. Meetings-By-Mail, which circulate at least four times a year, give each member an opportunity to take on leadership responsibilities. Whether as an officer or committee person, or simply to state problems or solutions relevant to homebased business, Meeting-By-Mail provides us with an opportunity for direct interchange and representation. We are proud to be an organization structured to hear and respond to each member's needs.

As a result of problems discovered through Meeting-By-Mail, ad hoc committees of NAHB have formulated and analyzed questionnaires and written summary reports on national advertising, national showcasing, and comparison product pricing. Presently, a study is being completed on national service pricing. We further facilitate contact between our members through the distribution of a yearly directory of all NAHB

> **❝I am so excited that NAHB exists, and I hope I can be part of it. It is such an inspiration to those like me who know what they would like to do but just need a little push to get started.❞**
>
> Interior Designer

> **❝Thanks ... to the National Alliance of Home-based Businesswomen for supporting me in gaining the national exposure that would not otherwise have been available to me.❞**
>
> Steel Broker

National Alliance of Homebased Businesswomen

members (updated every four months) and an annual general meeting with seminars and showcasing.

Occupations of our Alliance members are extremely diversified. Advertising agents, business consultants, computer technicians, artists, architectural designers, bakers, instructors, interior decorators, doctors, typesetters, craftspersons, publishers, salespersons, and manufacturers are among the wide variety of businesspeople represented.

Chapters give members the opportunity to gather together on a local level to exchange information, provide immediate business opportunities, and discuss prevalent local problems. Through chapter meetings: partnerships are forming; business requirements, such as secretarial, advertising, or consulting needs are being met; and local problems, particularly on issues such as zoning, are discussed and solutions found.

Alliance members on both national and chapter level have proved that a solid united voice of homebased businesspeople can indeed be taken seriously. Our efforts have been noted in *The New York Times, Family Circle, Vogue, Ms.,* and *Ladies Home Journal,* on *Good Morning America, Donahue,* and *Hour Magazine,* as well as many other national magazines, TV and radio programs, and newspapers.

Affiliation with the Alliance has benefited its members in more than business, publicity, and mutual support. It has provided homebased women and men with a newfound strength, dignity, and an opportunity to unite marvelous resources throughout this country.

We are an organization where every member in each occupation counts. We need each other to continue to grow both individually and nationally. Every homebased businessperson in this country can benefit from an affiliation with the National Alliance of Homebased Businesswomen, the first organization structured to represent the interest of homebased business owners.

NAHB Founding Members
Photographer: Ted Horowitz

Women have a special place in the home. There is no denying that. Since men first went off to fight wars in the name of gold, power, religion, or conquest, women have been left at home to manage the castle, the fief, the plantation, the cottage, the ranch, and the bi-level. They saw that the home fires were kept burning, crops were harvested, large numbers of slaves and ranch hands were fed, budgets were adhered to, and gardens were tended.

❝Guess I am a typical example of women raised during the fifties...it was just never suggested that there was life after kids or that we should seek anything other than settling into marriage and having our husbands look after us for life.❞

Knitter

Women later began to work outside the home as textile workers, teachers, nurses, secretaries, and riveters. The composition of the female labor force and the nature of the jobs women perform has increased dramatically in the past century. One might assume that this quantitative change has been so great that there has also been a qualitative change in social roles, but as women filled in the spaces in offices and factories, men did not, in like manner, take up the jobs in running a home.

Yes, we have heard that men have begun to take on more of these homemaker-type roles, and yes, we have heard about househusbands—but how many do you know? Most men still consider the home as the woman's place, and the tasks that must be done there as women's work. It is still the prerogative of most women to have the responsibility for maintaining the physical house as well as feeding, clothing, and nurturing those who live within it. That is hardly conducive to business, and therein lies our struggle—how to do it all and do it all well.

Our roles as homemakers and our inability to recognize our management skills handicap us in the world of business. Because most of us have never been trained to function in a business environment, we need all the encouragement we can get, as well as positive reinforcement and support from others. This was the basis for *Women Working Home*. This is why we must identify our needs, confront our areas of weakness, acknowledge our strengths, resolve our problems, and grow—individually and together.

Ann Marcelyn Caver
Artist

Entrepreneurial Profiles

Jane Poston

66My business is house sitting for absent homeowners, feeding their pets, watering their plants. I have retired people who augment their incomes and also vary their lives by doing house sitting. My business is called Housesitter Security Service.**99**

Jane Poston

"A man's home is his castle" is an old-fashioned saying, but it is just as true today as it ever was. I found this out speedily and thoroughly when I first went into the house-sitting business four years ago.

In the good old days, a housesitter was Aunt-Bertha-down-the-street or Cousin-Joe-who-lives-around-the-corner, but in these fast-moving days, people who have to travel most have often moved (or been moved by their companies) to strange new towns where they don't know anybody.

Thus was born a brand new business: housesitting. Such a business offers one magic ingredient: a sitter who is as dependable and honest as Aunt Bertha or Cousin Joe.

Housesitting is a delicate business in which sitters are matched up with clients with the exactitude of a dating or employment service. Homeowners are fussy—"a man's home is his castle."

How did I, an English teacher, get into the housesitting business? In 1977 I returned from two years with the Peace Corps on the island of St. Lucia in the Caribbean and found so many teachers looking for jobs that I realized I would be the last person to find one. I was fifty-four years old and, with my degrees plus experience, schools would have to pay me almost twice as much as a young beginning teacher; therefore, I would probably never get another teaching job in the U.S.A. in this lifetime.

What to do? I was too young to retire and perhaps too old to get a job of any kind; yet I had become accustomed through the years to having food and shelter. It suddenly occurred to me that one summer I had done housesitting for a friend and might be able to turn that into a business with an income!

Planning and luck helped. The local newspaper printed a half-page feature on my new, unique business. Almost immediately my phone began ringing. Potential customers and sitters poured in, and the business was off and running. It has been running ever since and has provided me with the necessary food and shelter.

The most important ingredient of a housesitting business is a good long list of reliable sitters. Through experience I have found that older people make the very best sitters. They know how to run a house; they have developed a respect for property; they often need the extra income to augment social security; and they like a change of pace. Most important of all, they like to stay home. Since jobs are hard to find when you are over fifty (and well I know!), it has been my policy to hire older people exclusively.

My sitters are not employees but private contractors; they are free to accept or reject any project offered. After the client pays, the sitter is paid without withholding taxes and without workmen's compensation insurance and other formalities.

When individuals call to express an interest in sitting, I make an appointment to visit them in their own homes. All sitters must own or rent their own homes, so they have some place to live between sittings; they must be residents of the community rather than transients just looking for a place to live; and they must supply three references. Most important is the home visit, where I am able to evaluate an older person's temperament and housekeeping abilities within their own homes.

At the end of the visit, I ask them to read and sign a housesitters' Code of Ethics. In it they agree to respect the privacy of the client's home and agree not to entertain any of their friends there while sitting. This is an important point, though it may seem cruel for a long sitting. The only problems have been with visitors rather than sitters. One cannot be kind about offering hospitality in another person's home.

After the visit, I write down my impressions, telephone the references, and then, if all results are positive, feel secure in placing the sitter in someone's home.

When clients first call, I never ask for name or address, because they are often reluctant to supply this information until they have made up their minds to accept the housesitting service. Instead, I ask about their pets and plants, how long they plan to be gone, and if they have any expectations of what kind of sitter would best suit them—a couple or single person, a smoker or nonsmoker, etc.

When they call a second time to accept the service, I obtain name, address, and convenient date for a visit with the sitter. The client has the option of refusing the sitter, but this has never happened in four years.

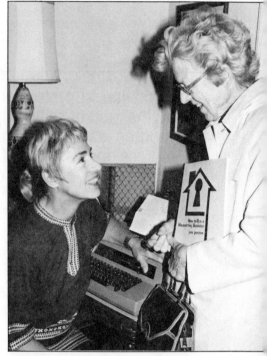

Jane Poston (seated)
House Sitter
Photographer: Hazel Froud

The formula for fixing the charges is complex. It depends on the length of absence, the numbers of pets to be cared for and plants to be watered, and what kind of service the client wishes. There are three types: first is the *Twenty-four-hour Vigil* in which the sitter moves in, bag and baggage, until the owner returns, only leaving the house to shop for groceries (sitters provide their own food). The second is the *Overnight* in which the sitter spends the day at home or at work but sleeps in the client's house at night. The fee for this service is only a little bit less than the Twenty-four-hour Vigil, because burglaries are more common in the daytime than at night and I don't feel comfortable with a house which is empty half the time. The third service is the *Drive-by*, which usually involves watering lawns and indoor plants, taking in the mail, newspaper, etc. The fee for this service is charged by the hour. Transportation for all three services is thirty cents per mile.

Because fee fixing is complex and because of many contracts and applications which have evolved over the years, I finally put it all together in a manual called *How to Run a Housesitting Business*. Details are described step-by-step in the book, which is divided into two parts: how to begin the business, and how to keep it running smoothly and profitably.

Although it sounds serious and complex, housesitting is really fun. I like to work with people, and those I meet in my work are dramatically different because they are either rich or old or both! This makes for strong variabilities and definite personalities; lots of salt and pepper in the stew!

And my experiences are often amusing. I now make it a practice to ask how big the family dog is. I once engaged a ninety-pound sitter to take care of a St. Bernard who was twice her weight! They got along fine, but I spent a few restless nights.

Incidentally, I telephone the sitter every day to be sure all is well. This keeps me feeling comfortable and provides some extra company for the sitter.

Let me close with the housesitter blessing for those who are establishing their own business: "May all of your sitters be homebodies, and all your clients travelers!"

Entrepreneurial Profiles

Doris L. Sassower, Esq.

66My advice to professional women contemplating the idea of setting up a working office in their homes is that you must make certain that the professional aspect of the environment is distinct from the personal aspect, so that each enjoys a separate status.**99**

Doris Sassower

A long, circular drive leads clients up to my Westchester County office—occupying one wing of a twenty-room house, set back on four acres in White Plains, New York. With a tennis court, grape arbor, and assorted pheasants, rabbits, and lesser creatures on the land, it's hard to believe that we're only a half hour or so from midtown Manhattan.

The reason I have attempted to create this atmosphere of sylvan serenity is that my field of divorce and custody litigation is one of the most highly charged, emotionally draining areas of law. This ambience quickly relaxes clients and other visitors—when the subjects at hand are often far from relaxing—but this took twenty years to achieve.

For the first ten years after graduation from law school in 1955, I lived and worked in New York City, then moved up to New Rochelle, another Westchester city, where I began developing a local clientele and eventually opened a New Rochelle office. Despite that, however, I thought the daily commute to my New York office would always be the necessary sacrifice to my legal career.

In 1970, a major fire in my home destroyed the entire third floor, and the extensive restoration required my personal supervision. This forced a switch to my homebased office, though I still continued to see many clients in Manhattan. It was then I realized the distinct advantages to this arrangement. It took another ten years for me to fulfill my dream, because I was using all my available time in the seventies mounting campaigns for equal rights for women.

A former president of the New York Women's Bar Association, I was coconvenor of the first Conference of Professional and Academic Women, held at New York University Law School in the spring of 1970. The meeting generated the start of respectable support for what became a movement for women's equality. Participating were many of today's well-known feminists, such as Kate Millett, Susan Brownmiller, Cynthia Epstein, and others who presented separate reports on the status of women in fourteen different fields.

During this period I immersed myself in writing, lecturing, and organizing for the women's movement. These endeavors needed freedom from distractions of telephone and office practice. After acquiring my White Plains estate, I made my home the principal base of operations, although still maintaining separate offices in New York and White Plains for more formal business meetings.

My advice to professional women contemplating the idea of setting up a working office in their homes is that you must make certain that the professional aspect of the environment is distinct from the personal aspect, so that each enjoys a separate status. This is especially important when clients are calling on a *woman* professional working at home. It is important that they realize they are not just visiting a housewife or making a social call. The image of the professional—the business-woman—must be protected.

The physical setup of the office, the separation from the home, is extremely important. The office must function as a real business. A woman working at home must try to avoid mingling her private with her professional life. This means eliminating children, animals, and everyday problems like broken vacuum cleaners and dishwashers from the environment. The next most important aspect is the need for a dependable staff who can keep nonbusiness interruptions and interferences from affecting the smooth operation of the office.

Liberated from the life of the commuter, I admit that I work ten times harder now—but I accomplish a hundred times more. I am also more relaxed even though I frequently work from 8:00 A.M. to 8:00 P.M. on days when I am in the office, rather than in court. A negative factor is that because it is so accessible, I sometimes find myself in the office at 11:00 P.M., 3:00 A.M., and even on weekends.

After nearly thirty years of practice, most of them commuting, I finally have achieved the ideal arrangement, permitting that much-sought-after balance between hard work and relaxation. With plenty of room for expansion, I can undertake more matters, not only in my specialty of family law and human rights, but other equally challenging areas.

I am a professional woman working at home—making my home work for me!

Doris Sassower
Attorney

Entrepreneurial Profiles

Joyce Friedland

66 Demand got greater, and I added three more helpers. The dining room was a sewing room, two bedrooms were dressing rooms, and a cutting table was in the foyer upstairs. I bought more machines after getting a small business loan. 99

Joyce Friedland

When I was nine I had polio; when I was thirteen I had artificial arches put in both feet. I married when I was seventeen, had my first child when I was eighteen, and was divorced with three children at twenty-three. At twenty-five I remarried and had another child—three sons, one daughter. This marriage lasted eighteen years and in that time I worked not only as a waitress, but also cared for twenty-four newborn babies from birth to adoption, sometimes two at a time. After discovering that my second husband was not the kind of decent person I thought he was, I divorced him and was again alone, with three of my children raised and a fifteen-year-old son at home. This was a tough period for me, and I worked again as a waitress to care for my son and to support myself.

One day I looked at myself in the mirror and saw a forty-two-year-old, 117-pound person with dark circles under her eyes. My normal weight is twenty pounds heavier. I looked like death warmed over, so I said to my reflection, "It has been a long time since you have been an individual. Who are you? Who do you want to be? What do you want to be?" I thought back to my younger years and all the things I had wanted to be then. I wanted to be a singer and had the voice for it; I wanted to be an artist and could draw very well; and, having been raised on a farm, I also wanted to be a veterinarian. In those days, however, my family felt that giving a girl an education was just a waste of time; she was supposed to get married and have kids. Having dreams was hopeless—that's why I quit school and got married, never graduating.

I remember very well a person who helped me when I decided to start the business of making custom-made shirts, using my talent in sewing. She was a lady at the employment office. When I told her my idea, she said she would arrange for me to draw unemployment for three months, then put me down for "cocktail waitress" with my only available hours from 6 A.M. to 2 P.M., knowing full well there would be no such position needed. I quit my job, took some of my unemployment money, and bought material. At that time I knew a man who could never get a shirt in his size and sleeve length because he was six-foot-six, nor could he get a choice of color or style. From this my business began in the home and became mine after the divorce. I promoted myself like crazy in whatever ways I could think of to get the word out. My young son took shirts to downtown stores where they were sold on consignment. After two months, ladies came wanting custom-made clothes, and I had to hire a lady to help me. Since I only had one machine, she had to bring her own. Demand got greater, and I added three more helpers. The dining room was a sewing room; two bedrooms were dressing rooms; and a cutting table was in the foyer upstairs. I bought more machines after getting a small business loan. Because I was not in a district zoned for business, I rented my first shop. At this point, I had five ladies sewing for me, while I did the major cutting and shirtmaking, janitorial duties, and bookkeeping. The huge windows in this store were filled with beautiful clothes designed by me and worn by eight mannequins. The shop front was filled with ready-to-wear men's leisure suits, jackets, ladies' clothes, and custom-made uniforms for waitresses and bartenders to match the decor of restaurants. I sewed for a total of ninety-eight major restaurants in Spokane. We then got into the entertainment costuming business, making matching shirts and outfits for performers. All were designed by me, and I had absolutely no training in design or business! I learned a great deal about sewing from the ladies that worked with me, because I wasn't really all that skilled when I started.

I named my shop The Style Builders and had separate names for the different things we made: ladies' clothes were "The Joyline" and children's wear, "Tif N' Todds," named for my first two grandchildren.

In 1977, when I was fifty-two years old, a truck coming out of a side street hit me as I was getting into my car and injured my upper right arm. Within six months after that, both my mother and father died, and I was diagnosed as having bio-carpral tunnel syndrome. Operations on both hands were necessary. With no money to pay for all this, I had to claim bankruptcy and close the door to my business. There were more medical expenses in the next two months, and I went on welfare.

Two years of seclusion passed, and I thought I had better find a way to get my life going again. My daughter was working at that time in a gift shop in Vancouver and, remembering my drawings of cross-eyed characters, suggested I make up a quality cloth doll using one of the ideas. I made one, then two, and three. The ideas kept coming, and I kept making dolls. I sewed the "Tif N' Todds" labels from my shop onto the dolls, signed each one, numbered them in sequence (we're up to number 1,016!) and later added a certificate of authenticity signed by me for collectors. My hands were getting the best possible therapy and so was my mind. Again I was doing what I love to do—creating with my own ideas. I now make a total of sixty-five different dolls, each one selling for $65–$80.

Joyce Friedland
Dollmaker
Credit: Repro Design
Denny Lippert

In May 1980 Mt. St. Helens blew! At the suggestion of my son, I created Baby Ashley, then added Baby Ashton, my best-selling doll. They have grey skin, eyes, hair, and print dress or shirt; their tongues are out (licking their chops, so to speak); and they hold a doll bottle filled with ashes—they are enjoying mothers' milk, concentrated ash. They are the children of Mt. St. Helens. All dolls, of course, have been copyrighted.

My business has been really rolling since May 1980, and I have sold dolls all over the U.S. and in other countries, as well. I am extremely proud of what I do and of myself right now.

Bad luck hasn't left me yet. I broke my right arm and wrist just before writing this, and there have been many personal family heartbreaks, but I did not work this hard to build a reputation for quality work and fast service to let anything stop me! Life surely hasn't been easy, but I am determined to succeed. My life is my dolls, and with each new one I create, I feel a renewed sense of pride and commitment. I want Joyce Friedland to stand out in a crowd and be counted a true individual in her own right. I think I deserve it!

Entrepreneurial Profiles

Rita Press

❝Although my labels could have been sold by professional sales reps, I chose to rep the product myself. It was important for me to get direct feedback and suggestions for additional products from the buyers.❞

Rita Press

Rita Press
Manufacturer
Photographer: Lynn Montlack

Who would think that an idea sparked by a college decal could lead to the development of a new business?.

I had a retailing background before settling into marriage, children, and community activities. As my three children moved through their teens, I often thought of starting a business but needed a product to market. Being a recycler by nature, I've always saved containers to store things but could never find attractive, quality labels for them. After speaking to some friends, I discovered they, too, had the same problem. Taking it a step further, I asked women in my community what they stored in jars and whether they'd buy a transparent, self-adhesive, washable label if one were available. Their responses were positive. Many suggested the product be dishwasher and freezer safe, adhere equally to glass, metal, and plastic, and be easy to read.

The idea may have been good, but converting it into a marketable product was a problem. The printers I searched out either couldn't transform the concept into a label at all or were overpriced.

I didn't know what to do next. Then one day, while washing the family car, I found the solution—the college decal could become a decal label. It was transparent, self-adhesive, and washable.

The first LABELeze* sheets containing twenty-six handsome, peel-and-apply decal labels for flour, pasta, cereal, popcorn, snacks, bran, etc., were test marketed at various community fund-raising affairs. The labels appealed to a wide variety of consumers—boaters, mobile home owners, young children learning to read, the visually impaired, creative recyclers, and organized women. I knew I had a winning idea.

The next steps were to create a product name, set up business and financial records, design a package, and map out a marketing plan. Moving from idea to packaged product took roughly eight months. If I knew then what I know now, it would have been only eight weeks. I was fortunate in being able to tap many business and marketing friends for advice; however, the final decisions remained mine.

Although my labels could have been sold by professional sales reps, I chose to rep the product myself. It was important for me to get direct feedback and suggestions for additional products from the buyers.

I've concentrated on selling to better housewares stores, many of which also sell attractive containers (that need labels, of course!). Continued success there will be followed by a larger sales and distribution network, mail orders, and trade shows. I also have plans, based on my initial market research and buyer feedback, to develop other kinds of labels, including institutional ones. By the time you read this, I hope you'll be able to purchase LABELeze* locally.

These days, I like to label my future growth "exciting"!

Entrepreneurial Profiles

Toni Goldfarb

As a writer with my own ideas, I'm always faced with the problem of becoming the right person with the right idea. If I'm working with a medical or social science publisher because that's my specialty, I'm the right person—but only if my ideas fit in with the usual work of the company. A book publisher will listen to a book idea. A journal publisher will welcome a journal article idea. I was stymied, however, when I came

> **66** Do we women really want to 'make it' in the male-dominated marketplace? Or are we willing to stretch our creative energies to build a more humane work world for ourselves, and for our families? As a homebased businesswoman, that is my goal. **99**
>
> Toni Goldfarb

up with a revolutionary, exciting idea for a medical newsletter that would report the latest scientific research findings direct to the general public. The trouble was, I didn't know any newsletter publishers! There was just one solution: I'd have to publish it myself. That's how a homebased freelance medical writer became not only a homebased businesswoman, but the chief executive of a publishing company—Communi-T Publications—and the editor-publisher of a brand new monthly, *Medical Abstracts Newsletter.*

In high school, I was a reporter and later editor-in-chief of the school newspaper and developed a monthly newsletter for twelfth graders. In college, the combination of a psychology major and a premed science program started me on the road to medical school until I came to a sharp detour—marriage! Combining studies and homemaking seemed almost insurmountable for a medical student, but not for a graduate student.

After graduate training in physiological psychology—"the biology of behavior"—I took my first job, as a psychopharmacology (literally, brain drugs) laboratory technician at Albert Einstein College of Medicine in New York City. I soon found that researchers' major efforts were focused on writing funding applications, research reports, and journal articles. I had found my niche—back at the writing desk.

Seeing my name at the top of published journal articles was indeed rewarding, but I knew that the name of a recognized researcher—my boss—had been more important than my own in getting into those publications. I wanted to become recognized for myself. And that wasn't easy! I began with a new job, working for one of the most prestigious cancer researchers in the New York area. But his glory had been built upon the ideas and efforts of others. Again I worked, and the boss got the credit. After many months of helping to write and design hospital programs for testing new anticancer drugs, I realized that I had acquired a unique combination of experience in both laboratory and hospital research. How could I make the best use of it?

Seeking a new job, I discovered a job title I had not considered before: medical writer. I decided to test out this new discovery by answering a few ads for free-lance positions while continuing my hospital job.

I soon had several assignments. Over the course of two years, I wrote college textbook chapters for a prominent New York publisher, summarized ("abstracted") medical journal articles for physicians' magazines, and edited and organized a descriptive brochure on an antidepressive medication for a top pharmaceutical company. Repeat assignments kept

Toni Goldfarb
Publisher

207

coming. Before too long, I realized I could not handle them all and still keep up with my hospital job, my family (we had two children by then), my community activities, and my sleep! I knew it was medical writing, not research, that really interested me; yet even with my free-lance experience, I still could not get the salary I wanted with a full-time writing job. The clear choice was leaving the hospital position and going off on my own as a full-time free-lance writer.

The security of a regular salary, benefits, and yearly increases was not to be discarded lightly, but the benefits of not having to commute, being at home when the children needed me, and best of all, being my own boss, won out.

Two years and many free-lance assignments later, I was ready to face the toughest employer I could imagine—myself! That's how I found myself with checkbook in hand, waiting on line at the office of the Bergen County Clerk. With the simple act of signing a $21.50 check, I was officially certified as the sole proprietor of Communi-T Publications, publishers of *Medical Abstracts Newsletter.*

My high school experience and my medical writing experience uniquely qualified me for the job ahead. Experience is the key to almost every business endeavor. Before trying a business on her own, any woman (or man) should have experience in doing the same thing for someone else. I gained "instant experience" in what I needed to learn about through reading books on newsletters.

Another major concern is money. Any business owner can get almost anything she needs, as long as she's got the money to pay for it. Trouble is, beginning businesswomen just don't have that kind of money. Having to write a check just to register my business should have been a sure tip-off, but it wasn't. I never realized how many checks I would have to write before my first issue hit the press.

Printing a run of 500 newsletters, 500 mailing envelopes, stationery, and some cover letters ran over $300. Add in almost $100 postage (stamps were 18¢ then), $10 for a half-year's rental on a small post office box, and $10 to register a copyright. That was the easy part; the *real* money went for advertising.

How much do you imagine it costs to run a tiny, inch-or-so square display ad in the back pages of a popular magazine? $100? $200? $500? Would you believe $1,000 minimum? I was astonished! At $1,000 apiece, there was no way I could fulfill my plan to run small display ads in four or five health-related magazines. I settled for the less-expensive classified ads—at over a hundred dollars apiece in any popular magazine. And ad agencies won't place them for you—it's too little dollar return on their time.

I was forced to start small and on my own. I wrote to several magazines for their rate sheets, chose the ones with the highest circulation for the least per-word ad cost, and then created what I hoped were tantalizing come-ons:

DOCTORS READ MEDICAL ABSTRACTS, you should, too! Monthly summaries of latest medical journal reports, all fields, now available to non-MD's. 6-month trial, only $10.

ARE YOU AN EDUCATED PATIENT? Each month, hundreds of medical journals report new breakthroughs in health care. Your doctor can't possibly read every report. Now, monthly *Medical Abstracts Newsletter* summarizes the *latest findings for you!* 6-month trial subscription only $10.

So few words to say so much, but at up to five dollars a word, believe me, each one was carefully chosen.

My first ads ran in *Prevention* and *Psychology Today,* and in one other publication I never thought I could afford, *The New York Times Magazine.* Its back-pages "Shopping Mart" provides some of the lowest display rates around. As with most magazines, the *Times* ad orders must be placed five weeks in advance of the date they're to appear.

At last, my ads were in; the first issue was written, typed, and printed; my press release went out; and I sat back exhausted, waiting for the letters to flood my post office box.

It was a long wait! Out of the initial 500 copies, 250 went out free with those press releases and with letters to everyone I knew in the medical field, publishing, and consumer affairs. And I sent one to every relative, friend, and passing acquaintance. Surely, most of them would at least spring for a six-month trial subscription; and some might even take the full-year offer. So that would be, say, 100 minimum. Then the ads. The combined circulation of *Prevention, Psychology Today,* and the *Times Magazine* was several million. Even at less than the 2 or 3 percent reply that direct mail solicitations are known to bring in, I could expect *hundreds* of subscribers. Right?

Wrong! My tally sheet for the June 1981 premiere issue showed thirty-seven responses from free copies, six from *Prevention Magazine,* five from *Psychology Today,* and twenty-six from the *New York Times Magazine.* Grand total: seventy-four, only three of which were full-year orders.

Not only had I failed to recoup the cost of my ads, I hadn't even covered the printer's bill for the second issue. It was the second issue that now concerned me. After you've done one, it is immediately time to begin work on the next. And the next! What had I gotten myself into?

That was June 1981. By December 1981, we had slowly but steadily doubled our subscribers' roll to about 200. And now the real test was at hand—renewals. Subscriptions taken during the initial June trial offer were now expiring. "Don't let your subscription STOP!" read the card we sent out. It contained a special renewal offer at "low charter rates." According to the Newsletter Association of America and other sources, a consumer newsletter renewal rate below 30 percent means you are dead; 60 percent says you are home free. In between the two, 50 percent means hang on and keep your fingers crossed; 40 percent looks like you are dying, but might pull out. Our rate that first year was 49 percent. On a small number like 200, it was not a clear sign of death *or* success, but it was enough to keep the business going.

Today, in the last quarter of 1982, after only one and a half years of publication, *Medical Abstracts Newsletter* has over 5,000 subscribers and some money on the plus side of the ledger!

To what do we owe our success? First and foremost, *a good product.* The newsletter is well written and targeted to an identified need; it provides the general public with the same scientifically proven medical information that previously was available only to doctors. It's an idea whose time has come in this health-oriented decade.

Second, it takes *dedication* to plug away month after month.

Third, we've improved our *marketing* through a combination of—

1. **Carefully selected ads.** More of the display-style ads that worked for us in the *New York Times Magazine.*
2. **Well-placed press releases.** The few that lead to in-print coverage make the whole process worthwhile. A few of our suc-

cesses: reviews in the *American Journal of Public Health*, the *Journal of Practical Nursing, American Libraries*, and even one "biggie"—*Changing Times* magazine ran our release in their "Things to Write For" section, which brought over 1,200 replies, 20 percent converted into subscriptions.

3. **Direct mail advertising.** Our newsletter was offered at a discount price (and at a loss to us—the company returns only fifteen cents for every dollar it takes in) through *Magazine Marketplace*. Through them we got literally thousands of new subscribers, but how many will be converted to full-price renewals? We continue to send free sample issues to anyone willing to send us a self-addressed, stamped envelope. If you're wondering how we can handle all this mail from a home office, we can't! Through the National Alliance of Homebased Businesswomen, I found a member's homebased business which does the work for us. And it's a great feeling to know that our profits are helping to expand another homebased business!

Where to from here? Onward and upward, I'm sure. The market for consumer newsletters is enormous. The problem still, for a small business person, is amassing the money needed to reach that market and, once reached, to keep the subscribers year after year. On the plus side, our present subscribers are a ready audience for related publications—I've started to plan at least two. In addition, the newsletter serves to introduce my writing abilities to publishers and businesses throughout the country. Many of them have contacted me with assignments. What a pleasant change from the old days of scanning the classifieds! And, with the newsletter as a financial back-up, I can be more selective about the assignments I take on. In short, I really am my own boss at last.

On the personal side, the expansion of my homebased writing business served as the impetus for my family to buy the kind of house we'd had our eyes on for a long time. Without my husband's substantial salary, we could never carry it; yet I know that my added income was the decisive factor in our move—and I'm extremely proud of that. I'm also proud that my children can see me at work each day, can listen in as I take important business calls, can help me (and even earn some pocket money!) by opening subscription mail and stuffing envelopes, and, best of all, can share my delight at being together with them while still pursuing my career goals.

Like many women today, I want to work—to make a "success" of myself, but I refuse to become a superwoman in the masculine work world. I've been there, and I know the pressures, competition, anger, and stress that cause ulcers, heart attacks, nervous breakdowns, and marital breakdowns. Is that what "liberated" women should be striving for? Not me, thank you!

I was fortunate enough to be elected as a delegate to the 1980 White House Conference on the Family. There, I heard first hand of the frustrations families face in these difficult economic times: dual-income families; single-parent families (most headed by women); practically nonexistent day-care facilities; employers unwilling to consider part-time or flex-time work options; inadequate tax deductions for work- and child-care-related expenses; meager social security coverage (and no disability coverage) for women who are "just housewives." Do we women really want to make it on these terms? Or are we willing to stretch our creative energies to build a more humane work world for ourselves and for our families? As a homebased businesswoman, that's my goal. And that's what I'm most proud of.

Bobbi Wolf

I write this for exceptional mothers working at home or thinking about the possibility. By exceptional I do not mean outstanding in their creative field or in their job as mother. By exceptional I mean the parent of a child who is not "in the norm." Exceptional, by law, includes children ranging from the gifted to learning disabled to severely retarded. I am an exceptional mother, and I am a woman working at home.

> 66Although my daughter's condition did not change, nor did the problem disappear, my state of mind improved...responsibilities and heartache did not lessen, but I have more strength to deal with the problems; and I have a much improved picture of my life.99
>
> Bobbi Wolf

I am the mother of three; my middle child is severely multiply handicapped. Having three children is a full-time job, but when one is handicapped, the job is more difficult.

As months and years were passing, I felt all my energies going to the care and concern of my daughter. I started to feel that I was missing something. I needed a diversion. I became active in my children's schools and found I had something to offer to those outside my home. After chairing a school bazaar, I sent thank-you notes in poetry to those who gave support and time to the cause. The response I received was terrific, and the wheels started to spin!

Here I was at home, unable to leave daily because of my situation but enjoying the sudden positive response I was receiving. I discovered I had a marketable talent. The obvious next step was to start a job at home. Consequently, Poemetrics began. I had the idea, the desire, and the support from friends who became my partners. Poemetrics has grown into a business of creative communications. We write personalized greeting cards for all occasions, invitations, and announcements. Poetry, calligraphy, and art design are combined to make a professional product.

Although my daughter's condition did not change nor did the problem disappear, my state of mind improved. My love for her was no longer struggling against an undercurrent of resentment toward her. Writing poetry, getting wonderful response from my customers, and receiving money for my work proved to be one perfect outlet.

Needless to say, my responsibilities and heartache did not lessen, but I have more strength to deal with the problems; and I have a much improved picture of my life. I think it is important for exceptional parents to talk and share their feelings.

I can honestly say that Poemetrics, plus other changes in my family picture, has certainly made a difference to me. I know and accept the fact that I am a working woman at home who has an exceptional job.

Barbara Bailine and Bobbi Wolf
Calligrapher and Poet
Photographer: Diane Actman

Entrepreneurial Profiles

Terri Tepper

❝Photographs have become an integral part of a growing effort to promote home business. Although change takes a concerted effort by all concerned, photography can make a substantive contribution toward influencing the public attitude which in turn affects the legal status of an issue.**❞**

Terri Tepper

One hot summer morning in 1907 Lewis Hine climbed a dark narrow tenement staircase. He was entering a world where families lived and worked from home to mass-produce merchandise. These first-generation Americans, living in these New York City tenements, had not long ago been funneled through Ellis Island, and they were desperate to make a living. Inevitably they found themselves around the kitchen table mass-producing such items as sock garters or synthetic flowers. For thirteen hours or more a day their children, too, worked at the same endlessly repetitive assembling tasks.

Lewis Hine saw the despair of parents as they forfeited, for themselves and for their children, dreams that promised a better life. He was not opposed to children working, only opposed to labor that didn't add to the growth of the child. Childhood was a time, he thought, to be learning skills and developing inner resources which would permit a young person to grow into an adult capable of earning a living with some time left over for enjoying life. In these stifling hot, primitive tenements with no running water, the mass-production work deadened a person. It involved the same kind of mindless, interminable toil Lewis Hine himself had experienced as a young person in Wisconsin.

As he walked up the dirty, dilapidated staircase, he carried with him tools which he felt certain would help change for the better the lives of the people who lived there—a 5″ X 7″-view camera, a tripod, and materials with which to create a flash bright enough to light up a dingy room. Hired by the National Child Labor Committee to photograph people in the tenements as they struggled to eke out a living, this was his first photographic assignment, and he was filled with enthusiasm and commitment. As a midlife career changer in his thirties, he had left teaching in a classroom for teaching on a broader social basis. He hoped that through photographs he would be able to educate the public about the reality of the insufferable living conditions in the New York tenements and thus, once educated, the public would pass legislation outlawing child labor and sweatshop conditions.

Starting in 1977, I, too, photographed home work. For many of the people in my home work environmental portraits, the struggle was every bit as intense as it had been for those photographed by Lewis Hine seventy years before. Although the standard of living had vastly improved, people still needed to earn a living to survive.

The ambivalent public attitude that Lewis Hine had had to deal with had changed, but it had not changed for the better. By the 1970s, it was assumed that home business was an extension of someone's hobby. In a society of corporate conglomerates, no serious businessperson would possibly work from home; so the public attitude had changed to one of condescension. In many cases, this meant home businesspeople, in order to be successful, had to conceal the fact that they worked from home.

Like Lewis Hine, I, too, had begun to photograph home work as a first photographic project in my mid-thirties and as an ex-classroom teacher. Because I was a home businessperson, I was driven to find out how others succeeded in a method of working where one not only

Photographer: Lewis Hine
Credit: International Museum of Photography at George Eastman House

concealed the milieu in which one worked but also was beset with distractions and intrusions necessarily an integral part of working from home and caring for small children. Since I anticipated that the only reason someone would work from home was because, like myself, there were small children to care for, I was surprised to find the number of single women—divorced, widowed, and without children—working from home. It astonished me that fully one-third of the nearly 100 women I photographed couldn't afford to work outside their homes in the kinds of jobs they could have had. For them, it was positively essential to make as much as possible since they were the sole support for the family. In addition to these breadwinners, I photographed women who had invited their husbands to join in their profitable ventures, as well as middle-class women who worked because they loved their work, not because it was profitable. There were also artists willing to live at a subsistence level in order to pursue their art. In each case, all the women were deadly earnest; their work should not have been dismissed as trivial. Public condescension was inappropriate and debilitating.

Like Lewis Hine, I hoped my photographs would lead to a change in the legal status of home work. While Hine sought protective legislation to end child labor and sweatshop conditions, I sought the removal of restrictive zoning laws. Laws had been enacted, even in New York City, that continued to permit a family to do the same kind of work Hine had photographed—that is, mass-producing goods around the kitchen table by family members. So while Hine's photographs led to protective legislation concerning children working outside the home, they did not alter the tenement situation. By the 1970s, with school compulsory, such laws were not needed. Strangely, however, by the 1970s laws had been passed limiting home business to family members. I found senior citizens, disabled people, single parents, modestly credentialed or unemployable, often needing help with their businesses, and, since they didn't have family members accessible to help, they hired others to work for them. These entrepreneurs operated in violation of local zoning laws because they were faced with either working from home to earn a living or not working at all. These and other restrictive zoning laws continue to be in force even when a home business does not alter the character of a neighborhood nor bother anyone.

Lewis Hine used captions to accompany his photographs to more poignantly bring out those conditions he wanted emphasized and for which he sought change. Sometimes he made a poster using several of his photographs along with large lettering directing the public's attention to the abuses being illustrated. I thought the women speaking for themselves would underscore the significance of their work within the context of their lives; so I excerpted quotes from their conversation to accompany photographs for photographic exhibitions, multimedia slide shows, and my book, *The New Entrepreneurs: Women Working From Home.*

Now, in the 1980s, concern for home business has resulted in the development of national organizations, books, and newsletters on the subject. Photographs have become an integral part of a growing effort to promote home business. Although change takes a concerted effort by all concerned, photography can make a substantive contribution toward influencing the public attitude, which in turn affects the legal status of an issue. It is my hope that my photographs may some day have the impact of removing unnecessarily restrictive zoning provisions as Lewis Hine's photographs had the impact of restricting child labor and ending sweatshop conditions.

Cheryl Gudinskas
Designer
Photographer: © Terri P. Tepper,
1979

Luz Holvenstot

❝I plan systems that incorporate various methods to save energy. Which ones to use naturally depend upon each particular project. ...Because solar heating must be individually designed for each building, the work is challenging and interesting.❞

Luz Holvenstot

The solar energy revolution occurred about 1974. The dramatic increase in energy costs coupled with the awareness that costs kept rising despite reductions in the amount of fossil fuels used (less driving, lowered building temperatures, and conserved electrical use), led scientists and do-it-yourselfers to examine free energy from the sun.

As a scientist I realized that solar energy was part of the wave of the future and wanted to join in this appropriate adjustment to rising energy costs and to avoid the dangers of nuclear power.

When I began to dig for information, there were no courses available, but the awakening was fast producing books on the subject, and close on the heels of these books came the first solar conferences. I read, attended conferences, talked to pioneers in the field, and visited experimental projects and inventors' backyards.

My first step in becoming a solar consultant was to teach a course in solar energy in an adult education system. I taught these courses for several years. When some class members began to ask me about their various projects, I became a solar energy consultant.

By 1979 my own experiments with solar collectors had progressed to the point where I was ready to build and install my own system on my home. I built a hot-air passive system, which presently heats my barn-studio of 18,000 square feet. From October 1979 to October 1981, I used 425 gallons of oil for backup heating, plus two cords of wood each year.

A consultant does not necessarily work full time in the strictest sense of the word. I wear many hats, but their brims all touch. My additional work as an environmentalist, scientist, artist, sculptor, and animal livestock judge brings me into contact with a wide variety of people in many areas. From time to time, these interests produce a solar energy project. As a consultant, I now advise on solar energy-efficient applications for new and existing buildings. Understanding the problems, applying good judgement, and following through with correct methods to build energy-efficient buildings involves the application of proper siting, insulation, location, greenhouses, wind protection, and actual building construction—with careful and responsible attention to the smallest detail.

I charge by the hour for pure consulting. Charges for drawings of building plans depend upon the time it takes to develop them. When I am the general contractor on a building job, I take a regular percentage and supervise construction. On local projects, I use local contractors that are trained and skilled in solar concepts.

With the building business in its present depressed state, we are doing more retrofits, or changes and additions on buildings. At present, the most popular additions seem to be sun rooms which increase living space, provide free heat to the entire home, add beauty, and make a home more salable in the future.

Because solar heating must be individually designed for each building, the work is challenging and interesting. Regardless of what the fossil fuel industries proclaim, this clean, effective solution for lowering costs of heating hot water and cooling and heating buildings is here to stay. As soon as the economy allows, we will see great growth in this field.

Luz Holvenstot
Solar Consultant
Photographer: Harvey L. Bilker

Entrepreneurial Profiles

Dora Back

When I started After 6 Secretarial Service in December 1976, I thought it would be a good idea to have a business to work at when I retired from my regular eight-thirty-to-five job. Now that retirement has arrived, the idea is better than ever! I could never have foreseen that the giant conglomerate I worked for, one of the Fortune 500, would have cash-flow problems and sell off my division. The employees are living with fear because they don't have jobs—some after twenty and thirty years of service. Many high-priced executives and professional people have told me how envious they are that I have a business to go to.

> **❝I look forward to retirement as a chance… to do all the things I once thought I might like to try yet never did because of a lack of time or energy. The key to successful retirement is self-understanding, a feeling of self-worth, and the will and ability to live life to its fullest.❞**
>
> Dora Back

There are many reasons I'm grateful for my business. One of the chief ones is that, as a child of the Great Depression, I hate being poor. Since women are more likely than men to be poor when they grow old, it is very important to know that I can always earn a living for myself.

Also, when I began my business, interest rates and inflation had not soared to the elevated heights they are now, and if I had not had an established business, I would have worried a lot more along the way to retirement. Retirement is a big step. It is scary. As my husband says, "You need a reason to get up in the morning."

When you leave a regular job, you lose quite a few things: acceptance, a built-in social life, and friends with interests in common; support systems; lunchtime socialization; a routine and framework to your day; the security of a regular paycheck and fringe benefits. However, you also gain some other things: self-determination; freedom from the tyranny of the time clock (you can work whenever you feel like it, even if it's 2:00 A.M.; the ability to turn down customers and work you don't want; a chance for adventure; and the opportunity to do different things instead of the same old day-in-day-out routine.

My business gives me a chance to use the knowledge and skills I have gained over the years. The secretarial/resumé-writing business requires skills such as communication, writing, ingenuity, imagination, selling, time management, economics, finance, credit, psychology, and a smattering of knowledge about many occupations.

As my business has grown, more equipment has been added to my office, each piece fully paid for when purchased. In retirement now, there are no large unpaid items. At present, I have three types of word processors and eight dictating and transcribing machines. All typewriters are compatible. If changes or corrections are needed when the client comes to pick up work, the type for that job can be matched. At the current cost of replacement, I have $15,000–$20,000 worth of equipment all paid for, and most of it by the business.

I look forward to retirement as a chance to try new things and spread my wings, to do all the things I once thought I might like to try yet never did because of a lack of time or energy. The key to successful retirement is self-understanding, a feeling of self-worth, and the will and ability to live life to its fullest.

As Barbara Walters once said, "To make it all come together somehow, sometimes, is what it's all about."

Dora Back
Secretarial Services Director
Credit: The News Tribune

Alice Hayes

> **66** Bringing in a partner was a great idea and has eased my anxiety about business decisions. We assessed our skills and discovered that she rounded out the needs of the company in a very complementary manner.... My partner helped move our company from a hobby status to a business enterprise. **99**
>
> **Alice Hayes**

"My business" is a concept and phrase that still excites me when I hear it, and I must confess that I have had my ups and downs with it since I started. Often I have considered abandoning the effort, but then a grateful customer infuses me with a new surge of enthusiasm and drive to carry on.

Bombay Fashion House, as my business is called, was hastily started in response to a friend's request to sell women's apparel on the East Coast, which her mother manufactured in Bombay, India. I had sold many things in my life by that time, so it was not to me an overwhelming request. As a matter of fact, I was ecstatic. The opportunity was a windfall because I had always admired her mother's designs and this connection allowed me to purchase firsthand her new arrivals for myself and for my customers.

During the first year of my business, I was also working full-time in the public relations office of a large trade association. In that position I was constantly coming in contact with people who liked my wardrobe and who wanted similar items for their wardrobes. I sold items on my lunch hour and had special selections during the Christmas season.

During this same period, I set up a salon in my home to accommodate customers who wanted to try on a range of outfits at their leisure. Such was the manner in which the home-show concept of Bombay Fashion House was conceived. Two of the upstairs rooms in my home were converted into salons, and I began to hostess a number of weekend showings. My primary objectives were highly personalized service, low overhead, and easy-wear, easy-care natural fibers. To encourage comfort and ease in shopping for our customers, we provided light refreshments during the shows. The number of invited guests at this time usually totalled ten to fifteen people; the length of time of the show was two to three hours. Our guest list was a mix of personal friends and business and professional acquaintances. From this initial group of people, we developed a larger roster of customers through word-of-mouth referral.

From the initial experience of having a business in my home, I learned a number of important requirements: parking space for customers; light refreshments for each show; a neat and clean house whenever customers would visit the salon; the need to be accessible to customers at all times of the day; and the inability to close and leave the shop. These requirements could be satisfied because of our location and because, at this period in my career, my husband and I had no children to complicate our schedules or to take time away from either my nine-to-five job or from my part-time retail business.

Initially the business specialized exclusively in imported fashions which I myself imported into the country. This is not a simple process. I was fortunate that my supplier and manufacturer were one and the same person; there was no middle person to complicate the expenses. In addition, I could trust my supplier completely because of my friendship with her daughter. I was confident that she would minimize risks in shipping the merchandise to me. She would ship the goods as inexpensively as possible to save both of us unnecessary shipping costs. Nevertheless, my trust in my supplier did not diminish the anxiety I felt whenever I went to customs to pick up inventory. My constant fear was that customs would charge an inordinate rate because of unusual detailing on the fabric. There was also a fear that the items would be returned to the shipper before my schedule would allow me to go to a distant airport to pick up the shipment.

Because of my mutual interest with my supplier in cutting shipping costs, I never knew when my merchandise would arrive or how long a shipment would take. Once I was delayed at customs for about three hours as one customs agent after another went through my papers to check the merchandise. Unfortunately, I was scheduled to fly to a conference in New York City at the same time that I was waiting at customs for a shipment. Three hours later, I had missed my conference and still had not received my merchandise.

It was about this time that I sought the assistance of a customs agent for importing my inventory. I was a little nervous about bringing a third party into my business. In addition, I was nervous about the additional expense that my company would incur each time I bought inventory.

Working independently without a partner, I found myself needing someone with whom to share my problems and decisions, so I looked around for someone to share the joys and difficulties of running an import business. Luckily, my sister was an available and willing candidate and had always been one of my best customers.

Bringing in a partner was a great idea and has eased my anxiety about business decisions. We assessed our skills and discovered that she rounded out the needs of the company in a very complementary manner. She had just completed a Sears sales management course and brought to our company actual retail experience and a sense of business order. My strength was as an image maker and a sales promotor, in buying inventory based on styles and on our customers' needs, and in having enough zestful enthusiasm for us both.

Alice Hayes
Importer/Saleswoman

My partner helped move our company from a hobby status to a business enterprise based on forms, schedules, checks and balances. Through her initiative, we sought out other distributors who could supply inventory and allow us to serve our customers better. No longer would we be limited to one supplier, but could broaden our base of operations and free us from the constant hassle of customs.

Just as we were getting comfortable, my husband and I bought a new house that also accommodated the business nicely. I now had plenty of parking and a neighborhood which any of my guests would love to visit. One problem was that we were just a little farther from downtown and from our working customers; therefore, we decided to take our fashions to our customers in a traveling caravan of clothing from India, Afghanistan, Kenya, Egypt, and Indonesia. Inventory was acquired through a combination of my buying trips, my husband's trips, my sister's trips, and wholesalers who bought items overseas for resale in the U.S.

The traveling fashion boutique was still called Bombay Fashion House, even though our wares came from areas other than India. Since our initial entry into the import business, we have struggled with the issue of a name change because the name has become too limiting.

The concept of taking the salon to our customers was a good one because it allowed us to reach a larger audience, and it provided us with a group of hostesses who could help us sell to their friends. My hostesses were people who liked our clothes, saw the idea of a fashion show as a novel way to entertain people informally in their homes, wanted to help us succeed, and were our friends.

To encourage volunteers to have showings, I devised a plan whereby each hostess would receive a special hostess gift, receive hostess discounts on her purchases, have an opportunity to see new fashion lines first, and choose between informal modeling during her show or simply displays of the clothes.

Another three years went by as we moved our traveling fashion shows throughout the Washington metropolitan area and across the country. By this time, however, I had two children, which meant my time was in more demand by my family, my house was in more disarray, and I had less energy to move our traveling fashion caravan from one place to another. Consequently, we are now focusing on larger shows for longer periods of time—shows lasting from three days to one week, with special inventory for each show. We would mail invitations to all our customers and would specify the hours, so that I could plan to staff it accordingly.

So here we are in 1982, and my business is seven years old. Looking back at its history, I can readily say that the greatest asset to having my own business is being able to decide where I would operate that business. I have found it to be a constant challenge and source of enthusiasm to devise ways in which I can operate it to suit my schedule, to meet my growing family needs, and to continue to strive for success. My interest in being a loving wife, a caring mother, and a professional continues to urge me to fulfill all of these roles.

Working out of my home allows me most comfortably to accommodate these personal needs and demands. It allows me, for instance, to interact during the day with my children on their schedule, permitting them to have a part of me in their lives also. In addition, it allows me to plan my time in conjunction with my husband's schedule so that we can have a more relaxed family life together.

Guatemalan Weaver
Photographer: Doranne Jacobson

Lorette Konezny

There I was, a former middle-school art teacher with a resumé of thirty-odd jobs by the time I was twenty-nine. I had few community connections and no formal business training. When my idea came, I managed to parlay it into a very successful business over a four-year period. It took that long because I had to learn everything from scratch—quite apart from the peculiar time requirements of my market. Business know-how, like pregnancy, is a long, continuous growth process. Nothing, it seems, is born overnight!

> 66 The keys to success? Listen to everyone who gives experienced advice, care about the people who work for you, and cherish your sales reps and accountant every minute of the day. Without them, you don't have a business! 99
>
> Lorette Konezny

My last job was teaching macrame and calligraphy to adult education classes. Drawing lines for calligraphy requires a special formula. One student, barely able to handle a ruler, much less a formula, kept demanding my help.

Later that night at home, it occurred to me that some sort of template might help this student. But a template made of what? It had to be durable, washable, and transparent. I bought some sheets of hard plastic, cut them to size, and silk-screened the calligraphic lines on them. It worked for the problem student; perhaps it could help others.

I quickly borrowed $466 for a tiny ad in *American Artists,* a consumer publication directed to artists who work at home. Not a bite!

My husband, a junior high school art teacher, had a colleague whose father was in the stationery business and who recommended the trade publication *Greetings.* When I saw the new-products section of *Greetings,* I called and asked how to get in. "Just send us a photo and release," they said. The two-inch caption I wrote pulled 300 inquiries, and my mail-order business was born!

My new calligraphy kit seemed a natural for art and hobby shops, but they rejected it because the price, based on my costs, was too high for their market. That forced me to try department stores. I found, however, that they prefer to deal with known sales reps who can certify production and delivery; and I had no idea how to find a sales rep!

Greetings publishes an annual nationwide list of department-store buyers. I just dialed through the list until one finally answered. The sales rep they recommended had his showroom in Manhattan but lived only a short drive from my home on Long Island. I was quite unaccustomed to city travel and persuaded him to see me at his home. The rest is history.

The gift-market rep advised me to focus on gift-market catalogs because they easily absorbed the higher price points and required no inventory buildup of a product untried by cautious buyers. Catalog product advertising also educates consumers about new products, thereby developing a future in-store market.

Lorette Konezny
Manufacturer
Photographer: Bruce Morgan

Designing new gift packaging to match the higher price point for the rep's first order from the art department of a major N.Y.C. department store was no problem. The scary part was gambling on a minimum 1,000-piece production run for a forty-eight-piece order. The gamble paid off when he then sold the new Pen Notes Italic Calligraphy Kit: The Designer Liner to the Christmas catalog of another department store (their biggest seller that year!) and put me in touch with the new-products sections of two more trade publications: *Gifts and Decorative Accessories* and *Giftware News.*

If I thought I'd make my fortune with the calligraphy kit alone, I quickly learned that reps and buyers wanted "lines," not single items. I worked up a "comp"—or artist's sample—for another kit, but didn't go into production until the market showed definite interest some months later. The Designer Liner Copperplate Script Calligraphy Kit ultimately proved as successful as the Italic kit.

Soon after I met the gift-market rep, I also hired an accountant to set up business records and give me much-needed personal and business tax advice; however, my accountant had other unsuspected talents as well. He was successful in pricing my products and arranging payment schedules with suppliers that protected my cash flow.

His willingness to become totally involved with my business has been a vital factor in its success; for instance, when I had exhausted all personal resources for financing production, he helped me make my first presentation to a bank. The loan arrived three weeks later!

Now, my accountant, my rep, and I meet regularly to develop new ideas, and to discuss prices for international accounts, special catalogs, and other negotiations. Our goal is to remain flexible enough to secure the sale while continuing to make a profit. It's my job to ship on time, spend according to schedule, and maintain an organized office.

One day while exploring the toy market, I met another rep who advised me to develop a children's writing product. I immediately called in a first grade teacher I knew, and our collaborative efforts resulted in *Learning to Print,* a book of twelve heavy-board pages with transparent wipe-clean plastic sheets between pages and its own nontoxic pencil. Children can trace over letters and words, erase, and repeat.

My rep brought an early comp of the book to a national mail-order catalog buyer, but she wouldn't look at a finished production copy from a new company until it established a track record and demonstrated financial stability and dependability. I discovered that track record means how a book is reordering elsewhere; financial stability is proving you have sufficient financial resources to manufacture and fill the orders; dependability is delivering on time while following their shipping instructions to the letter.

Not being dependable could be costly. If your package was pulled off their conveyer belt because it was improperly or carelessly marked, they'd bill you $10 per hour to correct it. If the catalog couldn't fill a customer's order within the time specified by federal mail laws (and must, therefore, refund money) *because* you delivered late, you're dead as a supplier to that catalog. Anything that's wrong can hold up their payment to you, ruining your cash flow for new production.

Almost a year later, we were ready with a production copy that was reordering very well in a national educational publication. This time the contact was successful—although we were not to see any profits until the catalog appeared months later and the orders came in.

The hard lessons here were planning and patience. Nothing in mail order is done quickly or haphazardly. If I wanted to make the Christmas

Lorette Konezny
President

(516) 868-5753 or 868-1966

Pen Notes

134 West Side Avenue
Freeport, New York 11520

catalog, I had to start setting up an appointment with a buyer to review my book ten months to a year earlier! Reviews are given only twice a year. If the buyer accepts it, the book is then passed to a committee for final review sometime in the following months. If the acceptances have been of a comp or hand sample, a production copy must be available for photography. It can be nerve-racking. A turndown means starting over for the next catalog.

Thanks to my advisors, I learned my lessons well by the time my second book, *Writing Script,* was ready. Both books are now sold nationally through department stores, retail chains, and mail-order catalogs, and can be bought in Canada, England, Hawaii, Alaska, and Puerto Rico. A third volume in the series, titled *Learning to Tell Time,* will be out in 1983.

The profits from these books paid off the original loan from my parents, as well as underwrote Pen Notes' total publicity, production, packaging, and delivery costs.

Advertising so far has been publicity. I have timed each year's new product for Christmas (the gift market's biggest selling season), successfully introducing it via photo and release to the trade magazines and with exposure in trade shows through reps and their showrooms. (Here I learned that trade shows are mainly for making contacts that lead to appointments where orders, hopefully, are then written.)

The hard work of these last four years has changed me from a very apprehensive novice into a much savvier businesswoman—who travels with ease in the city!

An important part of my growth was learning that it's okay to ask experienced people for advice and help. Men do it all the time in business without shame or guilt. Such networking has come a little harder for me, as I suspect it does for many women.

The keys to success? Listen to everyone who gives experienced advice, care about the people who work for you, and cherish your sales reps and accountant every minute of the day. Without them, you don't have a business!

Invoice no. _____

PO no. _____

Sales rep. _____

Ship date _____

Balance due _____

Dear Customer,

Your account is due.
Your prompt remittance is
greatly appreciated

Sincerely

Mr. Gerald Kaye
Credit Manager

Pen Notes   134 West Side Avenue   Freeport, New York 11520   (516) 868-5753 or 868-1966

A-Z Idea List

The following list of possibilities is set forth as a springboard for your imagination. These ideas are, for the most part, not listed elsewhere in the book—ideas to set you off on your own wondrous flights of fancy from A to Z.

Think about them. Think of what you can do that others cannot do (or cannot do as well). Think of saving people time, money, effort, or aggravation. Are any of the ideas potential moneymakers in your area? Are any of special interest to you?

Answering service—"Hello, Central!"
Appliances—fix-it shop for small items
Appraisals—antiques, books, collectibles, objets d'art
Aprons—different strokes for different folks— carpenters, cooks, gardeners, kids, painters, etc.
Aquariums—design and installation
Architectural design—blueprints, drafts, renderings
Awnings and shades—custom design and sales

Baby items—buntings, diaper bags, carryalls, bibs, toys
Babysitters—daytime sitters, especially—a working mother's best friend!
Bagels 'n' lox—personal delivery for Sunday brunches
Banquet coordinating—plus weddings and parties
Beauty services—hairstyling, manicures, pedicures, electrolysis
Bedding—handcrafted linens, quilts, pillows; coordinating accessories
Bees—keeping hives, selling honey, making beeswax candles
Birds—fancy feeders and cages—a feather in your cap!
Books—binding, collecting, trading, publishing, and sales
Boxes—big and little designs, but only big sales
Bridal services—gowns and accessories
Buttons—design and sales

Camps—information specialist and broker
Candy—homemade sweets for the sweet—who can resist?
Caricatures and cartooning—children's and adults' parties
Cars—driver education; customized interior and exterior decoration
Cellars—cleaning and organization
Chairs—caning, needlepoint seats and backs
Chickens and eggs—breeding, but which comes first?
China—painting
Clocks—collecting and sales; repairs
Cloisonné—jewelry, belt buckles, pictures
Coins—collecting and sales
Computers—hardware and software analysis, training, and sales
Copper—hand-tooled artifacts

Costumes—rental
Crafts—supplies

Dagwoods—hero sandwiches for parties, lunch hours, etc.
Découpage—furniture, boxes, and accessories
Decoys—carving, painting, and sales
Demonstrations—foods, appliances, cosmetics, etc.
Detectives—private eyes
Dinner deliveries—definitely delicious!
Designer—doghouses, dollhouses, and what have you!
Dolls—unique dolls, clothing, and repairs

Ear piercing and earring sales
Eggs—blowing, decorating, and sales
Electronics—sales and assembly
English—teaching English as a second language for conversation or citizenship; tutoring in composition and creative writing

Fabric—specialty fabrics and sales
Felt—designs for dolls, mobiles, pillows, puppets
Fish—breeding
Flies—designing and creating fishing flies
Flowers—preservation, arrangement, and instruction; creating artificial flowers
Foreigners—helping them resettle, adjust, become familiar with American systems (being bilingual is important)
Frames—one-of-a-kind frames for pictures and mirrors; also framing
Frozen foods—specialty items, precooked meals
Furniture—designing, building, stripping, refinishing
Furs—remodeling and repairing

Garage sales—organization and management
Garden furniture—rewebbing, repainting, repadding, reupholstering
Gifts—buying, wrapping, and mailing
Greenhouses—design and installation
Greeting cards—handcrafted
Groups—Lose Weight, Stop Smoking, Improve Your Memory, etc.

Hair—design and creation of unique combs, barrettes, clasps
Hammocks—handmade of rope, cord, canvas, webbing
Handwriting—analysis
Health foods—homegrown or package sales
Herbs—homegrown, dried or fresh, mixed or matched, creatively packaged
Hiking—guide and outfitter

Illusion—pantomime and magic
Indians—baskets, carvings, and handicrafts

Instruction—bridge, cooking, dance, fencing, gymnastics, judo, karate, languages, needlework, painting, sculpting, sewing, speed reading, shorthand, slimnastics, swimming, tennis, typing, etc.

Jams and jellies—homemade and creatively packaged
Jewelry—manufacturing, restyling, repairs, and sales

Kids—child care, play groups, trips
Kitchen—planning and organization
Kites—handcrafted
Kits—crafts, butterfly breeders, needlework, holiday items, dollhouse furniture and accessories

Lampshades—custom designed; handpainted lamp globes to match bases
Letters—correspondence for busy people who don't have secretaries, for elderly or ill
Library cataloging
Linens—handmade and coordinated napkins, tablecloths, place mats, and aprons

Mail—direct-mail marketing and lists
Maps and globes—antique and contemporary—collecting and sales
Marzipan—mouth-watering, edible art
Messenger service
Miniatures—handcrafted landmarks and dollhouse items
Mobile homes—rental or leasing
Monograms—personalized bags, aprons, handkerchiefs, clothing
Movies—8mm film or videotape biographies for special occasions
Murals—custom designed on walls and ceilings

Needlework—appliqué, crewel, crochet, embroidery, knitting, needlepoint, patchwork, sewing, stitchery, string art, trapunto

Omens—astrologers, nephrologists, palmists, tea-leaf readers

Paperweights—collecting and sales
Papier-mâché—toys and accessories
Pattern maker and tester
Pets—vacation care, grooming, supplies
Photography—people, places, things
Pillow furniture—handcrafted
Pillows—in lace, ribbons, fabric, needlepoint, batik
Plants—propagating, potting, and sales
Portraits—painted, photographed, or needlepointed—pets, people, residences

Quackers—breeding ducks (!)
Quilts—original designs, handcrafted

Rentals—Rent-a-picture, plant, sculpture
Restorations—antiques, artifacts, cars, homes
Roommates—matchmaking service
Rugs—custom designed—braided, hooked, and woven

Scarves—batiked, embroidered, handpainted, knitted, silk-screened
Scrimshaw—jewelry and belt buckles
Sewing—specialty clothes for hard-to-fit people; novelty items for special occasions
Shells—shell craft novelties
Shoes—repair and sales
Shopping services—groceries, gifts, clothing, whatever
Speech—therapy, dialect, inflection, pattern correction, diction
Spices—mixed or matched, creatively packaged
Stencils—on tin, plaques, walls, floors, ceilings, mirrors
Surveys—by mail or phone
Sweaters—knitted and crocheted; also mittens, socks, hats, scarves

Ties—handsewn of elegant and unusual materials
Totes—handcrafted designs
Tours—theme tours of your town or region
Transportation—for children, elderly, handicapped; to car inspection; service to airports

Umbrellas—handpainted, personalized
Unicorns and other stuffed animals in a variety of fabrics and fake furs
Upholstery—repair, recovering

Valuables—photographic records to provide householders with proof of ownership
Vans—customized
Vegetables—excess produce from home garden sold at roadside stand
Voice—teaching musical comedy and opera

Wastebaskets—painted, beribboned, découpaged, custom designed
Wigs—design, refurbishing, and sales
Windows—cleaning service and trimming

X-otic foods—specially prepared

Yarn—imports; naturally dyed sheep's wool

Zoot suits and zo forth—period clothing—restyling and sales

Bibliography

Planning Your Business

Cleaver, Claire M. *Step Into Sales*. Boyertown, Pa: Boyertown Publishing Co., 1981.

Dible, Donald M. *Up Your Own Organization*. California: Entrepreneur Press, 1974.

Lasser, J.K. *How to Run a Small Business*. 4th ed. New York: McGraw-Hill, 1974.

White, Richard M., Jr. *The Entrepreneur's Manual*. Pennsylvania: Chilton Book Co., 1977.

Managing Your Business

Brabec, Barbara. *Creative Cash: How to Sell Your Crafts*. Tucson: H.P. Books, 1981.

Catalog Sources for Creative People. Tucson: H.P. Books, 1981.
Lists more than 2,000 mail-order sellers of art/craft/ hobby supplies and materials.

The Thomas Register. New York: Thomas Publishing Co. Published annually.
Its several volumes include a listing of products in alphabetical order, with names and addresses of companies that make them.

Advertising, Marketing, and Promotion

Artist's Market. Cincinnati: Writer's Digest. Published annually.

Ayer Directory of Publications. Philadelphia: Ayer Press. Published annually.
Directory of print media listing editor, national advertising manager, publisher, circulation, advertising rates, etc.

Bacon's Publicity Checker. Chicago: Bacon's Publishing Co. Published annually.

Betancourt, Hal. *The Advertising Answerbook: A Guide for Business and Professional People*. New Jersey: Prentice-Hall, 1982.

Dean, Sandra Linville. *How to Advertise: A Handbook for Small Business*. Wilmington: Enterprise Publishing, 1980.

The Directory of Directories. Detroit: Gale Research Co., 1980.
An annotated guide to over 5,000 directories, rosters, lists, and guides.

Editor and Publisher International Yearbook. New York: Editor and Publisher Co. Published annually.
List of daily newspapers with their circulation, rates, executive personnel, editors, and department managers; also list of weekly newspapers, syndicates, and wire services.

Encyclopedia of Associations. 17th ed. Detroit: Gale Research Co., 1982. Published biennially.
Vol. I: National Organizations of the U.S.
Vol. II: Geographic and Executive Index
Vol. III: New Associations and Projects

Holtje, Bert. *How to Be Your Own Advertising Agency*. New York: McGraw-Hill, 1981.

Literary Market Place. New York: R.R. Bowker Co. Published annually.
Directory of 25,000 firms and individuals in U.S. and Canadian publishing.

McVicar, Marjorie and Craig, Julia F. *Minding My Own Business: Entrepreneurial Women Share Their Secrets for Success*. New York: Richard Marek Publishers, 1981.

National Directory of Shops/Galleries/Shows & Fairs. Cincinnati: Writer's Digest, 1982.

National Radio Publicity Directory. New York: Peter Glenn Publications, 1982.
Information on 3,500 U.S. and Canadian network, syndicated, and local talk shows for use in public relations. Lists coverage, station format, names of shows, contacts, etc.

The Newsletter/Yearbook Directory. 3rd ed. Rhinebeck, N.Y.: Newsletter Clearing House, 1981.

Photographer's Market. Cincinnati: Writer's Digest. Published annually.

Ries, Al and Trout, Jack. *Positioning: The Battle for Your Mind*. New York: McGraw-Hill, 1981.

Roman, Kenneth and Maas, Jane. *How to Advertise: A Professional Guide for the Advertiser, What Works, What Doesn't, and Why*. New York: St. Martin's Press, 1977.

The Standard Periodical Directory. 8th ed. New York: Oxbridge Communications, 1982. Revised biennially.
65,000 U.S. and Canadian periodicals arranged by subject and indexed by title. Contains names and

addresses of publishing companies, frequency, circulation, advertising rates, etc.

Standard Rate and Data Catalogs. Skokie, Ill.: Standard Rate and Data Service. Most published monthly. Eleven catalogs listing daily and weekly newspapers, consumer magazines, farm and business publications, TV and radio time, and mailing lists to facilitate planning and buying of media.

TV Publicity Outlets—Nationwide. Washington Depot, Ct.: Public Relations Plus. Revised triennially. Lists over 2,000 TV programs that use guests and publicity material.

Ulrich's International Periodicals Directory. 2 vols. New York: R.R. Bowker Co., 1982. Revised biennially.
Subject-arranged list of over 62,000 periodicals published throughout world. Entries provide price, frequency, editors' names and addresses.

Walker, Morton. *Advertising and Promoting the Professional Practice.* New York: Hawthorn Books, 1979.

The Working Press of the Nation. Chicago: National Research Bureau. Published annually.
Vol. I: Newspaper and Allied Service Directory
Daily newspapers, news services, newspaper supplements, photo services, special-interest and foreign newspapers. Contains names of department editors, index of editors defined by subject area, circulation figures, publication frequency.
Vol. II: Magazine and Editorial Directory
Service, professional, trade, farm, industrial, and consumer news publications. Contains alphabetical index, editors' names and areas of responsibility, telephone numbers, addresses, and lead times necessary for consideration.
Vol. III: TV and Radio Directory
Television and radio stations, newscasters, and program personnel.
Vol. IV: Feature Writer, Photographer, and Syndicate Directory
Feature writers, photographers, feature syndicates, photo sources, and publication requirements.

Writer's Handbook. Boston: The Writer, Inc. Published annually.
Instructions on free-lance writing and 2,500 markets for manuscript sales, with editors' names, addresses, payment rates.

Writer's Market. Cincinnati: Writer's Digest. Published annually.

Directory of 4,500 places where writers can sell articles, books, novels, stories, fillers, plays, gags, and verse.

Financial Advisory

Doyle, Dennis M. *Effective Accounting and Record Keeping.* New York: John Wiley and Sons, 1978.

Internal Revenue Service Publications. Free of charge.
#538 Accounting Periods and Methods
#587 Business Use of Your Home
#534 Depreciation
#508 Educational Expenses
#572 Investment Credit
#583 Record Keeping for Small Business
#552 Recordkeeping Requirements and a List of Tax Publications
#533 Self-Employment Tax
#334 Tax Guide for Small Business
#542 Tax Information on Corporations
#541 Tax Information on Partnerships
#589 Tax Information on Subchapter S Corporations

Kamoroff, Bernard. *Small-Time Operator.* Rev. ed. Laytonville, Calif.: Bell Springs Publishing, 1982.

Expanding Your Business

Directory of SBIC's. Available from the National Association of Small Business Investment Companies, 618 Washington Building, Washington, DC 20005.

1982 Directory of Venture Capitalists. Available from the National Venture Capital Association, 1225 19th St., N.W., Suite 750, Washington, DC 20036.

Gumpert, David E. and Timmons, Jeffrey A. *Insider's Guide to Small Business Resources.* New York: Doubleday & Co., 1982.

Franchise Opportunities Handbook. U.S. Department of Commerce, Bureau of Independent Economics and Minority Business Development Agency. For sale by Superintendent of Documents, U.S. Government Printing Office, Washington, DC 20402.

Lesko, Matthew. *Getting Yours: The Complete Guide to Government Money.* New York: Penguin Books, 1982.

Sources of Financing. Available from Office of Small Business Assistance, N.J. Department of Commerce and Economic Development, Trenton, N.J. 08625.

Bibliography

Special Reports

Cheever, Raymond C. *Home Operated Business Opportunities for the Disabled.* Bloomington, Ind.: Cheever Publishing, 1980.

Feingold, S. Norman and Perlman, Leonard G. *Making It on Your Own.* Washington: Acropolis Books Ltd., 1981.

Grebner, Marythea. *Business Management Training for Rural Women.* Newton, Mass.: Women's Educational Equity Act Publishing Center, 1982.

Income Generation for Rural Women. Washington: The American Home Economics Association, 1982.

Miller, Lynn and Swenson, Susan S. *Lives and Works: Talks with Women Artists.* Metuchen, N.J.: Scarecrow Press, 1981.

Ours, How to Organize a Consumer Coop. Free from the Cooperative League of the USA, 1828 L St., N.W., Washington, DC 20036.

Tepper, Terri P. and Tepper, Nona Dawe. *The New Entrepreneurs: Women Working from Home.* New York: Universe Books, 1980.

Small Business Enterprises for Workers with Disabilities. Falls Church, Va: Institute for Information Studies, 1982.

Marion Behr, Wendy Lazar, Arleen Priest
Photographer: Sally Cooney

Here we are again—Marion Behr, Wendy Lazar, and Arleen Priest—three women, each working from her own home to put together *Women Working Home: The Homebased Business Guide and Directory.*

In fact, this is the second edition of *Women Working Home* and our second collaboration. As in the first, the relationship and the combination of skills work well.

We have known each other many years, as childhood friends in Rochester, New York, and as students at Syracuse University. We continue to grow together—personally, professionally, and academically.

Survey Results from
Women Working Home, First Edition:

Of those responding, 56% have been in business for 1–3 years; 15% for 5–10 years. Almost half, 43%, knew something about their businesses before getting involved, while 39% knew a great deal. Start-up capital was needed by 68% of the women, but only 13% started with loans from a bank or other financial institution. Of the rest, 70% used personal savings and 25% borrowed from family.

Happily, 100% of the respondents enjoy what they're doing; 97% like working from home; and only 13% would move out of the home if they had the chance. Based on the returns, 79% are serious about their businesses, and 40% of these women also look upon their businesses as self-fulfilling. Businesses now support or, in the future, will support 60% of the respondents.

The neighborhood breakdown is interesting: 18% urban, 52% suburban, 18% small town, and only 9% rural. Of these, 74% own their homes.

Advertising works for 64%. Of those who hire employees, 3% use full-time help and 13%, part-time.

The age breakdown was as follows: just over half of the women were 30–39 years of age; 15% were 20–29; another 15%, 40–49; 13%, 50–59; and 3%, over 60. Married women comprised 78% of our survey; only 10% were divorced.

Almost half the women who answered the question about income grossed under $5,000 their previous year of business; slightly less, 44%, netted under $5,000, and 5% earned more than $10,000. A full 40% did not state earnings.

The majority of women, 49%, had completed college, and 25% had gone on for graduate training, while 9% were high school graduates.

Since our survey represents readers of *Women Working Home,* it cannot give the full picture of homebased business in America, but we found the results interesting and want to share these facts with you.

Jacqueline Rudolfer and Eva Birkner
Artists
Photographer: Sally Dorian

How to Use the Directory

Arleen Priest, Business Manager, WWH Press

This is the only national business listing for women working from home. Names and their occupations are listed alphabetically by state, then by product and service categories with more detailed information about each person's business. This is, after all, a business directory, and it is hoped that, through these listings, the women will be able to promote their products and services nationwide and expand their businesses because of that. Expansion may mean more publicity, greater sales, a new move toward consultancy, selling wholesale as well as retail, franchising, and/or networking nationally.

Readers may find the directory beneficial for purchasing products and services and for building contacts to exchange resources, business services, and products. Reach out to those businesses that may bring return business. You may want to send out a flyer, letter, or brochure about your business explaining what it can do for others. Mention where you saw the business listing and that you share a common work place. Reach out to businesses where there may be an exchange of ideas and sources. Reach out to similar businesses. A secretarial service with an overload of work may want to contact another local secretarial business for additional help with a big job. A public relations firm on the East Coast may need someone in another area of the country to provide transportation and backing for celebrity promotional tours. This is not competition but assistance, in what should be a mutually beneficial business arrangement. There are many who are pleased to support women in business, especially those who work from their homes, because of the many advantages this segment of the work force can pass on to the consumer.

We all would like to start a successful homebased business in the fastest and easiest way. How wonderful it would be to be locked in a room with someone who has the exact business that interests us and be able to pick her brain! Of course, this is unrealistic, unfair, and not smart for the businessperson, since we may become her competition. No one should be expected to spend unlimited amounts of time conveying information unless, of course, one is being paid as a business consultant. As always, time is money, and we are talking about *business!*

The following suggestions, however, will enable you to get information on starting a business. Contact people out of your geographical area. Introduce yourself through the mails, stating that you read their names in this directory. Give some background about yourself and perhaps an explanation of why you are interested in that specific type of business. Ask just a few questions that will require minimum answering time or suggest in the letter that, if she would prefer, the business owner may call you *collect.* If you telephone, remember to call during daytime business hours. Think through the questions before asking them, show intelligence and professionalism, and you will get intelligent, professional information in return. Just as you would have the business owner return your phone call collect, when you write, send a self-addressed, stamped envelope, so she has no additional costs.

Requests from respondents have changed the course of some businesses listed in the directory of our first edition. After being asked numerous times to help set up businesses exactly like their own, several women have decided to franchise. Others have become business consultants. To grow in business, one must never close any avenues for potential expansion. One might think that an artist's listing will bring only local sales, but an art dealer in another part of the country may contact that artist to represent her work. Mail-order businesses are often developed from products and services that originally sold locally.

You may find other ways to take advantage of the information within this directory. Let us know how the directory has helped you or your business, or send us other suggestions you may have. If you are not listed in this second edition, there will be space for you in the third edition, though a publication date has not been set.

We wish you much success and hope that your own business world develops to its fullest.

66 Knowing where to find a source is one of the most important factors in my business. I have to locate a tremendous variety of items and services when I'm working on a film. Since location shooting can take me anywhere, I need good resources in all parts of the country. **99**

Film Producer

State Directory

Tina Bobker and Carole Dlugasch
Accessories Manufacturers
Photographer: Janet Chill

State Directory

Constance Porte-Aigeldinger, Writer, "Kiddie Kassette," Photographer: Richard Aigeldinger

One thing is clear: small business owners wear many hats! Each one has a variety of job responsibilities and the skills and flexibility to move in many directions. Each woman listed in the directory sent us her occupational title and a description of her business. There were many instances, however, when the occupational title did not fully reflect the type of work being done. Therefore, we have chosen to list occupations in the State Directory but categorize by business description within the Product/Service Directory, so that readers might find information more readily.

The following list is a sampling of what can be done—and what is being done—by enterprising women at home.

ALABAMA

Margaret J. Pittenger
Pittenger & Associates
5568 Surrey Lane
Birmingham, AL 35243
205/991-7075
Publisher/Photographer

ARIZONA

Marjory Vals Maud
Single Impressions
642 West Zia Dr.
Tucson, AZ 85704
602/888-7176
Free-lance Writer, Publisher

Jane N. Poston
Housesitter Security Service
1708 E. 9th St.
Tucson, AZ 85719
602/884-8530
Personal Services Specialist

CALIFORNIA

Fawn DeMurl Carriker
Elite Business Services
3846 S. Shady Lane
Visalia, CA 93277
209/627-1782
Secretary/Typist

Barbara Deane
1675 Kasba St.
Concord, CA 94518
415/676-5930
Writer

Anita Dimondstein
Biobottoms
57 Grant Ave.
Petaluma, CA 94952
707/778-7945
Sales Manager

230

Arlene Marie Enos
Dental Engineers Inc.
PO Box 1367
San Bruno, CA 94066
415/334-5434
Dental Prosthetic Technologist

Nina Feldman
Nina Feldman Word Processing &
Editing
6407 A Irwin Ct.
Oakland, CA 94609
415/655-4296
Typist

Donna Gene Ferguson
The Typing Professional
PO Box 1152
Lake Elsinore, CA 92330
714/674-7220
Typist

Maxine Gottesman
SHEFA
24 Morrill Ct.
Oakland, CA 94618
415/652-5247
Home Business Consultant

Sarah Haddon
Sarah Craft
PO Box 663
Corte Madera, CA 94925
415/924-1553
Needlecraft Designer

B. Kirby Harrison (Bonnie)
The Portrait Place
953 Mountain View Blvd. Ste. 123
Lafayette, CA 94549
415/439-7375; 283-7620
Photographer's Agent

Connie Hunt
Pulsar Publications
PO Box 714
Lafayette, CA 94549
415/254-7535
Writer, Lecturer, Self-Publisher

Danielle R. Kennedy
DRK Productions
25108 Marguerite Pkwy., Ste. B-201
Mission Viejo, CA 92692
714/859-8440
Professional Platform Speaker

Melanie Ley
Melanie Ley's Quality Typing
3681 Hamilton
Irvine, CA 92714
714/552-8816
Typist, Bookkeeper

Catherine Linnerman, R.N., B.S., M.A.
Medication, Education, Diet, Support
(MEDS)
8384 Norfolk Way
Stockton, CA 95209
209/478-0854
Program Development Consultant
and Diabetes Nurse Educator

Carol Mastick
Carol Mastick Secretarial Service
1590 Sir Francis Drake
San Anselmo, CA 94960
415/459-4918
Free-lance Typist

Irene Hamlen Stephenson
Biorhythm Character Analysis &
Compatibility
PO Box 892-WWH
Chatsworth, CA 91311
213/347-6949
Analyst

Tamera Tate
Roses & Lollicards
9 Captains Landing
Tiburon, CA 94920
415/383-0638
Salesperson

Marianne Turlington
PO Box 23414
San Diego, CA 92123
619/566-3348
Bookkeeper

Christine A. Van Noy
The Wordshop
181 Paseo Del Rio
Moraga, CA 94556
415/284-4035
Typesetter, Graphic Designer,
Secretary

Maggie Weisberg
Inventors Licensing & Marketing
Agency
PO Box 251
Tarzana, CA 91356
213/344-3375
Marketing Consultant

Laurie Alexis Welch
The Box Office
Suite 890, The Courthouse Square
1000 Fourth St.
San Rafael, CA 94901
415/459-2697
Mail/Telephone Service Operator

Caryl Winter
Presentations with Impact
400 S. Beverly Dr., Suite 312
Beverly Hills, CA 90212
213/933-0933
Communications Consultant and
Author

Tamera Tate
Salesperson

CONNECTICUT

Ann Marcelyn Caver
109 Ripton Rd.
Huntington, CT 06484
203/929-8882
Artist/Designer

State Directory

Dolly Curtis
Architectural Textiles
35 Flat Rock Rd.
Easton, CT 06612
203/372-4511
Fiber Artist

Bette-Jane Hardersen
22 Burnwood Dr.
Bloomfield, CT 06002
203/242-8902
Accountant

Victoria Leisy
Elegant Threads
79 Rogers Lake Trail
Old Lyme, CT 06371
203/434-9681
Fabric Designer

Deborah Mitchell
Creative Expressions
43 Collinswood Rd.
Wilton, CT 06897
203/762-9690
Regional Sales Manager

Angela M. Mogin
Call A Wife, Inc.
48 McIntosh Rd.
Stamford, CT 06903
203/329-7600
Home Management Specialist

Frances Gildea O'Neill
Dantec Corporation
54 Taylor Ave.
Bethel, CT 06801
203/744-7375
Electronic Subcontractor

Marilyn Salmieri
Marilyn Salmieri, CPA
4 Baker Ave.
Westport, CT 06880
203/226-1900
Certified Public Accountant

Sarah Juniel Zaleski
Everywoman's Bookshelf
PO Box 104
Wilton, CT 06897
203/762-9426
Mail-Order Bookseller, Business
Consultant

DISTRICT OF COLUMBIA

Alice Hayes
Bombay Fashion House, Inc.
3206 Morrison St. N.W.
Washington, DC 20015
202/363-8183
Retailer

FLORIDA

"Danie" Bernard
Danie's Custom Poetry
8690 Gulf Blvd.
St. Pete Beach, FL 33706
813/360-5245
Free-form Writer/Poet

Diane Toby Deckinger
6850 N. Grande Dr.
Boca Raton, FL 33433
305/487-6028
Interior Designer

Delorus Whidden Eitel
National Sweepstakes & Contest
Guide
Box 2349
West Palm Beach, FL 33402
305/686-0617
Publisher

Jean Eitel
Palm Beach Needle-Painters, Inc.
912 Evergreen Dr.
North Palm Beach, FL 33408
305/622-1326
Fiber Artist and Quilter

Laura S. Kluvo
In Stitches
4041 N.W. 2nd Terr.
Boca Raton, FL 33432
305/392-3475
Mail-Order Salesperson and
Designer/Craftsperson

Mary Louise Pivornik
Mary's Typesetting
8512 Wooddrift
Tampa, FL 33615
813/886-6528
Typesetter/Graphic Artist

Marie A. Sherrett
Merrett Industries
7018 N. Cameron Ave.
Tampa, FL 33614
813/886-8971
Court Reporting Typist

GEORGIA

Ann F. Hurford
4384 Hale Pl.
Lilburn, GA 30247
404/921-3953
Typist

ILLINOIS

Elizabeth Carr
International Society of Fine Arts
Appraisers, Ltd.
PO Box 280
River Forest, IL 60305
312/848-3340
Fine Arts Appraiser

Jean Eitel
Quilter

Elaine A. Coorens
Coorens Communications
2134 W. Pierce St.
Chicago, IL 60622
312/235-8688
Computer Consultant

Janet V. Hansen
Koalaty Products Ltd.
118 S. Elmhurst Ave.
Mt. Prospect, IL 60056
312/253-9357
Mail-Order Entrepreneur, Designer

Patricia Kileen
Letters & Numbers
PO Box 223
Ingleside, IL 60041
312/587-2571
Graphic Designer/Calligrapher

Virginia W. Smith
Alphabetrics, Inc.
633 Breakers Point
Schaumburg, IL 60194
312/884-0091
Designer

Terri P. Tepper
261 Kimberly
Barrington, IL 60010
312/381-2118
Writer, Photographer, Speaker

Jo M. Wolf
The Cyclo-Scan Report
PO Box 712-WH
Chicago, IL 60690
312/874-0548
Astrological Consultant

Ea Zu-En
Zu-En Graphics Studio
8742 Luella Ave.
Chicago, IL 60617
312/768-2424
Graphic Designer and Astrological
Counselor

INDIANA

Sherrill Boggs
Anything Groes
RR 3
Columbia City, IN 46725
219/244-3247
Plant Counselor, Plant Finder

Rita J. Cassell
R/J Associates
4808 W. Peachtree
Muncie, IN 47304
317/288-2888
Photographer's Specialist

Myla D. Smith
Murals By Myla
1935 Crescent
Franklin, IN 46131
317/736-5442; 232-7811
Graphic Artist, Writer

IOWA

Carol Krob
Carol's Creations
1012 N. Summit—E
Iowa City, IA 52240
319/351-7854
Craftsperson/Graphic Designer

KANSAS

Karen Nash
The Best of Kansas City, Inc.
PO Box 7071
Shawnee Mission, KS 66207
913/341-8186
Salesperson

MAINE

Reesa Abrams
Reesa E. Abrams, Consultant
Lower Main St.
Freeport, ME 04032
207/865-3891
Software Quality Consultant

Vikkilyn Cambridge Griffin
The Cabbage Patch
20 Two Lights Rd.
Cape Elizabeth, ME 04107
207/767-4663
Clothing Designer, Seamstress

MARYLAND

Annette Collins, M.A.
Collins Associates
6128 MacBeth Dr.
Baltimore, MD 21239
301/435-1979
Nutrition Consultant

Betsy Heller
Canvas Creations
PO Box 84
Arnold, MD 21012
301/757-4682
Designer/Manufacturer

Dagmar Lemich
D. Lemich Custom Office Products
PO Box 7466
Silver Spring, MD 20901
301/587-6614
Manufacturer/Salesperson

Elizabeth Vandam
The Golden Needle Workshop
207 Wildewood Blvd.
California, MD 20619
301/862-2088
Quilt Artisan

Kay Winner
Kay Winner Studio
PO Box 610
St. Michaels, MD 21663
301/745-2606
Women's Exercise Instructor

State Directory

MASSACHUSETTS

Sandy Aponowich
Sandy Aponowich & Associates
54 Green St.
Charlestown, MA 02129
617/242-0306
Word Processor

Diane Elliott
Herbalife
55 Stadium Way
Boston, MA 02134
617/787-9626
Diet, Weight Loss, and Nutrition
Counselor

Margaret M. Feodoroff
Inspired Interiors
50 Brentwood Dr.
North Easton, MA 02356
617/587-0185
Interior Decorator/Designer

Juanita Gordon
Theological Threads
13 Washington St.
Beverly, MA 01915
617/927-7031
Religious Vestment
Designer/Manufacturer

Savoy Rose Jade
Day Tonight/Night Today
PO Box 353
Hull, MA 02045
617/925-0046
Editor/Publisher

Roz Shirley
49 Pleasant St.
Medfield, MA 02052
617/359-2944
Fiber Artist

Gail Pettiford Willett
Children Are Many Colors, Inc.
72 Chestnut St.
Cambridge, MA 02139
617/876-7665
Organization Director

Roberta H. Winston
Roberta H. Winston, Wordsmith
1431 Commonwealth Ave.
Boston, MA 02135
617/782-6499
Editor

MICHIGAN

Wendy Clem
Artbeats Unlimited
PO Box 461
Fraser, MI 48026
313/772-0173
Greeting Cards and Stationery
Designer

Barbara H. Goldman
Edit/Aide
14521 Artesian
Detroit, MI 48223
313/272-0256
Advertising/Promotional Writer

Jo Ann Miller
Sugar 'n' Spice Originals
4987 E. "T.U." Ave.
Vicksburg, MI 49097
616/649-2206
Designer/Manufacturer

N. Irene Sloan
G.G. Associates
PO Box 21343
Detroit, MI 48221
313/863-2813
Distributor

Nancy K. Steinbach
Mirrored Memories
15141 Floating Bridge Rd.
Three Rivers, MI 49093
616/279-2895
Craftsperson

Rosemary Summers
Rosemary's Health & Beauty Spa
16225 Greenfield #205
Detroit, MI 48235
313/837-8814
Health and Beauty Resource
Developer

Betty Vogel
Vogel's Demonstration Service
1254 Dickinson S.E.
Grand Rapids, MI 49507
616/452-0122
Microwave Cooking Instructor and
Food/Appliance Demo Specialist

Miriam Walton
Sunshine Press
3221 Bloomfield Park Dr.
West Bloomfield, MI 48033
313/626-3248 or 626-3223
Publisher

MINNESOTA

Sally P. Blumenfeld
First Class
5456 Fremont Ave. S.
Minneapolis, MN 55419
612/823-0719
Accessories Manufacturer

Edna L. Gonske
Studio G
20 E. 40th St.
Minneapolis, MN 55409
612/824-4737
Designer/Weaver

Pat Isaak
434 Hiawatha Ave.
Hopkins, MN 55343
612/935-5639
Writer

Edna L. Gonske
Designer/Weaver

Sandra Ostendorf
Airgraphics
13117 Valley Forge Lane
Champlin, MN 55316
612/421-1500
Photographic Airbrush and Retouch
Artist

MISSOURI

Barbara Brabec
Artisan Crafts
PO Box 10423
Springfield, MO 65808
417/882-9949
Crafts Publisher/Marketing Consultant

Kathy King
Kings
605 B Chipman Rd.
Lee's Summit, MO 64063
816/525-3668
Needlework Designer

Cheri Lynn Russell
Wicker Fixer and Caning
Rt. 1, Box 283B
Ozark, MO 65721
417/485-6148
Wicker Restorer, Chair Caner

Paula Ann Winchester
Herb Gathering, Inc.
5742 Kenwood
Kansas City, MO 64110
816/523-2653
Herb Supplier

NEW HAMPSHIRE

Audrey Nan Nelson
Nelson Crafts
RR 2, Box 212
Goshen, NH 03752
603/863-4394
Craftsperson/Artist

Kristen Rossi
K.L. Rossi Designs
McCurdy Rd.
New Boston, NH 03070
603/487-3345
Craftsperson

NEW JERSEY

Mary E. Archibald
21 Wayne Gardens
Collingswood, NJ 08108
609/858-5945
Free-lance Writer, Typist

by Audrey Nan Nelson
Photographer: Lars Nelson

"Weed people" are everybody's
*   And, like weeds, they are everywhere.*
They offer you a flower,
*   Because love springs in their heart.*
Each one suggests a smile,
*   As their purpose is to please you.*
And each is an individual,
*   Even as we are.*

State Directory

Dora Back
After 6 Secretarial Service
54 Johnson St.
Fords, NJ 08863
201/738-4670
Secretary and Resumé Writer

Roberta Bampton Beavers
BEAVER/S, Inc.
15 Jardine Ct.
Morris Plains, NJ 07950
201/285-9529
Management Consultant

Tina Bobker
Rainbow Artisans, Inc.
19 Troy Ave.
Livingston, NJ 07039
201/533-9081
Accessories Manufacturer

Audrey J. Boerum
Ideas Unlimited . . .
72 McNomee St.
Oakland, NJ 07436
201/337-7660
Communications Consultant, Writer,
Promoter

Iva L. Bramble
Sew Unique
PO Box 392
Hackettstown, NJ 07840
201/852-5370
Craftsperson

236

Mariana Hiser Burwell
9 Laketown Rd.
Long Valley, NJ 07853
201/876-4572
Sales Rep

Anne Cousineau
15 W. Circuit Dr.
Succasunna, NJ 07876
201/584-5208
Photographer

Ashia R. Covington
The Sewing Corner
Jersey City, NJ 07304
201/434-7282
Fashion Designer, Dressmaker

Jeanne Davis
The Designing Woman
679 Red Oak Lane
Smoke Rise, NJ 07405
201/838-6060
Graphic and Craft Designer, Lecturer

Fran Derlinga
Our Things, featuring The Paperdoll
27 Heather Lane
Mahwah, NJ 07430
201/529-4081
Interior Decorator

Carole Dlugasch
Rainbow Artisans, Inc.
35 Old Indian Rd.
West Orange, NJ 07052
201/731-6721
Accessories Manufacturer

Yvette Furman
Party Pizzazz, Inc.
10 Schindler Ct.
East Brunswick, NJ 08816
201/254-2646
Party Decorator

Bert Garino
Bert's Babes
559 Flock Rd.
Hamilton Square, NJ 08690
609/586-9083
Dollmaker

Toni L. Goldfarb
Communi-T Publications
586 Teaneck Rd.
Teaneck, NJ 07666
201/836-5030
Free-lance Writer, Consultant

Ceil Greco
Mary Kay Cosmetics
611 N. Washington Ave.
Dunellen, NJ 08812
201/968-7037
Beauty Consultant

Beverly Halperin
Rhyme Tyme
81 Oakview Ave.
Maplewood, NJ 07040
201/763-6319
Greetings Entertainer

Betty Hardy
Leadership Unlimited
178 Central Ave.
Madison, NJ 07940
201/377-0652
Leadership Consultant

Stella Hart
Stella Hart, Inc.
105 Shady Lane
Randolph, NJ 07869
201/895-3356
Public Relations Consultant

Luz Holvenstot
100 Naughright Rd.
Long Valley, NJ 07853
201/876-3614
Solar Consultant

Helen Keenan
Keenan Studio
135 N.E. Lakeside Dr.
Medford, NJ 08055
609/654-8470
Photographer

Muriel Kravette
The Wordworks, Inc.
236 Vreeland Ave.
Leonia, NJ 07605
201/461-0088
Word Processing Operator

Melissa Kuntz
Fabrics By Melissa
PO Box SB—404
Leonia, NJ 07605
201/592-6913
Salesperson

Dorothy E. Kurtz
Kurtz Krafts
PO Box 308
Hasbrouck Heights, NJ 07604
201/778-2968
Craftsperson

Beverly Lane
Graphics Lane, Inc.
22 University Rd.
East Brunswick, NJ 08816
201/257-8778
Typesetter

Helen Lurie, CTC
327 Lincoln Pl.
Waldwick, NJ 07463
201/652-5144
Travel Agent

Marie MacBride
100 Rock Rd.
Hawthorne, NJ 07506
Communications Consultant

Nancy E. Mack
Words in Process
PO Box 204
Ho-Ho-Kus, NJ 07423
201/445-9302
Word Processor

Barbara L. May
May Services, Inc.
PO Box 77
Norwood, NJ 07648
201/768-9379
Mail Order Fulfillment and Mailing
Service Operator

Lavinia Moore McKee
Moore, McKee Insurance Agency
21 Branton Dr.
East Brunswick, NJ 08816
201/254-7883
Insurance Agent

Margit Meissner-Jackson
"Margit" Designer Fashions
PO Box 5298
Atlantic City, NJ 08404
609/296-4367
Fashion and Costume Designer

Carol Motto
Fabricadabra
121 Pearl St.
Westfield, NJ 07090
201/232-2521
Seamstress/Designer

Anne M. Murphy
Functions Unlimited
14 Heighwood Trail
Sparta, NJ 07871
201/729-9704
Meeting and Function Planner

Patricia Parenteau-Eisemann
Dove Hill Weavers
70 Enright Ave.
Freehold, NJ 07728
201/780-1823
Crafts Innovator and Instructor

Arri Parker
The Woman's Newspaper of Princeton, Inc.
43 Southern Way
Princeton, NJ 08540
609/924-1330
Publisher

Lynne H. Pitcher
G.R. Pitcher, Inc.
35 S. First Ave.
Highland Park, NJ 08904
201/846-2021
Computer Programmer/Analyst

Cheryl Taub Pliskin, ACSW, MSW
82 Boothby Dr.
Mt. Laurel, NJ 08054
609/234-2195
Licensed Marriage Counselor, Family
Therapist

Donna Prostak
Suitability
520 Spring Valley Dr.
Bridgewater, NJ 08807
201/725-6597
Personal Shopper, Image Consultant

Leni Rabinowitz
Leni Distributors Ltd., Inc.
370 Willard Rd.
Paramus, NJ 07652
201/265-3126
Makeup Consultant, Salesperson

Rose Rogozinski
Jomark Corporation
RD 2 - Box 368 Dutchtown Rd.
Belle Mead, NJ 08502
201/359-8860
Exporter

"Margit" Designer Fashion
by Margit Meissner-Jackson
Photographer: Neal Preston
Camera Five

Mary Ellen Rohon
131 Madison Ave.
Englewood, NJ 07631
201/871-4548
Educational Consultant

Margaret Romanski
Moongotta Publications Inc.
PO Box 2023
Bloomfield, NJ 07003
201/748-9339
Publisher

State Directory

66 I am wearing many different hats and sometimes I have to ask myself whether I am the accountant, marketing director, typist/secretary, writer, publicist, or speaker that day. Still, I can decide which role to play, and my days are never dull with so many new skills to learn. **99**

Lecturer

Jacqueline Lemort Rudolfer
Sculpture Walls
44 Smith St.
Closter, NJ 07624
201/768-6470
Artist

Colleen Ruffini
Execu-Sec
PO Box 439
Allendale, NJ 07401
201/825-0357
Secretary/Word Processor

Anita Ruslin
15 Warwick Rd.
Edison, NJ 08820
201/548-5481
Stationer

Sunny Schlenger
Schlenger Organizational Systems
6 Aberdeen Pl.
Fair Lawn, NJ 07410
201/791-2396
Personal Systems Designer

Cynthia Schmid
Triskelion Collectibles
42 Arcadia Way
Hillsdale, NJ 07642
201/391-5069
Collectibles Dealer

Louise A. Seeger
Janus Express, Inc.
425 Broad Ave.
Palisades Park, NJ 07650
201/947-1200; 212/848-1025
Traffic Coordinator

Helen Seymour
Personally Puzzled
69 Edgemere Ave.
Plainsboro, NJ 08536
609/799-0845
Artisan

Dana Shilling
Plaintext
41 Mercer St.
Jersey City, NJ 07302
201/333-1173
Forms Designer

Dorothy "Eudora" Sinclair
Jo Dot Creations
848 Woodmere Dr.
Cliffwood Beach, NJ 07735
201/566-4704
Craftsperson

Stephanie Solodar-Katz
SSK Freelance Typing Service
7 Lee Ct.
Maplewood, NJ 07040
201/762-5937
Paralegal, Secretary/Typist

Joanne Stankievich
Executive Women's Council of North Jersey
107 Boulevard
Mountain Lakes, NJ 07046
201/334-7947
Business Management Consultant

Karen Starrett
Karen Starrett Graphic Design
27 Marshall Rd.
Ocean Township, NJ 07712
201/922-0810
Graphic Designer

Irene Stella
A Stella Show
162 Stuart St.
Paramus, NJ 07652
201/262-3063
Exhibition Manager

Anita L. Stellenwerf
Anita L. Stellenwerf, CPA
59 Winding Trail
Mahwah, NJ 07430
201/825-8197
Certified Public Accountant

Janet B. Summerville
J & W Associates
408 Route 17 S.
Carlstadt, NJ 07072
201/935-2353
Nutrition Consultant

Barbara M. Sunden
Mary Kay Cosmetics
411 Longview Ct.
Northvale, NJ 07647
201/768-2944
National Sales Director

Veronica Toker
Signs For The Times
PO Box 273
Rockaway, NJ 07866
201/627-2147
Engraver

Jessica Vermylen
Vermylen, Inc.
8 Gloucester Pl.
Morristown, NJ 07960
201/285-0468
Copywriter

Judith Wadia
707 Abbott St.
Highland Park, NJ 08904
201/985-2207
Artist

Vera Hollander Wadler
Vera Hollander Wadler, Public Relations
603 Kent Ave.
Teaneck, NJ 07666
201/836-6015
Public Relations Consultant

June Walker-Sloat
814 Leland Ave.
Plainfield, NJ 07062
201/753-1839
Budget and Tax Consultant

Marianne Wehrenberg
The Key Directory, Inc.
PO Box 562
East Brunswick, NJ 08816
201/254-6448
Publisher

Elizabeth P. Whittlesey, C.F.A.
Whittlesey Investment Corporation
PO Box 251
Princeton, NJ 08540
609/921-8382
Investment Advisor

Carol Zych
Infoserve
54 Park Ave.
Verona, NJ 07044
201/783-2900
Information Researcher and
Consultant

NEW MEXICO

Renita Freeman-Hubbard
Albuquerque Typing Service
Box 13133
Albuquerque, NM 87192
505/293-7083
Secretary/Typist

NEW YORK

Susan Abrams
Mary Kay Cosmetics, Inc.
116 Old Army Rd.
Scarsdale, NY 10583
212/548-3299, Ext. 554
914/968-7169, Ext. 554
Beauty Consultant and Lecturer

Miriam Monell Agresti, Ph.D.
11 Wren Dr.
Woodbury, NY 11797
516/921-3924
Psychologist, Family Therapist

Suzanne Baer
302 West 12th St.
New York, NY 10014
212/675-4165
Career Counseling Consultant

Toby Baron
Window Designs
1042 Webster Ave.
New Rochelle, NY 10864
914/725-1565
Interior Designer

Katherine T. Benassi
Career Development Concepts
9 Deer Lane
Wantagh, NY 11793
516/781-9528
Counselor

Virginia Bisanz
Mechanics, (A Writer's Quarterly)
PO Box 207
Hyde Park, NY 12538
Editor

Peggy R. Blumenthal
The "B" Hive
66 Skyview La.
New Rochelle, NY 10804
914/636-3222
Salesperson

Barbara Bonner
GPO Box 2608
Cadman Plaza
Brooklyn, NY 11201
212/858-9026
Free-lance Fashion Designer

Joanne F. Brown
The Schemers
67 Tintern Lane
Scarsdale, NY 10583
914/723-8867
Party Planner/Decorator

Judy Caden
Judy Caden Marionettes
180 Duane St.
New York, NY 07052
212/431-7627
Puppeteer

Ann Howard Calderwood
417 Riverside Dr.
New York, NY 10025
212/864-5532
Publishing Services Specialist

> **❝I am a thousand times happier working alone at home, watching my own creative ideas materialize, than I could possibly be in any other situation. Instead of waiting any longer for the 'right' job to come along, which would provide me 'experience' and self-fulfillment, I decided that the only sensible alternative was to create my own career. Handling all aspects of the business myself, I am definitely getting my share of 'on the job training.'❞**
>
> Craftsperson

Andrea N. Coggeshall
Accu-Records
80 Southern Hills Circle
Rochester, NY 14467
716/334-0677
Records Manager

Sally Cooney
Cooney Tunes
145 East 27th St.
New York, NY 10016
212/532-0353
Photographer/Designer

Ann I. Czompo
AC Publications
PO Box 238
Homer, NY 13077
607/749-4040
Typographer

State Directory

Sarah T. Donner
Sarah T. Donner, Inc.
54 Chaucer St.
Hartsdale, NY 10530
914/428-1483
Caterer

Joyce Dutka
Joyce's Janimals, Inc.
2600 Netherland Ave.
Riverdale, NY 10463
212/543-1567
Artist, Photographer

Betty Marx Dwin
Marx Enterprises Company
Suite 1008—510 E. 77th St.
New York, NY 10162
212/734-2552
Accessories Manufacturer

Zohar and Partner
Belly Dancer
Photographer: Robert Buchanan

240

Roberta Edwards
Watkins
115-40 Lincoln St.
South Ozone Park, NY 11420
212/529-3099
Dealer/Distributor

Ellen Eisner
716 Secor Rd.
Hartsdale, NY 10530
914/761-7116
Tag/Estate Sale Specialist, Household
Liquidator

Francine Fierstein
Aleph-Bet
12 Secor Rd.
Scarsdale, NY 10583
914/723-9390
Judaic Artist and Teacher

Judith Forward
Judy's
Cedar Lake
Clayville, NY 13322
315/839-5633
Fashion Consultant, Trainer

Mary Jo Gatti
Dayspring
Box 666
Plandome, NY 11030
516/627-2891
Giftware Consultant and Engraver

Rema Goldberg
Rema Goldberg Career Consultants
29 Tarryhill Rd.
Tarrytown, NY 10591
914/631-8165
Career Counselor

Chris Davis Haslinger
Communications Enterprises
35 Quarry Dr.
Wappingers Falls, NY 12590
914/298-8108
Editor/Writer

Marilynne Herbert
Marilynne Herbert Photography
88 Walworth Ave.
Scarsdale, NY 10583
914/725-5025
Free-lance Photographer

Roberta Hershenson
35 Hampton Rd.
Scarsdale, NY 10583
914/723-1891
Photographer

Sandi F. Howell
Mother Earth's Emporium
554 S. 10th Ave.
Mt. Vernon, NY 10550
914/699-4372
Craftsperson

Dianne Keesee
Hawley Rd.
North Salem, NY 10560
914/669-8325
Fashion Designer

Carol R. Klein
Advantage Typing Service
53 Clements Pl.
Hartsdale, NY 10530
914/949-6482
Typist

Lorette Konezny
Pen Notes, Inc.
134 West Side Ave.
Freeport, NY 11520
516/868-5753
Educational Publisher/Manufacturer

Joan Landsbergis
The Write Person For Advertising
and Public Relations
766 S. Long Beach Ave.
Freeport, NY 11520
516/378-7025
Marketing Communications Writer/
Consultant

Lillian P. Langseth, M.S.
Lyda Associates
Oak Tree Rd.
Palisades, NY 10964
914/359-8282
Communications Consultant, Writer

Shirley Liss
Jackpotunities, Inc.
102 Catherine Rd.
Scarsdale, NY 10583
914/723-6427
Editor/Publisher

Barbara L. Lobron
85 Hicks St.
Brooklyn, NY 11201
212/625-6648
Editor, Photographer

B. G. Mandel
70-20 108 St.
Forest Hills, NY 11375
212/261-1243
Salesperson

Mariacecilia Marambio-Hurtado
4 Tucker Ave.
New City, NY 10956
914/634-5887
Foreign Language Educator

Tamara J. Martin
Growing Free
PO Box 488
Yorktown Heights, NY 10598
914/245-5910
Bookseller

Vicki Mechner
OmniQuest, Inc.
PO Box 15
Chappaqua, NY 10514
914/238-9646
Business Consultant and
Information Specialist

Lurrae Lupone Meyers
SOLEMUSIC Company
241 Furnace Dock Rd.
Peekskill, NY 10566
914/739-4678; 739-1069
Marketing Entrepreneur

Angel Olivieri
Tax Relief
300 Saw Mill River Rd.
Elmsford, NY 10523
914/592-6857
Income Tax Preparer

Christine Pacchiana
Plant Care by Christine, Inc.
40 Whitlaw Close
Chappaqua, NY 10514
914/241-2678
Interiorscaper

Joan Peckolick
Joan of Art
135 W. 17th St.
New York, NY 10011
212/242-7409
Art Director/Graphic Designer

Marjorie Pollack
151 Rock Creek Lane
Scarsdale, NY 10583
914/725-5824
Moving Consultant and Organizer

Rita Press
Labeleze, Inc.
P.O Box 223
Baldwin, NY 11510
516/379-2978
Manufacturer

Arleen Gradinger Priest
41 Hampton Rd.
Scarsdale, NY 10583
914/725-3632
Publishing Consultant, Business
Consultant, Lecturer

Labarbara Mallette Pugh
Round Linens by Mallette, Inc.
PO Box 206
Monsey, NY 10952
914/425-1828
Manufacturer

Judith Pynchon
Box 26
West Sayville, NY 11796
516/589-7769
Human Resources Development
Specialist

Wilma Olivette Reid
Silver Phoenix
554 S. 10th Ave.
Yonkers, NY 10550
914/965-2332
Multimedia Craftsperson

Emily Rosen
Witty Ditty, Inc.
205 Rogers Dr.
Scarsdale, NY 10583
914/235-5590
Lyricist/Writer/Entertainer

Bryna F. Sarokin
Plus Five Marketing Services
1365 E. 23 St.
Brooklyn, NY 11210
212/258-7674
Sales Promotion/Advertising Specialist

Doris L. Sassower
Doris L. Sassower, P.C.
283 Soundview Ave.
White Plains, NY 10606
914/997-1677; 212/490-3866
Attorney

516 379-2978   RITA PRESS

LABELEZE INC.

P.O. BOX 223 • BALDWIN, NEW YORK 11510

Sharon Silverman
63 Walbrooke Rd.
Scarsdale, NY 10583
914/723-6279
Nutrition Consultant and Diet Consultant

Elizabeth Adams Smith
Adams Smith Productions
PO Box 52
Rye, NY 10580
914/967-0994
Audio-Visual Producer

Renee Soloway
1230 Pennsylvania Ave., #15H
Brooklyn, NY 11239
212/642-2356
Typist

Laura Spiegel
Zohar, Belly-Tellygrams, Inc.
64 Old Colony Rd.
Hartsdale, NY 10530
914/723-5252
Belly Dancer

Lois R. Stenzel
Word Craft
15-81 208th St.
Bayside, NY 11360
212/423-3480
Word Processing Specialist

State Directory

Helene Trosky
Yarmouth Rd.
Purchase, NY 10577
914/946-2464
Artist, Art Dealer, Educator

Cynthia Wallach
Pajama Party
2 Hickory Lane
Scarsdale, NY 10583
914/472-3808
Salesperson

Phyllis Wittner
Wittner Associates, Inc.
6 Pheasant Run
PO Box 271–Dept. 116
Larchmont, NY 10538
914/633-9307
Author/Publisher

Sylvia Wolff
Aleph-Bet
80 Ralph Ave.
White Plains, NY 10606
914/948-4314
Judaic Artist and Teacher

Myrna R. Youdelman
Gift Finders International
7 Tennyson St.
Hartsdale, NY 10530
914/948-6121
Manufacturer's Rep, Consultant on
Product Development

Suzanne Zilenziger
270 Nelson Rd.
Scarsdale, NY 10583
914/472-4676
Nutrition/Diet Counselor

NORTH CAROLINA

Jody Bryan
Scarborough Faire
Rt. 1, Box 280
Highlands, NC 28741
704/526-5314
Herbalist

Paula Baker Lohrmann
New All Over
307-A East Blvd.
Charlotte, NC 28203
704/376-3766; 847-6352
Image and Color Consultant

OHIO

Davie Strauss Hyman
Davie Hyman Designs
12908 Westchester Trail
Chesterland, OH 44026
216/729-3118
Needlepainting Designer

Julie Kozlow
Julie Kozlow, Business Services
7149 Natalie Blvd.
Northfield Center, OH 44067
216/467-9229; 467-8059
Secretary, Bookkeeper/Accountant

Marion Landis
Ultra-Fine Products, Inc.
21950 Byron Rd.
Cleveland, OH 44122
216/283-1033
Manufacturer

Myra G. Orenstein
MDG&O Advertising, Inc.
12900 Lake Ave. - Penthouse 8
Cleveland, OH 44107
216/529-1550
Advertising Consultant

Wilma C. Robinson
Career Action Planning
30 Pennsylvania Ave.
Waterville, OH 43566
419/878-4656; 877-5328
Career Consultant

OKLAHOMA

Corazon S. Watkins
1107 South Utah
Muskogee, OK 74401
918/683-0926
Craftsperson

PENNSYLVANIA

Claire M. Cleaver
CONCEPTS by Claire, Inc.
174 Popodickon Dr.
Boyertown, PA 19512
215/367-5481
Marketing Consultant

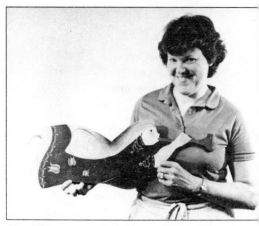

Terri Lipman
Folk Artist
Photographer: William J. Holland

Cynthia L. Euske
Central Penn Translation Services
488 Pine Ridge Circle
Lewisberry, PA 17339
717/938-1369
Translator

Brenda Utigard Hart
Hart Designs
330 Merion Rd.
Merion Station, PA 19066
215/664-4341
Illustrator

Terri Lipman
Terri's Folk Art
437 Lombard St.
Dallastown, PA 17313
717/244-8438
Folk Artist

Mary Mackin
Mari
56 Yeager Ave.
Forty Fort, PA 18704
717/288-5938
Artist

Patricia Norimatsu
Facemetrics, Inc.
Box 124
Plymouth Meeting, PA 19462
215/828-4865
"Pathfinder"

Carol Piper
501 Guard Lock Dr.
Lock Haven, PA 17745
717/748-5563
Calligrapher

FACEMETRICS
facial exercises for a fast facelift

Patricia Norimatsu

Constance Porte-Aigeldinger
Wordcraft
362 Prince Frederick St.
King of Prussia, PA 19406
215/337-2370; 337-2368
Writer

Nancy Thode
Camp Advisory Service
3201 Shawnee Green
Ambler, PA 19002
215/643-3325
Camp Consultant

Diane G. Wenrick
Diana Designs
Shavertown, PA 18708
717/696-3757
Sales Manager

Lois Winston
One Asbury Ave.
Melrose Park, PA 19126
215/635-3471
Needlecraft Designer/Illustrator

Bobbi Wolf
Poemetrics
228 Standish Rd.
Merion, PA 19066
215/667-5896
Poet

SOUTH DAKOTA

Linda M. Hasselstrom
Lame Johnny Press
Star Route 3 Box 9A
Hermosa, SD 57744
605/255-4466
Writer/Publisher

TENNESSEE

Beth Peck Cooper
Spatial Consultants
1455 Peabody Ave.
Memphis, TN 38104
901/276-9608
City and Regional Planner and
Interior Designer

Hilda M. Dorofee
Rt. 8, Branywood Dr.
Murfreesboro, TN 37130
615/896-2547
Craftsperson

TEXAS

Sara Addis
Sara Care Franchise Corporation
1200 Golden Key Circle, Suite 227
El Paso, TX 79925
915/593-5071
Franchisor and Home Sitter

Martha Anson
2615 N. Pecan
Nacogdoches, TX 75961
713/564-9754
Manufacturer/Craftsperson

Catherine E. Cole
Family Works
1014 Field St.
San Marcos, TX 78666
512/396-3890
Needlework Designer

Buffee Lewis
buffee originals
1602 Kindred Lane
Richardson, TX 75080
214/231-4964
Designer/Craftsperson

UTAH

Jan O. Steinbach
Janographics
6279 S. Clara Dr.
West Jordan, UT 84084
801/969-1100
Graphic Designer

Linda M. Hasselstrom
Publisher
Photographer: Steve Newnum

State Directory

Käthe Äna
Storyteller
Story Therapy
Story Tapes

Route 2, Pulaski, Wi. 54162
(414) 833-7163

VERMONT

Audrey Pudvah
Audrey's Designs
RD1
East Calais, VT 05650
802/456-7491
Needleworker

VIRGINA

Ingrid Bauer
1108 Moorefield Creek Rd. S.W.
Vienna, VA 22180
703/281-9539
Human Resource Developer

Virginia F. Dahlgren
Redbird Studio
PO Box 10264
Alexandria, VA 22310
703/971-3577
Artist

Clare H. Grosgebauer
Small Wonders Enterprises
10510 Acacia Lane
Fairfax, VA 22030
703/560-0577
Advertising/Marketing Consultant,
Writer

Laura B. Pryce
Contemporary Typing Service
4205 Lamarre Dr.
Fairfax, VA 22030
703/352-0625
Typist/Secretary

Gail S. Seredni
Small Business Systems
2303 Capehart Rd.
Richmond, VA 23229
804/285-9859
Tax Accountant

WASHINGTON

Mary Ellerman
R & M What Knots
23406 94th Ave. W.
Edmonds, WA 98020
206/542-1592
Tole Painter, Teacher

Roxie English
Evergreen Accents
1023 S. Adams, Suite 182
Olympia, WA 98501
206/943-9845
Mail-Order Sales Director

Joyce A. Friedland
Tif n' Todds
731 W. Knox
Spokane, WA 99205
509/327-3452
Designer/Manufacturer

Darla M. Sims
Unique Designs
312 S. Jackson
East Wenatchee, WA 98801
509/884-6092
Designer

Marilyn Warren
Warren Enterprises
N. 1318 Ella
Spokane, WA 99206
509/926-3736
Artist, Writer, Teacher

WEST VIRGINIA

Bette Sherman
The Hairy Beast
Rt 1, Box 334
Hedgesville, WV 25427
304/754-8443
Mail-Order Salesperson

WISCONSIN

Käthe Äna
Käthe Äna, Storyteller
Route 2
Pulaski, WI 54162
414/833-7163
Storyteller, Oral Historian

Susan C. P. Drake
119 S. Grand Ave.
Waukesha, WI 53186
414/782-2476
Bookkeeper

Patricia Durovy
Manifestation Management, Inc.
2437 N. Booth St.
Milwaukee, WI 53212
414/374-5433
Small Business Consultant

Joann Gerkhardt
Angelique
37308 Valley Rd.
Oconomowoc, WI 53066
414/567-7623
Quilter/Designer

WYOMING

Marian Bloss-Blaney
Butterfly, Inc.
4801 Yesness Ct.
Casper, WY 82604
307/265-2207
Advertising/Public Relations
Consultant

New Dimension Pillow
by Iva Bramble

Product/Service Directory

Typewriter
Photographer: Helaine Messer

Product/Service Directory

"Smeary Smooch"
Credit: © Helen Keenan Studio,
1983

Accessories

Sally P. Blumenfeld
First Class
5456 Fremont Ave. S.
Minneapolis, MN 55419
612/823-0719
Accessories Manufacturer:
manufacturing quilted travel
accessory bags, i.e., cosmetic
bags, jewelry rolls, sewing kits,
diaper bags.

Tina Bobker
Rainbow Artisans, Inc.
19 Troy Ave.
Livingston, NJ 07039
201/533-9081
Accessories Manufacturer:
manufacturing and distributing
infants' bedding and accessories. Had
feature articles in *The New York
Times, Newark Star Ledger, Woman's
Day* magazine, and *Hour Magazine*
TV show. Member: Board of Trustees,
National Alliance of Homebased
Businesswomen.

Carole Dlugasch
Rainbow Artisans, Inc.
35 Old Indian Rd.
West Orange, NJ 07052
201/731-6721
Accessories Manufacturer:
manufacturing and distributing
infants' bedding and accessories. Had
feature articles in *The New York
Times, Newark Star Ledger, Woman's
Day* magazine, and *Hour Magazine*
TV show. Member: Board of North
Central Jersey Chapter, National
Alliance of Homebased
Businesswomen, and Membership
Chair.

Betty Marx Dwin
Marx Enterprises Company
Suite 1008—510 E. 77th St.
New York, NY 10162
212/734-2552
Accessories Manufacturer: Ultrasuede
accessories for women, men, and
needlepointers—three separate
product lines. Member: National
Alliance of Homebased
Businesswomen.

Accounting Services

Susan C. P. Drake
119 S. Grand Ave.
Waukesha, WI 53186
414/782-2476
Bookkeeper: complete services—from
system setup through financial
statements, specializing in
custom-designed, inexpensive
systems. Long-distance (i.e., via mail)
services available for sole
proprietorships.

Bette-Jane Hardersen
22 Burnwood Dr.
Bloomfield, CT 06002
203/242-8902
Accountant: maintenance of financial
records for small businesses.
Accounting: original entry through
balance sheet and income statement,
quarterly reporting federal and state.
1981 graduate of Greater Hartford
Community College with Associate in
Science degree. Graduated Magna
Cum Laude. Charter member: Phi
Theta Kappa, national honor society
for two-year schools.

Julie Kozlow
Julie Kozlow, Business Services
7149 Natalie Blvd.
Northfield Center, OH 44067
216/467-9229; 467-8059
Secretary, Bookkeeper/Accountant:
services include typing (from
handwritten copy, machine dictation,
shorthand notes, and my
composition); full-charge
bookkeeping/accounting; payroll
preparation; and temporary office
help. The book *How to Start Your
Own Secretarial Services Business at
Home* (SK Publications, 1980),
detailed my business, originally
begun as Julie Kozlow, Secretarial
Services.

Angel Olivieri
Tax Relief
300 Saw Mill River Rd.
Elmsford, NY 10523
914/592-6857
Income Tax Preparer: complete
income tax preparation service.
Member: Elmsford-Greenburgh
Businesswomen's Chamber of
Commerce, chairperson of
Scholarships Awards Committee.

Marilyn Salmieri
Marilyn Salmieri, CPA
4 Baker Ave.
Westport, CT 06880
203/226-1900
Certified Public Accountant: tax
planning for individuals and small
businesses. Member: American
Institute of CPA's and Connecticut
Society of CPA's.

Gail S. Seredni
Small Business Systems
2303 Capehart Rd.
Richmond, VA 23229
804/285-9859
Tax Accountant: specializing in small
businesses' and individuals'
accounting and tax needs. Assist
small companies in setting up books;
provide tax advice and financial
statement preparation.

Anita L. Stellenwerf
Anita L. Stellenwerf, CPA
59 Winding Trail
Mahwah, NJ 07430
201/825-8197
Certified Public Accountant:
extensive experience with women's
personal and business accounting and
financial problems. Computerized
accounting capabilities available.
Former auditor with the IRS. Member:
Beta Gamma Sigma (National Business
Honors Society), New Jersey Society
of CPA's, American Institute of CPA's.

Marianne Turlington
PO Box 23414
San Diego, CA 92123
619/566-3348
Bookkeeper: over twenty years of
experience in accounting offices
through income tax returns. Monthly
bookkeeping services, including
payroll and sales tax returns.
Year-end bookkeeping and income
tax returns. Can recap the year's data
even if in "shoe-box" status.
Reasonable fees; monthly rates start at
$30 per month (with no employees).

June Walker-Sloat
814 Leland Ave.
Plainfield, NJ 07062
201/753-1839
Budget and Tax Consultant:
specializing in people in the
arts—writers, musicians, artists—and
other self-employed. Financial
guidance and planning for women in
the process of separation or newly
divorced.

Phyllis Wittner
Wittner Associates, Inc.
6 Pheasant Run
PO Box 271–Dept. 116
Larchmont, NY 10538
914/633-9307
Author/Publisher: HOME
RUNNER™—FINANCIAL RECORDS:
personal money organizer and how-to
workbook with systems and forms for
organizing and managing all personal
financial matters. Brochure available.
Wholesale prices for accountants,
financial planners/consultants for use
by clients. $14.95 plus $1.50
shipping, N.Y. State delivery sales
tax. Inquire about software program.

Advertising/ PR/Marketing

Marian Bloss-Blaney
Butterfly, Inc.
4801 Yesness Ct.
Casper, WY 82604
307/265-2207
Advertising/Public Relations
Consultant: all phases of commercial
advertising and promotion, including
political campaigns. Experience in all
media. Active civically, serving on
many local and statewide boards;
named to Outstanding Young Women
of America in 1980. Bilingual
(Spanish), ex-model, legislative
lobbyist, active in local theater,
member of dozens of associations,
director of retail association.

66 We value our freedom
to choose what we do
with any hour of the day.
We value our personal
growth in spirit and ability
which results from con-
stant exploration of our
potentials. We value our
ability to stand for what
we believe in and com-
municate to others by ex-
ample the possibilities
of enjoying a whole,
centered, independent
lifestyle. **99**

Craftsperson

Claire M. Cleaver
CONCEPTS by Claire, Inc.
174 Popodickon Dr.
Boyertown, PA 19512
215/367-5481
Marketing Consultant: CONCEPTS by
Claire, Inc., a creative marketing
agency providing business consulting
services on a national level,
specializing in image-building public
relations programs, training
publications, and seminars. Author,
public speaker, and seminar leader.
Selected for *Who's Who of American
Women*.

Stella Hart
Stella Hart, Inc.
105 Shady Lane
Randolph, NJ 07869
201/895-3356
Public Relations Consultant: working
with profit and nonprofit
organizations from concept through
completion, specializing in publicity,
promotions, promotional items,
projects. Provide clients with
brochures, celebrity appearances,
consultation services for fund raising
and other events; local, state, and
national magazine and newspaper
articles, newsletters, news releases,
photographs (working with Anne
Cousineau), and speechwriting.

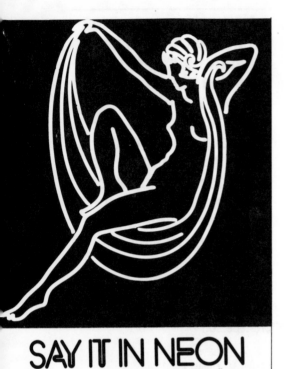

SAY IT IN NEON
custom neon gallery

Created by Bryna F. Sarokin
Advertising Specialist

Joan Landsbergis
The Write Person For Advertising
and Public Relations
766 S. Long Beach Ave.
Freeport, NY 11520
516/378-7025
Marketing Communications
Writer/Consultant: free-lance
concepts and copy—ads, brochures,
direct mail, promotions, video
scripts, commercials, catalogs,
rewrites. Public relations: feature
articles, product publicity, news
releases, speeches, newsletters,
annual reports. Corporate, trade,
industrial, consumer, business,
financial, retail.

Myra G. Orenstein
MDG&O Advertising, Inc.
12900 Lake Ave. - Penthouse 8
Cleveland, OH 44107
216/529-1550
Advertising Consultant: full-service
agency specializing in consumer
products: a creative cooperative of
which I serve as core figure handling
account services, media, copywriting,
and radio production. Staff
comprised of top creative people in
this area. The result? Top creativity at
a reasonable price!

Bryna F. Sarokin
Plus Five Marketing Services
1365 E. 23 St.
Brooklyn, NY 11210
212/258-7674
Sales Promotion/Advertising
Specialist: professional sales
promotion within budget for small
businesses creating and producing a
complete marketing plan or a single
promotion—brochure, flyer, direct-
mail catalog, newsletter, sales letter,
advertising, and/or press release.

Vera Hollander Wadler
Vera Hollander Wadler,
Public Relations
603 Kent Ave.
Teaneck, NJ 07666
201/836-6015
Public Relations Consultant: publicity
and sales promotion for companies or
individuals marketing products
and/or services. Programs include
media publicity (print and broadcast),
special events, newsletters,
brochures, press conferences, and
speechwriting. Extensive consumer
and trade experience in the following
areas: pets, toys, home furnishings,
and professional associations.

Maggie Weisberg
Inventors Licensing & Marketing
Agency
PO Box 251
Tarzana, CA 91356
213/344-3375
Marketing Consultant: licensing and
selling inventions to industry. Speak
to manufacturers' associations.
Publish books that deal with
inventions/inventing. Serve on
board of directors of Inventors
Workshop International, Geothermal
World Publications, and ILMA
Management, Inc.

Antiques

Cheri Lynn Russell
Wicker Fixer and Caning
Rt. 1, Box 283B
Ozark, MO 65721
417/485-6148
Wicker Restorer, Chair Caner: wicker,
rattan, baskets, and chair caning
restoration. Custom orders and
antique reproductions. Buy and sell.
Free advice and estimates with photo.
Call or send to this husband/wife
team. Feature articles in *Woman's
Day, Kansas City Star, Seattle P.I.
and Times, Today Florida,
Springfield News and Leader,* (MO.).
Lecturer.

Cynthia Schmid
Triskelion Collectibles
42 Arcadia Way
Hillsdale, NJ 07642
201/391-5069
Collectibles Dealer: limited edition
plates, figurines, lithographs, etc.
Write and publish quarterly
newsletter; sponsor of a collector's
club; teach course on collectibles to
adults and children. Member:
National Association of Limited
Edition Dealers.

Appraisals

Elizabeth Carr
International Society of Fine Arts
Appraisers, Ltd.
PO Box 280
River Forest, IL 60305
312/848-3340
Fine Arts Appraiser: professional
writer published nationally and
internationally in special fields of
art/antiques. Lecturer in art/antiques
in regional colleges and universities
in adult education classes.
Publisher/editor of quarterly
newsletter, *The Evaluator.* Member:
National Writers Club and numerous
specialized antique/art associations;
officer/director in many.

The Arts

Ann Marcelyn Caver
109 Ripton Rd.
Huntington, CT 06484
203/929-8882
Artist/Designer: not your usual etched glass. Multimedia artist specializing in etched glass murals, room dividers, and lighted columns. Also producing unusual pieces combining painting and etched glass, etched and stained glass and lit glass. Special effects consultant to architects and designers.
Media: oil, glass (etched and stained) wood, ink, acrylics, pastels, paper.

Dolly Curtis
Architectural Textiles
35 Flat Rock Rd.
Easton, CT 06612
203/372-4511
Fiber Artist: specializing in large-scale architectural weavings for residences and corporate buildings. Commissions installed in Chicago, New York, and Connecticut. Exhibitions in Soho, New York City, Paul Mellon Arts Center, Connecticut governor's residence, Pennsylvania State University Museum of Art, traveling museum shows. Artist Grant, Connecticut Commission on the Arts. Reviewed in numerous publications. Listed in *Who's Who of American Women, 1981–1982*.
Medium: fiber.

Virginia F. Dahlgren
Redbird Studio
PO Box 10264
Alexandria, VA 22310
703/971-3577
Artist: small original etchings, dollhouse size, framed in gilded or stained wood. Similar-size color block prints soon to be produced.
Media: drypoint etching, block prints.

Joyce Dutka
Joyce's Janimals, Inc.
2600 Netherland Ave.
Riverdale, NY 10463
212/543-1567
Artist, Photographer: personalized children's art. Names in animal letters, painted in watercolor. Choice of colors, mats, frames.
Medium: watercolor.

Jean Eitel
Palm Beach Needle-Painters, Inc.
912 Evergreen Dr.
North Palm Beach, FL 33408
305/622-1326
Fiber Artist and Quilter: design of needlepoint canvas and quilt patterns. Designer of fiber art works; author; consultant; lecturer and teacher on use of color in fiber arts field. Member of The National Needlework Association, South and Southwest Quilt Association, National Quilt Association, and Sand-Dollar Quilters.
Medium: fiber.

Mary Ellerman
R & M What Knots
23406 94th Ave. W.
Edmonds, WA 98020
206/542-1592
Tole Painter, Teacher: classes at home and around the country in different styles of folk art. Member: National Society of Tole and Decorative Painters; have taught workshops at their yearly conventions. Helped organize local groups of tole painters and rosemalers (Norwegian folk art); held offices in both these organizations.
Media: oils and acrylics.

Francine Fierstein
Aleph-Bet
12 Secor Rd.
Scarsdale, NY 10583
914/723-9390
Judaic Artist and Teacher: with partner, Sylvia Wolff, creating art works in fabrics and pen and ink, incorporating Judiac themes and Hebrew lettering. Works include marriage documents, bar/bat mitzvah commemoratives, Judaic games and toys, wedding canopies, Torah ark curtains and mantles, and wall-hangings for homes and synagogues. Present workshops and programs on Jewish art topics.
Media: gouache, pen and ink, fabric, yarn.

> **66** When I have worked for months on greeting/notecard designs and have taken them to the printer for the completion of this long process, my work put into their hands, and then the telephone call letting me know I can pick up my work—the smell of printer's ink is the sweet smell of success for me! **99**

Graphic Designer

Victoria Leisy
Elegant Threads
79 Rogers Lake Trail
Old Lyme, CT 06371
203/434-9681
Fabric Designer: creating original hand-dyed designs on 100% pure silk. Fibers preshrunk and permanently dyed for clothing, accessories, jewelry, quilts, and limited amounts of yardage. Wholesale and special order requests welcome. Member: Connecticut River Artisans Cooperative, American Craft Council, Society of Connecticut Craftsmen, National Alliance of Homebased Businesswomen.
Medium: dye.

Terri Lipman
Terri's Folk Art
437 Lombard St.
Dallastown, PA 17313
717/244-8438
Folk Artist: folk painting on wood, including silhouettes, furniture, small gift items, reproduction-type items and weathervanes. State-juried member of the Pennsylvania Guild of Craftsmen. President of the local decorative artists' chapter, named Keystone Painters. Also member: York Art Association, York, Pa., and several historical societies. Work sold to shops and at juried arts and crafts shops.
Medium: acrylics.

Product/Service Directory

"Terra"
by Jacqueline Rudolfer and Eva Birkner
Photographer: Sally Dorian

Mary Mackin
Mari
56 Yeager Ave.
Forty Fort, PA 18704
717/288-5938
Artist: watercolor paintings depicting sporting events; also pet portraits using client's photograph or snapshot. Juried exhibits include two regionals: some awards. Prices from $35. Patchwork quilts—traditional designs, machine pieced, hand quilted, hand bound. Custom orders accepted. Prices from $250. First and second prize at county fair, 1981.
Medium: watercolor.

Audrey Nan Nelson
Nelson Crafts
RR 2, Box 212
Goshen, NH 03752
603/863-4394
Craftsperson/Artist: one-woman shows: Passim, Cambridge, MA; Helen Winnemore's Gallery, Columbus, OH; League NH Crafts, Nashua, NH. Published articles on enameling and weaving. Member: League NH Craftsmen, American Crafts Council, Handweavers Guild of America. Listed in *Who's Who of American Women,* 11th and 12th eds.; *World Who's Who of Women, 1979, 1981.* Medium: Acrylics and ceramics.

Jacqueline Lemort Rudolfer
Sculpture Walls
44 Smith St.
Closter, NJ 07624
201/768-6470
Artist: design studio and workshop creating sand-cast tiles for interior and exterior design—murals, table tops, partitions, planters, panels, or walls. Work shown in *The Designer, AIA Journal, Florida Quarterly, Interior Designer, Newark Star Ledger, Business Restaurant, Restaurant Design.* Restaurant and private home installations.
Medium: sand sculpture.

Roz Shirley
49 Pleasant St.
Medfield, MA 02052
617/359-2944
Fiber Artist: hand-felted sculpture. Work shown in nationally recognized, invitational and juried exhibits at galleries and museums; also at market shows, including Rhinebeck 1980–82. Work in the collection of the Corning Museum of Glass. Work published in *Shuttle, Spindle and Dyepot* and *Soft Sculpture* by Hall. Member: ACC and HGA.
Medium: felt.

Myla D. Smith
Murals By Myla
1935 Crescent
Franklin, IN 46131
317/736-5442; 232-7811
Graphic Artist, Writer; portrait artist: people and pets; also scenic painter. Graphics, line drawings, logo design. Locally and nationally published writer, specializing in humor. Winner 1982 New Haven "Canal Days" medallion contest. Member: Indianapolis Art League, Johnson County Arts Association, National Alliance of Homebased Businesswomen.
Media: pastels, pen and ink, watercolor, oil, acrylics, pencil.

Helene Trosky
Yarmouth Rd.
Purchase, NY 10577
914/946-2464
Artist, Art Dealer, Educator: selling paintings, graphics, sculpture—modern and contemporary. Printmaker, papermaker, cast paper abstractions. Restore prints and pastels. Writer of art history, modern and contemporary art, and art scene today. Listed in *Who's Who in American Art.* Cited in *Complete Book of Handmade Paper.* Member: Silvermine Guild and Artists Equity of N.Y.

Judith Wadia
707 Abbott St.
Highland Park, NJ 08904
201/985-2207
Artist: custom designing stained glass and mosaic for private homes, offices, schools, and religious buildings. Work closely with clients on all phases from design and color selection to installation. Largest commission to date: a mosaic wall fountain for the State of New Jersey under the Public Buildings Arts Inclusion Act.
Medium: stained glass and mosaic.

Sylvia Wolff
Aleph-Bet
80 Ralph Ave.
White Plains, NY 10606
914/948-4314
Judaic Artist and Teacher: with partner, Francine Fierstein, creating art works in fabrics and pen and ink, incorporating Judaic themes and Hebrew lettering. Works include marriage documents, bar/bat mitzvah commemoratives, Judaic games and toys, wedding canopies, Torah ark curtains and mantles, and wallhangings for homes and synagogues. Present workshops and programs on Jewish art topics.
Media: gouache, pen and ink, fabric, yarn.

Astrology

Jo M. Wolf

The Cyclo-Scan Report
PO Box 712-WH
Chicago, IL 60690
312/874-0548
Astrological Consultant: twenty years' experience as a practicing astrologer, including a number of years spent as teacher, lecturer, astrological TV/radio personality, radio talk show hostess, and columnist. Personal and business services available and in typewritten presentation for easy reference. Inquiries welcomed with no obligation.

Ea Zu-En

Zu-En Graphics Studio
8742 Luella Ave.
Chicago, IL 60617
312/768-2424
Astrological Counselor: services include natal reports for adults and children; relationship analysis reports; solar returns and transits. Office consultations by appointment only—business conducted primarily by mail order.

Astrological Counseling
8742 Luella Ave. Chicago, IL. 60617
Ea Zü-En 312-768-2424

Beauty Services

Susan Abrams

Mary Kay Cosmetics, Inc.
116 Old Army Rd.
Scarsdale, NY 10583
212/548-3299, Ext. 554
914/968-7169, Ext. 554
Beauty Consultant and Lecturer: complimentary facials given to individuals and groups, male and female, ages 12 and up, including analysis of skin and prescription of individual skin care program and instruction in product usage and suitable makeup techniques. Reorders; career opportunities; specially tailored group programs. Also Manhattan location.

Paula Baker Lohrmann

New All Over
307-A East Blvd.
Charlotte, NC 28203
704/376-3766; 847-6352
Image and Color Consultant: specializing in the best personalized look for each man and woman. Analysis of total individual: career goals, wardrobe, skin care, hair, makeup, shopping, color usage, custom-clothing design, weight control, and nutrition counseling. Teaching techniques: individual consultation, lecture/seminar, color charts, demonstration, style analysis, personal shopping, merchandise.

Leni Rabinowitz

Leni Distributors Ltd., Inc.
370 Willard Rd.
Paramus, NJ 07652
201/265-3126
Makeup Consultant, Salesperson: with 40–50 salespeople selling unlabeled (private label) cosmetics at home parties, office lunches, beauty salons, door-to-door, and any other means of direct sales.

Rosemary Summers

Rosemary's Health & Beauty Spa
16225 Greenfield #205
Detroit, MI 48235
313/837-8814
Health and Beauty Resource Developer: providing general public, mainly women, with information on health and beauty issues, such as healing power of herbs, fashion, cosmetics, yoga, massage, hair.

Information provided by experts through seminar format. During year, individuals provided with six weekend getaways with dinner party, sauna, swimming, exercise, massage, manicure, facial, and seminar.

Books

Tamara J. Martin

Growing Free
PO Box 488
Yorktown Heights, NY 10598
914/245-5910
Bookseller: Books for those interested in exposing children to different lifestyles, with special emphasis on exploring nonstereotyped, nonsexist roles. Write for free catalog.

Gail Pettiford Willett

Children Are Many Colors, Inc.
72 Chestnut St.
Cambridge, MA 02139
617/876-7665
Organization Director: Children Are Many Colors, a nonprofit organization dedicated to providing books that reflect children's cultural and racial backgrounds. Books for children from preschool through high school. CAMC's philosophy: children must have books that reflect their cultures, teach their history, and expand their horizons. Book catalog available.

Sarah Juniel Zaleski

Everywoman's Bookshelf
PO Box 104
Wilton, CT 06897
203/762-9426
Mail-Order Bookseller, Business Consultant: specializing in helping an individual start her own successful small business. Send SASE for subscription rates for catalog of "How to Start Your Own Business" books or for news of small business workshops being conducted in Connecticut. Member: American Booksellers Association and Women's National Book Association (NY).

Product/Service Directory

Business Opportunities

Sara Addis
Sara Care Franchise Corporation
1200 Golden Key Circle, Suite 227
El Paso, TX 79925
915/593-5071
Franchisor and Home Sitter: selling sitting service franchises to women interested in operating businesses out of their homes. Coordinating start-ups for new franchises including training, sitting services brochures, sales kits, and advertising support. Designated Entrepreneur of the Year by Business and Professional Women's organization of El Paso. Member: NAFE, NAHB, and BPW.

Mariana Hiser Burwell
9 Laketown Rd.
Long Valley, NJ 07853
201/876-4572
Sales Rep: of Brite Music Marketing Program, a family-based financial opportunity—a new and growing direct-sales, multi-level program of beautiful, wholesome children's music featured in songbooks, stereo records, and cassettes. "Reach a child with a song." Teaches children appreciation for self, others, nature, and work.

Judith Forward
Judy's
Cedar Lake
Clayville, NY 13322
315/839-5633
Fashion Consultant, Trainer: selling quality women's clothing—three lines, four weeks yearly, at home, by invitation only—to friends and acquaintances from traveling sample sets of $30,000 valuation. No investment. Fun, easy, and lucrative. Have never had such a good time working and earning money.

Ceil Greco
Mary Kay Cosmetics
611 N. Washington Ave.
Dunellen, NJ 08812
201/968-7037
Beauty Consultant: Sales Director, Mary Kay Cosmetics, teaching skin care and makeup application to women. Help women bring out the self-confidence they have such a hard time finding and guide them step by step in making each of their Mary Kay businesses grow. No background needed; training provided for successful businesses.

Deborah Mitchell
Creative Expressions
43 Collinswood Rd.
Wilton, CT 06897
203/762-9690
Regional Sales Manager: for Creative Expressions, a direct sales stitchery company, teaching and selling needlecrafts at home workshops. Recruit women to be stitchery consultants who want a part-time business of their own. Also work with women interested in furthering their career into sales management. Member: Direct Selling Association, National Alliance of Homebased Businesswomen.

Angela M. Mogin
Call A Wife, Inc.
48 McIntosh Rd.
Stamford, CT 06903
203/329-7600
Home Management Specialist: providing total home services to members, fulfilling the need for someone to run the household while the primary homemaker is working, volunteering, or devoting time to family. Franchises available.

Arleen Gradinger Priest
WWH Press
41 Hampton Rd.
Scarsdale, NY 10583
914/725-3632
Business Manager. An easy way to earn extra money! WWH Press, publisher of this publication, *Women Working Home: The Homebased Business Guide and Directory,* looking for sales people to sell this publication to friends, neighbors, and local organizations on commission basis. Phone or written inquiries welcome.

Mary Ellen Rohon
131 Madison Ave.
Englewood, NJ 07631
201/871-4548
Educational Consultant: training educational advisors for Childcraft toys; selling toys that teach; demonstrating selection of appropriate educational toys to parents at home, P.T.O.s, and other organizations. Fund-raising possibility. Good commissions; growth potential.

N. Irene Sloan
G.G. Associates
PO Box 21343
Detroit, MI 48221
313/863-2813
Distributor: Aloe Vera Products for Forever Living Products, a people business built through sharing. Minimum investment $198. A multilevel plan helping many distributors earn $15,000–$100,000 a year. Approved by F.D.A. Clinical evidence available of Aloe Vera's healing effect and nutritional value. Member: National Alliance of Homebased Businesswomen.

Joanne Stankievich
Executive Women's Council of North Jersey
107 Boulevard
Mountain Lakes, NJ 07046
201/334-7947
Business Management Consultant: training women to develop and manage part-time businesses, specifically in the fields of business promotion gifts, beauty consulting, nutrition, safety, commercial and residential sales. Personal self-development, goal-setting, and skill training provided. Affiliated with Income Builders International. Member: National Alliance of Homebased Businesswomen.

Barbara M. Sunden
Mary Kay Cosmetics
411 Longview Ct.
Northvale, NJ 07647
201/768-2944
National Sales Director: Beauty Consultant for skin care and glamour products—teaching, motivating, and guiding women to develop their own businesses in relationship to Mary Kay products. Sales Director's role: to groom consultants to promote themselves up the ranks to management levels.

Business Services

Marian Bloss-Blaney
Butterfly, Inc.
4801 Yesness Ct.
Casper, WY 82604
307/265-2207
Advertising/Public Relations
Consultant: all phases of commercial
advertising and promotion, including
political campaigns. Experience in all
media. Active civically, serving on
many local and statewide boards;
named to Outstanding Young Women
of America in 1980. Bilingual
(Spanish), ex-model, legislative
lobbyist, active in local theater,
member of dozens of associations,
director of retail association.

Andrea N. Coggeshall
Accu-Records
80 Southern Hills Circle
Rochester, NY 14467
716/334-0677
Records Manager: managing personal
and independent businesspersons'
records and receipts for taxes,
reimbursement, budgeting, etc.
Member: Rochester Women's
Network, National Alliance of
Homebased Businesswomen,
Association of Records Managers and
Administrators.

Maxine Gottesman
SHEFA
24 Morrill Ct.
Oakland, CA 94618
415/652-5247
Home Business Consultant: assisting
clients in overcoming concerns that
may prevent them from achieving an
effective "office of the future at
home"—principally, comfort levels
with personal computers;
secondarily, the language used in this
process. Coach people in making
requests, promises, declarations, and
assertions which support them in
their work.

Barbara L. May
May Services, Inc.
PO Box 77
Norwood, NJ 07648
201/768-9379
Mail-Order Fulfillment and Mailing
Service Operator: order
processing—receive mail at PO box,
process order, deposit monies as
required, and mail out material
ordered. Also, screen reader inquiries
with requests for directions, advice,
etc. Mailing services include monthly
newsletters, promotional mailings,
and odd-sized mailing materials that
cannot be handled by machine.

Vicki Mechner
OmniQuest, Inc.
PO Box 15
Chappaqua, NY 10514
914/238-9646
Business Consultant and Information
Specialist: finding the resources you
need—unusual or hard-to-find
products, suppliers of services
(including free-lance and independent
contractors), and information
(anything from a single fact or figure
to complete market studies).
Problem-solving consultations help
clarify your goals, streamline your
production/information procedures,
develop new product/market ideas.

Louise A. Seeger
Janus Express, Inc.
425 Broad Ave.
Palisades Park, NJ 07650
201/947-1200; 212/848-1025
Traffic Coordinator: specializing in
package pickup and delivery—sizes
varying from envelopes to van loads.
ASAP Exclusives, three-hour rushes,
same-day normals, and storage
services available. Member: National
Alliance of Homebased Businesswomen, National Organization of
Women, Kappa Delta Pi.

Dana Shilling
Plaintext
41 Mercer St.
Jersey City, NJ 07302
201/333-1173
Forms Designer: designing and
publishing plain English forms for
lawyers, businesses, and consumers.
Also available for private language-
simplification assignments. Plaintext
forms reviewed in *Vogue, Glamour,*
and *Family Circle.* My first book,
*Fighting Back (Consumer
Complaints)* published by William
Morrow in September 1982.

> 66 My concentration is
> less when he's around,
> but I feel that it's worth
> sacrificing a bit of effi-
> ciency for us to spend
> this time together. I gener-
> ally figure my hours
> worked with Nathan (age
> 4½) at a different dollar
> value than those when I
> am alone. I am grateful
> that he is growing up with
> concrete experience of
> my work situation, some-
> thing we never shared
> with the breadwinner in
> my family when I was
> growing up. 99
> Industrial Seamstress

Elizabeth Adams Smith
Adams Smith Productions
PO Box 52
Rye, NY 10580
914/967-0994
Audio-Visual Producer: specializing in
general and technical training, sales
presentations, educational programs,
and speaker support visuals. Handle
all aspects of a production from
concept and/or training design
through scripting, graphics,
photography, narration, music
programming, recording, pulsing, and
duplication and packaging. Generally
work in slides, filmstrips, and small
multi-image formats.

Veronica Toker
Signs For The Times
PO Box 273
Rockaway, NJ 07866
201/627-2147
Engraver: attractive, custom-made
signs for offices, banks, and hospitals.
Badges, key tags, luggage tags, and
name plates engraved on sturdy
plastic.

Product/Service Directory

Betty Vogel
Vogel's Demonstration Service
1254 Dickinson S.E.
Grand Rapids, MI 49507
616/452-0122
Food/Appliance Demo Specialist: supplying demonstrators for food and appliance promotions in food, appliance, and department stores. Service covers northern Indiana as well as the state of Michigan. Hire part-time, mostly female, help; but do have some men available. Training, demo reports, payroll provided. Member: NAHB.

Laurie Alexis Welch
The Box Office
Suite 890, The Courthouse Square
1000 Fourth St.
San Rafael, CA 94901
415/459-2697
Mail/Telephone Service Manager: with a business service that lends a prestigious business address and has telephone answering, word processing, and other business-related services to help homebased businesses establish an "office" and out-of-town businesses a "branch office." Member: Northbay Women's Network and Marin Business and Professional Women.

Career Counseling

Suzanne Baer
302 West 12th St.
New York, NY 10014
212/675-4165
Career Counseling Consultant: private practice—individuals, groups; career/life planning specialist for women entering or reentering job market, second careers, or new careers after retirement. Career testing, job market information, and skills training. *Who's Who in the East, 1983*. Member: Career Development Specialists Network; Association for Psychological Type; American Personnel and Guidance Association.

Rema Goldberg
Rema Goldberg Career Consultants
29 Tarryhill Rd.
Tarrytown, NY 10591
914/631-8165
Career Counselor: for individuals and groups. Seminar presentations on career change, assertiveness training, stress management for corporations and educational institutions—IBM, Texaco, Manhattanville College. Member: ASTD, NAHB.

Wilma C. Robinson
Career Action Planning
30 Pennsylvania Ave.
Waterville, OH 43566
419/878-4656; 877-5328
Career Consultant: Career Action Planning, a self-directed approach for those seeking a change in life and work situations; an honest, practical approach outlined in ten easy-to-follow steps. Method based on research and on actual experiences of participants in my numerous seminars and workshops.

Catering and Food Suppliers

Jody Bryan
Scarborough Faire
Rt. 1, Box 280
Highlands, NC 28741
704/526-5314
Herbalist: culinary herb blends, decorative and fragrant items, sachets and potpourri; dried herbs; special programs, lectures, luncheons, and workshops on topics such as herb crafts, low-sodium cooking, gourmet cooking, and preserving herbs. Member: Herb Society of America.

Sarah T. Donner
Sarah T. Donner, Inc.
54 Chaucer St.
Hartsdale, NY 10530
914/428-1483
Caterer: full-service catering—weddings, bar/bat mitzvahs, confirmations, other occasions—in your church, synagogue, or home. Everything is homemade, including breads, cakes, and pastries. Rentals provided (linens, china, etc.). Excellent service (bartenders, waiters, and waitresses). Membership chair: National Alliance of Homebased Businesswomen, Westchester Chapter, and Westchester Association of Women Business Owners.

Karen Nash
The Best of Kansas City, Inc.
PO Box 7071
Shawnee Mission, KS 66207
913/341-8186
Salesperson: gathering foods and specialty items made in Kansas City, placing them in a basket with a bow, and selling them as gifts. Good for corporate or individual gifts.

Paula Ann Winchester
Herb Gathering, Inc.
5742 Kenwood
Kansas City, MO 64110
816/523-2653
Herb Supplier: providing fresh-cut herbs to restaurants and grocers; delivering within eighteen hours of cutting. Provide a line of twenty-six culinary herbs and unique "lettuce-like" produce. Hosted its first major potted herb sale April 30, 1983 with 10,000 plants. Herbal crafts and frozen herbs—another line of our expanding business.

City Planning

Beth Peck Cooper
Spatial Consultants
1455 Peabody Ave.
Memphis, TN 38104
901/276-9608
City and Regional Planner and
Interior Designer: limiting practice to
physical planning. Prefer assisting
small towns, neighborhood
associations, multi-municipal groups,
and regional organizations. Provide
historical research, goal-setting
assistance, survey of existing
facilities, analysis, future projections,
objectives alignment, implementation
adjustment, synthesis, and recurring
evaluations. Member: American
Planning Association.

Communications

Audrey J. Boerum
Ideas Unlimited . . .
72 McNomee St.
Oakland, NJ 07436
201/337-7660
Communications Consultant, Writer,
Promoter: designing, developing, and
consulting all types of
communications—publicity,
advertising, promotions, speeches,
articles, letters, newsletters,
brochures, public relations, and
more—for individuals, organizations,
business, and industry. Also match
people into business partnerships.
Member: NAHB, N.J. Press Women,
and N.J. Business and Professional
Women.

Chris Davis Haslinger
Communications Enterprises
35 Quarry Dr.
Wappingers Falls, NY 12590
914/298-8108
Editor/Writer; Communications
Specialist: editor, writer, producer of
newsletters, informational brochures,
sales promotions, specializing in
health benefits, retirement
counseling, medical information, and
women's issues. Top-notch in-house
organs created out of my home.
Articles have appeared in a variety of
newspapers, magazines, and
corporate publications.

Lillian P. Langseth, M.S.
Lyda Associates
Oak Tree Rd.
Palisades, NY 10964
914/359-8282
Communications Consultant, Writer:
specializing in food, nutrition, and
health sciences. Editorial services,
data synthesis, lecturing, liaison,
meeting coverage, technical writing.
24 publications in scientific, trade,
and popular journals; one children's
science book. Member: American
Medical Writers Association, Institute
of Food Technologists, American
Women in Science, Society of
Consumer Affairs Professionals,
American Management Association.

Marie MacBride
100 Rock Rd.
Hawthorne, NJ 07506
Communications Consultant: writing,
copy editing, proofreading,
organizational systems and forms,
adult education. Author and publisher
of *Orange Pages: A Directory of
News Media for Bergen County.*
Author of *Step by Step: Management
of the Volunteer Program in
Agencies.* Member of Board of
Trustees, National Alliance of
Homebased Businesswomen.

Caryl Winter
Presentations with Impact
400 S. Beverly Dr., Suite 312
Beverly Hills, CA 90212
213/933-0933
Communications Consultant and
Author: conducting workshops on the
art of business writing, making
effective presentations, dictation, and
follow-up techniques and developing
policies and procedures. Instructor,
UCLA; lecturer and organizational
speaker; author of *Present Yourself
with Impact* (Ballantine Books, 1983)
and writing a second book on
business-related skills.

*Paula Ann Winchester
Herb Supplier*

Product/Service Directory

Consultant

REESA ABRAMS

Lower Main Street
Freeport, Maine 04032

865-3891

Computer Services

Reesa Abrams
Reesa E. Abrams, Consultant
Lower Main St.
Freeport, ME 04032
207/865-3891
Software Quality Consultant: over
fifteen years' experience in many
phases of computer industry,
providing assistance in the areas of
quality assurance, management, and
software engineering. Specialties
include research and presentations in
systems measurements, quality
policy, and effective software
management. Policy and procedure
preparation customized to
corporation. *Who's Who of the West,*
1976.

Elaine A. Coorens
Coorens Communications
2134 W. Pierce St.
Chicago, IL 60622
312/235-8688
Computer Consultant: services,
consulting, and sales, specializing in
small business, individuals, and
not-for-profit. Database management
and word processing—lists created
and maintained, labels, repeat letters
and documents. Accounting
systems—billing, accounts
receivable/payable, and general
ledger.

Lynne H. Pitcher
G.R. Pitcher, Inc.
35 S. First Ave.
Highland Park, NJ 08904
201/846-2021
Computer Programmer/Analyst:
coowner, with George Pitcher of G.R.
Pitcher, Inc., offering computer
consulting, service bureau and
time-sharing services, as well as
system analysis, design, and
programming. Provide financial
systems and services for small
businesses and have pioneered in the
development of systems using bar
code scanners for order processing
and inventory control.

Crafts

Martha Anson
2615 N. Pecan
Nacogdoches, TX 75961
713/564-9754
Manufacturer/Craftsperson: large,
abstract-designed, silkscreened
pillows sold to carriage trade
department stores. Working at home
most enjoyable as I am a single parent
needing to support my family. As my
Cancer horoscope says—I am really a
homebody; I love my corner of the
earth.
Type of work: pillows.

Iva L. Bramble
Sew Unique
PO Box 392
Hackettstown, NJ 07840
201/852-5370
Craftsperson: have designed a New
Dimension Pillow. Trying to market it
most effectively. Have a copyright on
the pattern and have applied for a
design patent. Shown in New York
gift show and *McCall's Needlework
and Craft* magazine.
Type of work: fabric items.

Hilda M. Dorofee
Rt. 8, Branywood Dr.
Murfreesboro, TN 37130
615/896-2547
Craftsperson: fabric dolls and clowns,
felt mice and bunnies from existing
patterns and my own creations. Sold
wholesale and retail. Have a booth at
Christmas Village in Nashville, TN in
November, benefiting the Bill

Wilkerson Hearing and Speech
Center.
Type of work: fabric dolls and
animals.

Joyce A. Friedland
Tif n' Todds
731 W. Knox
Spokane, WA 99205
509/327-3452
Designer/Manufacturer: handcrafted
cloth dolls, all original, copyrighted
designs. Ashley and Ashton dolls,
children of Mt. St. Helens (only ash
dolls ever made), sold commercially.
Gone to several foreign countries and
other doll collections. 65 different
dolls available. Quality craftsmanship,
quality fabrics. All but five dolls
cross-eyed.
Type of work: dolls.

Bert Garino
Bert's Babes
559 Flock Rd.
Hamilton Square, NJ 08690
609/586-9083
Dollmaker: soft sculpture dolls with
handpainted faces. Won a first prize
for dolls at 1982 N.J. state fair. Wrote
an article for *Dollmaker* magazine,
appeared on A.B.C.'s *Good Morning,
N.Y.* to talk about homebased
business. Member: Delaware Valley
Doll Club; Princeton Area Chapter,
National Alliance of Homebased
Businesswomen.
Type of work: soft sculpture dolls
and toys.

Sandi F. Howell
Mother Earth's Emporium
554 S. 10th Ave.
Mt. Vernon, NY 10550
914/699-4372
Craftsperson: specializing in delights
for the senses—custom-blended body
oil, bath salts, potpourri, and scented
pillows. Also do herbal vinegars with
herbs grown in my garden, body
splashes, cream sachets. Member:
Third Generation, Black Woman's
Craft Collective, American Craft
Council.
Type of work: herbs, batik, kites,
pottery.

Laura S. Kluvo
In Stitches
4041 N.W. 2nd Terr.
Boca Raton, FL 33432
305/392-3475
Mail-Order Salesperson and
Designer/Craftsperson: Began
seriously by turning my college dorm
room into a quilt and clothing design
workshop. Business now primarily
mail order. Have received requests for
designs and workshops locally and
from major magazines. Have several
awards for original quilt designs.
M.B.A. degree in business.
Type of work: quilts, soft sculpture.

Carol Krob
Carol's Creations
1012 N. Summit—E
Iowa City, IA 52240
319/351-7854
Craftsperson/Graphic Designer:
designing and marketing a line of
counted cross-stitch kits, specializing
in greeting cards. Provide graphic
design and promotional services for
clients. Teach occasional needlework
classes and workshops for homebased
businesswomen. Also, free-lance
writer.
Type of work: cross-stitch kits.

**66As profits grow and
you become established,
the value of investing in
your own business be-
comes evident.99**

Entrepreneur

Dorothy E. Kurtz
Kurtz Krafts
PO Box 308
Hasbrouck Heights, NJ 07604
201/778-2968
Craftsperson: providing those very
special, personalized gift items that
make unique offerings at sensible
cost—mostly from ceramic pieces
with chocolates. Specializing in group
gift-giving—mugs with logos and
names, shower favors, calligraphy
plaques.
Type of work: personalized ceramics.

Buffee Lewis
buffee originals
1602 Kindred Lane
Richardson, TX 75080
214/231-4964
Designer/Craftsperson: various
one-woman shows and exhibitions of
my enamels and jewelry; participant
in many major Texas festivals. Works
featured in Guadeloupe collection.
Winner of numerous awards and
recognition for both jewelry and
enamels. Member: American Crafts
Council, Texas Designer Crafsmen,
The Dallas Craft Guild, The Enamel
Guild of Dallas.
Type of work: gold jewelry and
copper enameling.

Patricia Parenteau-Eisemann
Dove Hill Weavers
70 Enright Ave.
Freehold, NJ 07728
201/780-1823
Crafts Innovator and Instructor:
specializing in the collection and use
of natural materials. Basketry,
spinning, weaving, natural dyeing,
potpourri, dried and pressed flower
work, macrame, crochet. Creating a
harmony of crafts by merging their
methods into functional and/or
fanciful pieces. Mail order,
consignment, or outright sales to
individuals or stores. Reasonable
prices.
Type of work: basketry, weaving,
macrame, crochet.

**66Success, to me, is be-
ing able to truly enjoy the
work that you do, not to
let it take you over, to
have it under control.
Even if a person is financially successful, I feel it
is not true success unless
pleasure and satisfaction
are derived from the
work.99**

Interior Designer

Wilma Olivette Reid
Silver Phoenix
554 S. 10th Ave.
Yonkers, NY 10550
914/965-2332
Multimedia Craftsperson: specializing
in stylized jewelry using silver, brass,
copper, and semiprecious stones.
Customized rings, necklaces, and
earrings. Fabric coloring and batiks
for kites and wall hangings. Member:
Third Generation: A Black Women's
Craft Collective.
Type of work: metalsmithing, fabric
coloring, and batik.

Kristen Rossi
K.L. Rossi Designs
McCurdy Rd.
New Boston, NH 03070
603/487-3345
Craftsperson: designing and
handcrafting a collection of children's
clothing and accessories, specializing
in appliqué design. B.S. Home
Economics Keene State College,
Keene, N.H. President and owner of
K.L. Rossi Designs, children's country
clothing and accessories. Designs
marketed nationwide through retail
mail-order brochure, as well as
clothing stores and craft shops.
Type of work: children's appliquéd
clothing and accessories.

Product/Service Directory

Audrey Nan Nelson
Craftsperson
Photographer: Lars Nelson

Cheri Lynn Russell
Wicker Fixer and Caning
Rt. 1, Box 283B
Ozark, MO 65721
417/485-6148
Wicker Restorer, Chair Caner: wicker, rattan, baskets, and chair caning restoration. Custom orders and antique reproductions. Buy and sell. Free advice and estimates with photo. Call or send to this husband/wife team. Feature articles in *Woman's Day, Kansas City Star, Seattle P.I. and Times, Today Florida, Springfield News and Leader,* (MO.). Lecturer.

Helen Seymour
Personally Puzzled
69 Edgemere Ave.
Plainsboro, NJ 08536
609/799-0845
Artisan: wooden puzzles in varying original designs. Flat puzzles made from a variety of different woods with the natural color of the wood providing contrast. Standing puzzles, all pine, include three different trees and several animals.
Type of work: wooden puzzles.

Dorothy "Eudora" Sinclair
Jo Dot Creations
848 Woodmere Dr.
Cliffwood Beach, NJ 07735
201/566-4704
Craftsperson: trapunto and embroidered trapunto pictures, some of which are custom works. Also dress large bisque dolls—all sewing done by hand, using antique materials where possible. Member: Handcraft Guild of Central Jersey.
Type of work: needlework, doll dresses.

Nancy K. Steinbach
Mirrored Memories
15141 Floating Bridge Rd.
Three Rivers, MI 49093
616/279-2895
Craftsperson: learned the craft of working with mirrors in 1979. After many hours of trial and discoveries, have come up with a unique look and total new way of keeping that special moment forever! Any picture, wedding, anniversary, and baby announcement can be "Mirrored Memories."
Type of work: mirrors.

Elizabeth Vandam
The Golden Needle Workshop
207 Wildewood Blvd.
California, MD 20619
301/862-2088
Quilt Artisan: designing and creating infant crib-size quilts of bright gingham and calico fabrics. Designs and colors range from unisex to frilly, fluffy pink for girls to bright blues for boys. All quilts initially handsewn and eventually reinforced twice by machine stitching, machine washable, and guaranteed to be of the best quality.
Type of work: customized crib quits.

Corazon S. Watkins
1107 South Utah
Muskogee, OK 74401
918/683-0926
Craftsperson: decorative hand-thrown pottery.
Type of work: pottery.

Editorial Services

Barbara L. Lobron
85 Hicks St.
Brooklyn, NY 11201
212/625-6648
Editor, Photographer: writing and editing in photographic publishing. Copy editor, *Camera Arts.* Won first place honors, 1977, District One, International Association of Business Communicators, External Newsletter category. Listed in *Who's Who in the East, Who's Who of American Women.* Member: Authors Guild. First woman editor ever to attend 3M Annual Editors' Conference.

Roberta H. Winston
Roberta H. Winston, Wordsmith
1431 Commonwealth Ave.
Boston, MA 02135
617/782-6499
Editor: free-lance editor, specializing in women's issues and educational materials; emphasis on substantive editing and rewriting. Also provide writing and graphic design services.

Educational Services

Catherine Linnerman, R.N., B.S., M.A.
Medication, Education, Diet, Support (MEDS)
8384 Norfolk Way
Stockton, CA 95209
209/478-0854
Program Development Consultant and Diabetes Nurse Educator: developing health service organizations, patient education programs, in-house news publications, and standards for patient and professional education, specializing in development and evaluation of staff and patient diabetes education programs. Licensed continuing education provider. Copyrighted nursing education plan. Masters degree in the management of public organizations. Convention and lecture experience.

Mariacecilia Marambio-Hurtado
4 Tucker Ave.
New City, NY 10956
914/634-5887
Foreign Language Educator: specializing in tutoring Spanish and French to people who will be residing abroad. Also teach English as a second language to foreign executives and their families who will be transferred to the U.S.A.

Betty Vogel
Magic of Microwave
1254 Dickinson S.E.
Grand Rapids, MI 49507
616/452-0122
Microwave Cooking Instructor: teaching microwave cooking classes for appliance dealers and distributors, community education classes, and in-home party demos. Also do demos

for store promotions. Available for business, church, or club; luncheons or dinners cooked in microwave ovens. Factory-trained and updated. Consultant on proper dishes to use and recipes. Member: NAHB.

Marilyn Warren
Warren Enterprises
N. 1318 Ella
Spokane, WA 99206
509/926-3736
Artist, Writer, Teacher: My dolls, in conjunction with a series of books on feelings to be published this year, are a vital tool for professionals and institutions that work with children and are concerned about their emotional development.

Expositions and Meetings

Anne M. Murphy
Functions Unlimited
14 Heighwood Trail
Sparta, NJ 07871
201/729-9704
Meeting and Function Planner: coordinating events such as business or association meetings, conferences, open houses, holiday or anniversary parties, company picnics, galas. Member: Meeting Planners International; American Home Economics Association; National Alliance of Homebased Businesswomen; Business and Professional Women's Club; Chamber of Commerce.

Irene Stella
A Stella Show
162 Stuart St.
Paramus, NJ 07652
201/262-3063
Exhibition Manager: originating, organizing, managing, directing, promoting expositions, shows, sales, and fairs for promotional, public relations, and fund-raising events. Car shows, physical fitness, home and sports shows; antique shows and crafts fairs a specialty. Major clients: New Jersey Sports and Exposition Authority, Waterloo Village Foundation for the Arts, and shopping centers.

Exporting

Rose Rogozinski
Jomark Corporation
RD 2 - Box 368 Dutchtown Rd.
Belle Mead, NJ 08502
201/359-8860
Exporter: buying and selling products and merchandise to foreign companies and consumers. Started business career with Seneca Coal & Coke Corporation in New York City as a secretary, worked up to management, eventually took over business, and added Jomark Corporation. Moved office to home to combine homemaking and motherhood with business.

Fashions

Barbara Bonner
GPO Box 2608
Cadman Plaza
Brooklyn, NY 11201
212/858-9026
Free-lance Fashion Designer: Customers request very "Vogue"-type evening wear, although any other type of garment made also. Designing for new N.Y.C. boutique called Ivie Vancaces. Fashion Institute of Technology graduate, majoring in Fashion Design; also Long Island University graduate, majoring in Physical Education.

Ashia R. Covington
The Sewing Corner
Jersey City, NJ 07304
201/434-7282
Fashion Designer, Dressmaker: selling patterns, designing, and making ready-to-wear apparel (can be custom fitted). Monogrammed beach towels, potholder and apron sets, and stuffed toys. Also coordinate fashion shows and give fashion consultations and lectures.

Vikkilyn Cambridge Griffin
The Cabbage Patch
20 Two Lights Rd.
Cape Elizabeth, ME 04107
207/767-4663
Clothing Designer, Seamstress: action wear for infants, toddlers, children. From head to toe; specializing in 25–50% stretch fabrics, stenciled

clothing, quilted fashions, and soft sculpture novelties, including sock dolls, doll cradles, elephant strings for cribs, and clown mobiles. Member: Society of Southern Maine Craftsmen, National Alliance of Homebased Businesswomen.

Alice Hayes
Bombay Fashion House, Inc.
3206 Morrison St. N.W.
Washington, DC 20015
202/363-8183
Retailer: with partner and sister, Joan Coor, operate a traveling caravan of imported and domestic fashions sold at home parties, with emphasis on personal attention.

Dianne Keesee
Hawley Rd.
North Salem, NY 10560
914/669-8325
Fashion Designer: specializing in women's lingerie and children's wear, sizes newborn to 6X. Complete design services available from sketch to small quantities of "limited edition" items. Extensive background with top firms; manufactured lingerie line under own label for past five years. Holder of one slip patent. Member: Fashion Group.

Irene Stella
Exhibition Manager

Product/Service Directory

Margit Meissner-Jackson
"Margit" Designer Fashions
PO Box 5298
Atlantic City, NJ 08404
609/296-4367
Fashion and Costume Designer: trademark exquisite craftsmanship combined with beautiful fabrics, catering to discriminating women from all over the world whose age or figures make shopping for fashionable clothes difficult. Has appeared on television and radio; give workshops. Member: New Jersey Association of Women Business Owners.

Jo Ann Miller
Sugar 'n' Spice Originals
4987 E. "T.U." Ave.
Vicksburg, MI 49097
616/649-2206
Designer/Manufacturer: of little girls' fashions, specializing in the feminine look. Member: National Alliance of Homebased Businesswomen and the Kalamazoo Network.

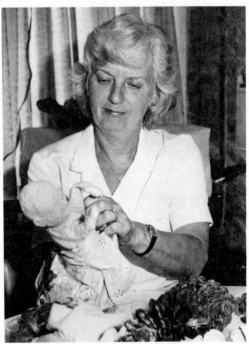

Jeanne Davis
Craft Designer
Photographer: Richard Davis

Cynthia Wallach
Pajama Party
2 Hickory Lane
Scarsdale, NY 10583
914/472-3808
Salesperson: designer lingerie sold with partner, Martha Kantor, at boutiques for fund-raising purposes—at schools, religious institutions, charitable organizations, selling our very fine line of lingerie with a commission on all sales going to the organization. Private house parties and trousseau orders.

Diane G. Wenrick
Diana Designs
82 Perrin Ave.
Shavertown, PA 18708
717/696-3757
Sales Manager: designer sportswear, classic suits, accessories, and designer bridal gowns.

Graphic Design

Sally Cooney
Cooney Tunes
145 East 27th St.
New York, NY 10016
212/532-0353
Photographer/Designer: graphic designer specializing in editorial, corporate image, and audio-visual work.

Jeanne Davis
The Designing Woman
679 Red Oak Lane
Smoke Rise, NJ 07405
201/838-6060
Graphic and Craft Designer, Lecturer: graphics, advertising, promotional art—logos, brochures, stationery, posters, displays. Christmas craft designs featured in national magazines. Member: Allied Board of Trade, Society of Craft Designers, American Craft Council, National Alliance of Homebased Businesswomen.

Patricia Kileen
Letters & Numbers
PO Box 223
Ingleside, IL 60041
312/587-2571
Graphic Designer/Calligrapher: conception, design, and production of both calligraphy and graphic artworks for corporate, public service, and institutional recognition, as well as for promotional purposes.

Joan Peckolick
Joan of Art
135 W. 17th St.
New York, NY 10011
212/242-7409
Art Director/Graphic Designer: covering all areas of design—logos, sales promotions, books (including *Women Working Home,* Second Edition), film titles, and magazines. Over a dozen awards for work in graphic design. Invited to lecture around the country on graphic design. Served as an Assistant Visiting Professor at Pratt Institute in New York.

Karen Starrett
Karen Starrett Graphic Design
27 Marshall Rd.
Ocean Township, NJ 07712
201/922-0810
Graphic Designer: creating printed literature—brochures, direct mail, business cards, and stationery—that distinguishes a business from the competition while enhancing customer awareness.

Jan O. Steinbach
Janographics
6279 S. Clara Dr.
West Jordan, UT 84084
801/969-1100
Graphic Designer: logos, brochures, publications, and other forms of graphic communication. Also free-lancing a project with a local television show producing sixteen segments (1:45 sec.) on "How to Start a Business in Your Home." Researched, wrote, and appeared in all segments, reflecting on own experiences, telling "nuts and bolts" of starting a business.

Ea Zu-En
Zu-En Graphics Studio
8742 Luella Ave.
Chicago,IL 60617
312/768-2424
Graphic Designer: illustrations/designs/logos. Have created a unique line of greeting/note cards sold mail order, wholesale, and retail.

Health Services

Diane Elliott
Herbalife
55 Stadium Way
Boston, MA 02134
617/787-9626
Diet, Weight Loss, and Nutrition
Counselor: independent distributor
and supervisor of Herbalife products,
an all-natural weight loss and
nutritional line, including skin care
products and an arthritic pain
reliever.

Catherine Linnerman, R.N., B.S., M.A.
Medication, Education, Diet, Support
(MEDS)
8384 Norfolk Way
Stockton, CA 95209
209/478-0854
Diabetes Nurse Educator and
Program Development Consultant:
developing, presenting, and
evaluating patient and professional
diabetes education programs.
Consultant for staff development in-
and out-patient courses. Copyrighted
education plan. Licensed continuing
education provider. Masters degree in
the management of public
organizations. Member: American
Association of Diabetes Educators and
American Diabetes Association.

Patricia Norimatsu
Facemetrics, Inc.
Box 124
Plymouth Meeting, PA 19462
215/828-4865
"Pathfinder": for health and
well-being. Self-publisher of
*Facemetrics, Facial Exercises for a
Fast Facelift,* and *Woman—From
Head to Toes,* a sourcebook for men
and women—from food facts to sex,
common boobytraps in vitamins and
minerals, reevaluation of research
studies for heart symptoms without
heart disease, migraines, constipation,
sexual dysfunction.

Sharon Silverman
63 Walbrooke Rd.
Scarsdale, NY 10583
914/723-6279
Nutrition and Diet Consultant:
counselor for the Cambridge Plan
International. Personalized counseling
for lifetime nutrition and weight loss.

Kay Winner
Kay Winner Studio
PO Box 610
St. Michaels, MD 21663
301/745-2606
Women's Exercise Instructor: "The
Shape of the '80s," exercise record or
cassette sold mail order—$11.95 ppd.
to address above. Graduate physical
education teacher. Have taught
exercises in N.Y. salons, adult
schools, YMCA's; given seminars for
exercise teachers, as well as lectures
and demonstrations for almost forty
years.

Home and Household Services

Sara Addis
Sara Care Franchise Corporation
1200 Golden Key Circle, Suite 227
El Paso, TX 79925
915/593-5071
Franchisor and Home Sitter: selling
sitting service franchises to women
interested in operating businesses out
of their homes. Coordinating start-ups
for new franchises including training,
sitting services brochures, sales kits,
and advertising support. Designated
Entrepreneur of the Year by Business
and Professional Women's
organization of El Paso. Member:
NAFE, NAHB, and BPW.

Ellen Eisner
716 Secor Rd.
Hartsdale, NY 10530
914/761-7116
Tag/Estate Sale Specialist, Household
Liquidator: advertising, pricing, and
selling household and personal items,
including jewelry and furs; providing
the client with a complete itemized
list of all merchandise for sale.
Delivery and cleanup services
available at a nominal charge.
Featured in *The New York Times.*
Member: National Alliance of
Homebased Businesswomen.

Marjorie Pollack
151 Rock Creek Lane
Scarsdale, NY 10583
914/725-5824
Moving Consultant and Organizer:
Call me to have your new home or
present one ready for you. Will line
your closets, arrange your furniture,
and subcontract any job, big or small.

Jane N. Poston
Housesitter Security Service
1708 E. 9th St.
Tucson, AZ 85719
602/884-8530
Personal Services Specialist:
introducing retired housesitters to
homeowners needing trusted persons
to care for pets, plants and protect
home and property while they're
away. Writer of book, *How to Run a
Housesitting Business,* sold mail
order, for those wanting to set up
and run a successful housesitting
business in their own communities.

*Joan Peckolick
Graphic Designer*

**❝I work at home be-
cause I found that I could
not successfully single-
parent two teenagers at
the end of a telephone
from a full-time job. Crazy
hours don't bother me—
the flexibility allows me to
play string quartets dur-
ing the day or take the
time for an occasional extended lunch with
friends.❞**

Word Processor

Product/Service Directory

Human Resources

Ingrid Bauer
1108 Moorefield Creek Rd. S.W.
Vienna, VA 22180
703/281-9539
Human Resource Developer: women's issues—special focus: women and leadership, women and the future. Qualities of women must be recognized and released in decision-making arenas around the globe. Especially interested in rural women. Honors: U.S. delegate to U.N. Mid Decade Conference on Women; first AAUW intern to Congressional Caucus for Women's Issues.

Katherine T. Benassi
Career Development Concepts
9 Deer Lane
Wantagh, NY 11793
516/781-9528
Counselor, Education M.S.: seminars, workshops, and training in women's programs, specializing in Future Women programs for women going back to work, stepping up the career ladder, homebased, or managing multiple roles. Also, Family Today program for singles, couples, and one-parent families emphasizing parenting as a career and encouraging effective, realistic approaches.

Patricia Durovy
Manifestation Management, Inc.
2437 N. Booth St.
Milwaukee, WI 53212
414/374-5433
Small Business Consultant: start-up and ongoing consultation for small businesses. Trainer in many learning techniques; seminar leader and public speaker; author of self-awareness programs, cassettes, and books. Numerous media appearances. Founder: Women's Resource Network; member of many professional organizations. Nominated Outstanding Young Woman of America, 1982.

Betty Hardy
Leadership Unlimited
178 Central Ave.
Madison, NJ 07940
201/377-0652
Leadership Consultant: leadership education and development through workshops, conferences, newsletters, and leaflets—assisting clubs and organizations in leadership training and guidance.

Judith Pynchon
Box 26
West Sayville, NY 11796
516/589-7769
Human Resources Development Specialist: versatile writing/consulting in HRD, from policy through training and career-path planning in sales, marketing, and industrial skills; special expertise in marketing/strategic planning for independent professionals. Member: American Society for Training and Development, Forum International, National Association of Female Executives, National Alliance of Homebased Businesswomen.

> **66** Since my parents' separation, I have gotten a good look at the business world. My mom opened her own home-based typing business after my father left, and through her clients, I have met a wide variety of businessmen and women. My constant association with them has given me an increasing interest in the field of business. I do not feel my interests would have necessarily turned in this direction if my mom had gone 'out to work'. **99**
>
> Secretary's Son

Insurance

Lavinia Moore McKee
Moore, McKee Insurance Agency
21 Branton Dr.
East Brunswick, NJ 08816
201/254-7883
Insurance Agent: Insurance sales and service. Licensed to sell: life, health, automobile, homeowners, bonds, and commercial casualty insurance. Member: Professional Insurance Agents Association.

Interior Design

Toby Baron
Window Designs
1042 Webster Ave.
New Rochelle, NY 10864
914/725-1565
Interior Designer: advising and designing window treatments with partner, Rochelle Bender; providing and installing custom-made vertical blinds, Levolors, woven woods, and all types of shades (balloon shades, Roman shades, etc.).

Beth Peck Cooper
Spatial Consultants
1455 Peabody Ave.
Memphis, TN 38104
901/276-9608
Interior Designer and City and Regional Planner: active in rehabilitating physical environments, particularly in adaptive reuse; specializing in interior work places and living spaces. Participating in all phases of the design process—including doing schematic drawings, site/structure analysis, proposal writing, plans development, detailed working drawings, textures and finishes procurement/installation, and scheduling/time management.

Diane Toby Deckinger
6850 N. Grande Dr.
Boca Raton, FL 33433
305/487-6028
Interior Designer: residential and commercial interiors. Member: National Alliance of Homebased Businesswomen.

Fran Derlinga
Our Things, featuring The Paperdoll
27 Heather Lane
Mahwah, NJ 07430
201/529-4081
Interior Decorator: graduate of New York School of Interior Design. Complete decorating service—furniture, windows, walls and floors, including wallpaper hanging. Lecture on decorating for club meetings. Also design wedding bouquets and prom corsages. Featured on *Hour Magazine* and N.Y. *Eyewitness News*. Lectured at N.J. Expo 82, "Starting a Homebased Business."

Margaret M. Feodoroff
Inspired Interiors
50 Brentwood Dr.
North Easton, MA 02356
617/587-0185
Interior Decorator/Designer: including floor coverings, wall coverings, window treatments, bed covering and decoration, floor planning, furniture selection. All coordinated with the occupant's lifestyle and preferences, which are given top priority. All appointments include at least one home visit, most are at homes under consideration.

Investments

Elizabeth P. Whittlesey, C.F.A.
Whittlesey Investment Corporation
PO Box 251
Princeton, NJ 08540
609/921-8382
Investment Advisor: providing investment advice to individuals on per-hour consulting basis, specializing in stocks, bonds, and mutual funds. Chartered financial analyst with over twelve years of experience in the investment field. Unaffiliated with any brokerage or other financial institution. Clients retain custody and discretionary control of their assets.

Jewelry

Arlene Marie Enos
Dental Engineers Inc.
PO Box 1367
San Bruno, CA 94066
415/334-5434
Dental Prosthetic Technologist: partner in prosthetic appliance manufacturing for dental profession and special effects facial prosthetics for film and theatrical use. Custom jewelry and miniature custom ornamental castings, using stainless steel, brass, and silver alloys. Knowledgeable in various rubber and plaster molding techniques for short-run manufacturing. Mail-order inquiries invited.

Legal Services

Doris L. Sassower
Doris L. Sassower, P.C.
283 Soundview Ave.
White Plains, NY 10606
914/997-1677; 212/490-3866
Attorney: Specialist, Divorce/Custody Litigation. Fellow: American Academy of Matrimonial Lawyers. Lecturer; columnist; author. NOW-N.Y.S. Special Award, 1980: "for her outstanding achievements on behalf of women and children and for her courage in efforts to obtain a just divorce law." Listed in *Who's Who in America, Who's Who in the World.*

Stephanie Solodar-Katz
SSK Freelance Typing Service
7 Lee Ct.
Maplewood, NJ 07040
201/762-5937
Certified Paralegal: providing on-call service to clients who do not have need for a full-time paralegal.

Manufacturing

Arlene Marie Enos
Dental Engineers Inc.
PO Box 1367
San Bruno, CA 94066
415/334-5434
Dental Prosthetic Technologist: partner in prosthetic appliance manufacturing for dental profession and special effects facial prosthetics for film and theatrical use. Custom jewelry and miniature custom ornamental castings, using stainless steel, brass, and silver alloys. Knowledgeable in various rubber and plaster molding techniques for short-run manufacturing. Mail-order inquires invited.

Dagmar Lemich
D. Lemich Custom Office Products
PO Box 7466
Silver Spring, MD 20901
301/587-6614
Manufacturer/Salesperson: custom rubber stamps (including novelty rubber stamps) and sales of fine business stationery, business cards, printing of all types. Designing letterheads and business cards. Manufacturer's rep for X-Stampers, self-inking stamps.

Frances Gildea O'Neill
Dantec Corporation
54 Taylor Ave.
Bethel, CT 06801
203/744-7375
Electronic Subcontractor: electronic design and assembly on a subcontract basis; technical writing and documentation on a subcontract basis; wire harnesses and cables on a subcontract basis.

263

Product/Service Directory

Rita Press
Labeleze, Inc.
PO Box 223
Baldwin, NY 11510
516/379-2978
Manufacturer: Labeleze kitchen decals and spice labels—transparent, washable, easy to read, pressure-sensitive labels that adhere to glass, plasticware, metal, and wood containers to beautify and organize a kitchen in minutes.

Labarbara Mallette Pugh
Round Linens by Mallette, Inc.
PO Box 206
Monsey, NY 10952
914/425-1828
Manufacturer: linens for round beds.

Needlework

Catherine E. Cole
Family Works
1014 Field St.
San Marcos, TX 78666
512/396-3890
Needlework Designer: designing and packaging, wholesale and retail, fine quality counted cross-stitch products, including ready-to-embroider hand-finished baby bibs and kits for toddler dresses, wall hangings, and pin cushions. Create and market appliqué and quilted items. Member: Counted Thread Society of America. Listed in *Who's Who in American Colleges and Universities.*

Jean Eitel
Palm Beach Needle-Painters, Inc.
912 Evergreen Dr.
North Palm Beach, FL 33408
305/622-1326
Fiber Artist and Quilter: design of needlepoint canvas and quilt patterns. Designer of fiber art works; author; consultant; lecturer and teacher on use of color in fiber arts field. Member of The National Needlework Association, South and Southwest Quilt Association, National Quilt Association, and Sand-Dollar Quilters.

Joann Gerkhardt
Angelique
37308 Valley Rd.
Oconomowoc, WI 53066
414/567-7623
Quilter/Designer: providing hand-guided outline quilting, such as used in custom-quilted bedspreads and upholstery quilting. Construct bedspreads, coverlets, reverse shams, fabric designer lamps, and accessories.

Sarah Haddon
Sarah Craft
PO Box 663
Corte Madera, CA 94925
415/924-1553
Needlecraft Designer: self-publisher of pattern booklets for crochet, knitting, sewing, cross-stitch. Specializing in miniature needlework scaled 1″ to 1′. Work featured in *Goodfellow Catalog of Wonderful Things.* Member: National Alliance of Homebased Businesswomen; Society of Craft Designers.

Betsy Heller
Canvas Creations
PO Box 84
Arnold, MD 21012
301/757-4682
Designer/Manufacturer: needlepoint and counted cross-stitch kits, specializing in nautical, geographical and sport themes, as well as custom designs. Kits featured in fine stores everywhere, as well as stitchery and gift catalogs.

Davie Strauss Hyman
Davie Hyman Designs
12908 Westchester Trail
Chesterland, OH 44026
216/729-3118
Needlepainting Designer: Embroiderers' Guild of America certified instructor; author; lecturer. Specializing in handpainted personalized designs and ecclesiastical commissions. Member: National Standards Council, American Craft Council, National Embroiderers Teacher's Association, Liturgical Art Guild of Ohio, Cleveland Museum of Art, National Textile and Research Center.

Kathy King
Kings
605 B Chipman Rd.
Lee's Summit, MO 64063
816/525-3668
Needlework Designer: running my own mail-order pattern company, offering an exclusive line of crochet designs, specializing in patterns for infants and children. Also, free-lance work for several craft and needlework magazines. Member: American Craft Council and Society of Craft Designers.

Audrey Pudvah
Audrey Designs
RD1
East Calais, VT 05650
802/456-7491
Needleworker: handcrafted hats, sweaters, scarves and vests.

Darla M. Sims
Unique Designs
312 S. Jackson
East Wenatchee, WA 98801
509/884-6092
Designer: handknitting or crocheting garments for national publications and yarn companies on a free-lance basis. Selling one-of-a-kind originals to shops. Style described as elegantly classic, often incorporating beads, pearls, or embroidery. Also produce booklets of knitting and crochet patterns.

Virginia W. Smith
Alphabetrics, Inc.
633 Breakers Point
Schaumburg, IL 60194
312/884-0091
Designer: with emphasis on geometrics, lettering, logos, and monograms. Three published books of graphed designs for needlework: *Alphabetrics, Alphagraphics, Minigraphics.* Member: The North Suburban Embroiderers Guild and The National Standards Council of American Embroiderers—both instrumental in stimulating my interest in a widening variety of fiber arts through lectures, workshops, seminars.

Lois Winston
One Asbury Ave.
Melrose Park, PA 19126
215/635-3471
Needlecraft Designer/Illustrator:
specializing in counted cross-stitch
designs for manufacturers, craft
magazines, and advertising. Author of
several books, leaflets, and a calendar
of cross-stitch designs. Work has
appeared in *Needlecraft for Today,
Needle & Thread, Needlecraft News,
Decorating & Craft Ideas*. Member:
NAHB.

Nutrition Counseling

Annette Collins, M.A.
Collins Associates
6128 MacBeth Dr.
Baltimore, MD 21239
301/435-1979
Nutrition Consultant: supervisor of
sales and training of own in-home
nutrition and skin care business,
offering nutritional counseling and
training for women desiring their
own businesses. Products all natural,
no sugar, no preservatives—in
harmony with nature and good
health. Business opportunity offering
good income, bonus car, group
insurance, wonderful trips.

Diane Elliott
Herbalife
55 Stadium Way
Boston, MA 02134
617/787-9626
Diet, Weight Loss, and Nutrition
Counselor: independent distributor
and supervisor of Herbalife products,
an all-natural weight loss and
nutritional line, including skin care
products and an arthritic pain
reliever.

Sharon Silverman
63 Walbrooke Rd.
Scarsdale, NY 10583
914/723-6279
Nutrition Consultant and Diet
Consultant: counselor for the
Cambridge Plan International.
Personalized counseling for lifetime
nutrition and weight loss.

Janet B. Summerville
J & W Associates
408 Route 17 S.
Carlstadt, NJ 07072
201/935-2353
Nutrition Consultant: managerial
training and development, nutrition
consultations, wholesale and retail
distribution of nutritional
supplements. Motivator in positive
self-dimension; beauty advisor,
Shaklee Corporation. Member: Society
of Public Health Educators (SOPHE)
American Public Health Association,
National Alliance of Homebased
Businesswomen.

Suzanne Zilenziger
270 Nelson Rd.
Scarsdale, NY 10583
914/472-4676
Nutrition/Diet Counselor: nationwide
independent counselor. Cambridge
Diet Plan International: 330 calories
daily including 100% U.S.R.D.A.
vitamins and minerals. Average
weight loss 16–20 pounds in four
weeks without hunger. Physician
supported. Lifetime nutrition plan for
heavy or underweight. Fun;
extremely easy. Business expansive;
very lucrative. Contact for
product/counselor information.

Party Planning

Joanne F. Brown
The Schemers
67 Tintern Lane
Scarsdale, NY 10583
914/723-8867
Party Planner/Decorator: theme
parties with emphasis on entirely
customized decorations—
centerpieces, posters, place cards,
favors, novelties of all sorts, table
arrangements of silk or dried flowers
or plants, calligraphy. Graduate of

New York Botanical Garden program
in floraculture. Member: National
Alliance of Homebased
Businesswomen.

Judy Caden
Judy Caden Marionettes
180 Duane St.
New York, NY 07052
212/431-7627
Puppeteer: performing at museums,
clubs, libraries, and birthday parties;
conducting workshops in puppetry
and crafts; exhibiting her sculptures.
Director of The Puppet Loft in New
York City.

Yvette Furman
Party Pizzazz, Inc.
10 Schindler Ct.
East Brunswick, NJ 08816
201/254-2646
Party Decorator: specializing in
theme parties for bar and bat
mitzvahs. Custom-created
centerpieces for any interest.
Coordinated favors, place card
displays, props, etc. Also silk flower
arrangements and balloon
decorations.

*Judy Caden
Puppeteer
Photographer: Barry McInerny*

Product/Service Directory

❝I work until the pain wakes me up at night; until I can't lift the dinner plates down from the cupboard; until I've made a vessel that makes my soul sing when I look at it. Then—only then—I am able to stop for a while.❞

Sculptor

Beverly Halperin
Rhyme Tyme
81 Oakview Ave.
Maplewood, NJ 07040
201/763-6319
Greetings Writer: personalized poetry greetings for birthdays, anniversaries, Mother's/Father's Day, weddings, retirement, organization events, etc. Original Rhyme Tyme invitations can cost even less than commercial "fill-ins." Special services, including calligraphy, special papers, illustrations, custom printing, and framing. Will create a party concept or coordinate with your theme. A unique personal gift!

Emily Rosen
Witty Ditty, Inc.
205 Rogers Dr.
Scarsdale, NY 10583
914/235-5590
Lyricist/Writer: personalized singing telegrams and balloons delivered by uniformed singers for all occasions.

Laura Spiegel
Zohar, Belly-Tellygrams, Inc.
64 Old Colony Rd.
Hartsdale, NY 10530
914/723-5252
Belly Dancer: offering a new way to send messages of love, congratulations, and birthday greetings. Belly-Tellygram: tastefully presented by a lovely female dancer or a handsome male dancer, suitable for all audiences and occasions. Serving greater New York metropolitan area and surrounding suburban communities.

Personal Services

Carol Motto
Fabricadabra
121 Pearl St.
Westfield, NJ 07090
201/232-2521
Seamstress/Designer: taking in all types of sewing and dressmaking projects right now; but planning to concentrate on appliqué work and patchwork. Developing a line of pillows using these two methods and will incorporate fabric paints into some of my designs.

Donna Prostak
Suitability
520 Spring Valley Dr.
Bridgewater, NJ 08807
201/725-6597
Personal Shopper, Image Consultant: specializing in business attire for men and women. Clients introduced to buying clothing in N.Y.C. at wholesale, plus a service charge. Seminars given for women on business attire, including wardrobe, makeup, color, and grooming. Speaking engagements to clubs and organizations. AMEX, MasterCard, and Visa.

Sunny Schlenger
Schlenger Organizational Systems
6 Aberdeen Pl.
Fair Lawn, NJ 07410
201/791-2396
Personal Systems Designer: a consulting service designed to help busy individuals manage their time and work space more effectively. Serve on the board of directors of the Women Entrepreneurs of N.J. and the Bergen County Girl Scout Council. Lecture extensively on the subjects of organization and success.

Photography

Rita J. Cassell
R/J Associates
4808 W. Peachtree
Muncie, IN 47304
317/288-2888
Photographer's Specialist: handling negative retouching color and B/W, transparency retouching, air brush, matting, framing, restorations, oils—heavy oil background and light oil, and composites. 1979 Indiana Court of Gold: Retoucher of the Year Award. Member: Board of Directors, Professional Photographers of Indiana; Chair of Professional Photographers Artists of Indiana 1980, 1981, 1982.

Sally Cooney
Cooney Tunes
145 East 27th St.
New York, NY 10016
212/532-0353
Photographer/Designer: portrait photographer working in the studio and on location, specializing in well-known people and those who plan to be well-known.

Self-Portrait
Photographer: Sally Cooney

Anne Cousineau
15 W. Circuit Dr.
Succasunna, NJ 07876
201/584-5208
Photographer: specializing in photography for newspapers and magazines in black and white or color, color slides for presentations, photography for brochures, newsletters, and news releases for local, state, national distribution. Work with profit and nonprofit organizations, individuals, corporations blending techniques developed to tell stories through photos. Work with Stella Hart, Inc.

Joyce Dutka
Joyce's Janimals, Inc.
2600 Netherland Ave.
Riverdale, NY 10463
212/543-1567
Artist, Photographer: custom color photography for portfolios, insurance, display, exhibits—jewelry, sweaters, travel exhibits.

B. Kirby Harrison (Bonnie)
The Portrait Place
953 Mountain View Blvd. Ste. 123
Lafayette, CA 94549
415/439-7375; 283-7620
Photographer's Agent: photography for schools, products, portfolios, family, children, weddings.

Marilynne Herbert
Marilynne Herbert Photography
88 Walworth Ave.
Scarsdale, NY 10583
914/725-5025
Free-lance Photographer: specializing in documentary, editorial, people, and places. Cited for work by One to One/Media Awards. Listed in *Outstanding Young Women in America,* 1979. Member: Pindar Gallery, N.Y.C., American Society of Magazine Photographers, National Alliance of Homebased Businesswomen.

Roberta Hershenson
35 Hampton Rd.
Scarsdale, NY 10583
914/723-1891
Photographer: free-lance photographic artist. Have exhibited widely and won numerous awards.

President of Ground Glass, a Westchester-based photographer's group. Teach photography to children. Commercial work: publicity, portraits, candids; specialize in black-and-white photography.

Helen Keenan
Keenan Studio
135 N.E. Lakeside Dr.
Medford, NJ 08055
609/654-8470
Photographer: specializing in children, groups, pets. Prints exhibited in banks and libraries, reproduced in several company employee publications and newspapers. Work featured at Radio City Music Hall, New York Coliseum, and *Ladies' Home Journal.* First prizes in professional photography contests. Work has appeared in pages and on covers of nationally circulated magazines.

Sandra Ostendorf
Airgraphics
13117 Valley Forge Lane
Champlin, MN 55316
612/421-1500
Photographic Airbrush and Retouch Artist: photographic airbrushing and retouching for studios, labs, department stores, and the general public, including restoration of old photos, corrective retouching, and airbrushing of recent professional portraits and photos.

Terri P. Tepper
261 Kimberly
Barrington, IL 60010
312/381-2118
Writer, Photographer, Speaker: Also, Director, Center for a Woman's Own Name. Author of *The New Entrepreneurs: Women Working from Home.* Multimedia slide presentation—Women Working from Home. One-woman photography show on environmental portraits of Women Working from Home. Coauthor: booklet for women wishing to determine own names after marriage. Member: NAHB, AAUW, Hadassah.

Plants

Sherrill Boggs
Anything Groes
RR 3
Columbia City, IN 46725
219/244-3247
Plant Counselor, Plant Finder: locating plants for customers and taking care of those that are sick. Introduce new people to my unique growing system. Also, have achieved a Master Gardener certificate from Purdue University, enabling me to identify plant problems more readily.

Christine Pacchiana
Plant Care by Christine, Inc.
40 Whitlaw Close
Chappaqua, NY 10514
914/241-2678
Interiorscaper: going into residential and commercial places and choosing plants that will do well, taking into consideration light, wind, exposure, etc. Also plant maintenance: cleaning, potting, pruning, doctoring, arranging.

Product Development

Myrna R. Youdelman
Gift Finders International
7 Tennyson St.
Hartsdale, NY 10530
914/948-6121
Manufacturer's Rep, Consultant on Product Development: representing gift items to the mail-order, premium, and fund-raising fields through a wholesale catalog published by Gift Finders International. Have chemical and design patents and manufacture a couple of the items in the catalog. Help others develop their products—taking them from conception through packaging, manufacturing, and sales.

Product/Service Directory

Public Speaking

Susan Abrams
Mary Kay Cosmetics, Inc.
116 Old Army Rd.
Scarsdale, NY 10583
212/548-3299, Ext. 554
914/968-7169, Ext. 554
Beauty Consultant and Lecturer: complimentary facials given to individuals and groups, male and female, ages 12 and up, including analysis of skin and prescription of individual skin care program and instruction in product usage and suitable makeup techniques. Reorders; career opportunities; specially tailored group programs. Also Manhattan location.

Jeanne Davis
The Designing Woman
679 Red Oak Lane
Smoke Rise, NJ 07405
201/838-6060
Graphic and Craft Designer, Lecturer: speaking on Christmas crafts—Holiday Happenings; fund raising—An Affair to Remember; decorating—Junking for Joy; becoming an entrepreneur—Getting Your Act Together. Member: Allied Board of Trade, Society of Craft Designers, American Craft Council, National Alliance of Homebased Businesswomen.

Danielle R. Kennedy
DRK Productions
25108 Marguerite Pkwy., Ste. B–201
Mission Viejo, CA 92692
714/859-8440
Professional Platform Speaker: sales training and motivational seminars for businesses and associations across the country. Program topics include: Communication, Success, Goals, Promotion, Prospecting, and Time Planning. Author and television personality. Member: National Speakers Association, National Association of Professional Saleswomen, National Alliance of Homebased Businesswomen.

Publishing

Virginia Bisanz
Mechanics (A Writer's Quarterly)
PO Box 207
Hyde Park, NY 12538
Editor: editing/publishing *Mechanics (A Writer's Quarterly),* a unique workbook/little magazine for and by writers. Also a free-lance writer of fiction, nonfiction, and poetry. Won Honorable Mention in the 1981 Writer's Digest Short Story Competition. Member: National Writer's Club, Mid-Hudson Valley Communicator, and NAHB.

Barbara Brabec
Artisan Crafts
PO Box 10423
Springfield, MO 65808
417/882-9949
Crafts Publisher/Marketing Consultant: publishing home business newsletter and special reports for those in the crafts/needlework/gift/garment industries. Sell books, directories. Offer author/publishing liaison service and private consultation to small business owners. Give marketing workshops nationally. Coordinate annual, cooperative advertising program for crafts businesses. Free "Information Sources Catalog" on request.

Ann Howard Calderwood
417 Riverside Dr.
New York, NY 10025
212/864-5532
Publishing Services Specialist: taking work to be published from rough manuscript through cold-type composition.

Delorus Whidden Eitel
National Sweepstakes & Contest Guide
Box 2349
West Palm Beach, FL 33402
305/686-0617
Publisher: monthly contest and sweepstakes newsletter, including new contests and sweepstakes each month, prizes offered, and exact directions for entering. Approximately 25 new national contests each month. Publisher personally won over $50,000 in cash and prizes from entering contests over the last eight years. $12 per year; $2 per sample.

Linda M. Hasselstrom
Lame Johnny Press
Star Route 3 Box 9A
Hermosa, SD 57744
605/255-4466
Writer/Publisher: works related to the Great Plains; also teacher, specializing in workshops on writing, independent press publishing and self-publishing. Featured in *Ms.* magazine, 1975; *SD Press Woman* nominee for National Press Woman of the Year, 1979. Publications include *The Book Book: A Publishing Handbook* and anthologies.

Connie Hunt
Pulsar Publications
PO Box 714
Lafayette, CA 94549
415/254-7535
Writer, Lecturer, Self-Publisher: reaching out to others through a book titled *Reaching,* also through radio/TV interviews and talks to business and community groups. The message: "Hope is instinctive; despair is learned." Sharing my positive views through media to be a bridge between the way it is and the way it could be!

Savoy Rose Jade
Day Tonight/Night Today
PO Box 353
Hull, MA 02045
617/925-0046
Editor/Publisher: of women's literary magazine; all stages, including correspondence, reading submissions, critiquing, editing, typing, paste-up, proofreading and mail distribution. Member: COSMEP and Feminist Writers Guild.

Lorette Konezny
Pen Notes, Inc.
134 West Side Ave.
Freeport, NY 11520
516/868-5753
Educational Publisher/Manufacturer: inventing, writing, manufacturing, and publishing calligraphy kits and books; writing and publishing children's educational books:

Learning to Print, Writing Script, and *Learning to Tell Time.* Presently under review for *Who's Who in Finance and Industry.*

Shirley Liss
Jackpotunities, Inc.
102 Catherine Rd.
Scarsdale, NY 10583
914/723-6427
Editor/Publisher: *Jackpotunities,* a sweepstakes bulletin. Write, publish, and mail it to subscribers from all fifty states with cousin, Harriet Levy. Former N.Y.C. schoolteachers (as is third partner, Steve Samtur), both enjoy working own hours from home to attend to the various school functions of their children and "do their own thing."

Marjory Vals Maud
Single Impressions
642 West Zia Dr.
Tucson, AZ 85704
602/888-7176
Free-lance Writer, Publisher: single parent and author of a cookbook-cum-guidebook for single parents—self-published, promoted, and advertised. Sold by mail order and also on consignment to shops. Also give workshops on personal, financial, and household management; now writing a series of workbooks on these subjects. Private consulting on organization of home, office, or personal affairs.

Arri Parker
The Woman's Newspaper of Princeton, Inc.
43 Southern Way
Princeton, NJ 08540
609/924-1330
Publisher: *The Woman's Newspaper of Princeton,* a monthly tabloid containing practical, useful information for women in the greater Princeton, N.J., area. Founded by two women in March 1982, the Paper has proven financially successful. The corporation now diversifying into books and seminars.

Published by Linda M. Hasselstrom

Margaret J. Pittenger
Pittenger & Associates
5568 Surrey Lane
Birmingham, AL 35243
205/991-7075
Publisher/Photographer: note cards with 3″ x 5″ photos, framed in colored mats. Themes available for gift packs or made into announcements, invitations. Wall calendars, 11″ x 14″, using twelve 5″ x 7″ oval-matted photos. Large spaces for daily notes; ivory stock; your photos or mine. Some photos award winners in local shows.

Arleen Gradinger Priest
41 Hampton Rd.
Scarsdale, NY 10583
914/725-3632
Publishing Consultant, Business Consultant, Lecturer: consultant and book packager to authors for self-publishing projects advising how to publish and distribute manuscripts. Expert in marketing and promotion. Available to speak before clubs or groups on "How to Establish a Successful Homebased Business." President and founder of Westchester Chapter, National Alliance of Homebased Businesswomen.

Margaret Romanski
Moongotta Publications, Inc.
PO Box 2023
Bloomfield, NJ 07003
201/748-9339
Publisher: one poetry book so far, *Bloomfield Rhythms,* written by me. Now looking for other local authors interested in small runs—under 500 copies. Provide typing, editing, contracts, printing, and delivery to your home. Member: Chamber of Commerce.

Miriam Walton
Sunshine Press
3221 Bloomfield Park Dr.
West Bloomfield, MI 48033
313/626-3248 or 626-3223
Publisher: *Entrepreneurial Woman Newsletter.* President of Michigan Chapter, National Alliance of Homebased Businesswomen; Member-at-large of Board of Trustees, National Alliance of Homebased Businesswomen. Member: International Platform Association, National Speakers Association.

Marianne Wehrenberg
The Key Directory, Inc.
PO Box 562
East Brunswick, NJ 08816
201/254-6448
Publisher: directories, magazines, journals, direct mail.

Product/Service Directory

Research and Information

Roberta Bampton Beavers
BEAVER/S, Inc.
15 Jardine Ct.
Morris Plains, NJ 07950
201/285-9529
Management Consultant: specializing in chemical marketing research, business development, and executive search. Listed in AWIS Registry of Women in Science. Member: American Chemical Society, American Entrepreneurs Association, Chemical Industry Association, Chemical Marketing Research Association, National Alliance of Homebased Businesswomen, Zonta International.

Vicki Mechner
OmniQuest, Inc.
PO Box 15
Chappaqua, NY 10514
914/238-9646
Business Consultant and Information Specialist: finding the resources you need—unusual or hard-to-find products, suppliers of services (including free-lance and independent contractors), and information (anything from a single fact or figure to complete market studies). Problem-solving consultations help clarify your goals, streamline your production/information procedures, develop new product/market ideas.

(914) 238-9646
Vicki Mechner
president

OmniQuest inc
specialists in finding
PO Box 15
Chappaqua
NY 10514

Carol Zych
Infoserve
54 Park Ave.
Verona, NJ 07044
201/783-2900
Information Researcher and Consultant: computer-based fact-finding service for marketing, financial, and scientific-technical subjects.

Sales

Peggy R. Blumenthal
The "B" Hive
66 Skyview La.
New Rochelle, NY 10804
914/636-3222
Salesperson: very unique personalized gift items for children and adults—such as clothing, desk accessories, wall hangings and pictures, picture frames, stuffed toys, glassware, stationery, napkins, invitations and announcements. Good prices and very special service. Full-color catalog available on request for $3; refundable with first order.

Anita Dimondstein
Biobottoms
57 Grant Ave.
Petaluma, CA 94952
707/778-7945
Sales Manager: with partner Joan Cooper—originators of Biobottoms marketing in U.S., principally a direct mail-order business. Biobottoms, woolen diaper covers, replace plastic pants and encourage parents to use cloth diapers, thus combating the unnecessary waste and expense of disposable diapers. Biobottoms easiest, healthiest, and most ecological system available today.

Roberta Edwards
Watkins
115-40 Lincoln St.
South Ozone Park, NY 11420
212/529-3099
Dealer/Distributor: Watkins Products, quality products since 1868. Extracts, spices, seasonings, household products, personal care products, health care items, and gift items. Sales made to individuals through house-to-house selling, home parties, and fund-raising programs. Also, commercial and business sale items.

Roxie English
Evergreen Accents
1023 S. Adams, Suite 182
Olympia, WA 98501
206/943-9845
Mail-Order Sales Director: specializing in decorator pillows. Color portfolio features pillows I designed and produced.

Mary Jo Gatti
Dayspring
Box 666
Plandome, NY 11030
516/627-2891
Giftware Consultant and Engraver: specializing in unique gifts of high quality at reasonable prices, most of which can be personalized with engraving or self-adhesive brass or aluminum plates in 32 colors. Serve mail-order customers and corporate clients through our gift catalog and/or scheduled appointments. Member: Long Island Direct Marketing Association, Inc.

Janet V. Hansen
Koalaty Products Ltd.
118 S. Elmhurst Ave.
Mt. Prospect, IL 60056
312/253-9357
Mail-Order Entrepreneur, Designer: specializing in fashion tops, T-shirts, aprons, and tote bags with original designs pertaining to various needlework techniques and other craft- and hobby-related fields. Also create designs or copy logos for companies and organizations according to their specific needs.

B. Kirby Harrison (Bonnie)
The Portrait Place
953 Mountain View Blvd. Ste. 123
Lafayette, CA 94549
415/439-7375; 283-7620
Photographer's Agent: photography for schools, products, portfolios, family, children, weddings.

Laura S. Kluvo
In Stitches
4041 N.W. 2nd Terr.
Boca Raton, FL 33432
305/392-3475
Mail-Order Salesperson and Designer/Craftsperson: Began seriously by turning my college dorm room into a quilt and clothing design workshop. Business now primarily

Melissa Kuntz
Salesperson
Photographer: Arieh Bellehsen

mail order. Have received requests for designs and workshops locally and from major magazines. Have several awards for original quilt designs. M.B.A. degree in business.

Melissa Kuntz
Fabrics By Melissa
SB–PO Box 404
Leonia, NJ 07605
201/592-6913
Salesperson: specializing in supplying fabrics to the home sewer, home economist, and student via a catalog with swatches. Advertise in pattern magazines, women's magazines, and newspapers. Also, consultant/fabric buyer for stores, designers, and craftspeople outside N.Y. area.

Marion Landis
Ultra-Fine Products, Inc.
21950 Byron Rd.
Cleveland, OH 44122
216/283-1033
Manufacturer: developer of "Mr. Glass" and "Mr. Chrome" cleaning products, distributed through major national mail-order companies, selected stores, and independent sales

agents throughout the country. Have had national TV publicity through *PM Magazine* and *Hour Magazine;* participate in business seminars.

B. G. Mandel
70-20 108 St.
Forest Hills, NY 11375
212/261-1243
Salesperson: mail-order distributor and manufacturer's rep nationwide. Discount prices; brand names only; dealer inquiries accepted. Magnifying lamps priced from $39.95–$99.95. Member: Embroiderers Guild of America.

Lurrae Lupone Meyers
SOLEMUSIC Company
241 Furnace Dock Rd.
Peekskill, NY 10566
914/739-4678; 739-1069
Marketing Entrepreneur: SOLEMUSIC—The Running Tape, a 60-minute cassette of original, pulsating music designed for runners, joggers, bikers, hikers, skaters, skiers, dancers, and rebounders; enhances aerobic activity. Chosen for score of "New York on the Run," the official 1981 N.Y.C. Marathon film. Product sold mail order, retail, and as a premium/incentive product.

Tamera Tate
Roses & Lollicards
9 Captains Landing
Tiburon, CA 94920
415/383-0638
Salesperson: candy greeting cards. Recently received my final product; now contemplating all possible markets. Should be sold in flower shops, gift shops, and card shops. Hope to market it through one of the national "flowers by wire" companies using theme song, "Roses and Lollipops," for Valentine's or Mother's Day.

Helene Trosky
Yarmouth Rd.
Purchase, NY 10577
914/946-2464
Artist, Art Dealer, Educator: selling paintings, graphics, sculpture— modern and contemporary. Printmaker, papermaker, cast paper abstractions. Restore prints and pastels. Writer of art history, modern and contemporary art, and art scene

today. Listed in *Who's Who in American Art.* Cited in *Complete Book of Handmade Paper.* Member: Silvermine Guild and Artists Equity of N.Y.

Myrna R. Youdelman
Gift Finders International
7 Tennyson St.
Hartsdale, NY 10530
914/948-6121
Manufacturer's Rep, Consultant on Product Development: representing gift items to the mail-order, premium, and fund-raising fields through a wholesale catalog published by my Gift Finders International. Have chemical and design patents and manufacture a couple of the items in the catalog. Help others develop their products—taking them from conception through packaging, manufacturing, and sales.

Secretarial Services

Sandy Aponowich
Sandy Aponowich & Associates
54 Green St.
Charlestown, MA 02129
617/242-0306
Word Processor: documents, company reports, multiple mailings, architects' specifications, and textbooks.

Dora Back
After 6 Secretarial Service
54 Johnson St.
Fords, NJ 08863
201/738-4670
Secretary and Resumé Writer: doing custom-written resumés and employment counseling. Furnish legal, technical, scientific (or whatever is required) typing, as well as automatic typing and transcription from machine dictation. Notary Public.

Product/Service Directory

Fawn DeMurl Carriker
Elite Business Services
3846 S. Shady Lane
Visalia, CA 93277
209/627-1782
Secretary/Typist: editing and preparing manuscripts, theses, and reports for the business and student communities; writing organization newsletters and publicity releases; preparing resumés and job applications. Short deadlines and last-minute projects welcomed. "Business typing with the personal touch."

Nina Feldman
Nina Feldman Word Processing & Editing
6407 A Irwin Ct.
Oakland, CA 94609
415/655-4296
Typist: word processing on a computer that stores text on a disk for easy revisions and updates. Resumés, reports, personalized multiple letters, mailing lists, labels, manuals, contracts, manuscripts, brochures, etc. Member: Professional Association of Secretarial Services, Independent Professional Typists Network, National Alliance of Homebased Businesswomen.

Donna Gene Ferguson
The Typing Professional
PO Box 1152
Lake Elsinore, CA 92330
714/674-7220
Typist: for nine major markets—professional writers, academic, advertising, business, engineering, legal, medical, statistical, and resumés. Complete secretarial and business writing service. Notary Public.

Renita Freeman-Hubbard
Albuquerque Typing Service
Box 13133
Albuquerque, NM 87192
505/293-7083
Secretary/Typist: typing, clerical duties, dictaphone transcription.

Ann F. Hurford
4384 Hale Pl.
Lilburn, GA 30247
404/921-3953
Typist: experienced legal secretary doing all kinds of typing in my home, with pickup and delivery available within 20 miles. One-day service in most cases. Materials provided. Quality of work guaranteed.

Carol R. Klein
Advantage Typing Service
53 Clements Pl.
Hartsdale, NY 10530
914/949-6482
Typist: experienced and flexible support service, supplying typing, cassette transcription, editorial and secretarial services to companies listed among the Fortune 500, as well as one-person consultant operations. Specializing in cassette transcription of conferences, seminars, interviews, and focus groups. Whatever your typing requirements—We're Your Type!

Julie Kozlow
Julie Kozlow, Business Services
7149 Natalie Blvd.
Northfield Center, OH 44067
216/467-9229; 467-8059
Secretary, Bookkeeper/Accountant: services include typing (from handwritten copy, machine dictation, shorthand notes, and my composition); full-charge bookkeeping/accounting; payroll preparation; and temporary office help. The book *How to Start Your Own Secretarial Services Business at Home* (SK Publications, 1980), detailed my business, originally begun as Julie Kozlow, Secretarial Services.

Muriel Kravette
The Wordworks, Inc.
236 Vreeland Ave.
Leonia, NJ 07605
201/461-0088
Word Processor: word processing service, specializing in work overflow, special projects, statistical reports, resumés. Work done by an experienced business teacher and secretary. Devoted to the small businessperson who does not have the need to hire additional secretarial help but frequently needs work completed quickly (weekends, evenings, too), accurately, and professionally.

Melanie Ley
Melanie Ley's Quality Typing
3681 Hamilton
Irvine, CA 92714
714/552-8816
Typist, Bookkeeper: specializing in small business bookkeeping and general typing, including layout and graphics for newsletters and flyers. Cited in *Irvine Today* newspaper, 1982, in an extensive article. To be listed in *Who's Who in California*, 7/83. Member: National Association Female Executives, Independent Professional Typists Network, National Notary Association.

Nancy E. Mack
Words in Process
PO Box 204
Ho-Ho-Kus, NJ 07423
201/445-9302
Word Processor: word processing and typing, transcribing, text editing, resumés, correspondence, mailing list maintenance. Intelligent, fast (usually 24-hour) service. Experienced legal secretary.

Carol Mastick
Carol Mastick Secretarial Service
1590 Sir Francis Drake
San Anselmo, CA 94960
415/459-4918
Free-lance Typist: providing typing and general secretarial services to a variety of clients in many different fields. Member: Independent Professional Typists Network.

Laura B. Pryce
Contemporary Typing Service
4205 Lamarre Dr.
Fairfax, VA 22030
703/352-0625
Typist/Secretary: offering professional typing, proofreading, and secretarial support. Name appears in one published book as the typist.

Colleen Ruffini
Execu-Sec
PO Box 439
Allendale, NJ 07401
201/825-0357
Secretary/Typist: comprehensive word processing and secretarial services at competitive prices. List management, newsletters, transcriptions, resumés, scholarly projects.

Marie A. Sherrett
Merrett Industries
7018 N. Cameron Ave.
Tampa, FL 33614
813/886-8971
Court Reporting Typist: typing for court reporters only. Article published in *The National Shorthand Reporters Journal,* June 1982 issue; article concerning my business appeared in September 15, 1982 issue of *The St. Petersburg Times;* also interviewed on WUSF Radio, University of South Florida. Member: National Alliance of Homebased Businesswomen.

Stephanie Solodar-Katz
SSK Freelance Typing Service
7 Lee Ct.
Maplewood, NJ 07040
201/762-5937
Secretary/Typist: offering complete and unique secretarial services, including telephone dictation hookups, word processing, printing, original advertising, and stationery setups. Also lecturer, writer, consultant, and certified paralegal in private practice, providing on-call service to clients who do not have need for a full-time paralegal.

Renee Soloway
1230 Pennsylvania Ave., #15H
Brooklyn, NY 11239
212/642-2356
Typist: professional typing and tape transcriptions; fast and personalized service. References on request.

Lois R. Stenzel
Word Craft
15-81 208th St.
Bayside, NY 11360
212/423-3480
Word Processing Specialist: an inexpensive alternative to typing services. Professionally prepared financial reports, personalized letters, resumés, mailing lists, legal documents, direct mail, and proposals. Typeset- or typewriter-quality print in over twenty different styles. Free disc storage.

Christine A. Van Noy
The Wordshop
181 Paseo Del Rio
Moraga, CA 94556
415/284-4035
Typesetter, Graphic Designer, Secretary: with a business support system providing full secretarial services, including word processing, transcription, letter composition, resumé writing, as well as typeset brochures, flyers, business cards, and stationery. Offer advice on planning a "paper wardrobe" to effectively portray one's personal and business image.

Solar Construction

Luz Holvenstot
100 Naughright Rd.
Long Valley, NJ 07853
201/876-3614
Solar Consultant: thrust of my consulting work in the area of energy efficient buildings—residential and commercial structures—that can be correctly, technically, and materially built so that energy costs are drastically reduced. Proper and well-designed, the building of tomorrow is being built today by application of all proven systems.

Stephanie Solodar-Katz
Secretary/Paralegal
Photographer: Stuart Katz

Stationery

Wendy Clem
Artbeats Unlimited
PO Box 461
Fraser, MI 48026
313/772-0173
Greeting Cards and Stationery Designer: unique, creative, and humorous greeting cards and stationery—a cut above the rest—with our special "Script-Tease" line geared toward adult humor. Custom orders are accepted with advance notice. Soon to be offered: the irony of sporting experiences, featuring the witty philosophies of Artbeats Unlimited. Work with partner, Diane Flynn.

Product/Service Directory

Beverly Halperin
Rhyme Tyme
81 Oakview Ave.
Maplewood, NJ 07040
201/763-6319
Greetings Entertainer: personalized poetry greetings for birthdays, anniversaries, Mother's/Father's Day, weddings, retirement, organization events, etc. Original Rhyme Tyme invitations can cost even less than commercial "fill-ins." Special services, including calligraphy, special papers, illustrations, custom printing, and framing. Will create a party concept or coordinate with your theme. A unique personal gift!

Brenda Utigard Hart
Hart Designs
330 Merion Rd.
Merion Station, PA 19066
215/664-4341
Illustrator: hand-painted greeting cards, stationery, invitations, note cards, and place cards. Designer of coordinated paper plates, napkins, table covers, and centerpieces, specializing in hand-painted holiday and gift items. Designs for needle art and crafts.
Medium: Gouache

Anita Ruslin
15 Warwick Rd.
Edison, NJ 08820
201/548-5481
Stationer: complete line of personalized invitations and stationery, specializing in design and originality; offering a full service to customers from calligraphy to napkins, etc. Also carry personalized gifts, party favors, silver, lucite, etc. After eleven years of experience, an important name in the industry.

Bette Sherman
The Hairy Beast
Rt 1, Box 334
Hedgesville, WV 25427
304/754-8443
Mail-order Salesperson: dog stationery sold mail order—more than eighty breeds. Also, one-of-a-kind advertising buttons—Billy Buttons—not advertised in catalog.

Storytelling

Käthe Ăna
Käthe Ăna, Storyteller
Route 2
Pulaski, WI 54162
414/833-7163
Storyteller, Oral Historian: through performances of folk tales, legends, and life stories, impart to children and adults enthusiasm for oral communication. Workshops for teachers, librarians, activities directors, and adult ed instructors using storytelling as a tool for discipline, learning, and healing. B.S. education/theater arts.

Therapy

Miriam Monell Agresti, Ph.D.
11 Wren Dr.
Woodbury, NY 11797
516/921-3924
Psychologist, Family Therapist: in private practice, specializing in divorce mediation and sex therapy. President of L.I. chapter of American Association for Marriage and Family Therapy. Listed in *Who's Who of American Women*, 1981–82, and *World's Who's Who of Women*, 1982. Ph.D. in Clinical Psychology, Yeshiva University.

Cheryl Taub Pliskin, ACSW, MSW
82 Boothby Dr.
Mt. Laurel, NJ 08054
609/234-2195
Licensed Marriage Counselor, Family Therapist: individual, couple, and family therapy, specializing in separation and divorce counseling. Pioneer in offering support groups for children of divorce. Member: Academy of Certified Social Workers, N.J. Association of Women Business Owners.

Irene Hamlen Stephenson
Biorhythm Character Analysis & Compatibility
PO Box 892-WWH
Chatsworth, CA 91311
213/347-6949
Analyst: character and compatibility analyst, researcher, teacher, matchmaker, and columnist. Editor, publisher, and writer of *The Truth* newsletter. Send stamped, long envelope for a free copy. Birthdates (month, day, and year) needed to get character analysis ($10 each) and compatibility ($15, two birthdates). Biorhythm numbering system used.

Translations

Cynthia L. Euske
Central Penn Translation Services
488 Pine Ridge Circle
Lewisberry, PA 17339
717/938-1369
Translator: in business four years translating French, Spanish, German (sources available for other languages). Clients mostly manufacturers and engineers, but also work for export firms, banks, advertising agencies, and state of Pennsylvania. Presently translating history book. Planning to install microcomputer and/or word processor in near future. Member: American Translators Association.

Travel

Helen Lurie, CTC
327 Lincoln Pl.
Waldwick, NJ 07463
201/652-5144
Travel Agent: certified travel
counselor, with certification from the
Institute of Certified Travel Agents.
Charter member of New Jersey Travel
Industry Professional Society (NJ
TIPS). Travel agent for twelve years.

Nancy Thode
Camp Advisory Service
3201 Shawnee Green
Ambler, PA 19002
215/643-3325
Camp Consultant: specializing in
placing children in private
independent summer camps and
travel experiences; discovering
parents' and child's interests, needs,
and hopes for summer programs; and
matching these with fine camps.
Worked in camps and schools for
twenty-five years. Possess first-hand
knowledge and experience. Member:
AAUW, American Camping
Association, NAHB.

Typesetting

Ann I. Czompo
AC Publications
PO Box 238
Homer, NY 13077
607/749-4040
Typographer: typesetting, layout, and
pasteup of all types of work—books,
newsletters, resumés, etc.,
specializing in educational materials
(manuals and textbooks) in fine arts
and crafts. Retired Associate Professor
of Dance. Listed in *Who's Who of
American Women, 1978–79,
International Who's Who in
Education, 1979.* Member: COSMEP.

Beverly Lane
Graphics Lane, Inc.
22 University Rd.
East Brunswick, NJ 08816
201/257-8778
Typesetter

Mary Louise Pivornik
Mary's Typesetting
8512 Wooddrift
Tampa, FL 33615
813/886-6528
Typesetter/Graphic Artist: working
primarily with printers (quick and
full line) by providing them with
typesetting and camera-ready layouts.
With select private customers, advise
on graphics, type design, and various
approaches that can be used to
promote their particular products or
services. Planning to form a small
publishing company in 1983.
Member: NAHB.

Vestments

Edna L. Gonske
Studio G
20 E. 40th St.
Minneapolis, MN 55409
612/824-4737
Designer/Weaver: specializing in
custom-designed liturgical garments
for clergy from handwoven or
commercial fabrics. Also
custom-designed fashion garments
and a line of handwoven accessories
for home or office. Create on
commission and available for
seminars, forums, and workshops on
Worship and the Arts, Liturgical
Vestments, and Design and Technique
for Banners.

Juanita Gordon
Theological Threads
13 Washington St.
Beverly, MA 01915
617/927-7031
Religious Vestment
Designer/Manufacturer: designing and
creating religious vestments and
mitres, altar cloths, banners,
tabernacle veils. Items available to
clergy, churches, and the general
public. Gift certificates available.

*Edna Gonske
Designer*

Writing Services

Mary E. Archibald
21 Wayne Gardens
Collingswood, NJ 08108
609/858-5945
Free-lance Writer, Typist: researching
and writing feature articles for
newspapers and magazines.
Personality features concerning
artists, musicians, conservation,
agriculture, and local history. Typing
of manuscripts, reports, letters,
business and academic papers.
College graduate with graduate school
training. Journalistic and educational
experience.

"Danie" Bernard
Danie's Custom Poetry
8690 Gulf Blvd.
St. Pete Beach, FL 33706
813/360-5245
Free-form Writer/Poet:
Dupes or praises a friend of yours
And custom writes the words to fit
Nice or humorous (your choice)
Incorporating the info you
Emit
$2/line plus $1.00 postage.

Barbara Deane
1675 Kasba St.
Concord, CA 94518
415/676-5930
Writer: magazine articles published in national, regional, and special-interest publications; coauthor of book, *Communicating Effectively, A Complete Guide for Better Managing* (Chilton). Specialties: business communications, health, education, human relations. Consultant in written communications. Creative writing teacher. Member: American Society of Journalists and Authors; Women in Communications, Inc.; AAUW, NAHB.

Toni L. Goldfarb
Communi-T Publications
586 Teaneck Rd.
Teaneck, NJ 07666
201/836-5030
Free-lance Writer, Consultant: in medical and social sciences. Articles, clinical reports, interviews, educational materials for professional journals, textbooks, popular magazines. Editor/Publisher of monthly *Medical Abstracts Newsletter,* summarizing latest medical breakthroughs and discoveries, as reported in over 100 scientific journals. Member: American Medical Writers Association; Newsletter Association of America; NAHB, Board of Trustees.

Barbara H. Goldman
Edit/Aide
14521 Artesian
Detroit, MI 48223
313/272-0256
Advertising/Promotional Writer: writing and rewriting of ad copy, catalogs, circulars, package inserts, letters, instruction manuals, press releases, invitations, brochures, and other promotional materials.

Clare H. Grosgebauer
Small Wonders Enterprises
10510 Acacia Lane
Fairfax, VA 22030
703/560-0577
Advertising/Marketing Consultant, Writer: specializing in free-lance writing services—books, brochures, advertising copy, marketing and educational materials. Author of two books, including *The Business Traveler's Survival Guide: Washington, D.C.* Many articles on women's issues and education topics published in *Working Woman, American Education, The Christian Science Monitor.* Listed in *Who's Who of American Women.*

Pat Isaak
434 Hiawatha Ave.
Hopkins, MN 55343
612/935-5639
Writer: author of *Helps for Leaders,* a book containing low-cost and no-cost ideas for crafts, games, service projects, and activities.

Carol Piper
Calligraphy
501 Guard Lock Dr.
Lock Haven, PA 17745
717/748-5563
Calligrapher: custom-designed calligraphy and lettering—certificates, menus, cards, letterheads, invitations, posters, announcements, etc. Demonstrations and workshops planned. Member: National Alliance of Homebased Businesswomen and The Pennsylvania Guild of Craftsmen.

Constance Porte-Aigeldinger
Wordcraft
362 Prince Frederick St.
King of Prussia, PA 19406
215/337-2370; 337-2368
Writer: personalized greeting cards, artistically scrolled in calligraphy on beautiful parchment paper; suitable for framing. Personalized songs and poetry, written or taped. Personalized cassettes. Professional equipment; professional staff. Recording music, messages, poetry, and educational information. Your thoughts in our words for a unique gift idea! Also, broadcast narrator and newspaper columnist.

Jessica Vermylen
Vermylen, Inc.
8 Gloucester Pl.
Morristown, NJ 07960
201/285-0468
Copywriter: free-lance writer specializing in complete direct-mail packages from concept to finished piece. Also design, write, and produce brochures, manuals, newsletters, space ads, and more. Member: Advertising Women of New York and American Advertising Federation.

Bobbi Wolf
Poemetrics
228 Standish Rd.
Merion, PA 19066
215/667-5896
Poet: creative calligraphy communications, a unique message service. With partner, Barbara Bailine, compose and create custom greeting cards, holiday cards, invitations, announcements, and stationery. Poetic messages mailed, telephoned, or delivered.

My life as a working woman at home is
  something to write about,
I'm either as proud as I can be, or I
  want to pull my hair out.
For years I wrote poetry for family and
  others I knew,
Then decided if my poems make people
  happy, they can make money too.

POEMETRICS
Merion, Pa.

Bobbi Wolf and Barbara Bailine
Poet and Calligrapher

Index

Do You Have a Homebased Business?

By filling out this questionnaire, you will enable us to collect important and needed statistics on women who produce goods or provide services from their homes.

We would also appreciate letters describing your work at home—hours, work place, problems, frustrations, joys, how you manage it all, your definition of success. These additional comments add dimension to our findings.

Some or all of the information may be published, so please sign the permission paragraph at the end and bracket all information you wish to be held confidential. Return the completed form to Women Working Home, Inc., 24 Fishel Road, Edison, NJ 08820.

Name: _____

Street Address: _____

City/State _____ Zip_____ Phone_____

1. Occupation:_____
2. What products are produced or services rendered?_____
   _____

3. What is your present field of small business?
   - 10 ☐ Agriculture/Forestry/Fishing
   - 11 ☐ Communications
   - 12 ☐ Construction
   - 13 ☐ Finance/Insurance
   - 14 ☐ Importing/Exporting
   - 15 ☐ Manufacturing
   - 16 ☐ Mining
   - 17 ☐ Real Estate
   - 18 ☐ Retail trade
   - 19 ☐ Transportation
   - 20 ☐ Wholesale trade

   Services:
   - 21 ☐ Administrative
   - 22 ☐ Business
   - 23 ☐ Educational
   - 24 ☐ Health
   - 25 ☐ Household
   - 26 ☐ Legal
   - 27 ☐ Personal
   - 28 ☐ Repairs
   - 29 ☐ Social

4. How long have you been in business?
   - 30–1 ☐ Less than 1 year
   - 2 ☐ 1 – 2 years
   - 3 ☐ 3 – 5 years
   - 4 ☐ 6 – 10 years
   - 5 ☐ 11 – 15 years
   - 6 ☐ More than 15 years

5. How much did you know about your business before you started?
   - 31–1 ☐ Nothing
   - 2 ☐ A little
   - 3 ☐ A moderate amount
   - 4 ☐ A great deal

6. Is your present business the first business you have ever owned?
   - 32–1 ☐ Yes
   - 2 ☐ No

7. Was start-up capital needed?
   - 33–1 ☐ Yes
   - 2 ☐ No

7A. Where did you get the initial investment/financing?
   - 34 ☐ Personal savings
   - 35 ☐ Retirement fund
   - 36 ☐ Husband
   - 37 ☐ Friends and relatives
   - 38 ☐ Partner(s) money
   - 39 ☐ Bank
   - 40 ☐ SBA
   - 41 ☐ Other _____

8. Do you enjoy what you are doing?
   - 42–1 ☐ Yes
   - 2 ☐ No
   - 3 ☐ Sometimes

9. Why do you work from home?
   - 43 ☐ Tax break
   - 44 ☐ Low overhead
   - 45 ☐ Convenience
   - 46 ☐ Flexibility
   - 47 ☐ Independence
   - 48 ☐ Children at home
   - 49 ☐ Parents at home
   - 50 ☐ Other _____

10. Do you like working from home?
   - 51–1 ☐ Yes
   - 2 ☐ No
   - 3 ☐ Sometimes

11. Would you move the business out of your home if you could?
   - 52–1 ☐ Yes
   - 2 ☐ No

12. Do you consider your business primarily
   - 53 ☐ Business
   - 54 ☐ Hobby
   - 55 ☐ Self-fulfillment
   - 56 ☐ Career
   - 57 ☐ Other_____

13. How much of the business do you own?
   58 ☐ 100%   61 ☐ 25 – 49%
   59 ☐ 75 – 99%   62 ☐ Less than 25%
   60 ☐ 50 – 74%

14. Are you satisfied with the amount of time you have to yourself?
   63–1 ☐ Yes   2 ☐ No

15. Do you think that a woman who devotes 10, 15, or 20 years to the full-time homemaker role takes a risk in future economic and emotional well-being?
   Economic 64–1 ☐ Yes   2 ☐ No
   Emotional 65–1 ☐ Yes   2 ☐ No

16. How satisfied are you in achieving the following personal success goals?

	Very	Moderately	Slightly	Not
Financial independence	66–1 ☐	2 ☐	3 ☐	4 ☐
Raising children	67–1 ☐	2 ☐	3 ☐	4 ☐
Job and career advancement	68–1 ☐	2 ☐	3 ☐	4 ☐
Physical well-being	69–1 ☐	2 ☐	3 ☐	4 ☐
Happiness	70–1 ☐	2 ☐	3 ☐	4 ☐
Social status	71–1 ☐	2 ☐	3 ☐	4 ☐
Self-understanding	72–1 ☐	2 ☐	3 ☐	4 ☐
Intellectual achievement	73–1 ☐	2 ☐	3 ☐	4 ☐

17. Does your business now support you or do you intend to make it support you?
   Now supports me   74–1 ☐ Yes   2 ☐ No
   Will support me   75–1 ☐ Yes   2 ☐ No

18. Is your business a
   76 ☐ Sole proprietorship   78 ☐ Corporation
   77 ☐ Partnership   79 ☐ Sub S Corporation

19. Is your community
   80 ☐ Urban   82 ☐ Rural
   81 ☐ Suburban   83 ☐ Small town

20. Is your neighborhood
   84 ☐ Residential   86 ☐ Industrial
   85 ☐ Commercial   87 ☐ Mixed

21. Is your home legally zoned for business?
   88–1 ☐ Yes   2 ☐ No

22. Do you   89 ☐ own   90 ☐ rent   your home?

23. Do you live in a   91 ☐ single family   92 ☐ multifamily building?

24. Do you advertise?
   93–1 ☐ Yes   2 ☐ No

24A. Where has advertising been most beneficial?
   94 ☐ Yellow Pages   99 ☐ Trade shows
   95 ☐ Newspapers   100 ☐ Flea markets
   96 ☐ Trade magazines   101 ☐ Craft fairs
   97 ☐ General magazines   102 ☐ Catalogs
   98 ☐ Direct mail   103 ☐ Other_____

24B. How else do clients and customers find out about you?
   104 ☐ Word of mouth   109 ☐ Networking
   105 ☐ Craft fairs   110 ☐ Cold calls
   106 ☐ Flea markets   111 ☐ Store displays
   107 ☐ Flyers/brochures   112 ☐ Bidders lists (government and prime)
   108 ☐ Consignments   113 ☐ Other_____

25. How many hours per week do you work?
   114____in your business at home   115____in business outside the home

26. How many paid employees do you have?
   116____Full time   117____Part time

26A. How many subcontractors do you use?   118____

26B. How many volunteers (including family members) do you use?   119____

27. How old are you?
    120–1 ☐ Under 20 years   5 ☐ 50–59 years
        2 ☐ 20 – 29 years   6 ☐ 60 – 69 years
        3 ☐ 30 – 39 years   7 ☐ 70 years and over
        4 ☐ 40 – 49 years

28. Are you
    121 ☐ Single, never married   124 ☐ Divorced
    122 ☐ Unmarried, living with partner   125 ☐ Widowed
    123 ☐ Married, living with spouse

29. Do you have children?
    126–1 ☐ Yes   2 ☐ No

29A. How many   127_____living at home   128_____living elsewhere?

30. If working full time, would you prefer to work part time in order to spend more time with your children, even though your income would be reduced?
    129 ☐ Yes   130 ☐ No   131 ☐ Not employed   132 ☐ No children

31. Do you have insurance coverage specifically related to the business?
    133–1 ☐ Yes   2 ☐ No

32. Are there local ordinances that have created problems?
    134–1 ☐ Yes   2 ☐ No

32A. Are there local ordinances that might create problems if enforced?
    135–1 ☐ Yes   2 ☐ No

32B. If yes, what are they?
    136 ☐ Zoning   139 ☐ Health code
    137 ☐ Permits   140 ☐ Other_____
    138 ☐ Noise restrictions

33. Do you currently draw income from any other business or company?
    141–1 ☐ Yes   2 ☐ No

34. Gross income last year from homebased business:
    142–1 ☐ Under $5,000   6 ☐ $25,100–$30,000
        2 ☐ $5,100–$10,000   7 ☐ $30,100–$50,000
        3 ☐ $10,100–$15,000   8 ☐ $50,100–$75,000
        4 ☐ $15,100–$20,000   9 ☐ $75,100–$100,000
        5 ☐ $20,100–$25,000   10 ☐ $100,100 +

35. Net income last year from homebased business:
    143–1 ☐ Under $5,000   6 ☐ $25,100–$30,000
        2 ☐ $5,100–$10,000   7 ☐ $30,100–$50,000
        3 ☐ $10,100–$15,000   8 ☐ $50,100–$75,000
        4 ☐ $15,100–$20,000   9 ☐ $75,100–$100,000
        5 ☐ $20,100–$25,000   10 ☐ $100,100 +

36. ☐ Compared to five years ago, how would you rate your financial situation?
    144–1 ☐ Better   2 ☐ About the same   3 ☐ Worse

37. Have you completed:
    145–1 ☐ Elementary school   4 ☐ College degree
        2 ☐ High school   5 ☐ Some graduate school
        3 ☐ Some college   6 ☐ Postgraduate degree

38. Do you think a college degree is essential to success?
    146–1 ☐ Yes   2 ☐ No

39. Have you taken any higher education course(s) in the past few years?
    147–1 ☐ Yes   2 ☐ No

39A. If yes, what was the objective?
    148 ☐ Improving skills   152 ☐ Enjoyment
    149 ☐ Learning a new field   153 ☐ Educational degree
    150 ☐ Career advancement   154 ☐ Other_____
    151 ☐ Intellectual stimulation

I give you permission to publish any or all of the above information, except as indicated by brackets [   ].
Date _____   Signature _____

National Alliance of Homebased Businesswomen

Purposes:

The purposes of the National Alliance of Homebased Businesswomen are to:

- Emphasize, encourage, and stimulate personal, professional, and economic growth among women who work from, or wish to work from, their homes
- Project a positive image of women with homebased businesses
- Provide a forum for the discussion and exchange of homebased business information and experiences
- Provide publications disseminating current information and exchanging views on mutual concerns
- Provide a support network of professional contacts, education, and encouragement for women with homebased businesses
- Showcase members' goods and services

Benefits to members:

- The *Alliance,* a quarterly newsletter, with articles about helpful business information, news of members' achievements, and information about new resources and ideas for businesses
- An Annual Meeting that includes seminars on business subjects, an opportunity for members to showcase their goods and services and to help decide the future directions and activities of NAHB
- A quarterly Meeting-by-Mail from the board of trustees, keeping members informed about what the board is doing for them and providing a place for members to speak out on issues that concern them
- An Annual Directory of all members published in November and updated quarterly
- Local chapters for networking with other members
- A certificate of membership, suitable for framing and displaying

Membership:

There are three categories of membership:

Member: A person with a revenue-producing homebased business; has the right to vote, to become an officer or trustee, and to become a member of a national committee.

Associate Member: A person who has not yet established a revenue-producing homebased business; may not vote or hold national office but may vote and hold office in a chapter if the chapter so rules.

Supporting Member: Any person not included under general or associate membership or any corporate body that gives tangible support to NAHB; may not vote or hold office in NAHB.

Membership fees can be deducted as a business expense. Membership is on an individual, professional basis, just as the benefits are on an individual basis.

Member: $30

Associate Member: $30

Supporting Member: a contribution of money, goods, or services.

NATIONAL ALLIANCE OF HOME-BASED BUSINESSWOMEN

Membership Application

_____   _____
(name)   (area code)   (telephone #)

_____   _____
(street address)   (city/state)   (zip code)

Name and nature of my business:_____
(for the NAHB Directory)

_____

My check for $___is enclosed for

☐ member — $30;
☐ associate member — $30
☐ supporting member

I would like to be affiliated with a chapter ☐
Make check payable to NAHB and mail to: NAHB, P.O. Box 95, Norwood, NJ 07648

WWH Press Order Form

Suggested uses for
Women Working Home:
The Homebased Business Guide
and Directory—
Marketplace for products and
  services
Resource information
Business guidelines
Idea catalyst
Textbook
Networking list

For Canadian buyers:
$15.50 (or $12.95 in
U.S. dollars), plus
$1.75 postage/handling.

WWH Press   **Order Form**
P.O. Box 237BK
Norwood, New Jersey 07648

Name _____

Address _____

     City _____ State _____ Zip _____

Area Code and Phone Number _____

Please send _____ copies of *Women Working Home: The Home-based Business Guide and Directory* at $12.95, plus $1.25 postage and handling, for each book. N.J. residents add $.78 sales tax. Enclosed is $_____. For information on quantity orders, write to WWH Press. Allow four weeks for delivery.
☐ Check.   ☐ Money Order.
Charge my ☐ MasterCard   ☐ Visa.

Card No. [| | | | | | | | | | | | | |] Exp. Date _____

Signature _____

- -

If you would like to be included in future directories, please print or type the following information. This will help us in our planning.

_____
Name

_____
Company / Business Name

_____
Address

_____
City, State, Zip

_____
County   Telephone

Occupation _____

Description of work _____

_____

_____